THE WANDERING JEW:

OR THE

TRAVELS AND OBSERVATIONS

OF

𝕳𝖆𝖗𝖊𝖆𝖈𝖍 𝖙𝖍𝖊 𝕻𝖗𝖔𝖑𝖔𝖓𝖌𝖊𝖉.

Comprehending a View of the most distinguished Events in the History of Mankind since the Destruction of Jerusalem by Titus.

With a Description of the

MANNERS, CUSTOMS, AND REMARKABLE MONUMENTS, OF THE MOST CELEBRATED NATIONS.

Interspersed with

ANECDOTES OF CELEBRATED MEN OF DIFFERENT PERIODS.

Compiled from a MS. supposed to have been written by that Mysterious Character.

By the Rev. T. CLARK.

LONDON:

PRINTED FOR JOHN SOUTER, AT THE SCHOOL LIBRARY, 73, ST. PAUL'S CHURCH-YARD.

1820.

PREFACE.

The object of this work is, under the disguise of a popular fiction, to present such a series of remarkable incidents as will enable the youthful Reader to form some notion of the moral, religious, and political, history of mankind during seventeen hundred years. The idea was suggested by the travels of the younger Anacharsis; but the method pursued is somewhat different from the principle adopted in that celebrated work. The Author considered it necessary to give his hero an individual character; and, while ascribing to him the sentiments of the authorities from which the incidents are taken, to assume the privilege of examining their reflections, in some instances, with the freedom of a reviewer. It therefore became expedient to introduce two parties, in order that the peculiar character of the principal might be preserved, when his national prejudices were likely to make him think differently from that impression which the events described have produced on posterity: and the part of a critical compiler seemed the most convenient and agreeable relief to the inherent solemnity of the supposed mysterious author of the Volume from which the extracts are ostensibly made. This, it will be perceived, has been in some measure adopted from the plan of Mr. Galt's tale of "The Majolo;" but, being on a more extended principle, it affords the advantage of introducing other facts, in addition to those embraced by the narrative, so as to present a view, as it were, of public history, in connection with the adventures of an individual.

PREFACE.

But, whatever may be thought of the plan, the work, in one respect, challenges approbation; for, in reviewing the manner of the ancient Romans, and of that odious race of tyrants who disgraced human nature in the imperial purple, the maxim that "Evil communications corrupt good manners," has been literally observed. It is time, indeed, that posterity should drop all notice of many circumstances in the story of Greece and Rome; and, that, in education, the ingenuous mind of youth should be taught to look only to those examples of virtue and heroism, which exalt the imagination, and tend to ennoble the sentiments of the heart.

Something perhaps of the nature of an apology is due, for those circumstantial descriptions of incidents which are supposed to have attended many of the historical events; but it will be perceived that, although they are for the most part fictitious, they are still in general probable. In representing the hero as an eye-witness, it was necessary to enliven his narrative with the notice of such minute accidents as were likely to fall within the observation of a person present. A dry series of extracts from the works of others formed no part of the design of this undertaking: but it will be readily discovered, that some of the notes from the imaginary volume of Hareach are almost literal quotations from the most distinguished and authentic historians of the affairs to which his reflections relate. In a word, that, with all the characteristics of a romance, this story of the Wandering Jew may lay some claim to be considered as a work of fact and history.

CONTENTS.

PART I.

	Page.
CHAP. 1. Some Account of the supposed Author of the following Work, and how his Book was found in a Monastery on Mount Parnassus	1
...... 2. The Burning of the Temple, and final Destruction of Jerusalem by the Romans; with the Discovery of the Jewish Leader Simon, and the Triumphal Return of Titus into Rome	7
...... 3. Of Roman Manners and Customs during the Reign of Domitian. Hareach visits Britain, and is present at the Defeat of Galgacus	13
...... 4. Some Account of the Manners and Customs of the Ancient Germans	22
...... 5. Anecdotes of Agricola, Pliny, and Tacitus; with some Account of the Death of Domitian, and the affectionate Conduct of his Nurse Phyllis	31
...... 6. The Antiquity and Grandeur of the Ancient Egyptians; with some Account of the Inundations of the River Nile	37
...... 7. Reflections on the Character and Religion of the Ancient Egyptians	41
...... 8. Of the Manners and Customs of the Ancient Egyptians	45
...... 9. Manners and Customs of the Pastoral Arabs	49
...... 10. The City of Petræa, and the Tombs of Abraham and Aaron	55
...... 11. History of Apollonius Tyaneus	58
...... 12. Biographical Anecdotes of the Emperor Trajan	62
...... 13. Anecdotes of the Emperor Adrian, and Reflections on the Magic studied in his Time	70
...... 14. Reflections on the State of Religion and Morals at the Death of Adrian	75

CONTENTS.

		Page.
Chap. 15.	Anecdotes of the Emperor Antoninus Pius	78
16.	Account of a Pestilence raging in an Ancient City	82
17.	The Death of Demonax the Cynic	85
18.	Anecdotes of Pertinax the Emperor, who reigned only Eighty-seven Days	89
19.	The Sale of the Roman Empire by Public Auction	93
20.	Hareach in India	98
21.	The Religious Opinions of the Hindoos	100
22.	The Hindoo Account of the Corruption of Mankind	103
23.	The Hindoo Account of the Third Epoch of Mankind	106
24.	Of the Pagodas of the Hindoos, comprehending a Description of the Caves of Ellora	108
25.	Religious Ceremonies	111
26.	Of the Origin of Hermits, and the Order of Anchoret Monks	113
27.	Hareach in the Desert	115
28.	State of the Roman Government	119
29.	Historical Sketch	122
30.	Anecdotes of the Emperor Maximinus	125
31.	Summary of the Roman History	128
32.	Rome in the Third Century	130
33.	Public Opinion among the Romans during the Third Century	135
34.	Of Authors and Publications in the Third Century	135
35.	The Falling of the Roman Empire	137
36.	The Opening of the Sibylline Books	139
37.	Zenobia Queen of Palmyra	142
38.	Longinus the Sublime	146
39.	Paul of Samosata	150
40.	The Resignation of Dioclesian	153
41.	Anecdotes of Dioclesian in Retirement	156
42.	The Family of Dioclesian	159
43.	The Building of Constantinople	162

PART

CONTENTS.

PART II.

	Page.
CHAP. 1. Decline of Classic Literature	165
2. The Christians persecute each other	168
3. Restoration of Idolatry	170
4. Anecdotes of Julian the Apostate	173
5. The City of Paris in the Fourth Century	177
6. Hareach at Daphne	179
7. The Attempt to rebuild the Temple of Jerusalem	182
8. The Misopogon	185
9. The Death of Julian the Apostate	186
10. Restoration of the Church	189
11. Anecotes of St. Athanasius	192
12. Adventures of St. Athanasius	195
13. The Inroad of the Barbarians	197
14. The Insurrection of the Goths	200
15. The Defeat and Death of Valens	203
16. The Massacre of the Gothic Youth	205
17. The Destruction of the Temple of Serapis	207
18. The Revival of Polytheism	210
19. State of the Roman Nobility	211
20. The Invasion of Alaric, and first Gothic Siege of Rome	216
21. The Second Gothic Siege of Rome	220
22. The Sack of Rome by the Goths	223
23. Summary of Events from the Sack of Rome by the Goths, till the Plundering of it by the Vandals	229
24. The Revolt of Bonifacius in Africa—His Union with Genseric the Vandal—Their Rupture—Rome plundered by the Vandals	231
25. The Last Day of the Roman Sovereignty	235
26. Establishment of the Salique Law in France	238
27. The Foundation of the French Monarchy	241
28. The Story of Chilperic and Fredigonde	244
29. State of the Eastern Church in the Age of Mahomet	248
30. Some Account of Mahomet before he assumed the Mission of a Prophet	252

CONTENTS.

	Page.
CHAP. 31. The Mission of Mahomet	255
32. The Flight of Mahomet from Mecca, and his Reception at Medina	259
33. Mahomet acts as a Conqueror	262
34. The Conquest of Mecca, and the Destruction of the Idols in the Caaba	264
35. The Final Abolition of Idolatry in Arabia	267
36. The first War between the Christians and the Mahomedans, and the Death of Mahomet	270
37. The Conquest of Alexandria by the Mahomedans; and some account of the Library destroyed by the command of Omar the Caliph	273
38. The Death of Hosein	275
39. The first Mahomedan Siege of Constantinople, with some Account of the cause of the Disappearance of the Greek and Roman Coinage, and the Introduction of our Arithmetical Cyphers	278
40. Second Siege of Constantinople by the Mahomedans	280
41. The first Decisive Indication of the Independence of the Papal Government	283
42. The Progress of the Mahomedan Religion arrested by Charles Martel in France	286
43. The Magnificence of the Caliphs, and their Encouragement of Learning	289
44. The History of the Caliph Montasser	293
45. Hareach among the Ruins of Babylon	296
46. Zingis Khan of Tartary, and the Conquest of China	299
47. Notes respecting the History of the Turks	303
48. The last Siege and Fall of Constantinople; with the final Extinction of all the Military and Imperial Institutions that originated with the Roman People	306

PART

CONTENTS.

PART III.

	Page.
CHAP. 1. The Retreat and Character of a Hermit in the Island of Samos	313
2. A general View of the State of Christendom about the Middle of the Fifteenth Century	318
3. The Story of the Hermit of Samos	322
4. The Brother of the Sultan a Prisoner at Rome—Pope Alexander VI.	326
5. State of Rome in the Fifteenth Century; with Reflections on the Causes that have contributed to the Destruction of her ancient Edifices	331
6. The Beginning of the Reformation	336
7. Hareach accompanies Cardinal Campeggio to England.—The public Entry of the Cardinal into London, and what happened on that Occasion; with Remarks on the League of London	341
8. The Meeting of the French and English Courts in the Field of the Cloth of Gold—The Reformation in England—Anecdote of the English House of Commons—Tax on Income	345
9. Anecdote of Wolsey respecting a Riot and Insurrection in the County of Suffolk	349
10. The Exchange of Francis the First for his Children	351
11. The Trial of Henry VIII. and Queen Catharine	352
12. Anecdotes of Cardinal Wolsey; with an Account of his House, and manner of entertaining Strangers	359
13. The Issue of the Trial of Henry VIII. and his Queen	363
14. The Fall and Death of Cardinal Wolsey	366
15. Notes respecting Francis I. and the State of the Protestant Religion in France when Mary Queen of Scots was married to the French King	377
16. The Massacre of the Protestants in France on the Eve of St. Bartholomew	382
17. Observations of the Editor on the Characters of Mary Queen of Scots, and of Queen Elizabeth, her Rival	38

CONTENTS.

	Page.
CHAP. 18. The Trial of Mary Queen of Scots	390
...... 19. The Execution of Mary Queen of Scots	394
...... 20. Hareach in Switzerland	398
...... 21. Some Account of the State of the Public Mind in London at the Time of the Trial of Charles I.	401
...... 22. The Trial of Charles I.	404
...... 23. The Execution of Charles I.	409
...... 24. The Funeral of Charles I.	413
...... 25. Sketches and Reflections on the State of Italy and Greece; with Pictures of Turkish Manners	416
...... 26. Hareach at Athens—A curious Mahomedan Ceremony	422
...... 27. Hareach in Persia—Permanency of the Asiatic Character—A Tribe of Turcomans—A Persian City—A Caravansera—A Cloud of Locust—Domestic Manners of the Persians—The characteristic Noises of a Persian City	424
...... 28. Pilgrimage to the Tomb of Noah's Mother—A Journey to Mount Ararat—Terrible Storm—View of Ararat—Reverie in contemplating the Mountain	428
...... 92. The Return of Hareach to Greece; his Journey to Mount Parnassus; with his Reflections on an Immortal Life and Death.—Conclusion	433

ERRATA.

Page 41, for *hemp-town,* read *hemp;* adding, " that is, as we would say, *hemp-town.*"

DIRECTIONS TO THE BINDER.

Plates.

Temple of Jerusalem—*Frontispiece*	1
Map of Europe	13
Egyptian Remains, *to face page*	48
The Wounded Arabian	118
Hareach in the Desert	118
Triumphal Arch and Temple of Peace	332
Turkish Barber and Muezzim	420
Athens	423
Mount Ararat	429
Map of Asia	165

HAREACH,

THE WANDERING JEW,

&c.

CHAPTER I.

Some Account of the Supposed Author of the following Work, and how his Book was found in a Monastery on Mount Parnassus.

On the eastern side of Mount Parnassus, above the road which runs from Thebes into Thessaly, stands a small monastery, inhabited by a few caloyers or monks of the Greek church. The steepness of the ascent prevents them from being often visited by travellers; and, living thus in a situation so very remote and high apart from the commonalty of mankind, they are more simple in their manners and notions than their brethren in other parts of the country. There is, indeed, something in the genius of their abode, calculated to inspire serene and religious sentiments. It commands, as it were from the clouds, a wide expansive prospect of the romantic scenery of Greece; and the hollow in which it is placed, among the precipices of the mountain, is so surrounded by inaccessible rocks, that it naturally awakens, in the mind of a stranger, all those associations of the imagination which delight to dwell on ideas of refuge, concealment, and repose.

Many years ago, a traveller, visiting this monastery, was so pleased with the hospitality and primitive character of the caloyers, that he remained with them several days. In appearance, he had but slightly waned from the vigour of life; but, in particular points of view, his aspect had a strange cadaverous expression, which gave him an air of supernatural antiquity, and he then seemed to belong to a different and older race than that of man.

As soon as he had taken possession of the little chamber which the good-natured friars prepared for him, he evidently shewed, by his reserved and unsocial manner, that he did not intend to hold any intercourse with them. During the day, he was commonly sullen, often peevish; and few nights passed, that they did not overhear him moan, and even howl, in his sleep. In fine weather, he would lie on the ground, with his hands under his head, looking to the clouds as they floated over him. At other times, he would shut himself up in his room, and stand leaning against the wall, with his arms folded, and his eyes fixed on the floor, never uttering a word. But, his chief delight was to sit on a jutting rock which overhung the precipices; and, with his chin resting on his hand, appear as if he was studying something in the distant horizon, while his eye-brows were knotted with the workings of thought. If he occasionally looked on the landscape below, it was with a swift and wavering glance, that followed some other object than the features of the earthly scene.

The monks, to whom this conduct seemed very extraordinary, began to entertain doubts of his being in his right senses; and they had good reason to do so; for, one evening, during a terrible storm, they could not persuade him to remain in the house. The wind, on that awful night, was full of preternatural lamentations; and when the moon, at short intervals, was discovered through the hurrying clouds, she appeared as if she had fallen from her orbit, and was bowling to ruin along the sky. In the midst of this tempest, while windows and doors could not be sufficiently fastened, and while fragments of rock, shattered from the cliffs, pealed as loud as the thunder in their precipitous descent, the mysterious stranger stood under the lea of the buildings, and often shouted, with impious satisfaction, as the wide sheets of lightning burst through the turbulence of vapour that rolled above, below, and around the monastery. The globe of the world, broken into pieces, and sinking amidst the black waves of chaos, could not present a more tremendous spectacle, than the scene which this awful being viewed with such blasphemous delight.

But, what chiefly grieved and disturbed the caloyers, was his total neglect of all religious duties; and, when they reflected on the disputations and divisions of opinion which his presence had occasioned among them, they durst not say to one another what they feared he was, till an incident occurred, which confirmed their worst and wildest apprehensions.

One morning, he left his chamber at the dawn, and went into the garden, where he dug a hole like a grave, and continued all the day after sitting near it, making violent gestures, venting appalling sounds, and frequently bursting into tears. In the evening he came into the refectory, and having taken some refreshment, he called for a draught of wine, which, when he had drank, he went to his own room; and, loading a pistol, returned and seated himself in the hollow which he had made in the earth.

In this situation he continued several hours, while the trembling friars, in great consternation, were at prayers in the chapel. What he did further, or what apparition rose to him, they never knew; but they heard the report of the pistol; and, soon after, the sound of his steps returning to his chamber. When they assembled in the refectory, he joined them, and partook of their supper with more cheerfulness than they had ever seen him assume; but it was remarked, that he had the pale and haggard look of a man exhausted by a great struggle.

When supper was ended, he requested to speak with the superior in private; but that pious character, before venturing to consent, thought it his duty to consult the brotherhood; and they were unanimously of opinion, that he ought not to comply, especially as there was such good reason to suspect that the stranger had held some horrible communion with the Evil powers—perhaps had undertaken to seduce the superior. On more mature consideration, however, they thought that, if he would kiss a picture representing God the Father which hung over the altar in the chapel, the superior might then safely hear what he had to say. Accordingly, two of the friars went for the picture, although one was quite sufficient for the errand; but it must not therefore be supposed that they were at all afraid, particularly as friar Theodosius said, that he only wished friar Jerom to go with him to hold the light, while he took down the picture from the wall.

The stranger having in the meantime retired to his room, the superior, when the two monks came from the chapel, took the picture from them; and, attended by the whole house, went to put his faith to the test, in the manner that had been agreed on. They found him stretched on his bed; but, as they entered, he rose and enquired what they wanted, in a tone so lordly and indignant, that the stoutest-hearted of them all quaked with fear.

The superior informed him of the test to which they were desirous he should submit his religious principles. He looked at them for a moment with a countenance so full of scorn, that the visage of Satan itself could not have been more dreadful; and, when the picture was offered to his lips, he dashed it from the hand of the superior, and kicked it after the horror-struck caloyers as they fled from the room.

There was no sleep in the convent that night. The trembling friars sat all together, and often prayed. At one time, they heard a low rustling sound pass near the door of the refectory, as if the wings of some demon had brushed along the passage; and they expected every moment, that the roof of the building would be carried off, and their limbs scattered like chaff before the wind. But, in the course of a few seconds, the noise died away, and was succeeded by a silence so solemn and profound, that it was as if every thing in nature stood still, and even the beating of the heart had been suspended.

Soon after day-break, three of the most courageous of the friars ventured to step softly to the stranger's door; and, hearing no breathing within, they said a short prayer, and entered.

The bed-clothes had not been turned down, and every thing was in its usual place in the room; but their attention was particularly attracted by a book on the table, as large as the volume of the Evangelists in the church.* In this book, one of the brethren had noticed that the stranger often wrote; and, upon looking at it, (for none of them dared to touch it,) they observed that the ink was still moist on the last passage. As they were thus contemplating with pious terror this mysterious volume, the stranger came into the room, and demanded why they had presumed to meddle with any thing of his; but, suddenly checking himself, he burst into a fit of laughter, and contemptuously ordered them to mind their prayers, and not trouble their heads with his affairs.

During the remainder of this day, he seemed disposed to be uncommonly social. He courted their company with the most conciliating affability, and endeavoured to entertain them with music, from an unknown instrument of the richest appearance, and which he played with the most exquisite skill; but they were on their guard against his tricks, and kept themselves aloof from his familiarity.

He spoke to them of their coldness and taciturnity: he pretended to make a thousand apologies for the indignity with which he had treated the picture. He sometimes affected to be jocular, and to chide them; at others, he endeavoured to command respect, by the coldness of his demeanour; but they persevered with religious constancy in their determination to shew him, that they were aware of his designs on their immortal souls.

Towards evening he again became thoughtful; and, soon after sun-set, left the refectory, where he had spent

---

* It is the custom, in all the Greek churches, to keep a copy of the Evangelists, of which one of the priests daily reads a portion aloud.

the greatest part of the day with the brotherhood; but, at supper-time, he returned, and had no longer the air and look of a mortal man. His eyes were inflamed, and had a fixed and glassy stare. His hand shook so much when he attempted to taste the wine, which had received the benediction of the superior, that he could not raise the cup to his lips. A green and mortified yellow overspread the wonted palour of his face to such a degree, that he was more like a Lazarus risen from the tomb, than one who had suffered no suspension of the functions of life. His whole appearance was indeed so ghastly, that the innocent caloyers trembled with dread when they looked at him, and thought that his spirit was actually departed, and that the faculties of the body, which he still exercised, were only kept in motion by the impulse of some wonderful excitement. Nor were they much mistaken in this notion; for, when he rose to leave them, as they thought only for the night, he fell on the floor; and, after a short convulsive quiver, which vibrated at once through all his frame, he stretched himself out, and stiffened apparently in death.

For some time, they did not venture to touch the seeming corpse; but it soon became so frightfully discoloured, that they were apprehensive it would fall asunder, and therefore, with the help of boards and sticks, they contrived to remove it to the garden, where they threw it into the grave which he had himself prepared, and rushed into the chapel, to implore the protection of St. John of Jerusalem, to whom their house was dedicated.

Whether the grand adversary of man, or a wolf from the rocks, had, in the course of the night, carried off the body, or whether the wretch himself had revived, and conscious that he could not hope to seduce any of these holy friars to the service of his evil superior, had secretly descended to the valley, and left them, was a point never satisfactorily settled among them. But those who entertained the latter opinion, were convinced that he was no other than Hareach the Jew, destined to wander, friendless, over the face of the earth, till the day of judgment: and really there appeared to be some reason for this notion;

for an English traveller, who afterwards visited the monastery, on looking at the unblest volume, which still remained on the table where it had been left, found that it contained a curious account of different nations and people, written as if the author had himself visited them, although the incidents and circumstances described related to different ages, and embraced a period of nearly eighteen hundred years.

Struck with the singularity of the narrative, and by the story which the caloyers told him regarding the author, he asked and obtained permission to take the book away; and it is to this curious production that we now call the attention of our young friends.

CHAPTER II.

The Burning of the Temple, and final Destruction of Jerusalem by the Romans; with the Discovery of the Jewish Leader Simon, and the Triumphal Return of Titus into Rome.

As the curious book of the unknown contained a variety of matter, in order to present a consistent narrative to our readers, we mean to extract only those passages which tend to throw light on the manners and customs of different nations, and to illustrate historical events. These extracts we shall give in the words of the author, which cannot fail to be the more interesting, as they serve to unfold his own mysterious character, and the singular feelings by which he was actuated. As a proper beginning, therefore, we beg leave to quote his description of the destruction of Jerusalem, in all the main circumstances, of which his account is corroborated by the historian Josephus.

"Omens and prodigies had long announced that

Jehovah was departed from the mercy-seat, but it was not till the 7th day of the month Elul, in the year of the world 4077, (A.D. 73,) that the daily sacrifice ceased for ever in the Temple. Titus the Roman, was desirous that the worship should have been continued; for it was an ancient maxim in the policy of his countrymen, to respect the religious rites, while they erased the history, of the nations which they subdued; but the remnant of our people, who had determined to perish with every thing rather than again submit to the Roman arms, rejected the representations which he made to them on this subject. Seeing them thus resolute, and in possession of the sacred edifice, which they had converted into a fortress, he prosecuted the siege with remorseless vigour. But desperate men, determined on death, resisted him with an energy new to his legions, and laughed to scorn the fury alike of the engines and the soldiery. For six days he endeavoured to batter down the walls which surrounded the temple, but was repulsed, with the loss of many of his bravest troops, and the destruction of their eagles. On the seventh, he set fire to the gates, which were plated with silver, and the flames communicated to the porticoes and galleries; but the besieged within answered to the shouts of the Romans with execrations, and made no attempt to extinguish the burning. Next morning, he ordered the legions to stop the progress of the fire, being still anxious to preserve so glorious a building; and having consulted his council, it was determined that, on the 10th of the next month, a general assault should take place. On the preceding night, however, my countrymen made two sallies, with partial success, which greatly exasperated the Romans; and I observed, from the terrace of the house where I had witnessed these conflicts, one of the private soldiers, after Titus had retired to take repose, mount on the back of his comrade, and throw a firebrand into one of the windows of the apartments that surrounded the sanctuary. Immediately the whole north side was in a blaze; and the Romans, on all sides, rent the air with acclamations. Titus, surprized by the noise, came running from his tent towards them, and prayed, and threatened, and even struck his men, calling on them to extinguish the flames. But, raging themselves with vengeance against the besieged, they paid no attention to his orders; continuing, on the contrary, to spread the conflagration throughout the whole edifice, and to sacrifice all the unhappy wretches within the reach of their swords.

"Titus having thus in vain endeavoured to preserve the temple, then entered the sanctuary, and took possession of the consecrated utensils of gold—the candlestick, the altar of incense, and the table of shew-bread; but when he penetrated behind the veil of the most holy place, he was struck with awe, and instantly retired. In the same moment, a soldier applied a torch to the sacred curtain, and the fire furling up for ever the veil of mystery, shewed that the God was not there! The Jews shrieked with horror, and a wail and lamentation spread throughout the city; even the Roman paused in consternation,—but it was only to return to the work of slaughter with redoubled fury.

"From the destruction of the temple the overthrow of the nation may be dated, although possession of the upper town was not obtained till the eighth of the month Elat (September,) when, as soon as the work of massacre and pillage was over, Titus ordered his army to demolish the city, with all its structures, palaces, and towers. He left nothing standing but a piece of the western wall, and the three towers of Hippicos, Phasael, and Mariamne; the former to serve as a redoubt to one of his legions which he left there to prevent any of the Jews from re-assembling, and the three latter as monuments to give future ages some idea of the strength of the city, and the valour that was necessary to the conquest. Thus was the bow of Israel for ever broken, and her quiver emptied; and, since that time, I have wandered among men, like a creature of another state of being, without communion of mind, without sympathy, without participation in any cares, without the hazard of any greater misfortunes, without the hope of any improvement in my solitary lot; a spirit interdicted from entering the social circle, living without any motive to action, my feelings seared up, and my purposes all done.

"But I felt myself fated to be the deathless witness of the ancient greatness of our holy people, and doomed to represent their homeless and outcast condition, till the terrible cycle of their sufferings was completed, and they had again assembled to reign in the land of their fathers.

"When the destruction of the city was completed, Titus ordered a tribunal to be prepared for him in the midst of the ground where he had encamped, and calling his officers around him, he addressed them from that lofty seat; commended their exploits in the siege, and rewarded them according to their respective rank and merits, with crowns of gold, and other precious ornaments. The army applauded this munificence to the skies. He then descended; and the Roman priests who attended the army having provided a number of oxen, a prodigious sacrifice was offered to the idolatrous gods of the Romans, and the remainder was distributed among the soldiery. The following day, leaving the tenth legion to prevent my miserable brethren from returning to the ruins of the city of their fathers, he marched with his army to Cesaria.

"When the main body of the Romans had been thus removed from Jerusalem some time, several of the inhabitants, who had been scattered by the issue of the siege, returned to look among the wreck of their habitations for any relics that might yet be found of their former property. One morning, as I was wandering among the ruins, observing these unhappy persons, and burning with indignation at the taunts which they endured from the Roman soldiers, I beheld a ghastly form, clothed in white, and wearing a purple cloak, rising out of the earth in the centre of the spot where the temple once stood. The soldiers, so loud in their derision, were struck with awe at the sight, and stood still for some time, believing that it was a supernatural apparition. Having however mustered courage, they approached, demanded who he was, and what he wanted. But the mysterious being, instead of answering, ordered them to call their captain. I now also advanced, and saw that it was no other than Simon, who had taken so large a share in the revolt against the Romans, and whom it was thought had perished in the burning of the temple. He had however concealed himself, with a few of his most devoted followers, in a secret cavern; and, having provided them with a stock of provisions, they had there remained until their stores were consumed. Terentius Rufus, the Roman commander, on being informed by the troops, hastened to the spot, and hearing from Simon his name, and former consequence, ordered him to be seized, and sent in chains to grace the triumph of Titus.

"My heart was greatly wrung by the fate of this man; for, although his factious spirit had raised many enemies even among ourselves, none laboured with more earnest spirit to break those galling shackles with which the Romans had held us in slavery, while they insulted our customs, and endeavoured to destroy the records of our national independence and glorious history. It is true, that by the revolt the nation was dispersed, and our kindred carried into captivity; but Jerusalem fell not without a struggle. The greatness of the vengeance of Titus bore testimony to the valour of Israel, and the indignities offered to Simon, was evidence of the fidelity and enterprise with which he endeavoured to redeem the independence of the nation.

"Seeing the melancholy condition to which Simon was reduced, and having myself no home, I resolved to pass with the captives to Italy; and reached the neighbourhood of Rome on the evening preceding the day appointed for the triumph decreed to Titus.

"Early in the morning, Vespesian the emperor, and Titus, who had rested during the night in the temple of Isis, came out crowned with laurel; and, clothed in the ancient purple robes of their dignity, walked to where a stage, with ivory chairs, had been prepared for them, and where the senate, the magistrates of Rome, and the members of the equestrian order, were assembled. When they had seated themselves, and received the congratulations of these public personages, amidst the acclamation of the soldiers and the people, a solemn sacrifice was offered to their gods, and the whole army feasted, according to the Roman custom, on the choicest portions of the victims. But the triumphal procession I cannot describe: my eyes were dazzled with the splendour, while my spirit mourned for Israel. I have therefore retained but a confused recollection of pictures embroidered by the Babylonians, the images of the Roman gods and of great men carried on superb chariots, and vast machines, towering above the houses, loaded with the richest trophies. I bowed my head to the earth when I beheld the sacred vessels of the holy temple borne along; and heard and saw not that this gorgeous train of ruin was terminated by a person bearing that copy of the law which had been preserved for so many ages in the hallowed archives of the sanctuary. Soon after, a terrible shout announced that the unfortunate Simon, who had been ignominiously dragged by a rope round his neck, was put to death in the forum.

"The Romans thus gloried in the victories of Titus, thus honoured his achievements, and erected monuments to perpetuate his fame; but the Jews, of all the nations that they subdued, alone preserved the integrity of their ancient character. We were broken, but not destroyed: scattered, but not lost!"

The history of Israel being thus for awhile closed, the author appears to have remained at Rome till after the spoils of Jerusalem were deposited in the Temple of Concord, which Vespasian at this period erected, to commemorate the universal peace then established throughout the Roman world.

EUROPE.

CHAPTER III.

Of Roman Manners and Customs during the Reign of Domitian. Hareach visits Britain, and is present at the Defeat of Galgacus.

The author appears to have remained a considerable time at Rome after the return of Titus from Jerusalem; for he describes the universal sorrow with which the death of that excellent prince overwhelmed the city. The injuries which the Jewish nation had suffered from the Roman arms, appears, however, to have warped his opinion of the Roman people, especially of the nobility; for he takes every opportunity of declaiming against their luxurious indulgences and their dastardly spirit, and to represent them as alike destitute of energy and public virtue. But let us quote his own words.

" No sooner had Domitian felt himself settled on the throne of his brother, than he began to insinuate malicious detractions against both Titus and his father Vespasian; and yet, at the same time, he certainly conducted himself as if desirous at least to be thought a magnanimous prince. He presented liberal gifts to his officers, that they might not have the pretext to accept bribes; but this, instead of allaying these parasites, only sharpened their avarice, and in the end had the effect of filling the mind of the emperor with a hatred of their baseness, that frequently vented itself afterwards in capricious acts of the cruelest tyranny. Domitian, however, had no resources within himself; and, constantly subject to the impulse of the moment, his conduct was alike unwise and disgraceful. His ideot practice of killing flies was an example of this; but the treatment which the senate submitted to endure at his hands, was still more degrading to the general character of human nature. He knew that these wretched representatives of the haughty republicans stood in continual terror of his cruelty, and he resolved to amuse himself with their fears. Having invited them, and some of the most distinguished of the equestrian order, to a banquet, they assembled at the appointed hour, each attended by a numerous retinue of servants. I was then in the household of Volusius Saturninus, and accompanied him to the party. As we approached the palace, we were joined by several of the other guests; and in the interchange of civilities at meeting, it was remarked by one of them, that, as the emperor had not for a long time been pleased to notice him, he was much surprised at receiving an invitation to the palace.

"This incidental observation, trifling as it was, chilled the hilarity of all present, and they walked onward in silence. On arriving at the porch, the servants of the palace received them with an audacious familiarity, felt, but could not be repressed; and they were conducted into the interior with a degree of mock solemnity, that mortified their abashed and pusillanimous pride. Still, however, they had the meanness to go forward, till they reached a spacious hall, hung with black, and illuminated with a few dismal lamps, which only served to discover a number of coffins, on which they beheld the names inscribed of all the guests who had been invited to the banquet. While they were standing in horror and amazement at this appalling spectacle, the doors suddenly burst open, and bands of naked slaves entered, with swords in one hand and flaming torches in the other. The despicable senators and knights suffered the agonies of death, as these tools of the most insulting despot danced in derision around them. When Domitian had thus diverted himself with their terrors, it was announced to them that they might go home, and tell how well they had been entertained at the palace.* And they did so: but the people were become insensible to the decorum of life, and the sufferings of these degraded cowards, instead of exciting sympathy or inspiring any indignation against the tyrant, only occasioned laughter and contempt.

---

* Dio Cassius, lib. lxvii.

"Soon after this humiliating affair, I availed myself of an invitation to accompany Marcus, the brother of Volusius, to Britain, where he was appointed to a command under Agricola, then governor of that island.

"The speed with which we travelled through Gaul allowed me no opportunity of observing the peculiar manners of the inhabitants; but, when we arrived in Britain, instead of that wild and savage country which it was believed to be at Rome, I found it fertile and well peopled, and the natives, under the judicious Agricola, fast rising into eminence in the arts of polished life. This wise commander, when the legions were not in active service, devoted his whole attention to the improvement of the people, and excited in them a taste for the Roman arts and magnificence. Their towns were adorned with stately temples and porticos; and their youth imitated the fashions of Rome, and put on the Roman toga with the pride of freemen, although it was but the badge of their slavery.*

"We arrived at the tent of Agricola while he was superintending the construction of a line of forts across the island, to prevent the inroads of the Caledonians, a fierce and untractable race, who possessed the mountainous regions of the north; and frequently, by their daring enterprizes, ravaged the civilized territories of the Britons. It was not one of the regular stations of the Roman army that Agricola then occupied, but a temporary encampment on the banks of an estuary of the sea, into which the river Glotta (the Clyde) empties its waters. No landscape that I have ever beheld exceeded in beauty the scene that presented itself when we reached the brow of the rising-ground where his tent was pitched. On the opposite shore rose a conical rock, a fortress prepared by nature, and occupied by a determined band of the hardy natives, who bade defiance to the Roman eagles. Beyond that lay a beautiful valley, watered by

---

* Ancient Universal History.

a spacious rapid stream;* and, in the distant perspective, the lofty ridges of the Grampian hills towered in alpine grandeur; while the western bound of the estuary was closed into the form of a lake, by a congregation of smaller but more rugged mountains, which the setting sun at that moment gloriously illuminated with his golden splendour.

"But my attention was soon called from the contemplation of that majestic prospect, by the approach of Agricola, who, being acquainted with Marcus, advanced to meet him with the cordiality of an old friend. The appearance of this respectable Roman, presented a striking contrast to the pompous ostentation of the ordinary generals of the empire. He had the air, frankness, and simplicity, of an older and better age. His dress (for he was without his armour, having been engaged in writing dispatches to the different legions then preparing to advance against Galgacus,) was plain, but worn with a grave and peculiar dignity. I was, however, chiefly struck by the sound of his voice, which had a degree of kindness in its tones, that bespoke at once confidence and esteem, and indicated warmth and benevolence of heart.

"Of all the Romans who had governed this province, Agricola, without question, had rendered the greatest benefits to the inhabitants. When he arrived in the island, he found them as fierce and untamed as the ancient Gauls, of whom they were no doubt descended; as they practised the same religious rites, and credited the same superstitions.† The strength of their armies consisted in their infantry, but some of the chiefs were accustomed to take the field in chariots; and a general partiality for equestrian exercises, was one of the characteristics of this bold and warlike people.

"The Caledonians, who occupied the north-eastern parts of the island, were evidently of German origin,

---

* The Leven, a river that flows from Loch Lomond.
† Tacitus.

easily distinguished from the Britons by their ruddy complexion and the lusty vigour of their limbs; and it was against this daring and heroic race that Agricola was then preparing to advance. We accompanied him soon after to the Grampian hills, where the enemy was posted in great force. Upwards of thirty thousand men appeared in arms, and their numbers were daily increasing. The youth of the country poured in from all quarters; and even the old men, proud of their past exploits, emulous of glory, and resolved to preserve their ancient independence, repaired to the standards of their chiefs, under the command of Galgacus.

" On the evening that Agricola reached the bottom of the hills where the Caledonians were posted, one of their soldiers was taken prisoner; and from him the Romans learnt that his countrymen were determined to defend their mountains to the last extremity. There was something in the demeanour of this man bold and singular; for, although only of the rank of a private soldier, his manner indicated that habitual consciousness of equality which is only found to exist amongst persons of eminent birth, and which those of a low origin, whatever their talents or acquirements may be, seldom attain. This peculiarity, I afterwards found, was one of the characteristics of the Caledonians; and it may be attributed to a notion which prevailed among them, that all the members of their several tribes were descendants of the same common parents, and that their chiefs were but the elder-born in the line of primogeniture.

" On the following morning, the Caledonian general addressed his army in terms full of spirit and virtue. From one of the Roman spies sent into his camp, Agricola obtained the following report of his speech:

" 'When I think of the motives that roused us to this war,' said Galgacus to his forces, 'I expect everything great from your efforts; and from this day I date the deliverance of Britain from the Romans. Ye are the men who never crouched in bondage; and beyond this land there is no refuge for liberty: for even the sea is shut against us, and the Roman fleet, hovering on our coasts, would deny escape, were we base enough to fly. The brave glory in drawing the sword for freedom; but, in our situation, cowardice itself would throw away the scabbard. From the battles that we have already fought, our countrymen trust their last hopes to our valour. They know us to be the noblest of the Britons, placed in the remotest recesses of the land, and unpolluted with the sight of the ignoble bondage in which the sons of the south are debased. But the Romans are in the heart of our country: no submission can satisfy their pride, but actual slavery,—no concessions appease their fury, but our entire overthrow. They are the only conquerors who make the rich and the poor equally their prey. Are the nations rich?—Roman avarice is their enemy. Poor?— Roman ambition drags them at the wheels of its triumphs. Children and friends are dear to all; but, when the Roman comes, where are they then? Wives, sisters, and daughters, mourn in the bloody track of the ravisher's career, branded with dishonour; or, if spared to be sacrificed on the altar of the hearth, it is to add the corruption of their minds to the pollution of their bodies. And, men! there are none where the Roman eagles are planted,—none like you erect in the ranks of glory; but dejected wretches, bent with the burdens of slavery, and doomed to perish in clearing woods and marshes. Manhood is wasted, that the articles of Roman luxury may be increased; and corn-fields and numerous flocks are substituted for virtue and a courageous race. This is called civilization! and this, Agricola and his legions offer to your acceptance. But we have no lands that can be cultivated, no mines of ore among our rugged mountains to dig for Roman avarice, no harbours to improve for the contaminating commerce of Rome. The fame of an unconquered ancestry constitutes all our riches; and the glory of subduing a race who never owned a conqueror, is a pride that the ambition of Rome burns to attain. What then should be our condition, were the universal enemy of national independence to triumph? Our virtue and courage are crimes that she is impatient to punish, for they mortify the consciousness of her own guilt. We have no mercy to expect, nor can we implore. Let us therefore dare like men. We are summoned by the great call of Nature, and placed here, in these everlasting rocks, to set bounds to the Roman aggressions. Here her haughty waves may beat and swell, but they shall pass no farther. From the bottom of our mountains, that deluge which has swept away all the independence of nations, will begin its ebb, never to flow again.'

"Agricola listened to the relation of this address in profound silence. A slight blush now and then tinged his cheek, as the excesses and vices of his countrymen were alluded to; and it was evident that he admired the enemy whom it was his duty to subdue. After a short pause, the legions having in the meantime advanced, he went forward; and riding out in front, as they halted within bow-shot of the Caledonians, spoke to them in these words:

"'It is now, fellow-soldiers, the eighth year of our service in Britain. During that time, the genius of Rome, with your assistance, has made the island our own. In every expedition, in every battle, the enemy has felt your valour; and, by your perseverance, the very nature of the country has been conquered. I have been proud of my soldiers, and you have had no cause to be ashamed of your general. In our long and laborious marches, when you were obliged to traverse moors, fens, and rivers, and to climb the rough mountains, it was still the cry of the bravest among you, When shall we be led to battle? when shall we see the enemy? Behold them now before you. Roused from their lairs, and raging from their dens and caverns, your wish is granted, and the glory of making these fierce barbarians your prey is now presented to your swords. But remember that a defeat here involves us all in the last distress. If we consider the progress of our arms to this point, to look back is triumphant: the tract of country that lies behind us, the forests you have explored, and estuaries you have passed, are monuments of your enterprize. But our fame can only be ensured while we press forward. If we retreat, we have the same difficulties to surmount again; and that success which is now our pride, will be converted into the worst misfortune. We are not well acquainted with the course of the country; but the enemy knows all the defiles and marshes, and where to draw the requisite supplies of provision. We however have swords and valour; and with these we may obtain everything. With me it has long been a settled maxim, that the back of a general, or of his army, is never safe. Which of you would not rather die with honour, than live in infamy. But life and honour are this day inseparable; they are fixed to one spot. Should fortune declare against us, we shall die here, on the limits of the world; and to die where nature ends, cannot be inglorious. If our present contest were with an enemy new to our swords, I should call to mind the example of other armies; but what can I present so animating as the splendour of your own exploits? I appeal to your own eyes. Look at the men drawn up against you: are they not the same who, under covert of the night, assaulted the tenth legion; and, upon the first shout of our army, fled? In woods and forests the fierce and noble animals attack the hunters, and rush on certain destruction; but the timorous herd is soon dispersed, scared by the sound and clamour of the chace. In like manner, the bold and warlike Britons have long since perished by the sword. The refuse of the nation still remains: they have not staid to make head against you; they are hunted down; behold where they stand motionless, caught in the toils. Here you may end your labours, and close the toils of fifty years by one glorious effort. Let your country see, and let the commonwealth bear witness, if the conquest of Britain has been a lingering task, that we at least have done our duty.'

"While Agricola thus addressed his men, a more than common ardour glowed in every countenance; and, as soon as he had ended, the field rung with shouts of applause. But I could not refrain from contrasting the lofty sentiments of the Caledonian with the dictates of the prudence and policy of the Roman. I was not however allowed much time for reflection. The battle immediately commenced.

The Caledonians kept possession of the rising ground; and, extending their ranks as far as possible, presented a formidable show of battle. The first line was ranged on the plain; the rest in gradual ascent on the acclivity of the hill. The intermediate space between both armies was filled with the chariots and cavalry of the Britons, rushing to and fro in wild career, and traversing the plain with noise and tumult. The Caledonians, with their long swords and small circular targets, eluded the javelins and darts of the Romans with astonishing dexterity. But neither their individual skill nor bravery, nerved with despair, could withstand the steady impression of the Roman discipline. They were routed and dispersed with tremendous slaughter; and many of them, with the wild sentiments of savage honour, laid violent hands on their wives and children, to preserve them from the indignity and passions of the conquerors. The following morning displayed the nature and importance of the cruel victory which Agricola had achieved over a bold and ancient people. Silence reigned on the hills. Towns at a distance were seen involved in smoke and fire. The inhabitants had vanished; the scouts of Agricola could not discover one;* and the Roman owned with a sigh that he had won the battle, but the enemy was still unsubdued."

Soon after this event, it appears that Hareach went with his master to Germany, where they remained some time with a noble Roman of the name of Lucius Sylvanus, who had then the command of the ninth legion. While they staid with him, the Jew had frequent opportunities of observing the manners and peculiar customs of the Germans; but, as his interesting account of that aboriginal people is of considerable length, it will furnish abundant materials for another chapter.

---

* Tacitus.

CHAPTER IV.

Some Account of the Manners and Customs of the Ancient Germans.

A. D. 98.

It was an opinion of the ancients, that the inhabitants of every country which possessed no literary monuments, were the immediate offspring of the soil; not that the Greek and Roman philosophers believed this to have been really the case; but, wherever the origin of a people could not be satisfactorily traced, it was assumed that they were the indigenous offspring of the country which they inhabited, and the folly of useless antiquarian conjecture was thus judiciously avoided. Accordingly, Hareach, in speaking of the ancient Germans, treats of them as an original race; but it must not therefore be supposed, that he believed they were the natural produce of the soil, and not the offspring of those migratory colonies which detached themselves from the primeval stock of mankind. With this brief explanation of an ancient notion,—a notion founded, we think, in a correct philosophy,—we may now proceed with his account of the Germans.

" During the reign of Domitian and his successors, for near a century, the Romans cherished the spirit of travelling; and it was fashionable for men of rank and erudition to visit the scenes of great events, and to explore the remains of former times. Under the influence of this spirit, as much perhaps as on account of the affection in which he held his relation, who commanded at Augusta Vindellicorum (now Ausbourg), Marcus was induced," says Hareach, in the manuscript, " to visit Germany before returning to Rome.

" We staid but a few days at that station; and Marcus, almost immediately on his arrival at the colony, evinced much impatience to view the interesting parts of that country; and he seemed more anxious to avail himself of the peace then existing between the natives and the Romans, than to enjoy the society of his friend.

"The appearance of Britain, contrasted with Italy, was that of a remote part of the same empire. We beheld there the Roman customs, and saw a country under the ameliorative influence of the Roman arts and laws; but Germany presented a far different aspect. The plains were uncultivated; extensive marshes, and woods of primeval antiquity, every where shewed that the inhabitants were still in the rudest state of barbarism.

"The pride of the ancient German consisted in the number of his flocks and herds, which to this day constitute the main portion of the wealth of the Hungarian nobility, in which country many characteristics of the ancient Germans may be traced. But I was struck with the comparative smallness of the cattle, and the singularity of their being without horns, the great ornament of the beeves that pasture along the shores of the Mediterranean. The precious metals were but little known, and where the use of them had been acquired silver was preferred to gold, not from caprice or fancy, but because it was more easily subdivided and applied in the purchase of the low-priced commodities which the frugal wants of the natives required. In the vicinity however of the Roman colonies, we found the coins and the vices of Rome: but even in these situations, the people retained much of their hereditary distrust of the Romans; for, although they consented to exchange their commodities for the Roman money, they would only accept the most ancient species of the coin, particularly that indented on the edge called the *serrati*, or that stamped with the impression of a chariot and two horsemen, and called the *bigati*. The *quadrigate*, or that which bore the impression of victory on a car drawn by four horses, had, in the reign of Domitian, become an antiquarian curiosity. The partiality of the Germans for the old money of the republic, was not without good reason; for it was the only pure coinage in circulation, and indeed only to be met with on the remote skirts of the empire. In the decline of ancient virtue, the senate, as if to transmit a monument of the national decay to posterity, mixed an alloy of brass with the silver; and the emperors afterwards debased it still more; so that the money no longer really represented that quantity of the precious metals which it professed to do; and it was on this account that the Germans, in their dealings with the soldiers, and other members of the colonies, refused to take the more recent coinage.

"One evening, after we had visited some of the most remarkable scenes of the Rhine, celebrated for their wild and romantic views, it became necessary to look for a place where we could pass the night; the sky, which had all the afternoon been overcast, having began to assume a very gloomy and lowering appearance. But for some time our search was fruitless; for the Germans had then no cities, and even their villages consisted but of a few scattered hovels, which, except when their hearths were kindled, and the smoke seen ascending from them, were not easily discriminated from the inequalities of the ground. At last however we came to a rude castle, situated on the edge of an abrupt rock, and which was the stronghold of one of the native chieftains. Habitations of the same kind, and in similar situations, we had several opportunities of seeing during our stay in Britain; but this was on a larger scale, and evidently belonged to a personage, if not of greater authority, at least of more extensive power, than the insular warriors.

"The frowning and troubled aspect of the heavens, afforded the best apology that we could offer for our intrusion. No difficulty however was made to admit us; on the contrary, we were welcomed with a frank cordiality, strangely at variance with the studied etiquette of more polished life.

"The chieftain was celebrating that evening the anniversary of a victory which some of his ancestors had gained over the Romans, in the series of conflicts that proved so fatal to the legions under the command of the unfortunate Varus. He perhaps exulted that Romans should be present at the recital of the songs in which the national bards had recorded the exploits of the victors;

but none of us, except the interpreter who had accompanied Marcus, understood the language, and its beauties or its satire was lost to our ears. But the performance of these heroic odes was exceedingly striking. One of the bards commenced the poem in a calm descriptive manner, and gradually, as he proceeded with what was probably a narrative, others joined in; and at regular intervals all present bore a part, with great vehemence and enthusiasm, producing an effect on the mind of the auditor equivalent to the shouts and uproar of battle.

"It was the custom of these barbarous warriors, not only to sing in this manner the praises of their ancestors, in order to cherish military valour in the bosoms of their youth, but on the eve of battles to sing war-songs, founded on the exploits of former days, and the glory of enterprize and energy in arms. They even drew, from the manner in which these latter odes were recited on the field, presages of the issue of the battle. In this respect, however, the superstition (if it may so be called) was not peculiar to the Germans, for it prevailed also among the Caledonians.* Nor indeed may it either be considered as local or national, for undoubtedly the pitch of the voice

---

* At the battle of Killicrankie, just before the fight began, Sir Ewen Cameron ordered such of the Camerons as were posted near him to make a great shout, which being seconded by those who stood on the right and left, ran quickly through the whole army, and was returned by the enemy. But the noise of the muskets and cannon, with the echoing of the hills, made the Highlanders fancy that their shouts were louder and brisker than those of the enemy; and Locheil cried out, " Gentlemen, take courage: the day is our's. I am the oldest commander in the army, and have always observed something ominous and fatal in such a dull, hollow, and feeble noise, as the enemy made in their shout; which prognosticates, that they are all doomed to die by our hands this night: whereas, our's was brisk, lively, and strong, and shews that we have vigour and courage." The event justified the prediction, for the Highlanders obtained a complete victory. Mr. Campbell, in his beautiful poem of " Lochiel's Warning," has finely availed himself of that peculiar poetical frame of mind which may be inferred from this curious anecdote of that noble Scottish chieftain.

D

of a multitude must in every place depend on the feelings of the moment. The soldier, when he is bold and sanguine, will articulate his feelings with force and animation; but, when his hopes are dejected by any circumstances that tend to weaken his confidence, a corresponding langour will be communicated to the tones of his shouts: and therefore the faith of the Germans in the spirit of their war-songs, was not without a basis in the principles of human nature, although that savage people did not reflect on the subject so curiously.

"During the intervals of these triumphal commemorations, we were entertained with large horns filled with a strong infusion of barley, fermented and mellowed by time. The chieftain, to do honour to his Roman guest, ordered a silver vessel,* of an antique form, to be brought; and, having filled it foaming to the brim, sent it by the hands of his cup-bearer for Marcus to drink. This officer was an old man of a singularly venerable appearance. Never having been in battle, and belonging to the priesthood, his hair and beard were hoary and flowing; for it was a consecrated custom amongst these people, not to shave their beards until they had proved their courage by killing an enemy in the field. The priests being exempted from military duties, were thus distinguished by the length of their beards; but no veteran would have been permitted to sit among the brave with such a badge of an ineffectual sword. In presenting the cup, the old man related that it was the gift of peace from a king of a distant land to an ancestor of his chief; and that, in consequence, it was only at the banquets of peace that it ever appeared. As the story embraced an account of all the persons and occasions for which the goblet had been filled to greet the presence of strangers, it might be said to be an index to so much of the oral traditions of the tribe; at least, it afforded a lively idea of the manner in which the Germans, without a written language, or any species of record or monumental trophy, preserved the circumstantial incidents of their national history, and

---

* Tacitus, section v.

cherished that devout affection for the memory of their fathers, for which they were celebrated over all the empire, and by the effects of which they preserved their national integrity unimpaired, and finally survived the Romans, who had so often, from the days of Julius Cæsar, endeavoured to reduce them to the Roman yoke.

"The Germans being greatly addicted to convivial indulgence on such occasions as the commemoration of their exploits, the drinking was prolonged till a late hour, and tumult and menaces arose. But it was a courteous maxim with that warlike people, to consider the stranger in their house as hallowed from all wrong; and, even though discovered to be an enemy, was protected by their hospitable usages from injury or aggression; so that, in their inebriated contention, we met with no insults, nor even incivility.

"But the point in which the manners of these northern barbarians differed the most from those of the Romans, and indeed from those of all the southern nations, was the delicate respect in which they held their women. The females only continued present at the banquet till the recitations commenced; and, when they retired from the hall, all the warriors stood up, and did homage to them as to superior beings. Nor was it surprising that they should do so, for the German women were distinguished for an Amazonian heroism, and more than Amazonian virtues. It is related, that after the victory obtained by Marius over the Cimbri, the conflict with the wives of the vanquished was not less fierce and obstinate. In carts and waggons they formed a line of battle, and from their elevated situation, as from so many turrets, annoyed the Romans with their poles and lances; and, when they found that all was lost, they resolved still not to be contaminated by the conquerors. They first sent a deputation to Marius, desiring that they might be at liberty to enrol themselves in a religious order; and their request being refused, they strangled their children during the night, and either perished by mutual slaughter or self-immolation; for, next morning, when the Romans looked towards the scene of conflict, they beheld only the dead bodies of mothers lying mingled with their children, or hanging from the boughs of trees suspended by the neck with their sashes.* And yet these heroic women were deeply embued with the beautiful tenderness of their sex: their days were spent in the exercise of the domestic virtues and in pious contemplation; and such was the purity and chastity of their manners, that they were much more fondly beloved by their male relations than the more voluptuous females of softer climates, insomuch that Augustus Cæsar, who excelled all princes in the depth of his policy, demanded from the conquered tribes of the Germans their women as hostages;† being informed that, to a German mind, the idea of a woman led into captivity was insupportable, and that the states which deliver the daughters of illustrious families as hostages, are bound by the strongest of all obligations.‡ It may indeed be said, that the respect of the ancient Germans for their women was inordinate, for it was tinctured with a degree of superstition that amounted to veneration; and in many instances, they ascribed to them the powers of prophecy. Perhaps it was from this prejudice that the belief in witches and sorceresses of later times took its rise; for there can be no doubt that Valeda, a prophetess of the Bructerian nation, who was taken to Rome during the reign of Vespasian,§ was a person of this description. Like others possessed of the art of divination, she was blinded to her own destiny.

"On the following morning I rose early, before the generality of the household was stirring, for the fumes of the preceding debauch had locked up their senses in unusual drowsiness; and, going forth to taste the freshness of the morning air, I walked to a dark grove of large and venerable trees; but, on approaching towards it, I was restrained by the sound of a low and wailing voice, and, as the Romans accused the Germans of offering human victims to their stern and invisible deities, I fled shuddering back to the castle, appalled with the

---

* Florus.   † Suetonius.   ‡ Tacitus.
§ Statius, Sylv. lib. i.

dreadful notion that the sound which I had heard proceeded from some such atrocious sacrifice, as the place was no doubt one of their consecrated groves, within the gloomy recesses of which the profane steps of the uninitiated were never permitted to enter. On mentioning what I had heard to the old cup-bearer, whom I found in the hall on my return, he informed me that I was mistaken in my apprehension; and that it was only on awful and calamitous occasions that human victims were offered, and even then in the mystery and darkness of midnight.

"The chief soon after entered, and Marcus, with his attendants, being ready to depart, went to thank him for the hospitality with which we had been treated; but the German expressed himself so anxious that we should spend another day with him, that it was impossible, without rudeness, to refuse his earnest request. And we had much reason to be pleased with the result, for it enabled Marcus to acquire a great deal of minute information respecting the manners of the people; by which, on our return to Rome, he enabled Tacitus to compose that eloquent treatise respecting the Germans, which is admired wherever the Roman language is cultivated.

"It happened that a public council of the tribe of which our host was the chief, was that day to take place. It had been announced, according to custom, to be holden some days prior to the festival; but, as it was a rule with the Germans never to obey a summons of this kind at the time appointed, lest it should be thought that they attended the command of their chief as much as the occasion of the meeting. The interval was spent in personal discussion among the different elders, or sages, who composed the council, by which a general notion was formed among them as to what was likely to be the issue of their deliberation, before they assembled.

"The feast of the preceding night having brought the councillors together, they met in the hall, all armed, exactly at noon-day. Silence being proclaimed by one of the priests, with whom the duty rested to preserve the traditions of their proceedings, the chief, in his capacity as president of the council, stated in a short speech the business they were called to consider; and such of the members as chose to deliver their opinion on the question, rose successively, but without any respect to rank, nobility, or fame, except such deference as one individual chose in courtesy to pay to another. No man attempted to dictate his opinion to the assembly, but only endeavoured to persuade. Sometimes the sentiments of the orator were received with murmurs of disapprobation; but when his arguments were satisfactory, the assembly signified their approval by brandishing their javelins. It was surprising to see with what powers of elocution some of those unlettered barbarians delivered their opinions, and with what dignity of gesture they enforced the accents of their voice. At the conclusion of the deliberation, when every one who was inclined to offer his opinion had spoken, the assembly divided themselves; those approving the business passing over to the right hand side of the hall, and those dissenting to the left. As soon as the question was determined by the majority, so far from any factious attempt being made to counteract it, as was often the case in the Roman senate, the minority acquiesced entirely in the decision; and even some of those who had very vehemently opposed the proposition, were appointed to carry the result into effect.

"There was thus evidently among the Germans the elements of a new species of political liberty, differing essentially from that of the Roman or Greek republics; for the members of the council did not consider themselves in the deliberation more than as individuals offering their own opinion on the subject, but in the voting they acted as the representatives of their respective corps; and when the question was settled by the sense of the majority, they considered it as of the force of a public law, which they were all equally bound to obey.

"After the council broke up, the members who had displayed so much intellectual talent in their deliberation, amused themselves in various ways; and it surprised me to see persons, who naturally possessed so much gravity and wisdom, engage with the earnestness of children in dicing and gaming, and in the ardour of their play betray all the impetuous passions of their wild and savage character."

These are the main particulars that Hareach has recorded of his observations on the ancient Germans. Soon after the adventure in the castle of the German chief, he returned with Marcus to Rome; and, as the incidents to which he was a party were in themselves interesting, and tend to throw some light on the manners of the Romans, we shall devote another chapter to that subject.*

CHAPTER V.

Anecdotes of Agricola, Pliny, and Tacitus; with some Account of the Death of Domitian, and the affectionate Conduct of his Nurse Phyllis.

"On our arrival at Rome," says the mysterious author of the manuscript, "we found Agricola there before us. He had not been recalled by Domitian; but, learning from some of his friends that the emperor was not satisfied at the renown he had acquired both by his civil measures and his victory over Galgacus the Caledonian, he determined, with his characteristic prudence, to resign a situation which had the effect of turning his virtues and merits into political offences: he therefore solicited, and obtained, permission to retire from the government of Britain.

"It was expected that, on reaching Rome, he would have been appointed to the command in Syria, then vacant by the death of Atilius Rufus; but the cold civility with which he was received by Domitian banished this expectation. By me it was felt as a misfortune, for I had calculated on passing with him to Asia, and to visit the desolate ruins of Jerusalem, and the land of Israel.

"My second visit to Rome was, however, not so full of painful reflections, as when I witnessed the triumphs that proclaimed the overthrow and dispersion of our sacred nation. Agricola being far advanced in life, (he was at this time in his sixty-sixth year,) and perceiving the jealousy with which his popularity and character shook the bosom of the tyrant, sequestered himself from public life, and gave himself up to the enjoyments of a virtuous sociality with his friends, such as well became the close of a career adorned by one continued stream of glory and benevolence.

"I went often to his house with Marcus, who was one of his most confidential visitors, and I had thus opportunities of sometimes meeting there the noblest characters in Rome; among others, with Tacitus, the son-in-law of Agricola, and whose historical works are justly famed for the sententious vigour of the descriptions, and the dark but profound knowledge which the author possessed of the human heart. Tacitus was without question a man of great solidity of judgment, but dogmatic in his opinions; and so disposed to think ill of mankind, that his many great qualities were obscured by this gloomy peculiarity, which rendered him more respected than beloved. He was nevertheless a very estimable character, and his misanthropy was perhaps but a natural effect of the outrages which his nice sense of moral propriety daily suffered, from the infamies of the court and the arbitrary violence of Domitian.

"Pliny the younger was also sometimes a visitor at the house of Agricola, but he had not then attained that eminence on which he reflected so much lustre. It was not, indeed, until the firmness which he displayed at the trial of Bebius Massa had attracted the public admiration, that the richness of his merits were valued or allowed, even by his most intimate associates. The story deserves particular notice.

"This Bebius was one of those characters so common in the decline of the Roman empire, who amassed prodigious fortunes by fraudulent accusations, and thrived by the ruin of others. While governor of Bithynia, he had practised a system of remorseless extortion, which so exasperated the Bithynians against him, that, when he returned to Rome, to revel in his ill-acquired wealth, they in their turn accused him of corrupt practices; and the senate appointed Pliny and Herennius Senecio to conduct the prosecution, which they directed should in consequence be instituted against him. This task these two able advocates managed with so much ability, notwithstanding Bebius employed all the means which his knowledge of the corruption of manners enabled him to apply with dexterity, that he was found guilty, and his whole possessions declared forfeited. But, before the warrants were issued by the consuls to take possession, he had contrived, by those practices in which he was so well skilled, to occasion so much delay in the proceedings, that Pliny and Senecio determined to demand the immediate execution of the sentence.

"Marcus was on a friendly footing with Pliny, and it happened, as I was going with him to visit Tacitus, who was then employed on his treatise respecting the Germans, that we met the two advocates on their way to the consuls; and, induced by the singularity of the business on which they were engaged, we accompanied them to hear the result.

"On entering the house, to our great amazement and indignation, we found the delinquent seemingly on a confidential understanding with the consuls, whom he had no doubt bribed to his purpose; for, when Senecio addressed them, requiring the sentence to be carried into effect, he burst with insolence into a furious passion, and loudly accused Senecio on the spot as a traitor to the emperor. All present were struck with astonishment at this false and audacious charge, but Pliny, who, with admirable presence of mind, turned round to him, and said, in a tone of contemptuous severity, 'I am sorry, sir, that you do not charge me also as equally guilty, because your forbearance may lead the world to imagine that I have not acted against you with so much zeal as my friend; and I should be grieved that any one should think I did not exert my utmost ability in this cause.' The effrontery of Bebius was confounded, and he shrunk away, conscious that his guilt and audacity were equally manifest.

"The behaviour of Pliny on this occasion deservedly raised him into great popularity; but his vanity was intoxicated with the applause which attended him whenever he appeared in public. Some time after, he was rallied a good deal by his acquaintances, in consequence of a letter which he had written to Tacitus, giving an account of the affair, and requesting him to insert it in the Annals, on which the philosophical historian was then engaged.

"But Pliny was soon exposed to much greater danger than the consequences of intoxicated vanity, or even the accusations of Bebius. The tyrant, conscious of his own great unworthiness, grew alarmed at the accounts which literary men might give of his conduct to posterity; and, having determined as far as possible to stop up the channels of historical truth, he put several of the most distinguished authors to death, particularly those who, not daring to speak justly of himself, had only ventured to state the truth respecting those whom he had condemned. He also obtained a decree from the degraded senate, by which all the teachers of philosophy were banished from Rome. The celebrated Epictetus was, in virtue of this infamous proscription of knowledge, driven from the city; and, among others, Artemidorus was also obliged to seek a concealed asylum in the country. In his retreat he was visited by Pliny, who held him in great esteem, and had done him many acts of favour and friendship. These visits were discovered by some of the emissaries of the notorious Metius Carus, who accused him to Domitian of infringing the law; but, from some cause that was never explained, the emperor forbore to proceed directly against him, and he thus escaped that vengeance which ruined so many of the best men of the age.

"But, why should I thus dwell on the records of Roman iniquity? why should I thus exult, with stern satisfaction, in relating so many instances of the dastardly subjection of that haughty people? They were the enemies of Israel, and their swords were yet red with the blood of Jerusalem! Of all nations, they were the least entitled to the respect of mankind; for their only ambition was conquest, the love of vulgar shouts, and plunder to supply their barbarian licentiousness. They were now in the decline of their fortunes; their temples were deserted: but all the base feelings of their idolatrous religion were as vigorous as ever. A series of prodigies about this time filled the city with consternation, and the oracles presaged calamities and slaughter. Conspiracies were formed against the tyrant, and in the end he was assassinated; an event which transported the senators with a joy as indecorous as their pusillanimity was, in his life-time, mean. They ordered his statues to be cast down and broken, his triumphal arches to be overthrown; they even published a decree ordering all inscriptions in which he was mentioned to be obliterated, his name to be struck out of the consular tables, and his body thrown into the Tyber. But these decrees were only so many monuments of their own baseness. The criminal, whom they thus so branded with everlasting ignominy, was one in whose offences they had themselves borne a deep and most infamous part. Nothing could more strikingly illustrate the despicable condition of the Roman people, both as to spirit and manners, than these flagrant acts of affected virtue in the senators. Had there existed any true sense of public honour in Rome, the senate would have shared the fate of the tyrant. But the moral sentiments of the world were at this period in a state of change; and the fermentation excited by the intermixture of larger conceptions of Deity with the old idolatrous superstitions, dissolved the ancient principles of conduct. Every man distrusted himself and his neighbour, and no patriotic combination was practicable. Thus, only the baser passions were called into action; and, when the citizens of Rome avenged the wrongs of human nature in the flagitious Cæsars, it was not for the noble purpose of vindicating the liberties of their country, but in revenge for slights or injuries which individuals had suffered. The tyrant of the day once disposed of, they cared not who succeeded, but tolerated the next oppressor as long as they could endure his oppression.

"This general depravity of the human character among the Romans, was however redeemed by one beautiful example of faithful affection, even towards the abhorred Domitian. On the morning after his death, as I was walking along the Appian road, at some distance from the city, glad to escape from the tumultuous exultation of the populace, I fell in with a humble bier, carried with a degree of haste and anxiety that attracted my attention. Surprised by a spectacle so unusual and indecorous, I went up to the attendants, and found they were labourers belonging to Phyllis, an old lady who had been the nurse of the emperor; and that the corse which they were bearing along with so much precipitation, was the body of Domitian. Phyllis had contrived to get it secretly removed from the palace, and her bondmen were thus conveying it to her country-seat, where it was that evening burnt, and the ashes secretly deposited in the mausoleum of the Flavian family, mingled with those of Julia the daughter of Titus, whom she had likewise brought up."

Hareach, after the death of Domitian, does not appear to have remained long at Rome; nor are the other incidents which he witnessed there important. But, from that time, he seems to have detached himself entirely from the rest of mankind, although the exact occasion is not noticed; for we find him moving among the characters, and in the transactions of subsequent years, like an invisible spirit, marking the motives and the events, but taking no part in them, unless the misanthropic bitterness of his sarcasms can be supposed to have originated in sentiments of sympathy or of interest. We shall therefore pass over those minute details respecting things which history has dropped as it were behind, as unworthy of preservation, and extract his account of the Egyptians, and some of the reflections in which he indulged on beholding the stupendous monuments of that mysterious people.

CHAPTER VI.

The Antiquity and Grandeur of the Ancient Egyptians; with some Account of the Inundations of the River Nile.

"The oldest historians speak of the monuments of Egypt as the senior antiquities of all the ancient works of human art. No tradition extends to the period in which the pyramids were constructed. They are so old, that they seem as if they had always been; and so strong, as if they would stand for ever. Are they relics of antediluvian labour that have withstood the Deluge?* Are the deserts around them but the alluvial deposit of the waters that swept away the language, and the archives which contained the records and chronicles of the kings and the priests by whom these everlasting edifices were raised? But, conjecture is lost among the Egyptian mysteries; and the genius of the country, like the sphynx in the desert, regards in monumental silence the prattle and the conjectures of the learned.

"The Romans, who derived their knowledge of history chiefly from the Greeks, found so strong a resemblance between some of the ceremonies of the Egyptians, and the worship which they paid to the divinities of their own mythology, that they made no scruple of giving the gods of Egypt the same names by which they distinguished the idols of the Pantheon. But, prior to the time of Alexander the Macedonian, there is no reason to believe that any intercourse existed between the Greeks and Egyptians, except the occasional visits of travellers actuated by the thirst of knowledge or the spirit of adventure. An arid and fruitless coast, rendered dangerous by many shoals and shallow sands, had prevented the offshoots of their interior population from settling along the shores of the Mediterranean. Till the building of Alexandria, the Egyptians preferred the banks of the

---

* Universal History.

Nile, and the skirts of the Red Sea, for the site of their towns, and the depositaries of their commerce; and, as their intercourse was chiefly with the Asiatic nations, their manners and customs bore but little affinity to those of Europe. They were, indeed, altogether of an oriental character; and, for this reason, on contemplating the diversity in the architecture of their religious edifices, and the different degrees of veneration in which their deities were held, it would seem probable, that the great works of Egyptian antiquity belong to an epoch prior to the introduction of that species of Paganism which is best known as the classic mythology.

"The Egyptians themselves possessed a very high notion of their originality; for they believed that the first men in the world, as well as animals, were produced in their country; and, to support this notion, they instanced the great numbers of mice which were every year bred out of the mud left by the Nile, on its retreat, some of which were said to be often seen but partially formed, the fore-part of the body only appearing animated, and the other without motion, as not being yet quite developed from the native clay. It is however probable, that these imperfect creatures are a species of animals or reptiles; said to be bred in other parts of that country with but two legs; and the vulgar, without sufficient examination, observing some of them entangled and struggling in the mud, have supposed them to be then coming to life."*

But, before proceeding further with the remarks which Hareach makes on the antiquities of the Egyptians, we should extract his account of the Nile, that remarkable river, whose fountain-head, and annual fluctuations, were long involved in as great obscurity as the history of the country.

"A short time before the summer solstice, the waters of the Nile had evidently increased; but, before that period, the inhabitants had taken no notice of the circumstance. On that day, however, the public crier announced that the

---

* Ancient Universal History.

waters had risen to the first mark on the Nilometer; and their progress became the topic of conversation, and was viewed with interest and solicitude.

"The overflowing of the Nile is the great source of the fertility of Egypt; but, as the river could not of itself cover the lands everywhere in the necessary proportion, the inhabitants have, with infinite labour, (the accumulated skill and industry of ages,) cut a countless number of canals and trenches, which intersect the country from the one end to the other. Each town and village has its canal, and from thence smaller veins open into the different fields. Where the ground is above the level which the waters commonly attain, they are raised to flood it by engines worked by oxen. The whole surface of the country is formed into various level spaces, surrounded with embanked trenches, supplied by these feeders with water. As the land is perfectly even, the gardens, which are the most fertile in the world, are formed into little square beds, surrounded, like the fields devoted to agriculture, also with trenches upon a small scale; and the gardeners, when they want to water one of these beds, open one of the trenches, which immediately furnishes the requisite supply; after which, they stop it up again: and thus they manage the rest.

"The Egyptians, in their agriculture, are not subjected to the laborious tasks of ploughing, digging, or breaking the clods. When the waters of their river have subsided, they have only to spread a little sand where the mud is left too deep and rich, and they then sow with little trouble, and with no other charge than the hire of the husbandman. Of old, it is said, they even spared themselves much of this expence, by sending in their herds of swine to tread the seed into the ground; but this practice, if it ever existed, had become obsolete before my first visit to that country. Their spring commences in the time of the vintage in Europe, when the waters begin to retire; and their harvest answers to the seed-time of Britain.

"But the fertilizing qualities of these annual benefactions of the Nile, are not confined to the earth; their influence extends to mankind and to animals. It has been found, by regular experience, that the new waters make women fruitful. They usually conceive in the two months immediately following the summer solstice, when the river is increasing, and are delivered in the Roman months of April and May. Cows have often two calves at a time, and sheep yean twice a-year, having generally two lambs the first time; and I have seen goats followed by four kids, which they had brought in six months.

"No two spectacles in nature can be more dissimilar than the appearance of northern countries in summer and in winter; but the contrast in Egypt, when the waters are out, and when they have retired, is, if possible, still more striking. I ascended the loftiest of the pyramids, while the river was at its highest flood. The country appeared like a sea of glass, studded with numerous villages, towns, turrets, and spires, intermingled with trees whose tops only were above the waters, and bounded by the distant mountains.* But, when the Nile has retired into his bed, and the ground is covered with the young herbage, the same prospect presents a universal meadow, with herds and flocks scattered in all directions, and the cheerful sight of husbandmen and gardeners busy in the fields and gardens. The air is then embalmed by the fragrance of a prodigious quantity of flowers, and the blossoms of the fruit-trees, and enlivened by the continual fluttering and voices of innumerable birds."

Hareach, after these general remarks on the country of Egypt, describes the various natural productions of the soil, and the animals and reptiles. It is unnecessary for us to extract them, as the description of such things does not fall within the scope of the present work. We shall therefore now attend him to the relics of ancient magnificence; topics that perhaps, in strict propriety, we should also omit, having only engaged to give his account

---

* The author does not seem to have visited any of the steeples in Holland, which present a view very similar to what he has here described.

of the manners and customs of the people that he visited in his long wanderings; but it is impossible to speak of the Egyptians, without recalling to mind the wonderful monuments of their former greatness, or indeed, to understand the object of many of their peculiar usages and notions, without referring to the age, the fame, and characteristics, of these astonishing structures.

CHAPTER VII.

Reflections on the Character and Religion of the Ancient Egyptians.

The Greek and Roman writers are not to be trusted in any thing that concerns the antiquities of other nations. They have assumed that the Trojan war, which owes all its dignity and all its consequence to the genius of Homer, was an event that influenced the destiny of the surrounding countries. It has doubtless done so, and even that of mankind, but only by the creative powers of the poet; for no satisfactory trace of the event can be discovered beyond the time of Homer.

We have been led to make this observation, by an incidental remark of our excursive author, who, in speaking of the environs of the city of Canopus, situated near one of the mouths of the Nile, says, "that, in this part of Egypt, flax and hemp were more particularly cultivated than in any other part of the country;" and he infers, from this circumstance, that the place derived the name of Canopus, which may be translated *hemp-town*. He does not seem to have been aware that it was alleged, by the Greek and Roman writers, to have been built by the Spartans, in honour of a pilot called Canopus, who was buried on the spot, at the time when Menelaus, on his return from the seige of Troy, was driven by contrary winds on the coast of Lybia.* A curious mythologian might discover, even in this tradition, the elements of a fable which referred to the cultivation of hemp, of which the cordage of vessels, in all ages, has been usually made. But, to resume our extracts.

"Their stupendous monuments not only prove the ancient Egyptians to have been a great people, but the wisdom of their laws, and the extent of their knowledge, placed them at the head of all the nations of the earliest antiquity. They are said to have been the first who found out the rules of government, and the art of improving the enjoyments of life—the true end of politics. The relics of their edifices, which still excite so much wonder, demonstrate that they must have possessed the means of supporting a very large proportion of their population, unconnected with the productive labours of agriculture; for they were not much engaged in foreign commerce. Of all their public works their harbours appear to have been the least considerable; and, what was their principal emporium, Alexandria, was formed long posterior to the epochs of their ancient greatness.

"But, notwithstanding the practical wisdom of their government, the Egyptians were deeper sunk in the moral degradations of idolatry than all the surrounding nations. In some respects, however, this folly was of a more refined character than that of the Geeks and Romans. It retained the emblematic principle more obviously in the ceremonies of worship. Their religion was, in reality, a symbolical commemoration of the phenomena of nature; and those festivals which they periodically celebrated, many of which the Greeks adopted without knowing their object, were originally established to mark the progression of time and the changes of the seasons. But the ancient astronomical ritual was corrupted by the reverence in which they held the memory of their great men, some of whom were commemorated by festivals illustrative of their actions, by which, in the end, they came to be ranked with the gods, and their festivals added to those which were purely religious.

---

* Tacitus.

"It was however an important part of the education of their priests, to discriminate between the festivals that were only commemorative, and those by which the knowledge of the laws of nature was at once taught and preserved; for the common people were apt to confound them; and the memory of a king was sometimes as much reverenced as the sun and moon, which they religiously regarded as the great causes of nutrition and generation.

"In what manner the worship of the stars, or the heavenly host, was first established, I could never ascertain. The origin had either been lost in the lapse of ages, or the priests, by their oaths, were forbidden to disclose it. I have sometimes thought, in looking at the signs of the zodiac, so frequently seen in their temples, and introduced among the hieroglyphics, that the mystery of their sacred animals, and many of their ceremonies, had an occult reference to those symbolic figures; and I amused my fancy in supposing that the zodiac itself was an allegorical comment on the progress of the year."

As there is some fancy in the account which Hareach gives of this hypothesis, we shall extract it; but the reader must be aware that it rests altogether on the ingenuity of the author. For, although the Egyptians held the bull of Apis in reverence, and as the representative of their god Osiris; though they considered the ram, as emblematic of Jupiter; and the goat, as symbolical of Pan, one of the most ancient of all the gods; though the dog, the crocodile, and different other animals, as well as plants, were held by these singular people in religious veneration; there is no sufficiently-authentic account of the times and ceremonies of their festivals extant, to support this effort of ingenuity.

"I supposed," says Hareach, "that the form of the symbols were derived from objects that marked on earth the periodical influence of particular stars. Thus, when the sun was moving through a certain constellation, it was observed that the sheep brought forth their lambs; hence, the name of that animal was given to the constellation. When he had passed into another, the bull was chosen as the symbol, conceiving, as oxen were employed in agriculture, that, by him the period for cultivating the earth was represented. To the sign of the bull succeeded that of the Twins, or the pair, which indicated the mating season of birds. In Cancer, the crab or tortoise, I could perceive the allegorical index of the spawning-time of fish, when those of the testaceous species come to deposit their eggs on the sand, to be hatched by the heat of the sun. In the Lion, I in like manner discovered an emblematic representation of the season, when young beasts of prey come abroad in the greatest numbers. Under the sign of the Virgin, the fittest season for marriage was typified; the preparatory labours of tillage being then over, and the harvest not yet come. In the Balance, I saw the period described, when the husbandman reckons the produce of his field against the seed and charge of labour. And, in looking at the Scorpion, I thought it indicated the increasing coldness of the weather, when such offensive creatures are apt to invade the hearths and couches of mankind. By the figure of the Hunter, it seemed to be denoted, that during the time the sun was passing over the stars which he represented, mankind was authorised, by nature, to kill those birds and animals for food, which, but for some such reduction of their number, would uselessly perish during the nakedness of the fields. In the sign of the Goat, I persuaded myself that the stormy season was described, conceiving his hoary hair, and the manner in which he tosses his head in butting, emblematic of the foam and motion of the waves. Aquarius, pouring water from his urn, seemed the evident symbol of the close of winter, when the snow on the mountains is thawed, and descends in torrents through the valleys. And the Fish, denoted still more strikingly, in my opinion, that the seas were again free to the navigator. Perhaps, however, the signs of the zodiac are of antediluvian origin, and were formed when the year consisted but of twelve revolutions of the moon."

CHAPTER VIII.

Of the Manners and Customs of the Ancient Egyptians.

"The priests of Egypt may have possessed the knowledge of the only one living and true God; but the people worshiped twelve fabulous deities. Osiris and Isis, are supposed to have represented the sun and moon; and the Egyptian Jupiter, was the spirit of life; Vulcan, fire; Ceres, the earth; Oceanus, moisture; and Minerva, the air.* But the apotheosis of their kings, and their emblematic worship, are so blended together, that the true nature of their religion will never be understood until the hieroglyphics can be read.

"While I was at Memphis, the bull of Apis died, and the carcass was deposited, with great funeral pomp, in one of the pyramids;† immediately after which, the priests, who knew the twenty-nine sacred marks that distinguished the bull of Apis, went in search of his successor over all the country; and having found him, he was brought with great joy, attended by an exulting multitude of all ages, to the banks of the Nile, where he was lodged in a house prepared for him, and fed for forty days with consecrated food. He was then embarked in a gilded vessel, and carried to Memphis, where he was purified by being made to pass through fire. When this was done, women only, for forty days, were allowed to see him; but, after that time, they were never more admitted to his presence.

"But, of all the Egyptian superstitions, the veneration in which they held the crocodile was the most degrading; for, of all creatures, a crocodile seems to be last to which

---

* Universal History.
† In opening one of the pyramids, Belzoni found, in a sarcophagus, several bones which, on being examined in London, proved to be those of a bull or cow.

mankind would ever pay divine honours; and yet the respect with which the people of this country regarded it, exceeds belief. I saw one that daily visited a temple on the banks of the lake Mœris. He was trained up to be tame and familiar: his head was adorned with strings of pearl, and his fore-feet with chains of gold. He was fed with dainties by the priests; and it was customary with strangers, who went to see him, to carry a cake for him of meat dressed with wine, or a drink prepared with honey. It was ludicrous to observe the native knavery of the creature, when the priests, with great reverence, offered him food. He seemed, as it were, conscious of the absurdity of their conduct, and would often, when they were feeding him, with the greatest affectation of solemnity, slyly snatch the offering from their hands, and devour it, with an expression of playful cunning in his eye, as if in ridicule of their folly.

"The Egyptians were a peculiarly serious people: they followed a method and a rule in all they did, often in despite, as it were, of reason. They ate and rejected different kinds of food, merely because they were allowed, or forbidden, by the priests; and, by way of an inducement to their guests to make merry, it was usual, after supper, before tasting the wine, to bring in a coffin with a mummy in it, to which the company were requested to look, while the steward of the banquet called aloud, 'Behold this, and be merry; for, such as this is shalt thou be, when thy days of life are ended.'

"In their dwelling-houses, the Egyptians were frugal, and even negligent. They were built of unburnt bricks, formed of the mud of the Nile, and considered by them as inns and places of temporary residence. But, in those everlasting edifices which they constructed in honour of their gods, they spared neither labour, skill, nor treasure; and their sepulchres were also constructed as their eternal mansions: hence it is, that the traveller in vain searches for the ruins of the domestic edifices of this wonderful nation. They have long crumbled into dust; and their residue constitutes no small portion of the sand and pulverised earth that covers so many of their sacred antiquities.

"The Egyptians believed that the soul lingered about the body after death, as long as it could be preserved free from corruption, and then entered into some other animal; and passing, by a continual metempsychosis, through the different kinds of animals, returned again into the human form, at the completion of a cycle, which embraced about three thousand years. For this reason, they endeavoured to preserve the body as long as possible, that the soul might continue with it; and hence, the origin of that unknown art, by which it has been said that they kept the dead in everlasting beauty. But, the origin of the notion that the soul, after the revolution of its fated cycle, returned again into the body, is not so easily traced. The priests, however, were great astrologers, and referred all terrestrial events to certain corresponding movements of the heavenly bodies; and hence, perhaps, they believed that they had discovered a periodical similarity in human affairs, and consequently inferred, that similar characters were always found under similar circumstances.

"The master of the house where I resided died; and, as he was a person of some consideration, the preparations for his funeral were according to the ancient and most honourable practice of the country. The women of the family, having their heads strewed with ashes, their bosoms bare, went into the streets, and, followed by all their female relations, deplored their loss, and recounted the virtues of the deceased with loud lamentations for his death. The men also formed a separate band, and mourned for him in the same manner; and this they continued daily till the embalming was completed, abstaining in the meantime from all enjoyment. I was however more curious to witness the process of embalming than to attend their fulsome affectation of sorrow; for, worthy and wise as their relation no doubt was, it was perfectly evident, that all this parade of grief had but little to do with the feelings of the heart.

"The embalmers having laid the body on the table, drew the brains out with a crooked instrument by the nostrils, and filled the vacancy in the head with odoriferous gums and spices. An incision was then made on the left side of the belly, by which the intestines were carefully removed. The hollow was then cleansed, and filled with aromatic drugs; and the entrails having been washed in wine of palms, gummed, and perfumed, were restored to their place, and the incision closed. The body was then steeped in an ointment prepared of wax and spices, where it remained upwards of twenty days; at the expiry of which, it was taken up, and bound in fillets of linen covered with gum, and placed in a wooden coffin. All this was done without disfiguring the body; so that the very hairs remained on the brows and the eye-lids, as well as the countenance, which was so well preserved as to be easily known.* As he was to be buried in the Island of Flowers, in the Nile, public notice of the day in which he was to pass the river was given, and the magistrates and the priests invited to attend the funeral. On the shore of the island, a select number of the priests at the time appointed were seated, and the body, having been embarked in a boat by itself, was rowed by a solitary old priest to the island.† Here, before it was allowed to be put on-shore, the chief priest demanded of the spectators, and persons forming the funeral assemblage, if they had any injury or wrong to allege against the deceased, why he should not be buried in the holy island.‡ No objection being made, the body was landed, and conducted with hymns of exultation to the sepulchre, which had been prepared for its reception."

---

* Universal History.

† The Grecian fable of Charon, and the river Styx, is evidently derived from this ceremony.

‡ This island is still a hallowed place in the eyes of the Egyptians. Mahomedans of a religious turn of mind sequester themselves in it; and Christian strangers are not permitted to land. Curtin, servant of Belzoni, was once on-shore there, and saw in the sepulchres several mummies which were not in coffins. It has been supposed that Herodotus, in speaking of the Egyptian funeral ceremonies, meant an island in the lake Mœris: I am inclined to think, however, that it was to this place he referred.

EGYPTIAN REMAINS

London Pub.d by J.Souter No.169.

CHAPTER IX.

Manners and Customs of the Pastoral Arabs.

HARBACH's account of the simple Arabs affords a curious contrast to the artificial manners of the Egyptians. We shall give it at length.

" Desirous of visiting the scenes which had been hallowed by the footsteps of Israel, in their journey from Egypt to the Land of Canaan, I passed over into Arabia, where I found many of the customs of the cotemporaries of Abraham still unchanged. In going to Petræa, which had then declined from its ancient consequence, but whose sculptured rocks and monumental edifices are not unworthy to be viewed, even after the everlasting piles of Egypt, the travellers that I had joined in the journey placed themselves under the protection of a tribe of Arabs; for the roads were rendered unsafe by the incessant predatory warfare of these sons of Ishmael—that people who, without any settled habitations, have preserved the most unchanged character of all the nations of the earth.

" They still live in tents, still worship as of old, and still preserve, in their songs and traditions, the religion and laws of their fathers. Their tents are formed of cloth of goats'-hair mixed with that of the camel, and coarse wool made by the women. Each tent is divided into two apartments, one of which is set apart for the men, the other for the women; and, in the latter, all the domestic operations of cooking, &c. are performed. These itinerant habitations are shifted with surprising celerity. The furniture consists of few, and these the most primitive, utensils: a wooden bowl, of the rudest workmanship; a common hand-mill; two or three kettles, of copper or of iron; a few goat-skins, to hold milk or water; and cushions and carpets, woven by the women, of a coarse texture, but not inelegant in the distribution of the colours. The place of honour in the tent, is marked by the saddle of the dromedary.

F

"The encampment of a tribe consists of a number of tents, arranged in a circular form, so as to enclose a considerable area. At sun-set, the flocks of sheep and goats are driven into this circle, and are stationed near the tents of their respective owners; the kids and lambs being fastened by a rope, pegged-down with nooses, to prevent them from sucking their dams. The camels are the last that come in, and the old ones, of their own accord, kneel down close to the tents of their masters. In the morning, the she-camels are first milked, and then driven out to feed upon the more scanty and distant herbage; afterwards, the sheep and goats; and the kids and lambs being liberated, they are turned out to graze near the camp.

"On the evening before we reached the city, we arrived at an encampment situated on the edge of a high precipitous cliff, at the foot of which stood an inconsiderable village, where we watered our horses. In front of us we saw Mount Hor, on the top of which stands the tomb of Aaron; and, at a distance, the hazy summit of Sinai was discovered in the remote horizon.

"While we were engaged in contemplating the magnificent prospect from this place, a dispute arose between the chief of our conductors and the sheikh of the camp, the latter declaring that we should not be permitted to pass through his lands. Our guide, seeing him so determined, called to us; and, mounting his horse, bade us follow his example. Grasping his spear, with a fierce and courageous look, he exclaimed 'I have set them on their horses, and let me see who will dare to impede their passage.' We then rode off, and the enemy prepared to follow us. In the course of about half an hour, we fell in with a party of the same tribe, who had undertaken to convey us safe to Petræa, which added fresh spirit to our bold conductor; and he swore that we should not only go directly towards the city through the lands of our opponents, but freely drink of the waters of a stream which lay across the road in that direction, and over which the inhospitable sheikh claimed the exclusive privilege of watering his herds and flocks.

"The enemy however had, in the meantime, taken another route, and was posted on the banks of the stream, to oppose our passage, before we arrived. Observing this, and being averse to bloodshed, we sent a messenger to the sheikh to say, that, if he would allow us to go over unmolested, we should not taste the water; and, after a long captious negociation, and the offering of presents, we at last were permitted to pass.

"This contest brought to my recollection a similar affair, in which Moses was engaged with the chief of the Edomites; for we were now in the land of Edom. 'Let us pass,' was the message of the patriarch to the king, 'I pray thee, through the country; we will not pass through the fields, or through the vineyards, neither will we drink of the water of the wells; we will go by the king's highway; we will not turn to the right hand nor to the left, until we have passed thy borders.' But Edom said unto him, 'Thou shalt not pass by me, lest I come out against thee with the sword.'*

"The pastoral life of the warlike tribes which inhabit this part of Asia, is favourable to their predilection for the indulgence of the imagination; and, accordingly, they excel in the invention of fictions, and the elegance of poetical conception. But it also tends to cherish among them the feelings of a vague superstition. They are great believers in fortune-tellers; and they even consider the camel, on some occasions, as an oracular animal, whose looks and voice are not to be disregarded with impunity. But, with this weakness of human nature, they possess a grandeur of mind that often excited my profoundest respect, even when it was shown under circumstances calculated to inspire lighter sentiments.

"One day, while I was with a tribe of the Bedoueens, a man, who had spoken contemptuously of his chief, was sentenced to be punished; and, while he awaited the preparations that were making for that purpose, his wife ran to the sheikh, and claimed his protection in the first place, and then solicited the pardon of her husband. The first

---

* Numbers xx. 17-18.

was readily granted: 'But (said the skeikh) your husband has done me an unpardonable wrong.'—'I acknowledge (said the wife) that he has done the offence that has been committed, and that it deserves the most exemplary punishment; but my husband is not altogether to blame.'—'How is that?' interrupted the sheikh.—'He is but half guilty, (replied the woman;) am not I his other half: I who never did you wrong,—and the guilty half is under the protection of the innocent,—and you cannot punish the one without harming the other.' The anger of the sheikh was disarmed by this reply, and the husband was pardoned.*

"On another occasion, I had an opportunity of witnessing a still more striking example of the magnanimity with which they often pardoned what might be deemed the greatest personal wrongs.

"One night, a Bedoueen having surprised the son of his chief with his wife, killed him on the spot, and threw the body into the middle of the area round which the tents were placed. At break of day the corse was found, and the father was informed of his loss by the grief and clamour of the tribe, with whom the young man was a great favourite. Instant search was made, and the murderer was discovered. Every Arab demanded immediate vengeance; but the father staid their fury, and requested time to examine into the circumstances of the crime. Two days past, and the murderer breathed only between life and death. On the third night, the chief went to him alone; interrogated him minutely respecting the whole transaction, and, being convinced of the irresistible provocation which the man had received from his son, exclaimed 'Brother, rise; profit by the sleep of the tribe,—fly; but, remember that it is the death of a son that I have forgiven.'

"When an Arab falls in battle, his wife does not abandon herself to grief, but glories as it were in his loss, and strives to gain the respect of all by her fortitude. Courage is, indeed, the great virtue of this undebauched

---

* Les Bédouins, par T. J. Mayeux.

people. Undismayed by darkness, storms, or beasts of prey, the Arab travels the pathless desert alone; and, in the field of battle, his wife attends him without dread, that she may be ready to assist him when he is wounded.

"A martial spirit pervades all the actions of the Arabs, and mingles with their amusements. Their dances are in imitation of combats, and their songs are distinguished for their heroic sentiments. But, with all the fine enthusiasm of their character, they have but a slight conception of music. It is only among the inhabitants of mountainous countries, that I have met with any impressive modulations of that delightful art, unconnected with poetry. The music of the Arabs pierces the ear, but it does not reach the heart; and yet their songs are possessed of wonderful merit. The verses are sweet, and full of pathos. The words are chosen with exquisite skill, and the stanzas closed with admirable precision.*

"In their diet they are remarkably frugal: their greatest luxury is the flesh of the kid or goat boiled in milk.†

"Their criminal justice is administered according to a principle of equivalents; an eye for an eye, and a tooth for a tooth,—precepts adopted in the Mosaic code, and executed with rigour. The impress of a divine legislation may be traced in their judicature, and in the maxims of their morality; but their manners and customs are corrupted with the infirmities of human nature.

"In marriage, they allow themselves the freedom of the patriarchal ages. Their manner of life is, indeed, in all things patriarchal, although it is not often the custom that the men indulge themselves with more than one wife, and divorce is rare among them; which has been ascribed to the practice of intermarriage among cousins and relations; the mutual adherence of the members of a tribe being thus secured, as it were, by the ties of natural blood. There are, however, certain distinct causes which may warrant divorce. Incompatibility of disposition,

---

* Les Bédouins, par Mon. Mayeux.
† Exodus, chap. xxvii. 19.

the waste of their property, misconduct, disobedience, repugnance in conjugal affection, and sterility. I speak not of adultery, for that is punished with death.

"The divorced are not permitted to be re-united, unless an intermediate marriage with another party has taken place; in which case, the conditions of the divorce are done away, and the original parties are considered as if they had never been man and wife.

"The obsequies of the Arabs are performed with simplicity, but the rites are very solemn. A primitive people, and immediate in the effect of all they do, they have no occult meaning in their ceremonies, like the Egyptians. What they perform at the funerals of their friends, is the natural expression of sorrow, heightened perhaps a little by the circumstances of public exhibition; and, when they consign the body to the earth, they practise no mystery indicative of any theological opinion.

"On one occasion, during my excursions in the neighbourhood of Petræa, I particularly remarked this.—The air was that afternoon close and sultry. The wind came from the south-east, but its breathings were languid, and loaded with disease. I was walking alone in the rocky environs of the city, and, weary with the oppression in the atmosphere, I sat down on a rock, overwhelmed with low and melancholy thought. The skies were obscured, but it could not be said that they were overcast. It was rather as if the vault of heaven had been filled with a thin, dingy smoke, than loaded with masses of cloud. While I was thus yielding to the melancholy reflections which my solitary state and the general dejection of nature inspired, I observed a band of Arabs approaching, bearing a corse on a litter. When they arrived at the place of interment, they laid the body on the ground; and, having dug a grave, consigned it to the earth with only a silent token of resignation to the will of Providence, and walked sorrowfully away. I was much affected by this scene: it struck me as transcendantly more sublime and appropriate than all the sumptuous pomp of an Egyptian funeral. They came before me with the soundlessness of a vision, and passed away as an apparition that had never been. The transit of the man from his birth to the grave, was not a thing of more insignificance than his obsequies; but yet, the silence of the ceremony thrilled my spirit as a spectacle of fearful sublimity."

Another Chapter must be devoted to Hareach's description of Petræa, and his visits to the tombs of Aaron and Abraham. We are not aware that any account of these interesting places is yet to be met with, out of the Volume which has furnished us with the particulars that we mean to transcribe. The narrative, therefore, does not only merit the attention of our youthful and ingenuous readers, but may challenge the antiquarian erudition of the grave and learned. How far it is correct we cannot judge. We state it in all essentials as it has met our eye, and future travellers alone must decide as to the fidelity of the descriptions. History coroborates the account of the chief incidents.

CHAPTER X.

The City of Petræa, and the Tombs of Abraham and Aaron.

[A. D. 106.]

"When Aulus Cornelius Palma, the Roman governor of Syria, reduced Arabia Petræa to the dominion of the emperor, the capital of the country was still a considerable city, though much declined from its former grandeur. It would seem as if all states and kingdoms, whether great or small, indicate, by a certain visible decay, the approach of their political death; but the city of Petræa, like the wonders of Egypt, possessed a sort of everlasting character, that was calculated to transmit the impress of its ancient kings to an interminable period. Desolation sat weaving in unmolested silence the cobwebs of oblivion in her temples, but Ruin was denied admission.

"The structures of this venerable metropolis have existed from an unknown antiquity. They are the works of the same epoch in which the imperishable fabrics of Egypt and India were constructed; nor can they be destroyed, but by the exertion of a power and perseverance equal to the original labour bestowed on their formation; for they are not built, but hewn, with incredible industry, from the masses and precipices of the living rock.

"We crossed a clear and sparkling rivulet, whose cool and delicious appearance irresistibly invited our horses to drink; and we halted to indulge them. We were then near one of the chief entrances to the town; but, instead of the busy circumstances which commonly indicate the vicinity of such a place, a solemn silence reigned in the air; while the drowsy chirping of the grasshoppers, and the lulling murmurs of the flowing stream, served as an accompaniment that deepened its awful effect.

"When we had again mounted, we rode forward without speaking; and the first object that attracted our attention was a magnificent mausoleum, the gate of which was open, as if ready for the reception of new offerings to oblivion. Two colossal sphynx stood at each side of the portal; but their form was defaced, and they seemed to be the monuments of a people that were greater and older than the race of man. We then entered a winding chasm between stupendous precipices, whose overhanging edges frequently darkened the path below. Above us, at a vast height, it was spanned by the arch of an aqueduct, from a small fissure in which, the water was continually dropping; and it sounded in my ears as if the genius of the place was mournfully reckoning the passing moments.

"The sides of this awful passage were, in some places, hollowed into niches; in others, dark openings into sepulchres yawned, from which a fearful echo within mocked the mortal sound of our passing, with accents so prophetic and oracular, that they thrilled our hearts with superstitious horror; and here and there masses of the rock stood forward from the wall, bearing a mysterious resemblance to living things: but time and ruin has wrapped their sculpture in an irremoveable and eternal veil.

"As we drew near to the termination of this avenue of death and oblivion, a tremendous spectacle of human folly burst upon our view. It was a temple to Victory, adorned with the pomp of centaurs and lapithæ, and the statue of the goddess, with her wings outspread as if just alighted. Perhaps it was placed there to commemorate the funeral triumphs of Destruction, whose innumerable trophies were displayed on all sides.

"But, although the architects of these works have perished, and their monuments have only outlasted themselves by being formed of a more stubborn substance, the inscrutable memorials of their greatness and power, of their wealth, intelligence, and splendour, still obscurely preserved in the legendary poetry of their descendants, serve to inspire high notions of their refinement; and the ruins of their metropolis bear witness to the truth of the suggestion."

To this we would add, that the genii and the talismans of their tales are, perhaps, but the spectral remembrance of the sages and the science that adorned the remote epochs of those kings by whom the temples and palaces of Petra were excavated.

After remaining some time at Petræa, our author appears to have visited the tomb of Abraham, distant about two days' journey from that city, and which he describes as covered by a consecrated building respected by the Romans as a temple, the architecture of which had all the vast features that characterise the first monumental edifices of antiquity, when durability was the principle chiefly attended to. The stones were of such a prodigious magnitude, that they could not be removed or destroyed without employing a constancy of labour,—such as men never have recourse to in the work of destruction.

Hareach then proceeded to Mount Hor, and ascended that ridge of the hills on which the tomb of Aaron (a simple stone monument) is still preserved. Here, while sitting on the mountain, and reflecting on the long course of miracles and events which had distinguished his nation since the time of that great high priest, an old pilgrim, who had come from Egypt, recognized him as having been at Alexandria many years before, and enquired if he was not the famous Apollonius Tyaneus.

What answer was given is not recorded; but, as the life and conduct of Apollonius tends to throw considerable light on the manners and opinions of that age, we shall suspend our extracts from the mysterious Volume, to give a brief sketch of his adventures and character.

CHAPTER XI.

History of Apollonius Tyaneus.

APOLLONIUS TYANEUS was born three or four years before the Christian æra, at Tyana, a city in Cappadocia. His birth was foretold, and accompanied with many prodigies, if we may credit Philostratus, who has written his Life. At the age of fourteen he applied himself to the study of the Pythagoric philosophy; first at Tarsus, the capital of Cilicia, and afterwards at Ægæ, another city of the same province, under the direction of one Euxenes. At the age of sixteen he retired to a house in the country, where, according to the principles of that sect, he led a life of great austerity, abstaining from animal food, allowing his hair to grow, going barefoot, and clad only in linen, that he might use nothing proceeding from any living creature. After some time, he removed from his country residence to the temple of Esculapius, in Ægæ, where he commenced censor and reformer of manners, exhibiting in his own conduct an eminent example of purity, disinterestedness, and benevolence.

By the death of his father he obtained a considerable inheritance, of which he reserved very little to himself, giving the major part to his brother, and other necessitous relations. By his persuasion, he appeased several seditious tumults in Cilicia, Pamphylia, and especially at Aspenda, where the populace threatened to burn the chief magistrate, for not obliging some of the wealthy inhabitants to sell their corn at a reasonable price during a famine.

He afterwards went to Antioch and Ephesus, and other cities of Asia Minor, where he revived the worship of deities, which had been long neglected; and he practised in all these places secret mysteries, to which those alone were admitted who had observed silence for the space of five years. The long course of abstinence to which he had subjected himself, began, it is alleged, to have an influence on his understanding; and he allowed himself to imagine and promulgate the most fantastic reveries, as revelations from heaven.

He assumed the character of a legislator, requiring nothing from others but what he had himself performed. He boasted of a thorough intuitive knowledge of all languages, and declared that the most secret recesses of the heart lay open before him. Still, he had but only seven disciples; and these deserted him when he proposed that they should go with him to India, and visit the Brahmins. He however set out himself, attended only by two domestics, and was joined at Nineveh by Damis, a native of that place, who, of all the disciples he ever had, proved the most devoted, and observed with care, and recorded with the minuteness of a Boswell, his most trifling words and actions. In his journey from Nineveh to Babylon, he was inspired with the notion that he had discovered the art of interpreting the oracles delivered by birds.

Upon his arrival at Babylon, he introduced himself to the magi of that city, and often conferred with them in private. In India he was received by a magnificent king named Phraothes, and introduced to Hiarchus, the chief of the Brahmins. Having spent four months with these priests, and attended them often in secret conferences to which Damis was not admitted, he returned by sea to the Trigs, deeply impressed with their wisdom. He then again visited Babylon, and thence passing through Nineveh, stopped a short time at Antioch; and finally settled in Ionia, residing sometimes at Ephesus, and sometimes at Smyrna.

The exemplary purity of his own life, and his indefatigable exertions, had, wherever he went, a beneficial influence on manners. He repressed licentiousness, and accomplished the reformation of great moral depravity.

Quitting Ionia he went to Athens, where he succeeded in abolishing the inhuman spectacles of the gladiators. He allowed no relaxation to his endeavors as a reformer; and not only at Athens, but at Corinth, in Lacedæmon, and in Crete, he achieved wonders. He subsequently went to Rome, but was banished by Nero. He then retired to Cadiz, where he encouraged Galba to revolt against that tyrant, and assume the sovereignty.

From Cadiz he crossed over to Africa, and soon after returned to Etruria, and thence passed to Sicily, where he received intelligence of Nero's death. He did not however go to Rome, but sailed for Greece, where he remained some time, and then went to Egypt, where he was followed by prodigious multitudes. Vespasian, while in Egypt, consulted him about the state of his affairs, and was instructed by him to govern with equity and moderation. He travelled into Ethiopia, intending to visit the sources of the Nile, but did not ascend beyond the third cataract. About the time that Titus took Jerusalem, he returned to Egypt; and the following year, having gone over to Greece, he met that conqueror at Argos, from which city he made a second and more extensive journey through the country; and then went to Rome, where he excited the people against the vices of Domitian.

From Rome he went to Asia, where Domitian, enraged at his seditious virtue in Rome, sent orders to the governor to seize and send him back in chains; but, before the order arrived, Apollonius was already on his way to the capital, undismayed by the knowledge of the emperor's hatred, or the edicts which had been published, banishing the philosophers. On his arrival he was arrested; and, after being imprisoned several days, was brought before

Domitian. His deportment must have been singular; for the tyrant declared him innocent, and immediately after admitted him to a private audience, and heard, with emotion of dread, the severity of his animadversions. Having warned the tyrant of the evil consequences of giving ear to informers, he added, " As for myself, I am not under the least apprehension: you may cause me to be seized; but, put me to death you cannot—that the laws of fate and my destiny will not allow." He then passed from the presence of Domitian, and was the same evening, it is said, seen at Patioli, distant three days' journey from the city. Thence he sailed for Sicily, where he remained two years, followed by vast crowds, whom he exhorted to virtue and benevolence; and, having a third time visited Greece, he again retired to Ionia, residing as before alternately at Ephesus and Smyrna.

On the day that Domitian was slain, he was preaching to a numerous assembly at Ephesus; and, at the very time that the blow was struck, he suddenly lowered his voice, apparently seized with fear, but nevertheless pursued his discourse, often however stopping, as if his attention were intent upon another subject. At length he left off speaking, fixed his eyes steadfastly on the ground, and, after a short silence, exclaimed " Strike home; strike the tyrant dead,—courage! dispatch the tyrant." The audience, astonished at this extraordinary rhapsody, stood in silence; but he soon recollected himself, and bade them rejoice, for Domitian was no more. The same story is told of him by Dio Cassius as well as by Philostratus; and he adds, that Apollonius even mentioned in his reverie the name of Stephanus, who actually struck the blow.

Nerva, who succeeded Domitian, was the friend of Apollonius; and no sooner had he taken possession of the empire, than he invited him to Rome; but the philosopher replied, that, by the decrees of fate, they were never more to see one another. He however wrote the emperor a letter filled with excellent political admonitions. This paper he sent by Damis his disciple, and in his absence embarked at Ephesus for Lindus, in the island of Rhodes, where he disappeared, and was never afterwards heard of.

No character in the Roman annals was involved in so much mystery as that of this philosopher; but the purity of his manners, and his disinterestedness, with his inimitable exhortations to reformation, rendered him an object of religious veneration to the people. As no person could give any certain account of his death, his countrymen, the inhabitants of Tyana, believed him immortal, and revered him as a divinity. His images were erected in many temples; and the emperors, instead of suppressing, countenanced this superstition. Adrian collected and preserved his letters. Antonius Caracalla honoured him with divine worship, and consecrated a temple to him; and the emperor Alexander Severus kept his image in a private chamber in his palace with those of Our Saviour, of Abraham, and other sages and kings, famed for wisdom, holiness, and justice. Vossius tells us that Aurelian, having resolved to give up the city of Tyana to be plundered, Apollonius appeared to him, and persuaded him to abandon the design; and adds, that the emperor, convinced by the apparition that Apollonius was a god, devoted to him an image, a temple, and a statue.

CHAPTER XII.

Biographical Anecdotes of the Emperor Trajan.

[A. D. 102–118.]

As the early years of the emperor Trajan were spent in the camps of the eastern provinces,* where he acquired the military reputation which afterwards contributed to raise him to the imperial dignity, it was natural, when he obtained

---

* Pliny's Pan.

the power, that he should seek to realise the plans of conquest that he had no doubt formed in his youth, while serving in those countries in an inferior station.* Accordingly, as soon as he had finished the war with the Dacians, he prepared for that campaign in Asia by which the frontiers of the Roman empire were extended to their utmost destined limits. Our excursive author appears to have joined him at Antioch, and to have accompanied him throughout the whole of his career. We shall therefore extract a few of the leading incidents which occurred in the course of that triumphant progress, especially his account of the emperor himself, whose character exhibited more of the best virtues of the ancients than any other of the Roman sovereigns.

"He seemed to be about forty-five years of age; but his appearance, notwithstanding the hardships in which his youth had been spent, was younger than his years. His countenance was open, manly, and majestic; his stature tall, and well-formed, and his air and manners at once noble and engaging.† Bred up in the tumults of a camp, he had not acquired that variety of knowledge which is distinguished by the epithet of learning, but he generously encouraged in others what he was conscious he himself wanted; and his good sense enabled him, on all occasions, to appear an accomplished prince. He was without question the greatest captain of his own age, nor inferior in this respect to the most celebrated of antiquity. In the duties of war he was indefatigable, and he delighted in its toils. He always marched on foot at the head of his armies, even after he was emperor; and crossed extensive countries without ever mounting a horse, or allowing himself the luxury of a chariot. In the frugality of his diet, he was an example to the common soldier; and the simplicity of his garb became the temperance of his table. He was the first officer, in his camp, abroad in the morning, and the last that retired to the couch in the evening; and, though a vigilant disciplinarian, he was

---

* Universal History. † Dio.

distinguished for that frank affability which commands the manly heart, and often conversed familiarly with the old soldiers, knowing them by name, and reminding them of the battles in which they had fought together. But, with all these military virtues, he was no less eminent in the talents which are requisite to govern well in peace. When he assumed the sovereignty, he declared that he did not think himself in that high station more exempt from the observance of the laws than the meanest of the people; and he took an oath to obey them, which he religiously observed. He lived with his people rather as a father with his children than a prince with his subjects;* and he advanced none to places of trust but the virtuous and the worthy. He possessed that fine sense of propriety which rejects flattery, and discouraged those servile offerings with which the sycophant spirit of that base age was so prone to intoxicate the vanity and worst passions of the Cæsars. His statues were in consequence few in proportion to his merits, but they were respected with feelings of religious veneration. And yet he was peculiarly alive to the sense of his own worth; for, when he returned from Germany to Rome, on his accession to the throne, he caused the expense of his march, and that of Domitian when he went into Gaul, to be computed and inserted in the public registers, that his successors might learn how to conduct themselves on similar occasions, and posterity appreciate the prudence of his economy.

"His palace was constantly open to persons of all ranks, whom he received with condescension, heard their applications with patience, and endeavoured, as far as possible, to dismiss none from his presence without satisfaction. He would not allow any person condemned on suspicion, however strong the presumptive evidence, to be executed; and was the author of that beautiful maxim, that 'it is better a thousand guilty should escape unpunished, than one innocent person suffer an ignominious death.' When he appointed the first captain of his guards, in presenting him, according to custom, with

---

* Pliny's Panegyric.

a drawn sword, the badge of his office, he used these memorable words: 'Employ this sword for me; but, if I deserve it, turn it against me.'"

Hareach then proceeds to shew the dark side of this bright and noble character; but we refrain from quoting his bitter animadversions. The frailties of the great and good often serve the profligate with a secret apology for their own offences; and that impartiality is dictated by an invidious love of truth, that would hold up to posterity the blemishes of a patrotic character, far less of a prince so illustrious as Trajan. It is only by contemplating the magnanimous qualities of eminent men, that the heart can be inspired with virtuous emulation. When the mind is directed to their human infirmities, all unworthy inclinations feel as it were countenanced, and become arrogant in their claims to indulgence. But it is time that we should resume our extracts.

"The patience and the virtue of Trajan were often put to the test, during his stay at Antioch, by the policy and craft of the neighbouring princes. They courted his favour with a servility and hypocrisy almost equal to that of the Roman senators. Augarus prince of Edessa, in Mesopotamia, was however an honourable exception. He sent the emperor many valuable presents, but declared, by his messengers, although he was sincerely desirous of living in friendship with the Romans, he was equally anxious to stand well with the Parthians, against whom the emperor was bent on war, and therefore he declined waiting on him in person. In the same audience, a prince, who came in person, presented him with a stately courser, which, on being brought before him, kneeled down, bowed his head to the ground, and seemed to worship him as a god. The emperor was amused by the docility of the animal; but he treated the ambassadors of Augarus with more respect than the owner of this four-footed sycophant.

"When he had thus received the homage of these treacherous Asiatic despots, he left Antioch, bending his march towards Armenia, ostensibly to avenge an insult which he had received from Parthamasiris king of

Parthia, but in fact to reduce the Parthians to the Roman yoke:—an ambitious project which he had formed in early life, when engaged against that bold and warlike people, who, by their power and enterprise, threatened the safety of the empire. The ground of the war was this: Parthamasiris had assumed the sovereignty of Armenia, although the Roman emperors, from the time that Nero crowned Tiridates at Rome, had claimed a right of disposing of that crown; and it was to vindicate this claim that Trajan advanced with the legions from Antioch to Elegia. Here he was met by Parthamasiris, who humbly requested to be admitted to his presence. Trajan received him on the throne, surrounded by his chief officers; and the king, taking off his crown, laid it at his feet, not doubting but the emperor would immediately return it to him. Trajan, however, received it as a regular resignation; which so enraged him, that he instantly left the tent, and endeavoured to escape. But the army, shouting with applause at the event, surrounded him on all sides; and the emperor gave orders that he should again be brought before him. Parthamasiris, no longer able to contain himself, exclaimed ' that he had neither been conquered nor taken prisoner; and that, believing no injury would have been offered to him, he had come voluntarily, expecting that he should receive his kingdom from Trajan as Tiridates had done from Nero.' The emperor heard him calmly, and replied, ' that as Armenia belonged to the Romans, it would receive a Roman governor, and be no longer a kingdom. As for you, Parthamasiris, king of Parthia, you are at liberty to quit the camp with your Parthian guards unmolested; but the Armenians in your train, being Roman subjects, must retire to their respective homes.' Parthamasiris submitted to this cool but dignified sentence with a frown of implacable resentment. But, on leaving the camp, he summoned his army, and for a time waged a fruitless war with the emperor, by which in the end he lost his life.

" When Trajan had thus reduced Armenia to a Roman province, he visited Augarus, the prince of Edessa, who had so courageously declared his resolution to remain neutral in the Parthian war. But the Parthians were not subdued by the death of their sovereign, and soon gave ample employment for the arms of the emperor. His fortune, and the discipline of the legions, were however constantly victorious, and he finally succeeded in driving them across the Tigris, where they resolved to make a last stand, at a place where the river was not fordable. But this he prevented. The woods of Nisibis lay behind him, in which he felled a great number of trees, and, conveying their trunks to the river, suddenly formed a raft, by which, in spite of the utmost efforts of the Parthian archers, he conducted his army across, and not only dislodged but dispersed them with great slaughter.

"When he had thus mastered the Parthians, he directed his arms against Assyria, and entered Babylon as a conqueror. Many circumstances contributed to make this an interesting event to me.

"The glory and fame of Babylon were spread throughout the earth. Whatever was considered great or magnificent in Egypt, or the regions of the west, were deemed insignificant, compared with the wonders and grandeur of this ancient capital: and it had been, in former days, the prison-house of our nation. The emperor was no doubt allured by the celebrity of its name to take possession of its ruins,—for it could only be considered as a wreck. The famous walls were crumbled into a mound, having been formed chiefly of earth faced with bricks dried in the sun; and the greatest of its edifices, of materials scarcely more durable: it was fast sinking into the condition predicted by the Prophets. Silence reigned over the largest portion of the vast space included within the circumference of the walls. The temples were roofless,—the courts of the palaces overgrown with weeds and brambles. I went with Trajan and his officers to see the house in which Alexander the Great died. It had been a sumptuous pile, but the walls were rent in many places. The roof had long been crashed by time; the columns of the arcades had been formed of bricks cased with a bright and shining plaster, which emulated the lustre and excelled the beauty of marble; but they were now stripped of this gorgeous covering, and shattered and fallen. We entered a lofty portal, and ascended a vast but ruinous flight of steps, which led to the chamber where the Grecian conqueror expired. The floor creaked beneath the tread of Trajan, and lizards, and other reptiles, disturbed by our approach, fled as we advanced. Every one was silent. I thought of Nebuchadnezzar. I remembered Jerusalem, and the dispersed and homeless of Israel. I looked at the imperial master of the world, then in all the majesty of pride and power before me; and contrasted his high and palmy state with the withered desolation that dwelt in the mansion of Alexander. His countenance saddened as he examined every thing attentively which the guides pointed out; and, when he returned home, he appeared thoughtful and melted with sorrow.

"On the following day, however, he reviewed the troops, distributed to them a liberal largess in honour of Alexander, and commemorated the exploits of that celebrated hero by a general festival, of which all the Babylonians were invited to partake. Immediately after, he returned to Antioch, where, during our stay, a dreadful earthquake shook the city into ruins, and overwhelmed a vast multitude of persons.

"The town happened to be crowded with troops, and strangers assembled from all quarters, either out of curiosity or upon business, and embassies. There was scarce a native, or a Roman, but shared in the calamity. The whole Roman world suffered by this event in this single city.* The day had been close, still, and gloomy; a fearful heaviness weighed upon the air, and oppressed the functions of life. Towards the evening it began to thunder: peal succeeded peal with increasing violence, till one continued rattle reverberated from all quarters of

---

* Dio Cassius.

the heavens, as if the pillars of the firmament had failed, and the dome of the skies was falling. Gusts of cold wind then burst in from every quarter, and a terrible subterranean sound, as if the chariots of Jehovah were approaching, was accompanied by a tremendous heaving of the earth. Houses were overthrown, and persons dashed against each other in the streets. The palace of the emperor was torn asunder, and he only escaped, by leaping from a window.

"This event was on many accounts received by the world as an omen of some great change. Many of the subjugated nations rebelled in the course of the spring; and that lofty structure of conquest and ambition, which Trajan had reared with such indefatigable labour, was shaken and rent from roof to foundation, like the edifices of Antioch. The emperor endeavoured, with all his activity, skill, and enterprise, to remedy the evil; but he was now declined into the vale of years, and adversity mocked the ineffectual efforts of the poor old man. The Parthians have revolted; the Arabians have revolted; the Armenians have driven forth your governor, and chosen for themselves a king; and Mesopotamia despises the authority of Rome:—such were the daily tidings that disturbed the last days of this warlike prince. And, as if to rebuke the pride of heroic achievements, his military career was closed by a swarm of flies, which forced him to abandon the siege of Atra, a city of Arabia."

CHAPTER XIII.

Anecdotes of the Emperor Adrian, and Reflections on the Magic studied in his Time.

[A.D. 118–139.]

THE crimes which historians have ascribed to the Roman emperors, are incredible miracles. They are, like all the other incidents of ancient history, the exaggerated reports of rumour and prejudice; doubtless, with some foundation in fact; but, in scope and circumstance, exceeding probability. Our author, in recording his observations during the reign of Adrian, the successor of Trajan, does not materially deviate from the writers of that time; but the colouring which he gives to the most remarkable transactions, is sometimes a shade lighter; and, at others, of a far deeper dye.

The mixed character of Adrian was however calculated to produce this, even with a mind less stedfastly settled in its own peculiar notions. What Hareach says, must therefore be received as the particular view of an individual; and, while the facts are admitted as unquestionable, as far as ancient history may be deemed authentic, due allowance must be made for the tinge acquired from the medium through which they have been transmitted. We shall omit, as we did in speaking of Trajan, the personal vices of this emperor, because the narration of such things taints the pure imagination of innocence; and the corrupted need not the example of the illustrious, to countenance them in iniquity. The grossness of the Roman manners, is a subject over which it is desirable that oblivion would draw a veil. A history of Rome, purged of the obscene infamies of her eminent men, is a desideratum in the literature of the schools. It is inconceivable, how so many grave and prudent teachers should have so long tolerated the indelicate pages of the classic writers, in the hands of youth. It is almost virtue, to be uninformed of vice. But, let us have recourse to our manuscript.

"Adrian was the most accomplished man of his time. With general talents of a high order, he possessed a memory so truly wonderful, that, by the powers of that alone, he might have been more distinguished than as the emperor of Rome. He could repeat the whole of the most difficult book, after having only once perused it. He recollected the name of every person to whom he had ever been introduced, and every face that he had once noticed, was indelibly impressed in his remembrance. He excelled in every branch of learning, and was without comparison the best orator, the best poet, the most correct grammarian, the most intelligent philosopher, and profoundest mathematician, of his time. In the fine arts he was an artist of the first class, and as a critic he had no superior. He sung with great effect, and performed on several instruments with exquisite sweetness and skill. He dictated to several secretaries, even while he was giving audience to his ministers, and discoursing with them on the most important affairs. He possessed the fullest and most particular knowledge of all the vast concerns of his empire; and yet, such was the singular versatility of his powers, that he was minutely acquainted with the smallest details of his household. He delighted in the society of the learned and ingenious, and took pleasure in debating with them respecting the topics with which they were best acquainted. Such is the account that the admirers of this extraordinary prince gave, on all occasions, of his acquirements and talents. But, much should be subtracted from this fulsome exaggeration. Flattery was the vice of the age; and the literary and the learned were among the greatest delinquents. One day, Adrian having, in a dispute, objected to an expression which Favorinus had made use of, the philosopher yielded to him, though he might have produced out of good authors sufficient authority for the words he had employed. His friends, after quitting the imperial presence, rallied him for so strange an instance of self-denial; for the Roman philosophers, like those of all subsequent ages, were little acquainted with the delicacies of good breeding. 'Do you think (said the prudent Favorinus) that I will pretend to be more learned than one who has the command of thirty legions.'

"This Favorinus was the friend of Plutarch, and celebrated for the facility with which he wrote; but his style was deficient in philosophical gravity. He was a native of Arles in Provence, and from his birth a eunuch. His works, however, were held in high estimation by his disciples, and he appears to have been a happy-tempered and amiable man.

"But, largely as the flatterers of Adrian swelled the measure of his accomplishments, they could not conceal his total want of personal dignity, though they described it as good-humour. His affability was familiarity; and, what should-have been condescension from his lofty station, partook of the nature of impertinence, although disguised by the conciliatory graces of his manners.

"A clamorous old woman having one day applied to him respecting a vexatious law-suit, he was teazed by her importunity, and said rather peevishly that he was not at leisure to hear her. 'To what purpose are you then an emperor?' exclaimed she, highly affronted. The spirit of this retort pleased him exceedingly; and, postponing the other business with which he was at the time engaged, he attended to her with patience, and finally dismissed her satisfied. This anecdote was repeated favourably of the emperor, and was creditable to his good-humour; but it afforded a striking instance of the easy indecorum of his public deportment."

Hareach appears to have been present, however, at a still more remarkable occurrence.

"The excellent temper of this prince, is his guardian god. This afternoon, when he entered the theatre, he was received with tumults of disapprobation. The voice of the populace was filled with contempt and opprobrium. I expected a riot; and many left the theatre, in dread of the guards, who stood impatient for orders to punish the insulters of majesty. But Adrian, instead of taking any revenge, listened for some time, with a serene countenance; the clamour, however, continuing to resound from all quarters, he at last rose, and, calling the public crier, (who was always in attendance,) ordered him to proclaim silence, with the imperious word *Tacete*, be silent,—first introduced by Domitian. The man had, either by the wonted familiarity of the emperor's manner lost part of his reverence, or dreaded the popular indignation; for, instead of repeating the command in the express words, said, with an air of diffidence and humility, 'The emperor begs you be silent.' The whole audience, being hushed from the moment that Adrian was seen to rise, in expectation of some very lordly communication, were so struck with the singular style of the imperial fiat, that they burst into a loud laugh. The monarch himself enjoyed the freedom of the translation; and was so far from resenting the liberty which the man had taken, that he commended his prudence, and rewarded it on the spot, which so appeased the popular fury, that he was applauded on retiring from the theatre."

We shall extract another instance of the indignities to which he subjected himself, by the equality that he affected, in despite of his rank.

"He was himself the architect of the temple of Venus and Rome,—one of the most magnificent structures erected during a reign, which surpassed all others in public works of that kind. Having exultingly shown the plan to Apollodorus, the most eminent architect then in the world,—to whom it was alleged he owed a grudge, in consequence of having received a rebuke from him, for pretending, in the time of Trajan, to give his opinion concerning certain buildings,—the artist considered himself as tacitly told, that he was not the only great architect; and said, with his habitual rudeness, 'The fabric is too low for the situation, and the statues of Rome and Venus too tall. You have taken care that the goddesses shall not rise and walk out.' Adrian was so offended at this freedom, that he banished him from Rome; and, with the implacable resentment of wounded vanity, took an opportunity soon after of causing him to be put to death."

Hareach appears to have been in Egypt at the time of

the death of Antinous, a youth whom the emperor afterwards commanded the Greeks to rank amongst the gods, and to worship with solemn ceremonies and the offering of victims. A mystery hangs over this incident; for, Adrian himself simply mentions that Antinous accidentally fell into the Nile and was drowned. But Dio Cassius assures us that the emperor, who had applied himself to the study of magic, being misled, by the execrable principles of that black Egyptian art, into a belief that his life would be prolonged by sacrificing a voluntary human victim to the infernal gods, accepted of the tender which Antinous made of himself, and sacrificed him accordingly. Our author's view of the matter is somewhat different.

"The Christian religion was now making a rapid progress throughout the empire, and the doctrine of the expiation of sin openly preached. The Egyptian priests, who pretended to all knowledge, affected to be acquainted with this also, and to explain its mysteries. Adrian was, by his taste and his vices, attached to the old religion, and could not endure doctrines which rendered personal purity indispensable to the attainment of immortal life. He was therefore an enemy to the Christians; but he trembled at the truths which Revelation had disclosed. His thirst of knowledge and his fears led him to consult the priests of Osiris and Isis; and they impressed on him a notion that the infernal deities possessed a claim on the soul of every man, which could only be satisfied by the propitiatory offering of a human being. This defaced exposition of the Christian atonement worked upon his credulity, and he became solicitous for a victim: all his friends and bondmen, however, were averse to die for him, till Antinous, moved by his anxiety, consented to be the propitiatory gift. It was for this devotion that Adrian ordered his memory to be hallowed with religious rites, believing that, by the magnanimity of his death, Antinous had actually attained an immortal and celestial destiny. For the magical mysteries taught the immortality of the soul; and, in the horrible sacrifices which the votaries of that shadowy knowledge originally offered to their infernal deities, a visionary forecast of the martyrdom on Calvary might be darkly discerned."

CHAPTER XIV.

Reflections on the State of Religion and Morals at the Death of Adrian.

Our itinerant philosopher appears to have fixed on the reign of Adrian, as that in which the new morality, introduced by Christianity, began to acquire an evident superiority over the ancient dogmas and mythological mysteries of the old religion. His reflections on this topic do not exactly coincide with the sentiments of the writers of that time: but, as they are supported by historical facts, and exhibit a very general view of the subject; such as might be expected from a person who had lived so long, and visited so many different parts of the Roman empire; we shall make a few extracts, in order to show the character of his opinions, as well as the state of the human mind, in this interesting crisis.

"It was evident, notwithstanding all the pains taken by Adrian to enlarge the pomp of worship, and to magnify the temples of the ancient gods, that the religion of the Pantheon was fast perishing in the estimation of the public. Whether among the Romans this obsolete religion ever possessed a purer character than idolatry, is difficult to say; but undoubtedly, at this period, the spirit of the age rejected the adoration of images, or only respected them as the visible representatives of immortal beings, of a higher order in power and intelligence than man.

"Among the Egyptians a faint notion had been preserved of the Omnipotent Creator of all things, but it was concealed in the incence of ceremony. Whether they had retained it from immemorial time, or had acquired it from the sacred traditions of Israel, could no longer be ascertained.

"A dim reflection of this expiring light might be seen in the religion of the Greeks, obscurely wavering amidst the clouds of a grosser superstition; but, among the Romans of Italy, it could no longer be discerned.

"It cannot be doubted that the Egyptians worshipped the Omnipotent, that they periodically celebrated the manifestations of his power in the return of the seasons, and that their initiatory rites consisted of some explanation of the reasons why this was done; and, among the Greeks, the mysteries sacred to Ceres at Eluesis possessed something of the same character. By the Bull, the former celebrated the vernal, and, in the adoration of the goddess, the latter the autumnal, equinox; showing, that so far their religion had sprung from the same common origin.

"But, a religion consisting only of anniversary festivals, and a worship that sought the approbation of deities, partial only to particular actions, could have no influence on the morals of the people. To this cause I would ascribe that singular peculiarity of the Romans, by which they were led to indulge themselves in all manner of personal vice with impunity, and without shame or remorse. They seem to hold nothing as vicious, which does not immediately harm others; and, although a few pure and virtuous sages see the anti-social nature of every species of self-indulgence, and raise their voices against it, the commonalty hear them not, and the oracles in the temples are silent on the subject.

"But a new æra has commenced. An alarm has spread throughout the world, that there is a terrible avenger of evil; and that, though he is not seen in this life, he is throned within the portals of death, and sternly demands, from all that enter, an account not only of what they have done, but of what they have omitted to do. In dread of this unknown god, the ancient temples are forsaken, and the old religion neglected. Men begin to enquire of one another, what are those things which he will punish? and human actions are no longer considered with reference to the pain or pleasure which they occasion, but as they are good or bad in their effects on the general system of the world. Virtue has ceased to consist in the magnanimity of manners, in courage, or fortitude, or temperance, or any qualities, constitutional to individuals; but, in doing that which is according to the will of God, as manifested in the laws of nature.

"This change of opinion, is certainly greatly owing to those persons who teach the doctrines of the Christian sect. It is no restraint on personal vice to know, that, if we injure our neighbour, he may punish us according to law; for, if he consents to what we wish, the only motive of restraint is removed. But it is a wonderful change,— a new creation in morals,—to know, that even the consent and concurrence of the whole world to any action contrary to the manifested will of God, will in no respect or degree lessen the enormity of the offence. The influence of this sublime doctrine must, in time, eradicate the vices at present openly practised in the Roman world. But the Christians have a great battle yet to fight, before their doctrines are admitted even to an equality with the opinions of the philosophers. The whole establishments of the priesthood are against them; and all the relations of the priests are interested in repressing that ascendency which they are inevitably destined to acquire. I think the proscription of the philosophers, and their banishment from Rome, was a part of the priestly persecution of the new opinions; for the emperors were the chief priests as well as the commanders of the army. It begins now to appear, that men may profess any opinions they choose with impunity, provided only that they call not in question the ceremonials of the temples:—and this is the only offence that the Christians commit; for, in all but in religion, they exhort to obedience, and forbearance, and patience, and benevolence, even towards their enemies. This, in time, must, gain the protection of the secular power; and, when that is obtained, the old religion, with all its pomp of solemn days, sacrifices, and ceremonies, will be consigned to the contempt with which many of the crimes that it forbade not, begin now to be regarded. At the death of Adrian, the thunderbolt fell from the hand of Jupiter; and the light of Revelation, penetrating into the recesses of the temples, showed that the deities, revered for so many ages, were but embodied metaphors, or the symbols of processes in nature, which, rightly considered, should have taught the world to know their Great Cause."

CHAPTER XV.

Anecdotes of the Emperor Antoninus Pius.

[A. D. 155.]

DURING the reign of the emperor Titus Antoninus, it is not easy to discover, from the materials before us, in what part of the empire Hareach resided. There is, however, a considerable abatement in the severity of his observations; and he seems to have enjoyed, like the rest of the world under the dominion of that excellent prince, a degree of comparative satisfaction. "Antoninus," he justly observes, " merited the empire;" for, with all the proper dignity that belongs to the imperial station, he unites great self-command, patience, and affability." When he went as pro-consul to Asia, on his arrival at Smyrna, he chose to lodge with Polemon the sophist, a proud and insolent man, who, instead of being gratified with the honour thus conferred on him, treated the representative of his sovereign with so much rudeness, that Antoninus was obliged to quit the house at midnight, and seek another lodging. Some years after, this arrogant sophist came to Rome; and, Antoninus being then emperor, Polemon went to court to pay his respects to him. It is not very clear that Hareach was present; but, the account which he gives of the interview might lead us to think so.

"Antoninus was sitting near the window, with his back to the light, hearing, with great attention a long-winded story which a poor old woman, who had presented a petition, was relating respecting the conduct of some one who had injured her. On Polemon being announced, he looked towards the door, and a slight emotion of surprise elevated his eye-brows, when he saw the sophist enter with a lordly and confident step. He, however, waved his hand, in which he held the poor woman's petition, with a look of cordial recognition; and, requesting one of his officers to place a seat for the stranger, turned to the petitioner, and desired her to proceed with her story. When she had finished, he made a mark with a pen on the back of the petition; and, giving it to one of his secretaries, nodded with an affable air to the old woman, and told her to follow the secretary, who, at the same moment, rose to quit the room.

"'Well, Polemon,' said the emperor, 'when did you come to Rome?'

"'This morning,' replied the sophist; 'and I have lost no time in coming to pay my respectful duty to your majesty.'

"'That is being very attentive,' said Antoninus, somewhat jocularly; 'and, as you cannot yet have had time to fix yourself in proper lodgings, I request you will take up your abode with me.'

"Polemon was astonished at this unexpected honour; and, without speaking, pressed his hand on his bosom, in token of acquiescence and profound respect.

"The emperor's condescension was not however altogether free from a tincture of revenge; for, with a smiling look, in which a certain slight expression of sly satisfaction was evident, he said to one of the domestic officers to take care that no one presumed to turn Polemon out of his apartment.

"The sophist felt the rebuke, and blushed exceedingly; but the emperor soon relieved his embarrassment, by entering into a free conversation with him respecting Asia Minor, and the health and welfare of some of the inhabitants, whom he had known when pro-consul in that country. The punishment did credit to the emperor, who, during the time that Polemon remained in the palace, treated him with the hospitable attention due from every host, whatever his rank and condition may be, to the guest whom he invites beneath his roof. The natural pride of Polemon was not however to be cured; and the civilities which he received from Antoninus served to augment it. His conduct in Rome, where he was but little known to the public, and unacquainted with the popular manners of that licentious capital, was in consequence often very absurd. On one occasion, being displeased with the performance of an actor, he obliged him to quit the theatre at mid-day. The player complained of this to the emperor, who laughed at the folly of Polemon, and pacified the comedian by saying, 'You have not so much reason to complain of him as I have had. He once drove me out of my lodgings at midnight, and, nevertheless, I made no complaint.'"*

These anecdotes serve to shew the amiable disposition of Antoninus, justly surnamed Pius; and the tranquillity of his prosperous reign, in which no sacrifice was made to the military ambition of Rome, is the best comment on the wisdom with which he ruled. The natural clemency of his character, led him to be indulgent to the Christians, against whom the wonted toleration of the Romans, in matters of religion, had been often suspended. During his time they were treated with liberality; and he has the singular glory of being the first who, uniting in himself the various prerogatives of high priest and monarch, granted indulgence to religious opinions at variance with his own.

Justin the martyr presented to him a copy of his first Apology for the Church; and Antoninus, having perused it with attention, was so moved by it, and by information which he had received from other parts of the empire, that he addressed a proclamation to the whole province of Asia in favour of the distressed Christians, concluding with these words: 'If any one, for the future, shall

---

* Universal History.

molest the Christians, and accuse them, merely on account of their religion, let the person who is arraigned be discharged, though he is found to be a Christian, and the accuser be punished according to the rigour of the law.' He also, at the same time, wrote in behalf of the Christians to the Athenians, Thessalonians, Larissians, and to the Greeks in general; and by these means put a stop to the persecution.

Our author, in noticing these circumstances, observes that " the persecution which the Christians suffered at this time, was owing to the influence of two opposite interests. The priests were vindictive at the diminution in the amount of the votive offerings to their idols, and possessing great influence with the magistracy, stirred them to harass the congregations who met to hear the preachers of the new doctrines. The spirit of bigotry among some of the old idolaters also had its effect. But the popular animosity was most excited by the universal and unmitigable condemnation of all their most favourite amusements, which the teachers of Christianity justly proscribed, as causes of the prevailing iniquities of the age. But, (exclaims Hareach,) though the cruelties practised by man at this time, and under the pretext of being propitiatory to the gods, fill my mind with horror in the recollection. How impotent was the calamity, compared to that awful pestilence which, during the reign of the successor of Antoninus, laid waste the greatest part of the Roman empire!"

Before giving his account of the plague, it may be necessary to mention that Ammianus Marcellinus says that it first broke out at Seleucia, where a party of soldiers, in pillaging the temple of Apollo, found a little golden coffer, which, upon their breaking it open, emitted a pestilential effluvia, that immediately infected the neighbouring country, and spread disease and death into most parts of the world.* But this story is not corroborated by our author, who simply states, that the contagion first appeared in Ethiopia, then in Egypt, afterwards among

---

* Ammian, lib. xxiii.

the Parthians; by whom, it is supposed, the army of Lucius Verus was infected: by that army, in its return to Italy, it was widely disseminated with the most fatal effects. He seems, however, to doubt that its ravages could be ascribed to the army, and thinks that the disease arose from some infection of the air. He appears to have been in some town in Asia at this time, but the exact place is not mentioned. From incidental expressions, we are led however to think it may have been one of those sumptuous cities, whose tenantless ruins alike astonish the Arab of the desert and the learned traveller.

CHAPTER XVI.

Account of a Pestilence raging in an Ancient City.

"I HAD not left my house for ten days till this morning: such is the influence of example; for what have I to fear from the plague? The waters of the sea fled from me, when I sought to extinguish my sufferings. The flames recoiled, when I rushed to their embrace. Why, since I am prohibited to enjoy the relief of death, am I thus tormented with the natural wants of man?

"My provisions were exhausted; my water done: I was hungry, and afflicted with a parching thirst; for I had confined myself at home, as others did, scarcely however so much to avoid the contagion, as to shun the frightful spectacles of disease and despair which were presented to view in every part of the city.

"When I went into the street, my heart was chilled with a strange appearance everywhere. Many of the houses were shut-up,—deserted on account of the plague being in the next. The doors of others were open, in which lay the bodies of persons who had died, abandoned precipitately by their friends on the first symptoms of infection. The few persons that I saw passing had a pale and alarmed look. They spoke not to one another, but passed by with a sidelong warding watchfulness of manner, more appalling than the excommunications of ignominy.

"Although the mid-day sun was intensely hot, I walked in the open street; but it was not from any feeling of precaution that I avoided the colonnades. I was compelled to do so from the smell of death in the adjoining houses, and the horrible swarms of large flies that issued from almost every open window, and filled the air with a rushing sound, that announced the presence of the destroying angel.

"Whether my confinement within doors had affected my eyes, or that there really was some peculiar modification of the air, I know not; but it seemed to me as if a vapour hung upon every object, and that every one who passed me was wrapped in a visionary veil, which at once magnified and obscured him. I walked in a state of stupefaction. Wandering onward, unconscious of any purpose, and looking at every thing as if it had undergone some strange transformation, I was suddenly roused from my reverie by a slow and solemn voice, crying, ' Bring out your dead ;' and immediately after, a deep low hollow rolling sound followed, that was more awful than thunder. I looked round, and it was the death-car coming along the street, in the front of which stood two felons; the one guiding the reins, and the other holding his hands at his mouth to augment the sound, crying, ' Bring out your dead.' Around this triumphal chariot of death, a number of other felons in fetters walked, to assist in loading the bodies.

"I stept aside, and allowed them to pass. While I was standing and looking at this tremendous apparition, (for, with its accompaniments, it seemed to be something more hideous than any furniture of this world,) a young female ran past me, bearing in her arms a crying infant, which she flung with a scream of horror into the receptacle, and staggering backward, as if she had been stunned by a blow, sat down on the steps of a neighbouring portico, and, covering her eyes with her hands, bent forward with her face on her knees, shaken with the most dreadful convulsions. I thought her frantic, and ran towards her. 'What is the matter?' I exclaimed.

"'Keep off, keep off,' she cried; 'the spots of death are on me: his father is dead, and I am dying.'

"'But, the child! Why have you flung your child among the dead?'

"She made no answer to my enquiry, but, starting up, gazed at me for a moment with a look so wild and woebegone, that I shuddered with horror; and, as if recollecting herself, she ran madly to the death-car, and, climbing its side, lifted out her infant, and, holding it from her by the clothes, with a frantic energy of alarm, exclaimed, 'Wretch! wretch!' and, dropping it on the ground, fell backwards among the mass of dead within.

"Two of the attendants came up at this moment: one of them lifted the infant, and it smiled in his face; the other seized the mother by her long flowing hair, and pulled her head into view;—but she was dead.

"I could not endure this scene longer. I ran from the spot, and, insensible to every object, knew not where I was, nor in what direction I had gone, till my progress was stopped by the stench of a horrible smoke that crossed my path.

"I turned aside to shun this smoke, and beheld the death-car loaded, approaching to the spot where the fire burned that sent forth the funereal vapour.

"The objects before me reeled in confusion; and I cannot describe what I saw,—a confused mass of things,—felons in chains, with lances stirring a fearful fire, among the embers and flames of which were indistinct fragments, that bore a frightful similarity to the heads and half-consumed limbs of many men, women, and children."

But we cannot venture to extract more of this appalling portraiture, which, consisting entirely of horrible circumstances, wherein no trait of that disinterested and courageous benevolence introduced by Christianity appears presenting a dismal picture of the selfishness of ancient manners, compared with those of the moderns, and serving to show how much the moral feelings of mankind have been improved by the diffusion of the Christian principles of virtue.

CHAPTER XVII.

The Death of Demonax the Cynic.

[A.D. 181.]

THE character of Marcus Aurelius as a man does not rise in estimation when compared with that of the pacific Antoninus Pius; but he was an active and plausible sovereign. To appear well before the public was the chief aim of his life; and this, where no craft or artifice is used, is only less than virtue. In point of talent, he was perhaps superior to his predecessor, and his literary abilities were highly respectable. But it would be difficult to prove that he was either a great man or a good prince.

Our wandering spectator has recorded no anecdotes of Marcus Aurelius, nor does he indeed appear to have seen him; and a considerable blank appears, during this reign, with respect to the proceedings of the Roman government. But we meet with a short notice of Demonax the Cynic, the master of Lucian, which is at once illustrative of the pride of the literary character, and the manners of the time, and is in itself affecting. We shall transcribe it at length.

" Demonax was a native of Cyprus, and had resided so long at Athens, that he considered that city as his home. At this time he inhabited a small house in a lane not far from the monument of Lysicrates,* close under the cliffs of the Acropolis. His apartment was mean, but kept with neatness, and, being on an elevated situation, the window commanded a fine view of the temple of the Olympian Jupiter, and other superb edifices in the hollow along the banks of the Ilyssus, beyond which rose the lofty summits of Mount Hymettus.

"His conversation was sharp,—I might justly say invidious; for he had looked narrowly into the motives of mankind, and judged with severity and suspicion. His paternal fortune was considerable, and he might have lived in affluence; but his humour, and the principles of his sect, prevented him from partaking of any luxury.

"In the cool of the evening I sometimes went to converse with him; for he was now exceedingly infirm with age, and could no longer take his wonted walk to the top of the Museum-hill, where, in the shadow of the monument of Philopapas, he was in the practice of discoursing with his friends and disciples.

"One evening when I happened to call, I found him alone, and pensively seated at the window. The air was serene, and the sun, at that moment on the point of setting, threw the shadow of the Acropolis over the city, and as far as the arch of Adrian; but the temple of Jupiter, and the mountain beyond, were still glowing with his departing radiance.

"Demonax did not take any notice of me when I first entered the room, but continued to contemplate the magnificent prospect from his window till the sun sunk beneath the horizon, and the twilight began to invest every object with that sober obscurity, which disposes the mind of the spectator to calm and lowly reflections.

"I sat down unbidden, and looked at the pale and venerable old man in silence. The fading light and the failing life seemed sadly in unison; and I was touched

---

* This edifice is now commonly called the Lantern of Demosthenes. The author made use of it as his study for upwards of two months.

with a sentiment of inexpressible sadness. When I had been seated some time, Demonax turned round to me, and said, 'I am glad to see you;—this is my last evening?'

"'How!' exclaimed I; 'do you then intend to kill yourself.'

"'No,' replied he, in his usual testy manner; 'I am not so tired of life; but the spirit, vexed with its falling house, is anxious to quit. It is four-and-twenty hours since I have tasted any food; and, were I now to indulge the craving of that voracious monster—the stomach, I should only voluntarily incur pain; and I do not wish to go out of the world making ugly faces at those I leave in it, however much they may deserve it.'

"'But, my friend,' continued the philosopher, assuming a sedate and grave manner; 'I wish to ask you a question. You are a person of much experience; and I have been surprised often at the knowledge you seem to have acquired as a traveller. Can you tell me what that vain fellow, Adrian, meant by erecting yonder sumptuous heap of stones,—that something to which we have given the name of Jupiter? Piety it was not; for he as little regarded Jupiter as I do the Bull of Memphis.'

"'It was, no doubt,' said I, 'to perpetuate his name, and to become famous with posterity.'

"'I thought so,' replied Demonax, with a sarcastic smile; 'I thought so;—but, when these marbles are shaken down by time, and converted into mortar by the barbarians that will then inhabit Athens, where will be the renown of Adrian?'

"'The works of poets and historians will commemorate his glory: and by them the fame of his liberality and magnificence will be transmitted to future ages. In that way (said I) Adrian will be rewarded.'

"'Rewarded!' exclaimed the old man with contempt; 'poets and historians—I grant you, may speak of them to future ages; but they also are human, and their voices are circumscribed. There is a circle in the theatre of time beyond which they cannot be heard. The fate of Adrian, and all like him, is this:—the present age admires his structures; the next will do so too; in the third, the religion to which they were consecrated will be neglected; other temples will then be frequented. These will fall into decay; the priests will desert them,—for the revenues will diminish. The buildings will require repair; the weather will get in: by and by it will be dangerous to enter beneath the roof;—a storm will then put his shoulder to the wreck, or an earthquake will kick it down. The stones will lie more ready to the next race of builders than the marble of Pentilicus. Hammers and hands will help the progress. By this time Athens will have dwindled into a village;—her arts and genius no more;—poets and pilgrims from far countries will come to visit her. They will come again, to revive the magnificence of Adrian by their descriptions. But the language in which they write, will, in its turn, grow obsolete; and other Adrians, and their edifices, will arise, to engross the admiration of the world, and to share the fate of ours. Nature ever works in a circle. It is morning, noon, and night;—and then morning comes again. It is Adrian,—renown and neglect;—and then another Adrian. It is birth, life, and death;—and then another takes our place. There is a continual beginning,—continual ending; the same thing over again, and yet still different. But the folly is in thinking, that, by any human effort, the phantom of immortality can be acquired among mankind. It is possible that an individual may spring up with such wonderful talents as that his name may last on earth five thousand years. But, what are five thousand years, or five millions, or five hundred millions, or any number that computation can reckon, when compared with what has been, and is to be?'

"In saying these words, the philosopher appeared worn out, and almost on the point of expiring. I rose hastily to bring him a little water; but, before I had done so, he somewhat recruited, and told me that he would not belie the principles on which he had so long acted, by accepting of any assistance from another. He then rose, and, tottering towards a pallet of straw covered with a piece of hair cloth, stretched himself down, and ordered me peevishly to go away. 'I will return in the morning, and see how you are,' said I, in taking leave.—' No, don't,' said he; ' do not come till the evening, by which time I shall have become a nuisance, and the neighbours will be glad to assist you to put me in a hole.' Next day he was dead.

"It was evident (observes our author) that Demonax felt very much like other men, notwithstanding his apparent indifference; for I noticed, on leaving the room, that he followed me with his eye, with a languid and pathetic cast, that expressed more than words could have done; but I could not disturb his last moments by any attempt to violate the principles of his philosophy."

CHAPTER XVIII.

Anecdotes of Pertinax the Emperor, who reigned only Eighty-seven Days.

[A.D. 192.]

WE shall pass over the brief notice which our author has taken of the iniquities of Commodus, the son and successor of Marcus Aurelius. The tyrant disgraced human nature; and his name should only be remembered in the list of extraordinary criminals. It is a mistaken notion, that a faithful history of any ancient state can now be written, or, if it were possible, that it could be of any service to mankind; in order, however, to connect the different parts of our author's reflections together, it is necessary that we should supply some account of the reign of Pertinax, the successor of Commodus.

"Lætus and Eclectus, who had accomplished the death of Commodus, determined to offer the empire to Pertinax; and went to his house as soon as they had disposed of the body. By this time it was midnight, and Pertinax was asleep in his bed. He was roused however by their entrance; and, believing they had come with orders from the tyrant, prepared to meet his fate with firmness. He desired his domestics to admit them into his room; and, upon their appearing, without rising from his bed, or betraying any emotion, he said, that as Pompeianus and he were the only friends of Marcus Aurelius left alive, he daily expected to fall a sacrifice to the cruelty of the emperor; and with great firmness bade them put their orders into execution.*

"Lætus, admiring his constancy, told him that the tyrant was dead, and that they were come to offer him the empire, as the person in the senate the most worthy of that dignity. He immediately rose; and, having ascertained that there was no treachery in their offer, he accompanied Lætus to the camp of the prætorian guards, where he was immediately proclaimed emperor.

"This fortunate man, as he was then deemed, sprang from a very low origin; his father, having either been himself a slave or the son of a bondman, followed the mean profession of drying wood and making charcoal. Pertinax at first was inclined to prosecute the business of his father; but, having received a superior education for his condition, was induced to quit Alba, his native place, and go to Rome, where he commenced his career in life as a schoolmaster. In this situation he was not successful, and enlisted as a common soldier, and served with the army in Syria, during the reign of Antoninus Pius, with so much distinguished bravery, that he was soon raised to the rank of a centurion.

"Under Lucius Verus, the colleague of Marcus Aurelius, his merits attracted still more attention in the Parthian war; and he was promoted to the command of

---

* Universal History.

a cohort; and afterwards employed in Britain, Mœsia, Italy, and Germany. From Germany he was sent into Dacia, where, upon some malicious information, he was deprived of his employment by Marcus Aurelius: but the emperor being soon after convinced of its falsehood, created him a senator, honoured him with the ensigns of prætor, and gave him the command of the first legion, which he led against the Germans, and recovered the countries of Noricum and Rhætia from them in one campaign; for which eminent service he was advanced to the dignity of consul. He was afterwards sent into Syria, but soon recalled from thence to guard the banks of the Danube, and command the army in Illyricum. He was subsequently preferred to the government of the Two Mœsias; then to that of Dacia; and lastly, to the government of Syria, which he held in the reign of Commodus, when he returned to Rome. From the capital, notwithstanding his great merits and services, he was exiled to his native country, where he remained three years, during which time he embellished it with several fine buildings; and it is a pleasing trait of his affection, that he would not allow his father's cottage to be touched, although it stood in the midst of them. His enemies attributed this to pride; but those who knew him better, were convinced that it sprang from a purer and better feeling. He was recalled to Rome after the death of Perennis, the insolent favourite of Commodus, and sent into Britain, to restore the discipline of the legions,—a command of great delicacy: but he effected the reformation,—not however without danger. From this duty he was recalled, at his own request, to the capital; and, after receiving various minor public trusts, was, at the death of Commodus, governor of the city.

"His elevation to the imperial dignity afforded satisfaction to all but the prætorian guards, whom he offended by attempting to restrain their licentiousness. These insolent terrors of the state, justly dreading that he would endeavour to revive the ancient discipline, on the third day after his accession to the empire, had the audacity to proclaim another senator; but he, escaping from them while they were taking him to their camp for this purpose, ran to Pertinax, assured him of his loyalty, and then fled from Rome. They afterwards attempted to raise Falco the consul to the empire; but in this they were also defeated. In this daring and rebellious conduct, the prætorians were secretly encouraged by their commander Lætus, who did not think himself sufficiently rewarded for the share he had in raising Pertinax to the empire; and who, to exasperate their mutinous spirit to the utmost, caused some of them to be publicly executed for being concerned in the conspiracy, pretending that he only obeyed the orders of the emperor.

"Their disaffection being thus inflamed, about three hundred more daring than the rest, quitted the camp with drawn swords, and marched directly to the palace, which they entered without opposition. Pertinax, in the mean time, knew nothing of what was passing, till his wife in terror came rushing into his apartment, and told him that the prætorians had revolted, and were already in the palace. Lætus was at this time, among others, with him, and also his father-in-law Sulpicianus, the governor of Rome. He ordered the former to oppose the band that had presumed to violate the imperial residence, and sent the latter to the camp, to appease the tumult there. But Lætus, covering his face, that he might escape unknown, instead of obeying the emperor's orders, retired to his own house. The palace rung with alarm and consternation. The wife and friends of Pertinax entreated him to conceal himself, till the people, by whom he was greatly beloved, could come to his assistance. But he magnanimously replied, that to save himself by flight was unworthy of an emperor; and immediately presented himself before the rioters, and asked, with a calm and undaunted countenance, whether they, whose duty it was to defend the emperor's person, were come with an intent to betray or murder him. At the same time he remonstrated with them on the heinousness of their crime with so much dignity and freedom, that many of them began to relent; and, sheathing their swords, turned to retire. But a Hungarian named Tausis, at this critical moment, threw his javelin at the emperor's breast, and cried, 'The soldiers send you that.' This was followed by rage and clamour. Pertinax made no resistance; but, covering his head with his robe, fell, pierced with many wounds, calling upon Jupiter the Avenger."

After this tragical event, an occurrence took place,—one of the most singular recorded in history,—the sale of the Roman empire by auction; but we must quote our author's account of the transaction.

CHAPTER XIX.

The Sale of the Roman Empire by Public Auction.

[A. D. 193.]

"How often do I meet with remarkable things that I would describe to my early friends;—but they are all gone. I have to-day witnessed the most extraordinary spectacle which this earthly stage of human actions ever exhibited;—but there is no one to whom I can communicate the sentiments with which it has effected me. I walk the streets alone, elbowing my way through the riotous multitude,—solitary in the crowd, unknown,—though known to all. They speak not to me; but, whenever I am observed, they make way with solemnity, and suspend their ribaldry as I pass. This silent reverence is the most dreadful of all excommunications. The exclusive condition of the sceptred monarch, is but one stage of interdict and exile short of mine, and yet it is deemed enviable; and, in spite of all its cares, crimes, and dangers, in the fluctuating state of Rome, is coveted as the reward and ornament of life.

"The murder of Pertinax sealed the fate of the Roman empire. It was the last exploit of the lawless power, by which that stupendous monument of military virtue was founded, raised, and so long maintained preeminent. By the event of this day, the ancient genius of Rome has been voluntarily changed, and sordid motives openly adopted by those entrusted with the custody of her honour, in place of that superb ambition by which she acquired such renown in arms, and led into slavery the greatest of all the earth.

"Flushed with the blood of their sovereign, and insolent with the success of their guilt, the three hundred prætorian traitors, bearing the head of Pertinax on a spear, returned to the camp. Their audacious companions welcomed them with acclamations. Sulpicianus, whom the emperor had sent to appease the rebellion, was in the camp when they arrived, and seeing that his son in law was slain, offered himself a candidate for the imperial dignity, and a large pecuniary reward to those who would proclaim him emperor. But the soldiers, conscious of their power, not satisfied with his terms, and knowing well how many in the city, rich in the plunder of the provinces, would give them much more, resolved to expose the empire to sale; and accordingly proclaimed, from the ramparts of the camp, that it should be sold to the best bidder.

"The news of this singular proceeding excited the greatest ferment in Rome. A countless multitude of all descriptions of persons, who at the time filled the streets loudly lamenting the death of Pertinax, rushed towards the camp. I went in the stream, no less attracted by the same motives of curiosity and wonder.

"On reaching the camp, we found the ramparts thronged with the military, and over the gate, instead of the eagle, the head of Pertinax:—a spectacle, which ought to have appalled ambition, was exhibited as the ensign of their cause.

"The gates were shut; and Sulpicianus, who happened to be within when the proclamation was resolved on, was, at the moment of our arrival, haranguing the soldiers. I heard his voice, and occasionally a few broken sentences; but he was often interrupted, sometimes by shouts of applause, but oftener with groans and yells of disapprobation. The immense multitude without, listened in profound silence. There was a strong expression of shame and sorrow in every countenance; and, when Sulpicianus ceased to speak, and it was doubtful how the soldiers had decided, a muttered and deep low murmur of indignation rolled through the crowd, like the menace of an earthquake.

"At this moment Didius Julianus, the wealthiest man in Rome, attended by many of his friends, with whom he had been sitting at a banquet when the news of the proclamation arrived, and by whom, in the midst of their mirth and jollity, he was advised to offer for the purchase, came forward. Something like a feeling of disgust certainly operated with the people when his object was announced; for they sullenly recoiled on both sides involuntarily, and left an open passage for him and his attendants to pass on close to the gate.

"Independant of the qualification which Julianus derived from his great wealth, it must be admitted that he had some well-founded claims to public distinction. He was descended of an illustrious family; he had been educated by the mother of Marcus Aurelius, and was by that emperor, who had a particular affection for him, created first quæstor, then ædile, afterwards prætor; and subsequently, he gave him the command of the twenty-second legion, then quartered in Germany. He afterwards appointed him governor of Belgic Gaul, where, with an unequal force, he so effectually repulsed the Chauci, who had made an irruption into the Roman territories, that he was rewarded with the dignity of the consulship. When he had discharged that office, he was sent into Illyricum, which he defended against the barbarians with such success, that he was soon after preferred to Lower Germany, and subsequently appointed to the important task of supplying Rome with provisions. Commodus gave him the government of Bithynia, and he was a second time named consul, with Pertinax for his colleague. In all these various and important trusts, he had not only conducted himself without blame, but with commendable merit.

"His character, however, was of that mixed kind, which allows the greatest scope to the malice of enemies, for he was by turns profuse and avaricious, luxurious and mean. By some he was charged with gluttony, drunkenness, gaming, and every vice of prodigality; and by others, with covetousness, and all the abject dispositions allied to that base passion. Nor could it be denied, that particular instances of these opposite vices might be easily cited from his actions; but his general deportment was undoubtedly affable, tempered with much kindness, and he had both the capacity to understand the importance of his public duties, and the ability to execute them with effect and address.*

"When the soldiers were informed that Julianus was a candidate, they received the information with shouts of satisfaction, for they knew his vast riches, and anticipated a prodigal offer. They crowded towards that part of the ramparts nearest the gate where he was standing, and he spoke to them with considerable elocution and plausibility. Without setting forth any merit of his own, he represented to them that he was a preferable candidate to Sulpicianus, who, as the father-in-law of Pertinax, whatever his present professions were, would, no doubt, if raised to the throne, take some opportunity in future of avenging the death of that prince; and he concluded by assuring them, that were they, on the contrary, to choose himself, he would restore them to all the freedom and privileges in which they had been circumscribed by Pertinax. This latter promise had more effect on the licentious and dissolute soldiery than the dread of vengeance by Sulpicianus, and, at the conclusion of his speech, they filled the air with acclamations. They would perhaps have at once declared him emperor; but an audacious private waved his hand, and, requesting silence, reminded them that the sale had not yet commenced, calling to Sulpicianus within the camp, and to Julianus at the gate, to make them an offer.

---

* Universal History.

"The two candidates, entering into the vulgar humour of the soldiery, by whom the proposal was received with peals of laughter, and in mirth, but truly, in effect, with the derision of the most poignant satire, respectively offered an insignificant price; and in the same spirit continued for a short time to bid against each other. Some symptoms of impatience however beginning to appear, Sulpicianus offered five thousand drachmas a man; upon which Julianus at once bade twelve hundred more, ready-money: the other immediately resigned the competition, and Julianus was admitted into the camp, and proclaimed emperor.

"This unprecedented transaction was marked by one solitary instance of virtue on the part of the soldiers. Before proclaiming Julianus, they stipulated with him, that he should forgive Sulpicianus for having been his rival, and never resent his aspiring to the empire.

"But nothing could extenuate, in the opinion of the people, the state of degradation to which he had reduced the majesty of Rome, by daring to purchase the sovereignty. When he returned to the city, invested with the purple, they loaded him with reproaches and execrations. They reviled him with the epithets of parricide and usurper; and, when he went to perform the inaugural sacrifice in the capitol, they menaced him with maledictions, and implored the gods never to grant him any favour."

CHAPTER XX.

Hareach in India.

HAREACH, with all his disgust against the Romans, seems to have lingered among them, as the most interesting portion of mankind; for, although by his book he appears from time to time to have made excursions to the most remote parts of the earth, we ever find him in Europe, and present at all the great events which affected the destiny of Rome. After the sale of the empire, he appears to have immediately quitted the capital, and, after wandering from place to place, to have at length reached India, and taken up his abode for some time with the Brahmins. It is not very obvious what induced him to undertake this far excursion, but it would seem, we think, that the commerce between the eastern provinces of the empire and India, had excited the cupidity and curiosity of the inhabitants of Italy, and that our author, incited by the reports that were from time to time spread of the riches and grandeur of the oriental world, was induced himself to pay a visit to those distant countries. In the course of this journey, and his interviews with the Hindoo priests, his wonder was abundantly excited; but, being under the influence of Jewish prejudices, his account of what he saw and learnt, must be received with some qualification. We shall however quote from his own words, using the freedom that we have hitherto done, of pointing out what appears to us fanciful, or at least not corroborated by other authorities.

"The oldest things in all nations," says Hareach, "are matters of religion, and therefore the people of India set forward no peculiar pretension to greater antiquity than the rest of mankind, when they assert that the history of their religion commences with the beginning of the world. Any religion that takes a later date, virtually confesses that it is of human origin, or is at most founded upon some human pretension. The true religion is coeval with the creation of the world; and all other religions, however modified by a greater or a lesser portion of human errors, at least affects to have an origin equally primitive and antient. But, the religion of the Hindoos is so obviously derived from that of Israel, that it may be justly regarded as springing from the same pure fountain-head, although the stream has been much troubled and stained with the intermixture of other tides."

After some reflections of this kind, to the effect that, granting the Hindoo religion to have been of the same divine origin as that of the Jews, it still could not be the genuine revelation, and the other the corrupted, because it contains more dogmas at variance with the laws of nature; he proceeds to give the following account of the Hindoo faith and religious discipline.

"The Hindoos, like almost all other nations, affirm that their religion is of divine origin, and that its doctrines are contained in a book called the Vadem, which they believe was delivered to their great law-giver, Brahma, by the Deity himself. In this respect they show great wisdom; for the principles of equity, and of justice, are emanations of the Divine intelligence, and laws, unless founded on them, must be contrary to nature,—for nature is God. It was therefore wise in them to adopt it as a truth as indisputable as the divine legation of Moses,—that their laws were derived from Heaven.

"Their sacred volume, their Bible, is divided into four books; the Rogo, Issura, Sama, and Adera. The first treats of the first cause and the beginning of things, of spirits, the soul, future rewards and punishments, the generation and dissolution of organized creatures, of what sin is, how it may be pardoned, by whom it is remitted, and upon what conditions. The second relates of temporal powers and authorities, the necessary privileges of superiors, and of the rights of the governed. The third embraces all matters that concern the actions of daily life, the distinctions of moral obligation, and the reciprocities of the different members of society. The fourth treats of rites and ceremonies, and those acts of personal discipline and periodical commemoration, which are equally required for the maintenance of good order and the preservation of religious knowledge.

"The precepts contained in these holy writings are known to but a few of the priesthood; it is even alleged that the book relating to rites and discipline has been lost; enough however remains, and is known, to satisfy me, that the materials of their Vadems have been drawn from the Pentateuch.

"Besides the Vadems, or rather a compendium of what is contained in them, the Hindoos have the Shâster,* a work no less venerable among them, which may be described as containing the system of their theology."

As if to contrast the rationality of their religion with that of the Jews, and to show its inferiority, Hareach gives the following abstract of the Shâster.

CHAPTER XXI.

The Religious Opinions of the Hindoos.

"THE great God being alone, and resolving to make his excellency and power manifest, by creating a world stocked with intelligent animals, made four elements, earth, air, fire, and water. These elements being confusedly mingled together, he next divided them, and formed the several parts of the sensible world, in the following manner.

---

* A copy of the Vadem is said to have been procured by Calmet for the French king's library, in the year 1733, but this we doubt. The Shâster was brought entire to England first by a Mr. Fraser, but what use was made of it we know not. Our account of the Hindoo Cosmogony of the world, is an abstract of the Shâster, obtained by Lord, about the beginning of the seventeenth century.

First, by a cane or some similar instrument, he blew upon the waters, which, rising in a bubble or round form like an egg, and spreading gradually to an immense space, made the firmament, which, so beautiful and so transparent, encompasseth the world.

"Of the sediment which remained, the Creator formed a ball or globe; the solid parts became the earth, and the liquid the seas; and this globe he placed in the midst of the firmament, every way equidistant from it, and called it the Lower world. He then created the sun and moon in the firmament, to distinguish the times and the seasons.

"The four elements being thus separated, and assigned to their proper places, began to discharge their several offices. The air filled up whatever was empty; the fire nourished with heat; and the earth and the seas brought forth creatures congenial to their respective natures, to whom the Creator conveyed the power of generating their species.

"In the last place, Man was made, superior to all other creatures, and endowed with a capacity to contemplate the works of God. He rose from out the earth, his head first appearing, and then his body, formed with all its parts complete. Being then inspired with life, his lips began to redden, his eyelids to disclose the two lights of nature, his limbs to take motion, and his understanding to worship the glory of God.

"That this man, who was made a sociable creature, might not live alone, a woman was formed to be his companion, who resembled him in the qualities of the body and of the mind. His name was Pourous, and hers Parkouti, and they lived together, feeding on the fruits of the earth, without the destruction of any creature.

"In process of time, this, the primeval pair, had four sons, named Brammon, Kuteri, Shudderi, and Weyz, who differed in their nature, according as the elements prevailed in them. Brammon, being of an earthy constitution, was therefore melancholic; but, being also ingenious, he was appointed by God to impart his precepts and laws to the people; and a book was delivered to him by the hand of God, containing the forms of divine worship, and the principles of religion.

"Kuteri was of a fiery temper, and had a martial spirit, and he was invested with power to rule kingdoms, and to bring mankind into order; for which purpose the Deity placed in his hand a sword, as the emblem of victory and dominion.

"Shudderi, being of a phlegmatic constitution, was mild and conversible; it was therefore appointed that he should be a merchant, and enrich the commonwealth by commerce; and, that he might never forget the end for which he was created, a pair of scales were put into his hands, and a bag of weights hung at his girdle.

"And Weyz, who was of an airy temper, was endowed with invention, and capable of forming with facility any mechanical contrivance to abridge labour. He was accordingly furnished with a bag, containing a variety of tools and handicraft instruments.

"It did not please the Creator to give Pourous and Parkouti any daughters; but, that the work of generation might be free from impurity, he made four women for these four men, and, for the better dispersing their offspring, he placed them in the four quarters of the world,—the east, the west, the north, and the south: and the sons of Pourous and Parkouti were ordered to travel each in a different direction, to find the wives who had been thus provided for them.

"Brammon travelled eastward, and found Sawatri, and married her, conformable to the rules prescribed in the book which he had received. Kutteri, proceeding westward, met with Toddikastie, and, after a terrible struggle between them which lasted three days, she submitted, and consented to become his wife. Shudderi took his matrimonial journey northward, and, after discovering pearl and diamond mines, lighted upon Visagunda, whom he married. And lastly, Weyz, after crossing seven seas in a vessel built by himself, landed on the coast of Dupe, where he built a house, and, walking one day on the shore, met with Jijunogunda, and paid his addresses to her: but she treated him with scorn, until Weyz prayed to God that he would turn her heart towards him, which request was granted, on condition that he would erect pagodas for worship, and adore images under green trees: the Almighty having in their shade manifested himself to him by vision.

"The four sons of Pourous and Parkouti, after having in this manner began to people the earth, resolved to return to the place of their nativity, in order to see their parents; so, leaving their families behind, they went back to the middle of the earth, where, on their arrival, they were received by Pourous and Parkouti, and entertained with banquets and rejoicings.

CHAPTER XXII.

The Hindoo Account of the Corruption of Mankind.

"In process of time, the four brothers and their wives became parents of many generations, who strictly conformed to their division into four tribes, without mixing, and followed the instructions of their respective ancestors. But numbers and abundance begat evils. Brammon grew negligent in his piety; Kutteri became cruel and arrogant; Shudderi cheated his brethren with false weights; and Weyz set exorbitant prices upon his wares, to maintain his extravagance. Brammon envied Kutteri's greatness, and Kutteri contemned the quiet and sequestered spirit of Brammon, and forbore to pay him the respect due to his birthright; he even carried his contempt so far as to prefer his own laws to those of God. He delighted in wars and bloodshed, laid taxes on Shudderi, and drained the profits of Weyz's labours; whilst they, to indemnify themselves for his injurious treatment, defrauded and exacted in every possible manner. Weyz also sought to introduce a new form of religion concerning the worship of images, with other ceremonies, which he affirmed had been communicated to him in vision; but, as they differed essentially from what was prescribed in the book given to Brammon, a great dispute arose whether they should be received as canonical. Weyz, however, swearing that he had them from God, they were admitted as part of the canonical law.

"These seeds of corruption grew to great excess, and ripened into all manner of iniquity, till the Deity could no longer endure to look upon the earth. At length he resolved to suffer them no more, and caused the heavens to put on a face of darkness and terrror. Thunders rolled, and lightnings flashed. The seas swelled, and overwhelmed the dry land, and swept away the whole race of mankind; but, although their bodies were destroyed, their souls returned into the bosom of the Almighty:— and thus ended the first age of the world, named Kurlayn.

"But God did not intend that the purposes of creation should be rendered abortive by the wickedness of mankind. He therefore determined to renew the human race, and begin the second age with three persons, of greater perfection and excellence than the former. Accordingly, he descended on a great mountain called Meropurbati, and said 'Rise up, Brahma,—the first of living creatures in the second age;' and the earth brought forth Brahma, who immediately did homage to his Maker; and, in like manner, Vishnou and Rudderin were summoned into being, and obeyed.

"The design of making these three persons was, that they might act as deputies to Omnipotence in the work which he was about to perform. To Brahma was assigned the office of making the creatures: and for this purpose he was endowed with the powers of creation and production. To Vishnou was given the charge of preserving the creatures; and for this end he was constituted lord o' the sun and moon, of the hills and valleys, of the weather, and of the seasons: he was likewise made the conferrer of riches, health, honour, and whatever conduced to the well-being of man, and other animals. And lastly, Rudderin was vested with a commission to destroy the creatures, because God knew that they would be wicked, and deserve punishment; for this purpose he was appointed lord of death and judgment, and disease, and famine, and war, and pestilence; and every evil that might be deemed a punishment for sin, was given to him, as the avenger of divine justice.

"To each of these three persons was allotted a time for remaining on earth, conformable to the nature of his office. Brahma remained one age, in which the work of creation was finished; and, at the end of that period, he was taken up into heaven. Vishnou was to remain double the time of Brahma, and Rudderin three times as long as theirs.

"These three persons, conscious of the powers with which they were endowed, resolved to execute the purposes of their creation; and Brahma, consulting with himself how to discharge his commission in the best manner, was seized with such extraordinary pain in all parts of his body, as foreboded some great alteration to ensue,—as in effect there did; for he fell in labour, and the burden, forcing its way from both his sides, twins sprung forth, male and female, at full growth. These two having given glory to God the Creator, and to their producer Brahma, called the man Manow, and the woman Seteroupa, and sent them to the mountain of Mundurpurral, where they begat sons and daughters, that multiplied and peopled the earth.

"All things had a good beginning in the second epoch of the world. Religion was cultivated; prayers were offered to God, and to Brahma, Vishnou, and Rudderin. But evil again was engendered as mankind multiplied; and the Lord, again provoked by the iniquity of the world, sent Brahma down from heaven, to warn the inhabitants that, unless they repented of their sins, he would destroy them. For a time the admonition of Brahma made a salutary impression, but, by degrees, they returned to their old course of wickedness. But Brahma interceded with God for the human race;—the Almighty, however, would not be pacified; and the time of the intercessor's abode on earth being expired, he was removed into heaven and the bosom of Omnipotence.

"God then made known his displeasure to Vishnou, who, in virtue of his office as the preserver, also interceded for them; but the Lord would not be entreated. He therefore commanded Rudderin the destroyer, to cause a wind to rise out of the subterranean abysses of the earth, and sweep the nations as dust from the face of it. Rudderi, in obedience to the Omnipotent order, set the winds in a violent commotion. The frame of the earth trembled;—the day vanished into sudden darkness, as if the breath of death had extinguished the flaming light of the sun. The mountains were heaved from their foundations, and the Ganges, rolled from his channel, sought another course. The race of mankind were borne like chaff and ashes away, and all perished but a few, whom Vishnou was permitted to cover with the skirts of his mantle from this terrible tempest, as a reserve for the propagation of mankind in the third epoch. Thus concluded the second race or period called Duaper."

CHAPTER XXIII.

The Hindoo Account of the Third Epoch of Mankind.

"RUDDERIN having fulfilled the Divine will, put reins upon the tempest, and bridled the furious winds. But the desolation that covered the earth was more appalling than when the seas burst their bounds, and deluged the dry land. The dead carcasses of men and animals were seen scattered in all places. Some were found clasping with their skeleton arms the rocks of the mountain-tops; others, that could not cling to any steadfast hold, were discovered dashed in pieces. The waters were filled with the bodies of the dead, and Silence sat with Death upon the circle of the earth,—and Rudderin the destroyer looked around where all living things were wont to be, and he was grieved:—for such was the desolation, that he deemed his power no more.

"The seed however preserved by Vishnou, began again to grow, and the earth was again filled with inhabitants; but, as the period of that primeval person's sojourn on the earth was terminated, the Lord put down his mighty hand from on high, and lifted him up into heaven:—and the race of man are now subjected to the sole domination of Rudderin the destroyer. How long he will be content to chastise sin with only disease, and famine, and wars, and pestilence, is not known; but, as mankind are by nature prone to wickedness, and will continue to grow worse, his power in the end will be provoked to the utmost, and a third final destruction of all things will take place by fire. The moon will be kindled into a fiery orb; the sun will send forth flames of brimstone instead of light; the skies will be furled away and rolled up in darkness, while the four elements of which the world was originally formed, disengaged from the laws of order, will rush into everlasting conflict and confusion. The souls of mankind, having come from God, then separated from the materials of the body, and purified from all blemish and earthly corruption, will mount into heaven, and be received into the Divine bosom.

"There is much in these religious notions of the Hindoos that indicates a common origin with the Jewish religion. Did the Hindoos derive then their opinions from the lost ten tribes?"

But we cannot venture to quote the speculative opinions of Hareach. In matters of fact, his statements uniformly appear borne out by the best and most authentic histories; when he indulges in conjectural inferences, we are however, not prepared to allow the same weight to his opinions. His account, however, of the pagodas, rites, and priests, of the Hindoos, is highly curious; and, as it relates to the religious belief of a large portion of British subjects, it cannot fail to be interesting; and it is undoubtedly instructive.

CHAPTER XXIV.

Of the Pagodas of the Hindoos, comprehending a Description of the Caves of Ellora.

"THE pagodas or temples are low and flat, without windows, or any light, excepting what comes in by the doors. The pagoda is divided into three parts: the first consists of an aisle supported by pillars, beset with statues of stupendous animals, and open to all comers; the second part is shut with a strong inclosure, and contains awful images with many heads and hands,—the emblems and representatives of circumstances commemorated in the worship; and, in the third, the statue of the god is kept to whom the temple is dedicated; for, notwithstanding the plain text of their vadems, or sacred books, the purity of the ancient worship of God is lost in gross idolatry.

"Round these temples is an open space of ground, or court, inclosed with walls, on which are built several small pagodas.* The most holy of all these mysterious edifices are those of Ellora, which, being formed from out the living rock of the mountains, are the most appro-

---

* Universal History.

priate mansions that ever mankind consecrated to the worship of their gods. Whatever may have been the absurdity of the Hindoos in their mythology, it was a sublime idea of them, to construct their temples within the everlasting mass of the globe, and to make them as it were a portion of the frame of the eternal universe. In this respect they have excelled in taste the Egyptians, and turned the beautiful fabrics of the Greeks and Romans into perishable and temporary filagree.

"The works at Ellora make an impression, on the mind of the cursory traveller, somewhat analogous to the reverence of the sincere worshipper, who believes in the truth and divinity of his religion. The first sight of these wonderful monuments is not particularly striking; compared in effect with the Egyptian edifices, they are indeed far inferior; but, in the examination, they grow upon the mind, till the imagination, lost in atonishment, abandons the attempt to conjecture how the first conception arose of hollowing the mountains into temples, and confesses the power of a superior genius, with the mingled emotions of gratitude and awe.

"The sides of hills, for the extent of two miles, are excavated into vast halls and chambers,—the abodes of the priests and the students of their religion. But the chief object of veneration is the temple of Keylas. The approach towards it is not remarkable: a gateway, having apartments over it, connected with the sides of the precipices by two walls, with rude battlements, apparently built across an ancient quarry, is the first object that presents itself.* On a nearer approach, a confused and superb mass of pagodas and obelisks is discovered within; and the stranger is surprised to find so many stately buildings crowded into so narrow and obscure a space. On advancing, under this impression, his eye wanders over the surface of the wall, unconsciously in quest, from habit, of the separations that divide the stones; and he

---

* Fitzclarence's Journal.

discovers that the whole is formed of the solid rock. On entering the gate, the appearance of a colossal monster, surrounded with various emblematic sculptures, and two elephants, joining their trunks over his head, begin to awaken the fancy; and the spectator moves forward, endeavouring in vain to divest his mind of a strange chill, that affects his very blood, arising from the succession of amazing objects that present themselves at every step,— such as elephants, and lions, and chimerical animals, starting from the rocks in fierce conflict, and sustaining, at the same time, the temples on their backs.

"On entering the great temple, I unconsciously stooped, as if the stupendous ceiling was too low for me to stand upright:—such was the effect of the enormous columns that uphold the mountainous mass above. But, why should I attempt to describe these awful scenes? It is by the feelings they awaken that the heart owns their greatness; and description, however minute, is beggared in the effort to convey any notion of their sublimity. They remind me of the fiat at which the world rose into being; and they awaken fearful thoughts of creative intentions, abandoned before the living principle was imparted to creatures prepared for life."

CHAPTER XXV.

Religious Ceremonies.

"The religious worship of the Hindoos is attended with a great number of ceremonies;—such as observing festivals and fasts, of which they have several in the course of the year. Their washings and purifications are reckoned of no small efficacy. They strew themselves with consecrated ashes, as a protection from misfortunes, and a charm against evil spirits. Pilgrimages are also enjoined, as undertakings of great holiness; and penances, as expiatory duties, of the most blessed consequence. Some of the penitents will sit, others stand, in the same posture, for years together: some carry vast loads; and others drag heavy chains. I have seen a man, who held his fingers so long clenched, that his nails had penetrated through his hands, and were rivetted as it were on the back.* Some expose themselves to the scorching sun; others are seen hanging before a fire, with their heads downwards;† while others, no less ambitious of the reputation of sanctity, suspended by hooks, are swung from elevated beams, showering flowers on their admirers below, as if in the actual enjoyment of beatitude‡. The Hindoos, of all fanatics, have alone demonstrated the extent and capacity of human fortitude.

"By such severities inflicted on the body, by good actions, benevolence, and sincere repentance, the Hindoos hope that the wrath of God will be appeased, and their sins forgiven.

"They believe in a future state, with rewards and punishments. They also believe that there is a purgatory, and in the devil, and sorcerers, and apparitions.

---

* Fitzclarence's Journal.
† Universal History.
‡ Fitzclarence's Journal.

"They entertain different opinions concerning the human soul. Some hold God to be the soul; while others hold it to be an emanation, or a part of God. A third party conceive, that, at the creation, the Deity made all the souls at once which were designed for the race of mankind; others say that the soul is begotten by the parents; and a fifth class imagine that it is compounded of five elements; and, in general, they believe the soul to be eternal as well as immortal, thinking that it remained in a state of sleep before the world was created. But, those who hold the soul was not from eternity, say it was formed the first of all things, and lodged in the Divine essence. Many, however, think that man has two souls: the one superior, immortal, and pure; the other merely animal life,—the sensitive principle of pleasure, and pain, and love, and all other passions and appetites.

"But the most singular of all these metaphysical notions of the Hindoos, is their opinion, that the soul, both of men and animals, is of the same nature; and that the cause of the difference between them, is owing to their respective structure and organization, by which one species of creatures possess an advantage over others.

"The doctrine of transmigration is generally entertained by all the people of India; and they think that those souls only which are pure go immediately into heaven. The impure transmigrate, or pass into several bodies successively, in order to obtain a perfect purification, which requires many generations. Sometimes the translation is from a better body or state to a worse; and sometimes from a worse to a better. But the souls of very impure persons migrate into reptiles and venomous insects, or into beasts of burden, that are punished by severe treatment for faults committed in their state of man."

CHAPTER XXVI.

Of the Origin of Hermits, and the Order of Anchoret Monks.

[A. D. 256.]

How long our author continued in India, or what other eastern countries he visited, in his first excursion to that part of the world, is not very easily traced; but, it appears that he returned westward during the reign of the emperor Decius, and was landed on the Egyptian shores of the Red Sea. His description of the coast, and his journey to the Nile, contain a number of impressive circumstances, particularly his account of a Hermit whom he met in the Desert, and who appears to have been no less a personage than Paul, the founder of the Anchoret order of hermits. It is necessary, however, to give some explanation of the causes which, undoubtedly, more than the example or opinions of any individual, occasioned the institution of this anti-social sect.

The Roman emperors were not only commanders of the forces, and the heads of the civil government, but they also, in their persons, comprehended the functions of the high priests. It was therefore an important, indeed a necessary, part of their public duty, to set themselves at variance with all doctrines that tended to impair the power and emoluments of the priesthood. To this cause alone, and not to any objection in principle, were they the early declared enemies of the professors of Christianity. Although perhaps of all the various tyrants ever invested with sovereign authority, the series of Roman potentates were the most deficient in public or private integrity, it should not be imagined, that, when they persecuted the Christians, they were actuated with any respect for their own idols, or by any other hatred of Christianity than as it was opposed to their pontifical authority.

Decius was no so sooner invested with the imperial ensigns, than he conceived himself bound to uphold the declining cause of Paganism, which he saw fatally undermined by the indefatigable exertions of the teachers of the Christian doctrines. Accordingly, he resolved to extirpate, if possible, the whole sect, and enacted the most cruel edicts against all the professors of the new religion. The fury to which the magistrates were, in every part of the empire, incited by the Pagan priests to carry the edicts into effect, produced alike horrors and consternation. The most distinguished of the Christian teachers were seized, tortured, and required to recant their opinions. The scaffolds streamed with the blood of their executions, and the air was polluted with the smoke of their burning. Rome and Antioch, at that period, afforded spectacles of atrocity, that were not exceeded by those of London during the conflict of the Reformation. Great numbers of the persecuted Christians fled to the mountains, choosing rather to trust themselves with wild beasts, than to the merciless fangs of bigotted idolaters. Among others, Paul, an inhabitant of Alexandria, withdrew into the Egyptian deserts, where he led a solitary life for the space of ninety years; and, by his meekness and piety, threw such a lustre on his patience and self-denial, that, in times of less affliction, it was deemed glorious, by many holy men, to imitate his sublime abstinence by a voluntary sequestration, equally joyless and austere.

As our author returned from India soon after the persecution had been instituted by Decius, and crossed that part of the desert where Paul had sought an asylum, we think, the hermit of whom he speaks could be no other than that celebrated character. It is true, that he describes the person he met with as a young man, while all the extant accounts of Paul represent him as venerable by his age no less than his appearance; but, it should be recollected, that these relate to the old age of the saint, when he had acquired renown, by his sanctity and long-suffering. Without, however, attempting to institute any controversy on this point, we shall give the description of the desert, and the interview with the hermit, as it is recorded by our author himself, leaving it to antiquaries to compare his statements with the facts of history.

CHAPTER XXVII.

Horeach in the Desert.

"The appearance of the Egyptian coast from the Red Sea is the most inhospitable in nature; and, on landing, I found it a suitable vestibule to the desert, which I afterwards traversed. At break of day, when we first discovered it from the deck of the vessel, it seemed, illuminated by the rising sun, to be a brazen-coloured cloud, floating on the sea, and stretched along the horizon. On nearer approach, and, as the sun ascended higher in the firmament, it became more distinctly of a sandy hue, with dimmer spots scattered here and there, which all on-board hoped would prove verdure; but they were only hollows in the shadow of the hills.

"It was the evening before I was put on-shore; and the place where I disembarked, with the merchants going to Alexandria, was a small village, at which it was understood we should find camels to cross the desert; but, in consequence of a numerous band of Roman officers having arrived the preceding night from Arabia, only two were remaining; and these I was allowed to take; the one for the guide, and the other for myself,—the merchants having determined to wait the return of the rest of the camels.

"As it is desirable to travel as far into the desert during night as possible, in order to avoid the glare and heat of the sun, we departed about two hours before midnight. Never having been before on the back of a camel, I found the motion of that animal excessively disagreeable, arising, I conceive, from its moving two legs on the one side at the same time; but I gradually became accustomed to it, and, in the course of a few hours, felt myself in comparative ease.

"I had pictured to my imagination that the desert was a wide expanse of sand, but I found it a congregation of rocks, with only patches, or, as they might be called, lakes of sand, between them. The path along which we travelled winded among these rocks, and, during the darkness of the night, presented no object that rendered the appearance of the country different from that of any other. But, as the moon rose, the scene became awful in the greatest degree. Her silver light, tinting the tops of the innumerable rocks, suggested the idea of the ocean heaved into billows by the tempest; but, the profound silence which reigned over all, and the dead stillness of the air, made it a spectacle of inconceivable horror. It was as if the world had been destroyed, and only myself, the guide, and the two camels, were left among the ruins.

"In the midst of this scene of supreme dreariness, and while the very pulses of my life were almost suspended with the feeling of dread, the guide, exulting in the rising splendour of the moon, began to sing a cheerful song, with a clear voice and a light heart. This incident, in itself the effect of habit and familiarity, affected me in so strange a manner, that it seemed to me as if the solemn genius of the desert was insulted, and my spirit for a moment shrunk and cowered into its cell, as if in apprehension of some terrible apocalypse bursting into view.

"When we had travelled about four hours, we came to one of the watering-places, where, according to custom, we rested some time. The camels, after being refreshed, knelt down beside the spring, and the guide also stretched himself on the ground, and was soon asleep. The moon was now high in her journey;—the air was deliciously fresh;—and the stars shone with unwonted brilliancy. All was still;—and, except the breathing of the man and the camels, the regions of the dead could not be more silent. The silence might, indeed, be said to be augmented by those low sounds of sleep and repose; for they seemed possessed of a strange and wonderful audibility. It was like the first principle of life, indistinctly stirring among the rudiments of the world, before the creation of animals or living things.

"While I was thus listening and ruminating, I heard at a great distance the noise of footsteps and voices; and, after the lapse of a considerable time, a band of travellers arrived at the spring, and my guide, being roused by their approach, got up, and we again departed. Our object was to get to the next watering-place, which was six hours of the camels' pace distant, and to remain there till the fervour of the day abated. But in this intention we were frustrated; for, soon after sun-rise, we passed the mouth of a cavern,* where, feeling myself fatigued and overcome with sleep, I proposed we should wait till the afternoon. The guide was averse to this, and said that it would subject us to the risk of passing, at a dangerous time, the open waste between the rocks and the cultivated land of Egypt,—a district of country much frequented by banditti and Arabian robbers. But what had I to fear? Fate protected me from the possibility of dying by their hands. I had nothing to lose; and it was not their custom to injure the guides, knowing that, without them, their prey, the travellers, would cease to pass the deserts. Accordingly, after some persuasion, he consented to stop; and we turned aside to go into the cavern.

" I alighted, and stepped forward, leaving the guide with the camels. The glare without had so affected my sight, that, when I entered, the darkness within appeared almost palpable; and I hesitated to advance. In this situation my attention was startled by a deep sigh near me, and I recoiled two or three paces backwards. In the same moment, a young man, of a wild and haggard appearance, but withal of a mild and sublime aspect, came forward, and stood in the entrance, without speaking, seemingly in expectation that I would address him first.

" The guide, who had now observed him, instantly came forward, and kneeling, said ' Holy man of the desert, give me thy blessing.'

" The hermit immediately lifted up his staff, on the top of which was a rude cross, and, raising his hands and eyes towards the heavens, bestowed his benediction on my companion.

---

* Fitzclarence's Journal.

"I now knew, by the emblem which he held in his hand, that he was a Christian, and one of those zealous members of that sect who had been compelled to fly the persecution of the emperor as the great high-priest of the Roman gods.

"When he had concluded his prayer I spoke to him; and he requested me, with much meekness, to come into the cave. 'I can give thee,' said he, ' the cordial of the desert, and dates that were gathered yesterday. They were given to me by the travellers that you must have met at the fountain.'

"I went in; and he placed an earthen vase before me filled with delicious water; and, in spreading a few dates on a stone near to where I had taken my seat, he said, ' I do not prefer this solitude for fame, like the cynics, but to suffer for Christ. Not that he delights in suffering: but by this I testify to my faith in him; and his favour to me is all-sufficient.'

"He then, in a strain of holy enthusiasm that was often pathetic, and sometimes tenderly touching, declaimed on the sacrifice that he had been forced to make of all the ties, and hopes, and endearments, of his youth, and concluded with saying, 'The earth now contains nothing interesting to me. All the fallacies of life,—those lambent bubbles that glittered before my young eyes,—have burst, and are dissolved into a drop that is a tear. I have but the choice of two things,—to live with Man in the city, or with God in the wilderness; and who, with a broken heart, would not do as I have done, although in the first instance this sequestration from the world was dictated by necessity.

"He would, perhaps, have continued to address me longer; but, observing how heavily the needful sleep pressed upon my loaded eyelids, he ceased. When I awoke, about two hours after, the guide told me that he was gone abroad, to wander, according to his custom, among the rocks, and that, perhaps, we should meet with him at the next spring;—but we fell in with him no more."

THE WOUNDED ARABIAN.

HAREACH IN THE DESART.

CHAPTER XXVIII.

State of the Roman Government.

[A. D. 193–211.]

That the reader may be enabled to enter with proper spirit into the observations of our desultory author, especially in what relates to the state of the Romans on his return from India, we shall endeavour to give a summary view of the history of the empire, from the ignominious transaction of the sale.

Julianus, the purchaser, had, during his short reign, great reason to repent of his splendid bargain. The people despised him; and, although he bore their patriotic insolence with extraordinary mildness of temper, he could not conciliate in any degree their fluctuating affections. Pesennius Niger, who commanded the legions in Syria, revolted, and was acknowledged emperor by the eastern nations of the Roman world; and Septimius Severus, then governor of Illyricum, was also at the same time saluted by his troops with the title of Augustus, and all the cities and legions from Gaul to Byzantium followed their example. Julianus, on the first intelligence of this defection, repaired to the senate, and induced that pliant body to declare Severus a traitor, and his soldiers rebels and enemies to their country, unless they abandoned his standards in a limited time. The senate also sent deputies, to persuade the legions to desert the party of Severus, and acknowledge Julianus as emperor; but the deputies, instead of executing their trust, joined Severus, exhorted the soldiers to revenge the death of Pertinax, urged them to advance for that purpose to Rome; and accordingly they went forward, amidst the acclamations of the country. The prætorians were dismayed at the news of their approach; and Julianus, seeing they were not to be trusted, caused his palace to be fortified, determined, if he fell, to close his life with dignity. Had he done no more he would have merited commendation; but he was superstitious, and a believer in the influence of magic; and, it is alleged, that he sacrificed children, and made use of their blood in mysteries, which, he expected, would constrain the purposes of eternal fate, and change the inevitable issue of his ambition and his fortune.

"In the meantime, Severus, advancing to Rome, had reached Ravenna. Julianus fled in consternation from his cauldrons and sorceries, and implored the senate to declare Severus his partner in the empire. The decree passed without opposition; and the captain of the prætorians was sent to deliver it to Severus; but he rejected it with scorn, and ordered the bearer to be immediately put to death. This sealed the doom of Julianus. The senate declined to assist him with their advice. In despair he armed the gladiators; he entreated an old man, Pompeianus, to become his partner: but the troops sent to guard the passes of the Apennines declared for Severus, and the prætorians also abandoned him. Deserted on all sides, he shut himself up in the palace; and the murderers of Pertinax were delivered to Massala, (then consul,) who immediately assembled the senate, and procured a decree to pass, depriving Julianus of the empire, sentencing him to die, and acknowledging Severus as emperor. When this was carried into effect, a hundred of the senators were appointed to meet Severus, and to congratulate him upon his accession to the empire. But he received them in armour, at the head of his troops, and ordered their persons to be searched, as if he suspected their fidelity,— a tacit and tremendous reproach on the integrity of the Roman legislators. He then continued his march to the capital, ordered all concerned in the murder of Pertinax to be executed, and the prætorian guards to meet him without their arms, and in the attire which they wore when they attended the emperor at great solemnities. His orders were obeyed. The soldiers, imagining that they were only to adorn his public entry, came to the camp, and were instantly surrounded, in their defenceless state, by his army.

Severus then ascended the tribunal, and reproached them in the bitterest terms for murdering their sovereign; for selling the empire by auction, to the everlasting disgrace of the Roman name; and even for abandoning, like so many cowards and traitors, Julianus, whom they had themselves elected.—'For such enormous crimes,' he exclaimed, 'I can inflict no adequate punishment: but, quit your horses, and all military badges; and, if one of you is ever found within a hundred miles of Rome, he shall be instantly put to death.' They were thunderstruck, and forced to comply. The troops dragged them from their horses, stripped them of their tunics and ornaments, and sent them from the camp with howls and execration of contempt and infamy.

Severus, having performed this magnificent act of justice, marched to Rome, attended by his legions, bearing the standards of the degraded prætorians reversed. He advanced to the gate on horseback in his military habit; there alighting, and having put on the purple robe, he entered the city on foot, accompanied by the senators, with crowns of laurel on their heads, which the people, who on this occasion were all clothed in white, also wore. The streets through which Severus walked to the capital were strewed with flowers; the fronts of the houses adorned with carpets and tapestry,—and, for a time, all was triumph, and splendour, and festivity. But the soldiery, taking-up their quarters in the temples, porticos, and other public buildings, and no provision having been made for them, became riotous, committed great disorders, and would not be appeased, without being paid by the senate as large a sum as the troops that attended Augustus to Rome received, demanding it as their right.

The fortitude and address of Severus having subdued this dangerous mutiny, and new prætorians having been formed for the protection of the city, he again put his troops in motion, and marched against Niger, who, having in the meantime heard of his success, was advancing to meet him.

Niger having taken possession of Byzantium, Severus laid siege to it, and was vigorously resisted: in the end, however, Niger was subdued; his adherents and children put to the sword; Byzantium, with all its stately edifices, laid in ashes, the walls razed to the ground, and the inhabitants sold for slaves. By persevering in this stern course of vengeance and resentment, Severus made himself the entire master of the Roman world,—exterminated his enemies, but gained no friends. He was, if not one of the greatest of the Cæsars, the most inflexible of princes; and his reign, although not distinguished for superior wisdom, was eminent for the vigour with which all the functions of government were administered.

He died in Britain; and his body was burnt with great solemnity at York, from which the ashes, in a golden urn, were carried, with great funeral pomp, to Rome, and deposited in the superb mausoleum of Adrian, now better known as the Castle of St. Angelo."

CHAPTER XXIX.

Historical Sketch.

[A. D. 211–234.]

THE sons of Severus, Caracalla and Geta, succeeded him in the empire. They ruled without unison; and the infirmities which had begun to appear in the frame of the state were rendered daily more manifest. Caracalla, ambitious of reigning alone, and hating as well as dreading his brother, formed a plot against his life; and Geta was stabbed in the arms of their mother. The remainder of Caracalla's reign was one continued series of public wrongs and private crimes: the people were loaded with taxes, to supply his profusion; the coin of the empire was forced into circulation at a price far above its intrinsic value; and the haughty majesty of Rome so far declined from her former greatness, that she was content to purchase a peace from the Germans with a large sum of money. Such is the summary that may be given of the government of Caracalla, who was assassinated in the thirtieth year of his age, and the seventh of his reign.

He was succeeded by Opelius Macrinus, a native of Africa, by whom the downfall of the military grandeur of Rome was not arrested. The Parthians, under Artabanes, invaded the empire; and Macrinus was compelled to purchase his forbearance, under the name of peace, at the price of fifty millions of drachmas. But, if the splendour of the Roman name was thus fading away, a better virtue than heroism was beginning to appear; and the reign of Macrinus is honourably distinguished for the impartial severity with which crimes were punished, and many popular vices proscribed, for the first time, as public offences,—a clear indication of the influence of that improved morality diffused by the propagation of the Christian religion.

But, the elevation of Heliogabalus to the imperial dignity is a sufficient proof of the strength and licentious genius of the old religion. He was set up in opposition to Macrinus. The whole of his transactions should, however, be erased from the records of history, and therefore we pass them over as unworthy of farther notice.

Alexander, the cousin to this blot of human nature, was, after his death, proclaimed emperor, in the fourteenth year of his age. His mother, Julia Mamæa, is supposed to have been a Christian, and she was undoubtedly a lady of singular purity of manners in that corrupted age. His father dying when Alexander was very young, she brought him up with great care, and employed only such persons as his instructors who were distinguished for their probity as much as for their acquirements. His abilities were certainly of a high order, but his assiduity was still greater; and the mildness and generosity of his disposition, with the simplicity of his manners, rendered him an amiable man, and an accomplished prince.

He did not openly profess the Christian religion, but he adopted publicly its leading maxim, 'Do as you would be done by;' and caused it to be engraved over the gates of his palace. In many respects he appears to have borne a striking resemblance to Edward the Sixth of England, who succeeded to the throne in circumstances singularly similar; for the Popish religion was then in a state of abrogation, and the Protestant not more settled than the Christian in the days of the Roman emperor.

As Alexander advanced in life, the solidity of his character often appeared to great advantage; and there was a principle of utility and benevolence in all his measures, that made them shine with the lustre of virtue and wisdom. But nothing could arrest the decay of the Roman state.

Other nations were rising in strength and power along the frontiers, and the energies of the warlike Persians, which had slept for ages, were again awake, and stirring for action. Artaxerxes, their king, sent four hundred of the tallest men in his army, well mounted, richly caparisoned, and magnificently clothed, to acquaint the Romans and their emperor, that he ordered them to retire immediately from Syria and Asia, and all the countries between the Euphrates and Ægæan Sea, which had formerly belonged to the Persians. Alexander listened to this with undisturbed equanimity; and, having ordered the messengers to be stript of their armour and apparel, sent them, under a guard, to till the ground in Phrygia, and immediately prepared for war. The oriental monarch, determined to carry his threat into effect, advanced towards the frontiers, at the head of an army, consisting of an innumerable anarchy of foot-soldiers, one hundred and thirty thousand horse, eighteen hundred chariots of war, armed with scythes, and seven hundred elephants, bearing towers on their backs, filled with archers. This vast array, the greatest in point of number that ever the Romans encountered, Alexander totally defeated, and returned to Rome in triumph. But, although defeated, the Persians were not subdued; on the contrary, their ambition was inflamed with the spirit of revenge, and many years did not elapse till they again appeared with refreshed vigour, and more than vindicated the disgrace and chastisement which the arrogance of Artaxerxes received from Alexander.

CHAPTER XXX.

Anecdotes of the Emperor Maximinus.

It is a remarkable feature of the Roman government, that, although its general institutions were formed with great wisdom, and the inferior magistrates called to office, according to the routine of an old and settled system, the imperial dignity was left a prey to every daring adventurer. Notwithstanding the excellence of Alexander's administration, his popularity with the citizens, and, what perhaps was of more consequence to an emperor, the affection with which he was regarded by the soldiery, Maximinus, an illiterate barbarian, who was only distinguished among the vulgar by his gigantic stature and amazing strength, had the audacity to aspire to the throne, and succeeded. But, before relating the result of this conspiracy, it may be proper to give some account of Maximinus.

He was of mean extraction, and in early youth a shepherd among the mountains of Thrace. In stature he exceeded the height of eight feet, and his limbs and the structure of his body were formed in admirable symmetry and proportion. His strength was no less extraordinary, and his speed and courage were incredible. When he was about twenty years of age, Severus, in passing through Thrace, exhibited some military games and exercises; and Maximinus, coming to the camp a spectator, entreated permission to enter the lists as a competitor for the prizes. The emperor, struck with his size, matched him,—not with the soldiers, but some of the strongest slaves; and he overcame sixteen successively. A few days after, Severus happened to fall in with him as he was riding, and, to try if Maximinus could run as well as wrestle, put his horse to the gallop, and rode round the camp, followed close by the gigantic shepherd, till his horse was quite tired.

"Thracian," said he, "art thou now disposed to wrestle?"—"Yes; as much as your majesty pleases," replied Maximinus. The emperor immediately dismounted, and ordered some of the stoutest soldiers and best wrestlers in the army to try him,—of whom he overcame seven with as much ease as if they had been children. Pleased with this wonderful activity and strength, Severus presented him with a golden collar, placed him among his guards, and conferred on him many favours, appointing him extraordinary allowances,—the common pay not being sufficient to support him; for his appetite was even more amazing than his vigour.

Caracalla made him a centurion; and, in the time of Heliogabalus, he was raised to the rank of tribune: but he always declined, under some pretence or other, to attend that monster. He appears, indeed, while in a subordinate station, to have conducted himself with modesty and prudence. By Alexander he was treated with much kindness, appointed to the command of a legion, and created a senator; honours which inspired him with ambition, and called into action all the latent bad qualities of his nature.

Soon after the return of the emperor from the Persian war, news arrived at Rome, that bands of the northern nations had passed the Danube in great numbers. At this time Maximinus commanded a body of Pannonians in Germany. Alexander placed himself at the head of the army in that country, with the determination to chastise the barbarians; but he found the discipline of the legions so much relaxed, that it was necessary, before venturing to take the field with them, to restore their neglected exercises. This irritated the licentious soldiery; and Maximinus, with equal ingratitude and address, fomented their discontent, inveighing against Alexander as a weak and pusillanimous prince, governed by his mother, and unfit to conduct a war with the hardy myriads of the north. When their allegiance was thus poisoned, the emperor being at a town in the territory of Treves, with only a small detachment of troops with him, Maximinus thought the opportunity favourable for carrying his ambitious project into effect. He accordingly imparted his wish to some of the boldest and most devoted of the soldiers under his command; and, by promises of large preferment, in the event of succeeding to the empire, he induced them to undertake the murder of Alexander. They immediately set out for the place where the emperor resided, which they contrived to reach about an hour after mid-day, when the attendants were withdrawn to refresh themselves (according to the Roman custom) with a short sleep after dinner. At their appearance the soldiers on guard fled with precipitation. The virtuous Mamæa, (the emperor's mother,) hearing the noise, alarmed, and running out, was struck down and killed on the spot, with the captains of the guard, who had also been roused by the tumult. The assassins then entered the imperial apartment with their swords drawn; and Alexander, who was unarmed and alone, threw his robe over his face, and received, without uttering a word, the many blows with which they dispatched him.

Such was the tragical end of this estimable prince;— and by these means was Maximinus raised to the empire.

CHAPTER XXXI.

Summary of the Roman History.

[A.D. 234–249.]

SUCH is the inherent disposition of human nature to err, that ignorance is almost vice; for, knowledge is the only guide to justice, integrity, and honour. Maximinus was free from many of the worst stains of his time; and, till raised to honour and command, his native modesty and ingenuous character conciliated many friends. But, as he advanced in life, and was promoted in fortune, the virtues of his youth were absorbed by ambition,—the passion which contends with avarice for the dominion of our riper years,—and, being unfurnished with the requisite knowledge to guide the decisions of his judgment, he was degraded from the dignity of a brave and honest soldier to the rank of a Roman tyrant.

He was no sooner invested with the sovereign power, than he dismissed all the meritorious officers employed by his predecessor, and filled their places with a base herd of his own, as little qualified as himself, by education, for the trusts to which they were appointed. Determining to rule with vigour, it was natural that such a man should become ferocious; and, accordingly, in the catalogue of his crimes as a monarch, we find that, being ashamed of his humble parentage, he ordered all who were acquainted with any of his family in their original condition to be put to death. The adherents of Alexander, as a matter of course, were also massacred; and, in the pretexts of plots against his life, or to obtain money for his warlike enterprises, his cruelty rioted in promiscuous slaughter. The consequence was, that he soon exhausted even the abject submission of the Romans. The Africans revolted, and proclaimed Gordian emperor, who immediately wrote to the senate and people of Rome, acquainting them with what had taken place. The people and senate received the communication with joy; and Maximinus, with his son, whom he had associated with himself in the empire, were declared enemies of the public, and a price set upon their heads.

Maximinus, who was at this time in Thrace or Sarmatia, on receiving intelligence of his ejection from the empire, was seized with transports of rage, and, with the terrible violence of his great strength and savage simplicity, beat his head against the walls of his apartment, threw himself on the ground, and, tearing his imperial robes into tatters, uttered the most dreadful vows of vengeance against the senate and his enemies.. His officers thought him bereft of understanding, and disarmed him with much difficulty. When this paroxysm had subsided, he however summoned his council, and consulted them with more equanimity than might have been expected from a man so void of self-command; and the result of their deliberation was, that he should immediately march for the capital. In this attempt, he was murdered by a party of his own soldiers.

The details of the political conflicts of the Romans, from the abortive election of Gordian to the death of Balbinus and Maximus, possess no interest with posterity; nor does the history of Antonius Gordianus, their successor, offer much, although he repulsed the Persians, who, under the command of Sapor, the son of Artaxerxes, had again invaded Syria. He was a young prince of excellent dispositions; but the empire was too easy a prize to any one who had the courage to seize it; and he was soon put to death by Philip, the captain of his guards, the son of an Arabian robber.

Philip had undoubtedly some talent for the imperial office; and the Christian religion, which was in his time openly preached, and which it has been supposed he professed, must be allowed to have had some influence in the public suppression of those infamous personal vices, which, till the reign of this emperor, had been flagrantly practised in Rome without shame, and without punishment. But his reign was not long. He, in his turn, was put to death, and succeeded by Decius, in whose time Hareach returned from India; at the period, as we have mentioned, that the persecution of the Christians was revived with so much fury, so as to oblige many of their most eminent teachers to take refuge among the rocks of the mountains and the caverns of the desert.

We shall now recal the attention of the reader to the Volume of Hareach, who appears to have been in Rome about the two hundred and fiftieth year of the Christian era.

CHAPTER XXXII.

Rome in the Third Century.

" IF the morals of the Romans," says our author, " have not improved since I was last among them, there is an evident disposition to arrest at least the progress of corruption. Vices, which were wont to walk abroad in naked effrontery, now scarcely dare to venture forth but in the dark of the twilight, and even then, in sequestered places. This merit is due to the anathemas against sin so courageously preached by the Christians; for the priests of the idolatry no longer pretend that their fictitious deities favour any offence against decency and good morals.

" Letters arrived to-day from Decius to the senate, informing them that he was desirous they should re-establish the office of censor; and they have unanimously appointed Valerian, a man of blameless conduct, and popular with all parties. He is at present with the army in Thrace, and some people are of opinion that he will not accept the office.

"When the duties of censor were limited to Rome, it as an office of some utility; but, in what manner they re now to be administered over a hundred nations, contituting a state where the whole power is vested in the rmy, is a problem not easily to be solved. But the evival of this venerable officer, indicates a consciousness f the necessity of some attempt to recal the purity of ncient manners. To recal!—that cannot be. The imple virtues of the golden age of the republic were he fruit of an unaffected faith in the influence of the ods that were then adored. But this faith has expired, and with it all the influence and efficacy of the institutions which owed their sacredness and authority to its dogmas. The setting-up again of the censor, is an act of senseless gnorance. They may as well place the urn with the ashes of Marcus Junius in the consular chair, and expect that it will award justice with the virtue and wisdom of the living man. No:—a change must take place in the theoretic principles of morality, before there is any improvement in manners; and this change is growing to effect by the propagation of the new religion.

"The more I look around, the more I am convinced that the fate of Rome is sealed, and her greatness sinking —never to rise again. The public edifices, for want of money, are falling into decay. The priests belonging to many of the temples, no longer supported by the offerings of the votaries of their idols, have been obliged, for the means of subsistence, to allow the fruit-sellers and dealers in toys to erect booths and stalls beneath the porticos. Some of the temples are utterly deserted. A common carrier has obtained permission, from a priest, to make use of one near his stables as a warehouse. He brought my luggage from Ravenna; and when I went to bring it away, I found part of it on the altar. A mat was wrapped round the statue of the deity to keep him from profanation; but he will never be revered again.

"The decay of general opulence is also visible every where. The theatres are less frequented than formerly, and their decorations are greatly in need of repair. Many of those sumptuous private palaces, which, a hundred years ago, were the ornaments of the world, have been deserted, either on account of the decline or confiscations of their owners, and are now occupied by several families, who, in appropriating them to their respective uses, have distorted their symmetry and defaced their architecture.

"There are fewer equipages in the streets, and the servants are less splendidly dressed. The magnificence of the shops has also suffered in the general impoverishment, and many dissimilar articles of merchandise, showing that the dealers have been necessitated to entice retail customers, now lie in scattered and dusty heaps, in those superb magazines which were once filled with the riches of whole nations.

"For many years no new streets appear to have been added to the city, but its general magnitude is not contracted. This, however, cannot long fail to take place; for I observe many empty houses, and others no longer habitable. I passed to-day a mason, who was breaking a statue of Augustus to burn for mortar, to help him to convert what had once been the porter's-lodge of a palace into a shop for a dealer in old utensils and furniture. I asked him if he knew the statue?—and he replied it was an idol.

"These spectacles infect me with melancholy thoughts, and yet I know not why it should be so. Rome has had her fame and her greatness, and must follow in the train of Thebes, and Babylon, and Jerusalem. Some other will rise to dominion in her stead,—and, like them, also pass away."

CHAPTER XXXIII.

Public Opinion among the Romans during the Third Century.

WE shall continue our extracts from the Volume of Hareach. He appears to have felt, with the energy of new sensations, the impressions which the various objects in Rome made on him at this time; and, although his reflections are corroborated by history, yet they possess so much of an individual character, and are so greatly different in their strain from those of all the cotemporary writers, that they place many things in a new light.

"The fortune of Rome," he observes, "has no doubt passed the full, and is now waning. In proportion as its splendour fades, other luminaries begin to appear;— few, far between,—and scattered certainly; but still they are of the same divine origin, and destined to run their appointed course, however circumscribed their spheres.

"Formerly the army was every thing to the Romans, and all public virtues partook of some affinity to military discipline. Actions were not esteemed virtuous so much on account of their utility as their resemblance to exploits of war; and fortitude, under the shocks of adversity, was only admired in proportion to the resemblance which it bore, compared to the manner that the soldier withstood the brunt of battle. But now the current of partialities run in another direction; and, it is not what is admirable, grand, or heroic, that the public esteem, but what is useful and benevolent.

"Men no longer address each other with the abrupt rudeness of the plain matter-of-fact, but temper their intercourse with suavity, and endeavour to sheath as it were with gentleness even their quarrels. Society has altogether become more civil and mild in its etiquettes;

and, although there is less force of character now displayed, and less originality to be met with, there is probably more rational enjoyment, as there is undoubtedly much less party acrimony.

"But, the most curious change of all is the indifference with which the army is considered, and all its movements. It is regarded as an evil demon that rules the destiny of the state, whose authority and domination no one thinks of resisting, nor dreams that it is possible to resist. All act, however, as if they considered it not; and, if the expression may be allowed, are atheists in practice towards that ruling power. A thousand daily frequenters of the porticos and places of recreation may be asked where the emperor is, and whether it is war or peace in Germany and Asia? and scarcely one will be found who can answer the question correctly.

"The emperors, by having become the creatures of the army, are obliged to conciliate the soldiery at the expense of the citizens. As the rising nations around the frontiers are daily growing into greater vigour, when the armies are conquered, the state will be no more; for all that is national is abandoned to the armies; and there is no principle of public union cherished among the people.

"They do indeed complain of grievances; they cry out for the reformation of manners; they pine beneath the loads of taxation; and, to deprecate an increase of burdens, they are willing to unite. They pretend even to be anxious for the extirpation of the many evils that prey upon the vitals of the state; but they have lost the relish of renown, and hear with equal carelessness the preparations of the Persians, the inroads of the barbarians, and the defeat of a Roman army. They take no interest in the general concerns of the commonwealth, but only think of the circumstances that press upon each other individually. It was formerly their boast to deem no sacrifice too great for the majesty of the Roman name, but every thing that is now required of them for the public service is grudged, as so much subtracted from their means of personal enjoyment; yet, at no period was ever charity perhaps so liberally dispensed. Almshouses, schools, and hospitals, are numerously endowed; and still poverty and ignorance seem strangely to increase. At this time, throughout the whole extent of the Roman empire, compared with the writers of the Augustan age, there is not one author, who, either by the choice of his subject, his style, or his manner of managing what he inculcates, rises beyond mediocrity; while hundreds of experimenters in taste and philosophy are endeavouring to strike out some new and splendid course. Their endeavours only prove that the topics of antiquity have become trite."

After indulging at some length in reflections of this kind, always tinctured with a sentiment of contempt, our author gives a description of a literary character, which, perhaps, may be taken as a picture illustrative of the state of authors at Rome during the third century.

CHAPTER XXXIV.

Of Authors and Publications in the Third Century.

"THE suppers of Toxotius* are the most delightful repasts in Rome. Every man of celebrity is welcome to them; and the accomplishments of the host, though neither superior nor interesting, qualify him so well to

---

* The only person that we have been able to trace of this name, about this period, in Rome, was a senator related to the family of Antoninus Pius, who wrote several poems that had merit enough to be preserved and read in the time of Constantine the Great;—they are now lost. He married Junia Fadilla, who was betrothed to the son of the emperor Maximinus.

conduct conversation agreeably, that all his guests are afforded an opportunity of appearing to advantage, by speaking on the subjects with which they are best acquainted. In other houses, men of greater talent are occasionally met with than the generality of those who frequent the table of this amiable man; but they are there either on business, or to gratify the vanity of the feast-giver.

"Last night we were gratified by the publication of a new book—a short account of the Life of Maximinus,* by a young man who evinced considerable ability. Toxotius gave a special banquet on the occasion, and invited a numerous assemblage of his friends; for he was desirous of obtaining their patronage to the author. The best public reader in Rome was engaged, for the author himself was too diffident to do justice in that way to any work before so large a company; and, in order that nothing might be wanting to give due eclat to the publication, the manuscript had been carefully perused by the reader some time before.

"The history was written with commendable brevity, and no one disputed the correctness of the facts, or the views which the author took of the principal incidents; but he dwelt too strongly on the transactions of Maximinus after he became emperor; and it was generally thought that he adopted too much of the vulgar opinion respecting his strength, appetites, and ferocity.

"The reader acquitted himself so well that he was much applauded at the conclusion; and the friends of Toxotius expressed themselves so pleased with the book, that the author was requested to furnish them with copies; and, that he might be able to employ the most elegant penmen, they presented him with a very liberal contribution of money.

"During the time of the reading, the author watched the faces of the company with great anxiety, and was often apparently much distressed, by the curious and inquisitive looks which were from time to time cast towards

---

* Ælius Sabinus wrote the Life of Maximinus. Can this refer to his work?

him, when his expressions were not exactly according to the rules of approved taste, or his statements not in unison with the common opinion. It was however of great use to him to undergo this trial, painful as it no doubt was; for, it enabled him to see where he failed in producing due effect, and to correct his text and narrative before committing the work to the penman."

How far this account of the mode of publication among the ancients may be trusted, we have not the means of judging; but, it is at least plausible; nor, indeed, is it easy to conceive any other effectual method of making a literary work known to the public, prior to the invention of printing.

CHAPTER XXXV.

The Falling of the Roman Empire.

[A. D. 251-260.]

"The misfortunes of Rome increase daily in magnitude and ignominy. Decius the emperor, with his son, have been killed in battle by the Goths, and the imperial army routed. Gallus, one of his generals, is elected to the vacant dignity, and has concluded a dishonourable peace, instead of revenging the disgrace of the Roman arms. But he could not revenge that disgrace; and the senate and citizens, while they repine at what he has done, in consenting that the triumphant barbarians should be allowed to retire unmolested with their spoil and prisoners, and an annual tribute, forget that he was in no condition to make head against them ——— * * * * * *

"He has declared vigorous war against the new opinions, and the Christians are attacked as public enemies. A plague rages in different parts of the empire, and the continued drought of the spring threatens a general famine. Omens of evil are glaring everywhere —— * * *

"The reign of Gallus has not been a year and six months, and his fate has been the common one of an emperor. Æmilianus, a moor, was chosen in his stead, and the senate approved the choice; but the army, under the command of Valerian, who had been named Censor by Decius, preferred their own leader; and Æmilianus was killed, after nominally reigning between three and our months —— * * *

"The senate and people are intoxicated with joy; and the virtues of Valerian cannot be questioned; but, whether they are of a kind sufficiently firm to withstand the temptations of imperial power, and bold enough to stem the rushing ebb of the Roman destiny, a short time will determine —— * * *

"The enemies of Rome continue to increase. Every day brings an account of some new nation that has ventured to invade the empire. The Franks have only in the course of the present year been heard of for the first time, and they are already formidable. The Persian king is again ravaging Mesopotamia and Syria; and Valerian has set out in person to oppose him. In the meantime, the Romans exult in the success of a few inconsequential skirmishes with the barbarian myriads; and day after day expect the restoration of their ancient glory. What they however deem the dawn, is but the twilight of the evening; and the victories of Aurelian Probus are but as the last beams of day on the clouds of the gathering storm of night. The barbarians are as flies, and the empire a carcase:—they will have their prey; for, as often as they are disturbed, their swarms return with augmented numbers —— * * *

"Valerian has been defeated by Sapor the Persian king, and taken prisoner. The chief and representative of the Roman greatness has been carried in chains, to grace the return of that haughty monarch,—almost as haughty as those consuls and emperors, who so often compelled the captive kings to drag their chariots along the streets of Rome ——— * *

" Sapor was not content with exhibiting Valerian in chains, nor with making him his footstool whenever he mounted on horseback, but, after his death, ordered his body to be flayed, and the skin preserved in salt, and exposed in a temple, as a lasting trophy of the Persian monarch's power ——— * *

" It is only the unwieldy bulk of the Roman state that prevents it from being utterly overthrown. It is so great a mass, that time, as well as all the force that can be employed against it, is requisite to break it up. The indifferency with which the fate of Valerian was heard throughout the whole extent of the empire, demonstrates the universal extinction of public principle,—that life of a nation, without which there is no certainty in law, no security to property, no freedom to the subject, honour to the magistrate, charity to man, nor homage to God."

CHAPTER XXXVI.

The Opening of the Sibylline Books.

[A. D. 261-267.]

THE narrative of Hareach is so broken, during the twenty years which followed the disastrous fall of Valerian, that his reflections cannot be affixed to any particular events. Nor is this to be wondered at; for, even the most meagre chronicles would labour in the confusion of the multitude of incidents, that render the history of that period almost unintelligible. We are told of no less than thirty pretenders to the imperial dignity, starting in different provinces, and at the head of as many armies, and, by aspiring to the same object, tending still to keep together the empire, which, had they been content with the rank of kings, and formed states for themselves by the power that they actually possessed, would naturally have fallen asunder. Revolt and invasion resounded on all sides, and frightful portents and calamities seemed to indicate that universal nature sympathised with the political convulsions which shook the Roman world. The sun was overcast with blackness, and a preternatural night continued for the space of several days, attended with peals of thunder, not in the air, but in the bowels of the earth, which opened in many places, and swallowed up towns and villages, with all their inhabitants.* The sea swelled above its boundaries, and drowned whole cities, and a pestilence raged in Egypt, Greece, and Italy. These tremendous visitations of Divine wrath had an awful effect on the populace of Rome; and the description which Hareach gives of the opening of the Sibylline books, may be extracted as the final act of national adoration paid in Italy to the genius of the classic mythology.

"It is now the third day, and the sun has not appeared. The clouds hang so low, that they seem to rest like masses of black marble on the roofs of the city. It is not darkness, but an obscurity much more terrible, that fills the whole air, for still all things are visible, as distinctly so as in the brightest sunshine, but they are covered with an ashy-coloured wanness, that is the more appalling, as no light can be seen from whence it proceeds.

"The Christians expect the day of judgment, and are at prayers openly; and the magistrates tremble and forbear to enforce the edicts against them. The senate has assembled, and, unable to apply any authority to repress the menaces of God and Nature, decrees that the books of the sibyls shall be consulted.

"The preparatory sacrifices are slain, and the offerings

---

* Universal History.

to Jupiter laid upon the altar. A prodigious multitude of all ranks and ages has assembled round the capitol, and in the streets leading to the temple of Apollo, where the books were deposited by Augustus.

"It is announced that the sacrifice is consumed. The portals of the capitol are thrown open; and the senators, in their robes, in the great chamber, are standing to receive the books. All is profound silence;—the priests and vestal virgins approach;—the crowd fall on their knees as the procession passes; and the senators, with their hands crossed on their bosoms, bend forward with reverence, as in the presence of a coming God.

"On a golden salver, borne on the head of a child, and covered with a veil that conceals the face of the bearer, is the sacred casket which contains the prophetic volumes. The chief of the college, with whom they are deposited, and who alone can read the venerable language in which they are written, walks reverentially behind.

"The priests and vestals form a lane from the porch of the capitol and down the stairs, beyond the bottom of the hill, and the child and the interpreter ascending to the hall of the senators, the ranks close, and follow them up the steps.

"The procession has filled the area of the hall;—the veil is raised by Faustinius;*—the casket is opened;— and the volumes are unfolded.

"The countenance of the consul is pale with anxiety and dread. The pontiff, who explores the books, searches them in vain. The last of the three volumes is in his hand, and every eye is fixed on him as he turns over the leaves; but he returns it also into the casket with a sorrowful look, and Faustinius covers it with the veil.—In the same moment, a dreadful clap of thunder was followed by a sudden shuddering of the earth, and the doors of the capitol were closed with tremendous violence by a blast of cold and furious wind. The multitude, horror-struck by the thunder and the earthquake, fled in all directions; and the senators, priests, augurs, and vestal

---

* He was consul at this time.

virgins, no less terrified, came rushing from the doors and windows, and precipitated themselves down the steps as if driven out of the building by some avenging demon. It was soon known, that, although this was but the effect of fear, inspired by the convulsions of Nature, the prophetic wisdom of the Sibylline books offered no consolation to the public despair. The report indeed is, that they are all blank, the writing having entirely vanished from the pages, and this the Christians suppose indicates, that the end of the world is come; while the idolators consider it as the evidence of the Gods having abandoned the protection of Rome."

CHAPTER XXXVII.

Zenobia Queen of Palmyra.

THERE is undoubtedly much of a vindictive spirit in the strictures which our wandering Jew makes on the Romans and the Roman government. He rejoices evidently in the progress of that strong current of adversity, which was flooding the empire with calamities both physical and political; but still there are glimpses of a better spirit scintillating through his work, and the strong workings of a generous mind may be discerned in his most misanthropic animadversions. His account of Zenobia, the queen of Palmyra, may be taken as an example; for, although history confirms the elevated picture that he has drawn of her pure and noble character, it is untinged with that admiration with which he appears to have contemplated her conduct.

"She affected to derive her pedigree from the Cleopatras and the Ptolemies for it is the weakness of splendid minds to seek an adventitious consequence from hereditary honours, even while they have shone forth with greater lustre than the merits of all the ancestry to which they lay claim. The family of this illustrious woman was undoubtedly one of the most honorable of the eastern provinces, but she was the most distinguished of her race. She was accomplished in all the polite languages, possessed of more science than most men, and enjoyed such high and clear notions of religion, that, if in this she was not a daughter of Zion, she might have been justly classed with the Christians.

"She had the good fortune to be married to a man worthy of herself, and who not only sympathized with all her lofty conceptions of royalty, but in his own conduct exhibited a splendid example to princes. Odenatus, her husband, having been slain on the shores of the Euxine, in a campaign against the Goths, she resolved to assert the rank that was due to her lineage and her genius. The first act of her widowhood was a frank declaration to the world of the grandeur to which she destined her children. Odenatus having been partner in the empire with Gallienus, she arrayed her three sons, Herennianus, Timolaus, and Vhaballet, in the imperial purple, and caused them to be acknowledged by all the eastern provinces as joint emperors of Rome; obliged them to conform to the Roman customs, and to use the Latin language instead of the Greek, which was spoken by the other eastern princes. As they were boys under age, she governed in their name, with the magnificent title of Queen of the East; and discharged all the various duties of her station with the delicacy of a woman and the intrepidity of a sovereign. Her councils were wise, her resolutions steady; kind and generous to persons of merit, she was inexorable where severity was just. She lived in the full exhibition of oriental magnificence; and, like the Persian monarch, would not be addressed on any occasion but with worship and prostration. Her banquets were as gorgeous as those of the emperors at Rome; and, on such occasions, she seemed to consider the indulgence in luxury as a public duty. For she was naturally temperate in her private mode of living, and chaste, even to singularity. She was without question the most illustrious personage of her age; but it was offence enough that she had set herself in opposition to the coarse and insolent Aurelian.

"This stern soldier, who had nothing but military exactness to recommend him to the greatest throne in the world, having in different engagements obliged Zenobia to retire within the walls of Palmyra, laid siege to that city. He at first attempted to carry it by storm, conceiving that his enterprise would intimidate her at once to surrender; but her preparations, her pride, and her courage, repulsed him in the first onset, and he was obliged to solicit by siege, what he had presumed to seize by bravery. The garrison, animated by the great example of their queen, showered upon his soldiers such clouds of missiles and arrows, and upbraided him with such taunts when they saw him passing under the ramparts, that, instead of venturing to renew the attack, he insulted her by letter, with an exhortation to surrender. To this she replied,

'No man, before you, ever made such a demand; it is not by letters, but valour, that you must induce me to submit. You cannot but know that Cleopatra chose rather to die than to live subordinate to Augustus, notwithstanding his promises. I expect daily the Persians, the Saracens, and the Armenians, who are all hastening to my relief; and what will then become of you and your army, whom the robbers of Syria have already put to flight? You will then lay aside that pride and presumption with which you command me to surrender, as if you were the conqueror of the world.'

"The vulgar Aurelian was so enraged at this answer that he immediately ordered a general assault; but the courageous Zenobia stood on the ramparts, and so directed her soldiers, that he was repulsed with great loss.

"Negociation was the virtue of Aurelian; and, although not without talent, his mind was of the basest kind. He felt not the emanations of the sublime spirit with which Zenobia, in the despair of her fortune, was animated; and having defeated the Persians, and corrupted the Saracens and Armenians, who were coming to her aid, he counted her as his prize. But, their defection did not subdue her courage. At the dead of night, carrying with her jewels and treasures, she secretly quitted the city. Aurelian having received notice of her flight, dispatched a party of cavalry, who, coming up just as she was on the point of embarking in a boat to cross the Euphrates, arrested and carried her back to Palmyra.

"The native coarseness of the man did not desert him on this occasion. Disregarding her rank, her birth, and her great talents, he asked 'What had instigated her to take up arms against the emperors of Rome?'—'To you, (she replied,) who have conquered me, I am bound to submit; but, as for your immediate predecessors, I never thought them worthy of the name.' Success, and her triumphant spirit, which adversity could not subdue, had such an effect on Aurelian, that he endeavoured to soften the degradation to which his pride had subjected her. At his triumph, she was loaded with riches and gems, such as Rome, in all the plenitude of victory, had never witnessed; and, when he allowed her to retire to a private station, with her daughters, at Tebar,* he treated her with more courtesy and respect, than might have been expected from a man so little sensible to any virtue beyond the performance of military duty."

---

* Now Tivoli.

CHAPTER XXXVIII.

Longinus the Sublime.

THE severity with which our author speaks of the emperor Aurelian, requires some qualification; for, although he was an illiterate man, and had sprung from the rank of a common soldier, he possessed many of the qualities essential to the character of a great prince. He was firm, and judiciously liberal; and the people held him in great respect, on account of the rigour with which he acted, and the ability he had shown in restoring the empire, after the troubles with which it had been almost shaken asunder by the captivity of Valerian. His treatment however of Longinus, the author of the celebrated "*Treatise on the Sublime,*" may be considered as an exception to the general justice of his administration. The account of that transaction, in our manuscript, without differing materially from what is recorded in other histories, is more circumstantial.

"The fate of Dionysius Longinus has lessened the satisfaction which would otherwise have been felt at the conquest of Palmyra. Having been invited from Athens by Zenobia, to instruct her in the Greek language, and, perhaps, to assist in the education of her sons, his eloquence, integrity, and wisdom, raised him so much in her esteem, that she made him a member of her council about the time that Aurelian advanced to lay siege to the city. His mind being elevated with the noblest conceptions of heroism and virtue, he acquired a deserved ascendency over the other counsellors, and certainly obtained at least the reputation of having approved of the magnanimous determination of the queen not to submit until compelled by conquest. The emperor, therefore, considered him as a main cause of the resistance which Palmyra opposed to his arms; and was so enraged against him, on receiving the letter of Zenobia,—for he considered it as written by Longinus,—that he vowed to punish him as a rebel. Accordingly, when the city surrendered, one of his first acts was the arrest of Longinus, whom he ordered to be brought before him.

"The centurion and guard sent to execute this duty, found the philosopher in his study, reading the works of Homer. He had retired thither when it was determined by the magistrates to surrender, and waited with calm sublimity the issue of an event which he could no longer control, expecting that the Roman soldiers, exasperated by the repulses they had sustained, would, on their entrance, abandon themselves to licentious revenge. But, the discipline which Aurelian has restored, prevented any excess; and the Roman guard entered the residence of Longinus without noise or opposition.

"On going into his apartment, the centurion, a young man of an ancient Italian family, was so struck with the serene resignation of the philosopher, that he halted the guard at the door; and stepping forward, with an air of respectful commiseration, informed him for what purpose he had come. Longinus rose, with the book in his hand, and saying he was ready to attend him, they walked to the palace together.

"On going into the open air, he looked towards the skies, and observed 'that it was a beautiful night;' expressing his satisfaction at the tranquillity which reigned throughout the city, so different from the tumults and outrages that might have been expected from a victorious army; and he praised the excellent discipline with which the emperor held in subjection the violent passions of the soldiers. 'But,' said he, 'it is thus with all evils which we see coming in the sunset of fortune,—we measure their stature by their shadows.

"When they reached the palace, Aurelian was at supper with his generals. The prisoner being announced, he was ordered to be brought in. The officer, by whom he had been arrested conducted him into the chamber where the company were at table, and stopped at the door, while Longinus stepped forward, still holding the volume of Homer in his hand, and made the customary reverences to the emperor.

"The simple and easy dignity with which this was performed overawed Aurelian for a moment, and he rose from his seat, actuated by an impulse of involuntary respect. The generals, seeing the emperor rise, also started up, and for the space of two or three minutes there was a considerable degree of embarrassment among the imperial party. But, Aurelian recovering his presence of mind, happily extricated them, by an act of decision and propriety, strikingly characteristic of the man. Instead of resuming his seat, he left the table, and walked into another apartment, desiring Longinus to follow; by which adroit expedient, he rendered it in some degree doubtful, whether his first rising proceeded from the irresistible effect of the philosopher's dignified deportment, or from a determination immediately to decide his doom.

"On entering the inner room, the emperor turned quickly round, and said, with a sharp voice, that indicated suppressed agitation more than anger, ' Longinus, you are a Roman subject, and, having been found aiding the cause of the enemy, you must prepare to die.' Longinus bowed at these words, in token of resignation. Aurelian repeated them in a more vehement tone. ' It is your majesty's pleasure, and I must therefore submit,' replied the philosopher.

" ' Have you nothing else to say?' enquired the emperor, chagrined that the sentence was heard so calmly. ' What can I say? You are here the conqueror, and I am a prisoner. It is your pleasure to order me to be put to death. I have no means to resist the execution of this determination.'

" ' But, what do you say for yourself in being a traitor to Rome,' exclaimed Aurelian, still more disturbed.

" ' If that were the only offence that I had committed, in the eyes of your majesty, I do not think you would condemn me to die.'

" ' Let him be executed to-morrow,' cried the emperor, turning away from him, and walking hastily into another room.

"Longinus was then conducted to a strong chamber in the wing of the palace, where the imperial guards were quartered. The young officer who attended him, was so deeply affected by his prepared and collected mind, that he requested permission, as an honour, to be allowed to sit with him. 'Cheerfully,' said Longinus; 'if you will order in a little supper. Mental exertion has, I think, much the same effect as corporeal exercise: at least, this trial has made me feel more than usually hungry.'

"The officer looked at him with surprise, and said diffidently, 'Is it possible that you have not been agitated?'

"Longinus smiled at the question, and replied, 'I have certainly not been agitated; but it required no little effort, to prevent myself from being so.'

"When supper was brought in, the philosopher ate of several things with relish; but the officer could not taste a morsel: and, when he attempted to swallow a little wine, it was with great difficulty.

"Longinus observed his agitation, and turned the conversation to the Iliad, which he had laid on the table during supper, remarking, that Homer, in all his various pictures of death and dying men, had not given an example of martyrdom; and lamented that the state of opinion, in his age, did not furnish him with materials for an incident so magnificent. He then observed, that this was a species of the sublime in action, which had been introduced by the persecuted professors of the Christian faith.

"After speaking in this manner some time, he began to feel heavy, and requested the officer to leave him. The other, in rising to do so, looked at him for a short time, and, bursting into tears, drew his sword, placed it on the table, and immediately moved towards the door. Longinus called him back, and, taking the sword in his hand, said, 'Put it up:—it is Aurelian's will that I shall die; but, there is nothing in my condition, to make me wish for death. The Roman youth took back his sword; and Longinus, embracing him with tenderness, bade him good night."

We need extract no more. On the following day Longinus was conducted to the scaffold, where he suffered with the same sublime firmness, consoling his friends, who were much affected by his misfortunes.

CHAPTER XXXIX.

Paul of Samosata.

[A. D. 270.]

HISTORICAL justice requires that the character of Aurelian should not be dismissed with the harsh impression which the death of Longinus is calculated to leave on the mind of the reader, especially as his conduct, in the case of Paul of Samosata, the last splendid instance of the tolerant spirit of the ancient religion of Rome, affords a striking contrast to that tragical event.

Recent as the introduction of Christianity had been, gross corruptions, both in doctrine and discipline, were already become prevalent. Simony was openly practised; and it appears that even bishoprics might be purchased. A pious and wealthy lady, of Carthage, of the name of Lucilla, bought the see of that city for her chaplain, at a price equal to two thousand four hundred pounds of our money; but Paul, whose character and conduct we have now to notice, was, in his venality, less actuated by religious motives.

He had been appointed bishop of Antioch while the East was in the hands of Zenobia and her husband; and his wealth was soon so great, that it alone was sufficient evidence of his venality and rapacious extortions, since it was neither derived from the inheritance of his fathers, nor acquired by the arts of honest industry. He considered the service of the church as a lucrative profession; and, by his pride and luxury, rendered the Christian religion odious in the eyes of the Gentiles. His council-chamber and his throne, the splendour with which he appeared in public, the suppliant crowd who solicited his attention, the multitude of letters and petitions to which he dictated his answers, and the perpetual hurry of business in which he was involved, were circumstances much better suited to the state of a civil magistrate, than to the humility of a primitive bishop. When he harangued his flock from the pulpit, *this* Paul affected the figurative style of the Asiatic sophists, while the cathedral resounded, like a theatre, with acclamations, in praise of his eloquence. Against those who resisted his pretensions, or refused to flatter his vanity, he was arrogant, rigid, and inexorable; but he relaxed the discipline and lavished the treasures of the church, in the pleasures of the table and two young and beautiful women, the companions of his leisure.

Not content with bringing scandal on the church by his flagitious life, he attempted to introduce some peculiar heresies of his own,* which roused all the orthodox clergy from Egypt to the Euxine against him. Councils were held, confutations were published, excommunications were pronounced, ambiguous explanations were by turns accepted and refused, treaties were concluded and violated; and, at length, he was degraded from his episcopal character, by the sentence of seventy or eighty bishops, who assembled for that purpose at Antioch, and who, without consulting the rights of the clergy or the people, appointed a successor of their own authority.

The irregularity of this proceeding increased the partisans of Paul, who, being supported by the favour of Zenobia, kept possession of the episcopal house and office. But the conquest of Palmyra changed the face of things; and the two contending ecclesiastical factions were

---

* Mosheim.

summoned to plead their cause before the tribunal of Aurelian. As a Pagan and a soldier, it could scarcely be expected that the emperor should enter into the merits of the doctrinal opinions at issue between the parties. His determination, however, was founded on the principles of equity and reason. He considered the bishops of Italy as the most impartial and respectable judges among the Christians; and, as soon as he was informed that they had unanimously approved the sentence of the council, he gave orders that Paul should be compelled to relinquish the temporal possessions belonging to an office, of which, in the judgment of his brethren, he had been regularly deprived.

There was without question an impartial administration of justice in this case; and the merits of Aurelian's award will be the better appreciated, when it is considered that the cause of the trial was a difference of opinion on a theoretical point of doctrine, which, whether true or false, was equally at variance with his own religion, and inimical to the ecclesiastical institutions which he was bound to maintain as the most sacred in the empire. It is remarkable in other respects; for it serves to show, that, at this period, the church had acquired consequence, property, and establishments, which were acknowledged, if not by law, at least, by the magistrates and the government.*

---

* Gibbon.

CHAPTER XL.

The Resignation of Dioclesian.

[A. D. 305.]

THE next memorable incident which we find in the Volume of Hareach, after the death of Longinus, is an account of the Abdication of the Empire by Dioclesian. A continued tide of prosperity flowed during the whole period of his reign; and, when he had vanquished all his enemies, and accomplished all his designs, he came to the singular resolution of resigning the most splendid throne in the world, to enjoy in a private station, as it were, with posterity, the fruit of his public measures as a sovereign. During the winter, he had been confined to his palace at Nicomedia by ill health; but, as the spring advanced, he found himself better, and determined to carry into effect the resolution which he had long meditated.

"The city of Nicomedia," says Hareach, "is situated on the northern shores of the gulf, and rises in successive tiers of stately mansions, from the edge of the water to the summit of the hills. In appearance, the edifices are worthy of being compared with those of Rome; but they are constructed of perishable materials; and posterity will in vain look for the relics of a metropolis, that boasts of rivalling the capital of the world in magnificence.*

"About three miles eastward from the town, there is a spacious plain, surrounded by a swelling ground, that may be described as resembling the form of a theatre, having the sea and the successive promontories of the

---

* The author visited Nicomedia in 1811; and, though it is still a considerable city, it exhibits but few remains of ancient grandeur.

gulf as a stage and scenery, extending in long perspective before it; and it was here that preparations were made for the resignation.

"The army, from a wide extent of country, were assembled, and the city had poured forth from all her gates the whole population, to witness the ceremony. At break of day, it was understood, the emperor would leave the palace; for, in his infirm health, the heat of the sun oppressed him; and arrangements were made, that, when the solemnity was over, he should proceed on his journey to Dalmatia, where he had erected for himself a retreat, befitting his greatness and the renown of his fortune. But the sun was risen before he appeared. A murmur of respect, intermingled with accents of regret, announced his approach to the throne, which had been raised in the midst of the plain; and, soon after, he passed between the ranks of the military, in an open chariot, attended by two of his principal officers; several of his physicians and domestics following on foot, with vases and canisters, containing medicines and cordials. He appeared pale and emaciated; and the expression of his countenance, as he looked around on the respectful multitude of his subjects, was calm and dignified, but softened with a shade of paternal sorrow.

"He alighted from the chariot without assistance, and ascended the throne with a firm step; but the exertion seemed to have exhausted him; for, on taking his seat, a bustle was seen among the attendants, and they hastily placed their vessels on the ground, seemingly with the intention of opening them. He observed their anxiety and preparations, and said to them a few words, which I could not hear; upon which, they lifted the vases, and retired to a short distance behind the throne. A pause of three or four minutes then ensued, and he addressed the vast assembly to the following effect:

"'When it pleased the gods, the army, the senate, and the Roman citizens, to raise me to this high dignity, it was my duty to act as became a man sensible of so eminent a fortune, and to the best of my ability: while I had health of body, and energy of mind, I have endeavoured to do so.

But, sickness has fallen upon me, and old age is fast approaching; and you see, that, so far from being able to perform the great trusts of a Roman emperor,—to uphold the majesty of the Roman name, to defend the empire, and to see the laws executed with justice,—I am no longer in a condition to help myself. Were I therefore to retain possession of the imperial dignity, since I am become incapable of performing any of its duties, you might have just cause to regard me as a public enemy. Of all arts, the most difficult is the art of reigning; and a sovereign, while possessed of the greatest power to do wrong, is, without any corresponding check, placed in the thoroughfare of every temptation. How often is it the interest of four or five ministers to combine together to deceive their prince? Secluded from mankind by his exalted rank, the truth is carefully withheld from him: he can see only with their eyes, and hears only their misrepresentations. Misled by them, he confers the most important offices upon vice and weakness, and disgraces the most virtuous and deserving among his subjects.* This, at all times his situation, how much more dangerous does it become, when infirmity and old age obscure his faculties, and he is reduced, like me, to a helplessness more distressing than that of childhood:—for time, that gives strength and wisdom to youth, increases the infirmities of age. As the last and greatest favour in my power now to bestow on the Roman people, I have resolved to resign that sacred trust, while I can do it unblamed, and it has received no injury during the time that I have held it.'

" He then rose from the throne, and, with extended arms, implored the gods to protect the empire. The whole of the vast multitude was, at this action, melted to tears; and, when they saw him divest himself of the purple, and lay it on the throne, and take the diadem from his brows, and place it on the robe, a universal sob

---

* Vospicius learned these observations from his father.—*Gibbon.*

of grief burst from all present. In the same moment, a close carriage, which had been drawn up behind the throne, was brought to the foot of the steps, into which he immediately entered, and was driven off at full speed. Before the army or the people had time to recover from the emotion with which they were affected, he was already a considerable way towards the city, which he traversed without stopping."

CHAPTER XLI.

Anecdotes of Dioclesian in Retirement.

THE abdication of the empire by Dioclesian, was the the result of a determination which he had long formed. When, with his colleague Maximian, and their successors, Constantius and Galerius, he enjoyed the honours of a triumph, he exacted from Maximian a solemn promise in the capitol, ratified by an oath before the altar of Jupiter, that he would descend from the throne, whenever he should receive the advice and example. Accordingly, on the same day that Dioclesian resigned the diadem and purple at Nicomedia, Maximian also abdicated the imperial dignity at Milan. But this act, on the part of the latter, being an obligation, and not voluntary, he never ceased to repine at his compliance. The following year, when a favourable opportunity presented itself, he burst from the retirement to which he had reluctantly consented to withdraw, and again resumed the reins of government.

In the meantime, Dioclesian had quietly retired to the mansion which he had prepared for himself at Salona, in Dalmatia; and we shall now give our author's description of the place, and the manner in which the emperor usually spent his time.

"The situation of Dioclesian's palace is very delightful; the soil around is dry and fertile; the air pure and wholesome, and not exposed to those sultry and noxious winds to which some parts of Italy are so much exposed. The views are no less beautiful than the soil and climate are inviting. Towards the west lies the richly-cultivated shore that stretches along the Adriatic, in which a number of small islands are scattered, in such a manner as to give this part of the sea the appearance of a great lake. On the north side is the bay, which leads to the city of Salona; and the country beyond it, appearing in sight, forms a fine contrast to that more extensive prospect of water, which the Adriatic presents both to the south and to the east. Towards the north the view is terminated by high and irregular mountains, situated at a proper distance, and, in many places, covered with villages, woods, and vineyards.*

"The edifice itself is of great extent. The form is quadrangular, flanked with sixteen towers. In the one direction it extends about two hundred and fifty paces, and in the other cannot be less than three hundred. The whole is constructed of beautiful freestone, almost equal to marble, brought from quarries in the neighbouring hills. It is subdivided into four courts, and the approach to the principal apartments is by a stately entrance called the Golden gate. The general mass of the buildings is augmented by a superb square temple to Esculapius on the one side, and a still more magnificent octagon edifice of the same kind dedicated to Jupiter, on the other. All the chambers of the palace are on one floor; and the state-apartments, which are in the south-west wing, open to a spacious colonnade, that extends along the whole of that side of the building, before which a beautiful garden, adorned with arbours of fragrant shrubs and flowers, presenting a constant succession of blossoms, is disposed with an equal prodigality of luxuriance and art. In this

---

* Adams's Antiquities of Dioclesian's Palace.

colonnade the imperial philosopher commonly walks in the cool of the evening, or, reclining on cushions, enjoys the conversation of his officers and visitors. His mornings are devoted to the superintendance of his gardeners; for he has but little relish of books, and he is not much inclined to listen to the news of the day. But, when he is visited by any of the young officers,—for, in passing, all consider it their duty to pay their respects to him,—he exerts himself for their advantage, and turns the conversation on military affairs, of which he is, without doubt, a great master.

"An incident took place this morning, strikingly characteristic of his tranquillity and taste. The confidential bondman of Maximian brought letters from that restless old man, containing accounts of discontents at Rome, which his own wishes have magnified, and pressing Dioclesian to resume the purple. At the time the messenger arrived, the philosopher was seated in his garden, giving directions to his labourers respecting the preservation for seed of some cabbages of a superior species, which, under his own superintendence, they had cultivated with great success. He read the letters with grave attention twice. 'What answer shall I bear?' said the man. Dioclesian paused for a moment, and then, with a smile somewhat expressive of compassion, said, 'Tell Maximian, that, if I could shew him the beautiful cabbages which I have raised myself, he would refrain from urging me to relinquish the enjoyment of happiness for the pursuit of power.' He then returned the letters to the bondman, who immediately withdrew."

CHAPTER XLII.

The Family of Dioclesian.

CONTENTED however as Dioclesian was in his retirement, he could not escape the grasp of misfortune. He had given his daughter Valeria in marriage to Galerius, his successor, who, with her mother, Prisca, at the death of the emperor, was residing at Nicomedia. Her riches excited the avarice, and her personal beauty the desires, of Maximin, who succeeded her husband in the imperial dignity, and, with no respect for the decorum of her situation, he immediately informed her that he would divorce his wife; and requested that, in the meantime, she should submit to his embraces. The answer of Valeria was such as became the daughter and widow of emperors; but it was tempered by the prudence which her defencelessness obliged her to observe. She represented to the persons whom Maximin had sent with his shameless proposal, 'that, even if honour could permit a woman of her character and dignity to entertain a thought of second nuptials, decency at least must forbid her to listen to his addresses, at a time when the ashes of her husband and his benefactor were still warm, and while the sorrows of her mind were still expressed by her mourning garments;' adding, 'How little confidence can I place in the professions of a man, whose cruel inconstancy was capable of repudiating a faithful wife.'

On this repulse, the love of Maximin was converted into fury. He confiscated her estates, tortured her domestics to accuse her of infidelity and crimes, condemned her, with the aged matron Prisca, her mother, to exile from Nicomedia, and they were ignominiously hurried from place to place, and confined to a sequestered village in the deserts of Syria. Dioclesian, overwhelmed with their misfortunes, made several ineffectual efforts to alleviate their sufferings; and, as the last return for the favours which he had conferred upon Maximin in promoting him to the empire, entreated that they might be permitted to share his retirement at Salona. But, as he could no longer threaten, his prayers were rejected with disdain.

At the death of Maximin these illustrious and unfortunate ladies, in the hope that Licinius, his successor, would treat them with more lenity, left the place of their exile, and repaired to his court, where they met at first with an honourable reception. But the fallacious hopes thus inspired, were soon dispelled by such a train of bloody executions on their friends, that Valeria and her mother fled again from Nicomedia, and wandered among the provinces, in a state of unvaried alarm and distress. They were at last discovered at Thessalonica; and, as the sentence of their death had been already pronounced by proclamation, they were immediately beheaded. The account which Hareach gives of this tragical story differs entirely from that of every other historian, and assigns a motive for the reiterated persecution of Valeria and Prisca, which has hitherto been overlooked.

"Valeria having no children of her own, had adopted Candidianus, an illegitimate son of her husband, and invariably displayed towards him the tenderness and care of a real mother. At the death of his father he was approaching his twentieth year; and Maximin, on being repulsed in the offer of his affections to Valeria, endeavoured, by threats and cruelty, to suborn the servants of the empress to accuse them of adultery. But, failing in this infamous attempt, he seized on her wealth, and banished her, with Prisca, her mother, to Syria.

"After the death of Maximin, Licinius, who knew their innocence, seemed disposed to treat them differently; and, when they arrived at Nicomedia, where Candidianus was already before them, he received them with the distinction due to their elevated station. But his jealousy soon became alarmed; and the same motive which prompted him to put the two young children of Maximin, with the son of Severus,* to death, in order to extinguish all competitors for his throne, led him to execute Candidianus, and to pursue Valeria and Prisca, as traitors who had conspired to raise him to the empire.

"These disconsolate women, after wandering through the provinces nearly fifteen months, without friends, and not daring to divulge their rank and misfortunes, were last night seized, in the disguise of plebeian habits, as they were on the point of embarking in a common passage-boat, and taken, like the basest criminals, to the citadel. The people knew not at the time who they were, but their mournful dignity of deportment excited a sentiment of profound respect towards them; and, since it has been known that the prisoners are the wife and daughter of Dioclesian, the alarm and ferment in the town has been very great.

"The victims have been executed: their bloody and headless trunks have passed in a cart, and are thrown into the sea."

---

* This Severus was raised to the dignity of Cæsar by Dioclesian.

CHAPTER XLIII.

The Building of Constantinople.

THE jealousy of Licinius, instead of being appeased by so many victims, involved him in new troubles; and he was at length engaged in a war with Constantine, his brother-in-law, and partner in the diadem, or rather sovereign of the western empire; for, from the time of Dioclesian and Maximian, the Roman world was virtually divided between two independent potentates. This quarrel ended in a total defeat, on the banks of the Bosphorus, on the heights above Chrysopolis, (the modern city of Scutari;) the results of which were an abject submission to Constantine, the establishment of Christianity as the religion of the empire, and the transfer of the seat of government from Rome;—an event which, while it ended the military domination of that proud metropolis, was the cause of her acquiring, under the pretext of religion, a power and influence still more extensive and supreme.

As Hareach appears to have been present when the foundations of the new capital were laid, we shall extract his account of the ceremony; and, with it, conclude the first Part of our desultory narrative.

"The situation is the finest in the world. The Bosphorus, like a vast river, rolls in front from the Euxine. To the west extends the open sea of the Propontis, which branches into the interior of Asia as far as Nicomedia, and flows to the Mediterranean by the straits of the Hellespont. On the north, an estuary of the Bosphorus forms one of the best and safest harbours that commerce could desire or art imagine.

"It is reported that the emperor has been induced, by a vision, to prefer this situation to that of Troy, which he had previously chosen. As he slept within the walls of Byzantium, which is still a considerable town on the extremity of the headland that projects into the Bosphorus, he dreamt that the tutelar genius of the place, a venerable matron sinking under the weight of years and infirmities, was suddenly transformed into a blooming maid, whom his own hands adorned with the symbols of imperial greatness.*

"This morning, before day-break, the whole army, with a vast multitude of persons, drawn by curiosity from all quarters, assembled on the shore of the Propontis, and, at sun-rise, Constantine left his tent. He was in light armour, clothed with the purple, wearing the diadem on his brows, and holding in his hand a spear. Going down close to the lip of the sea, without speaking to any one, he appeared for some time rapt in prayer. He then turned slowly round, and, trailing his spear, made a motion with his hand, as it were to some awful personage to marshal the way, and walked onwards with a steady step,—the end of the spear leaving a mark on the ground, which his officers ordered the crowd to consider as sacred.

"As soon as it was observed that the emperor was moving, the whole crowd were in motion, and followed him till he reached a rising ground, about half way between the Propontis and the harbour. The space he thus traced was so extensive, that the people could not believe it was intended for the city; and one of his officers said to him, he had already exceeded the most ample measure of a great capital. 'I shall still advance,' replied Constantine, 'till *he*, the invisible guide who marches before me, thinks proper to stop;'—and he proceeded till he had reached the edge of the water, at the head of the estuary destined for the harbour. Here he again halted, and invoked the blessing of heaven on his undertaking. When this was done, guards were stationed along the whole extent of the line which he had traced with his spear; and, on those parts of the ground where the impression

---

* Gibbon.

was broken, the spaces for the gates were marked, and the multitude ordered to enter only at those places.

"The building of a new metropolis for the Roman world is a magnificent undertaking, and perhaps it is rendered necessary by the change in the religion of the state. Constantine himself, a Christian, has, by his open protection of the new religion, completed the downfall of the old; but, so many of the institutions, habits, and customs, of Rome, are still associated with the rites and ceremonies of Paganism, that it will be almost impossible to prevent something of the nature of a union between them. In the new capital the chance of this is not great; the temples to be raised in Constantinople will, from their foundation, be Christian; and the priests that will serve in them, are more likely to be chosen from genuine and original professors of that religion, than from such interested proselytes as have, for the preservation of their emoluments, cast out their ancient idols, and ostensibly embraced the principles of the new faith."

END OF PART I.

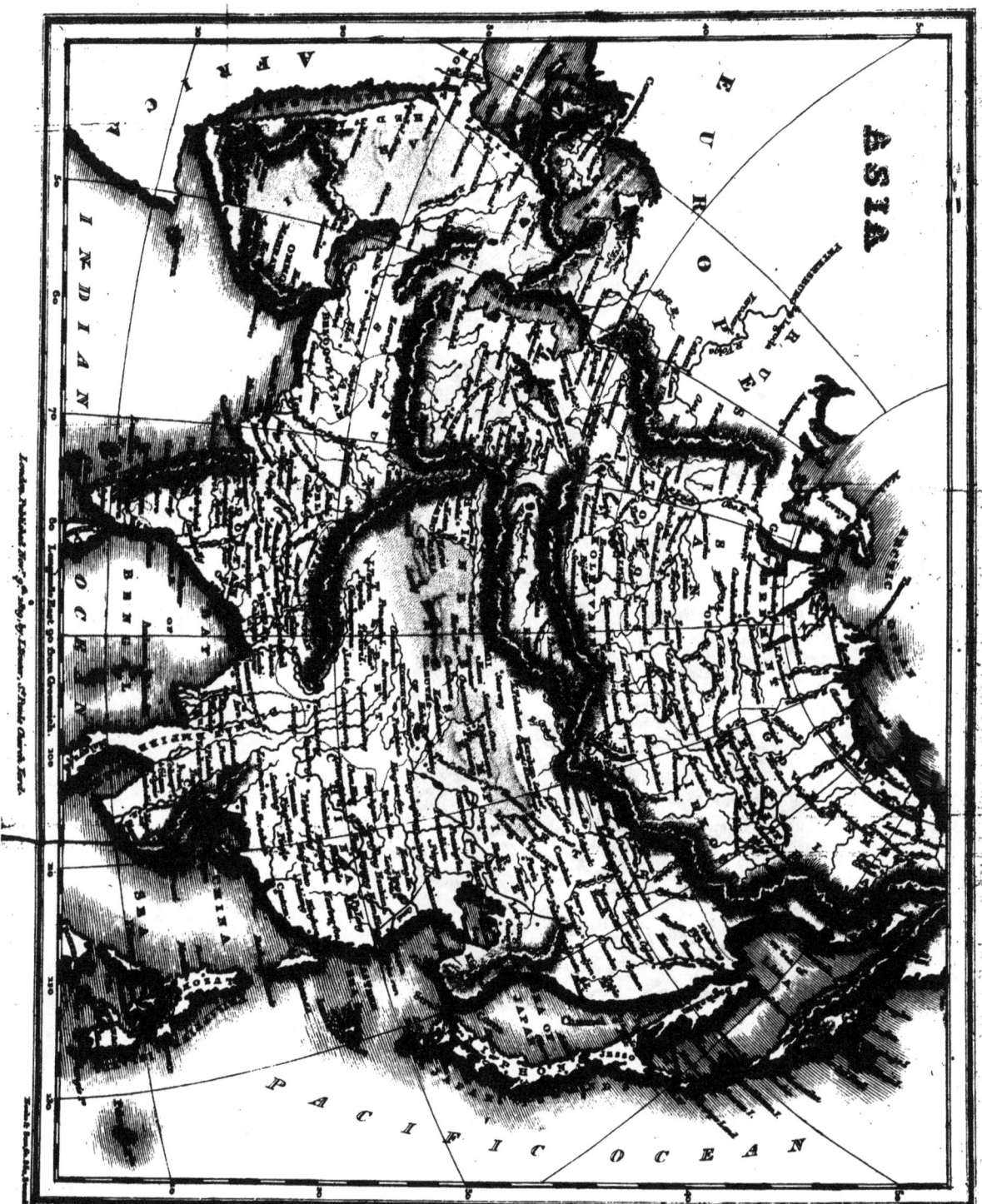

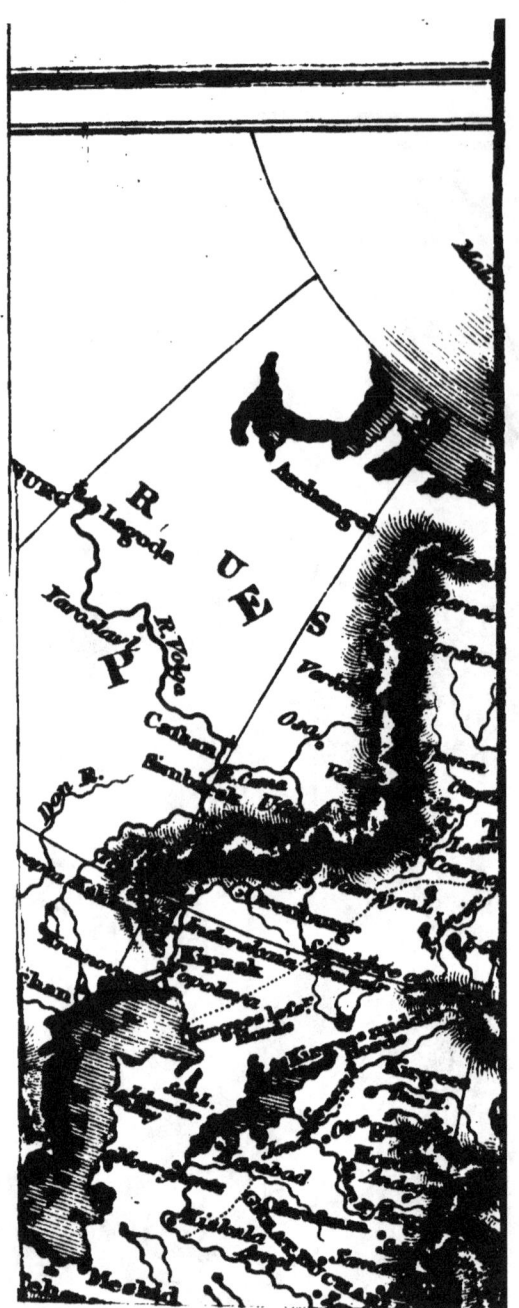

PART II.

CHAPTER I.

Decline of Classic Literature.

Before resuming our extracts from the Volume of the mysterious visitor to the Caloyers of Parnassus, it is necessary to direct the attention of the reader to the state of the European world, at the era of the Building of Constantinople.

The reign of Constantine the Great constitutes the grand chronological boundary between the ancients and the moderns, speaking in that comprehensive sense in which they are distinguished from each other in manners, religion, laws, and literature. We no longer hear of the same sins and crimes being openly practised; the human partialities of the gods are things unknown; and justice is administered according to principles that affect the interests of society; but literature, long declining from its classic elegance, becomes a mere vehicle of facts and notions, in which truth is more attended to than taste, and reason less exercised than in periods of inferior information.

In the time of Constantine, that simplicity in social intercourse, which had survived the Roman republic, gave place to the formalities of Oriental etiquette, from which may be deduced all those multifarious degrees of rank and personal titles, which were finally established as essential distinctions by Charlemagne, and continued unquestioned as such till the period of the French revolution. By abolishing the mythological worship, and establishing Christianity as the national religion, and by removing the seat of government from Rome to Constantinople,—a measure, originating probably in those inconveniences which the venerable but deranged machine of the ancient senate sometimes occasioned in the exercise of that arbitrary power so uniformly usurped by all the emperors,—Constantine established the supremacy of the imperial edicts in such a manner, that, simple and unsanctioned by any other authority than that of the sovereign, they acquired the force of laws.* Hence new principles of personal rights and of property were gradually developed; but, the maxims of Christianity being acknowledged to be from a higher authority than any temporal power, the successors of Constantine were compelled at least seemingly to regulate their edicts by those divine maxims. It does not however require any argument to prove the moral effects of the change that could not but take place, by the removal of the seat of government, with the abrogation of an old, and the establishing of a new, religion. The consequences however to literature were less obvious; and it has been supposed, that the progress of the human mind was suspended during what are usually called the dark ages.

In so far as the taste and science of the classic writers were concerned, we may grant, that, from the removal of the seat of sovereignty, until the revival of ancient literature in the pontificate of the second Julius, the rules and modes of reflection, which attained their meridian in Greece in the days of Pericles, and in Rome in those of Augustus, were not studied. But this is all that we can concede; and we will briefly explain the principle upon which we even grant so much.

The taste of every nation takes its tone from the court or the government,—not by authority, but by that in-

---

* Edinburgh Monthly Review, vol. i. p. 358.

fluence of example, which is happily described in our own language by the various modifications of the term fashion. In Constantinople, this influence however was, for a long time, necessarily very weak; and, when it had there acquired its natural ascendancy, such changes had taken place in other parts of the world, that its effects were circumscribed to its immediate limited sphere, even before the empire had dwindled into that insignificance, which left the name and office of the Cæsars scarcely known beyond the walls of the capital.

The inhabitants first planted in Constantinople, being a mixed race, drawn together from all parts of the empire, formed a new general language, which had necessarily every imperfection of a barbarous tongue, though composed in a great measure of Greek and Latin. The language of the capital, in process of time, became that of the court; and the mingling of the traditions of Asia and Europe, which took place from the same cause, materially changed the topics of polite literature. The abolition of idolatry had also the effect of suspending the rehearsal and the study of those beautiful compositions, which classic piety and genius had consecrated to the gods of the Pantheon; so that, among the populace, who in that age had no other means of acquiring a knowledge of the elegant poetry and fables of their ancestors but from theatrical representation, all recollection of them soon became extinct. In place of the ancient mythological subjects new legends were substituted. The priesthood, falling into corruption, and converting Christianity to dark and crafty mysteries for their own advancement, engrafted on the sublime simplicity of the worship instituted by the Apostles many of the ceremonies of idolatry; and finally succeeded, as we shall have occasion to show, from the notes of our author, in forming a system of apotheosis, with respect to saints and martyrs, which differed in nothing essential from the superstitions of Pagan antiquity.

CHAPTER II.

The Christians Persecute each Other.

[A. D. 325.]

THE Christians having suffered severely from the persecutions which the emperors, as the high priests of the Pagan religion, had deemed it expedient to institute, for the preservation of the immunities of their inferiors, seem to have determined to retaliate as soon as they had it in their power to do so. But it must not therefore be supposed, that this was according either to the precepts or spirit of the divine benevolence which it is the professed object of Christianity to inculcate. The fact is, that, early in the third century, as we took occasion to show, in the case of Paul of Samosata, great corruptions had crept into the practice of the church, and even its doctrines were not those which had been taught by the holy Apostles. Therefore, although it is usual to consider Constantine the Great as the potentate who first established the supremacy of the religion ostensibly taught in the name of Jesus, it must be borne in mind, that the worship which he patronized, was something very different from that moral charity of which the doctrines and testimonies are contained in the New Testament. The religion established by the edicts of Constantine was, in reality, one of form and ceremony, and the study of it consisted in discriminating certain speculative opinions, which taught any other sentiments than those of " peace on earth, and good will to man."

The imperial recognition of Christianity, however, as the state religion, was an important boon to the world, if so daring an expression may be employed to characterise any act of man towards an emanation of Omnipotent goodness. It is time, however, to return to the work of Hareach; and the first extracts we shall make relate to events that took place soon after the foundations of Constantinople were laid.

"The Christians appear to be falling into the mistake, of confounding the glosses of their preachers with the purposes of their religion, and to think that, if they negatively believe certain dogmas, they may act like the rest of the world. They are now waging war as strenuously among themselves as they were persecuted by the ancient priesthood; thus establishing the worship of the idol of human opinion, and abandoning the religion of which they still retain the name.

"Constantine has returned from the council of Nice, where he presided in person, and assisted in condemning the doctrines of Arius, Eusebius, and Theognis, and banishing these bishops from their temporalities. But, will his sentence prevent them from cherishing their opinions? and have they not formed their opinions by what they conceive a right interpretation of the Scriptures? What is this but assuming the blasphemous authority of deciding for God. It is by his life and conversation that the true Christian can alone make himself known to the world; and not by any such rigorous and bigotted maintenance of speculative opinions. With all this busy interference with the faith of others, Constantine shows but little Christian virtue in his own conduct; he has, however, rooted out the last weed of the criminal amusements which grew out of the ceremonies of the man-worship of Paganism, by prohibiting the combats of gladiators, and ordering the criminals, instead of being devoured in the arena of the amphitheatre by wild beasts, for the amusement of the populace, to be condemned to hard labour or public works, and in the mines. This edict has originated in Christian principles; but, what can be said of his treatment to his son Crispus?

"Fausta, the stepmother of the prince, urged by the implacable demon of disappointed love, has renewed in the palace of the Christian emperor the tragedy of Hippolitus and of Phædra.* She accused Crispus of insulting her chastity; and has secured, at least, the reversion of the empire to her own children, by procuring his death.

"No one believes the story of which Fausta was the author, and her conduct belies its truth. Nor would it have received any credit from the emperor himself, had his judgment not been warped by his jealousy of the popularity of the prince; yet, he affects to have acted from motives of religion. It is strange, that a man can pretend to be just before God, and, even though invested with supreme authority, be ashamed to disclose his motives to man."

CHAPTER III.

Restoration of Idolatry.

[A.D. 330.]

THE building of Constantinople was carried on with great vigour; the walls and public edifices were raised with amazing rapidity: the latter, however, being chiefly constructed of timber, were not calculated to last long; and accordingly, it appears that, in the course of a few years, they were in a state of evident decay. But, there is one important circumstance connected with the history of this metropolis, respecting which we must quote our author.

"The Christians boast that the founder abolished the worship of images, and established their religion; that he has forbidden, by his edicts, consecrating idols; and

---

* Gibbon.

that he is only intent to exalt the glory of the church, and the service of God. But, what answer can they make to those, who enquire why he has dedicated the new city to the Virgin Mary; and what warrant has he, from the testimonial books of the religion, that she possesses any power to protect it? Still more, why has he ordered that for ever, on the anniversary of the foundation of the city, a statue of himself, bearing in its right hand an image of the genius of the place, shall be carried in a triumphant car, attended with all the pomp of military and ecclesiastical glory, to the throne of the reigning emperor, who shall rise and do it homage?* Is not this an institution of self-worship, as idolatrous as that of Alexander the Great, Nero, or Caligula? and, in what respect does the consecration of the city to the Virgin, differ from the principle on which the Athenians and Ephesians were wont to regard Minerva and Diana, as their tutelary deities?

"The new religion is like the moon when first seen after the change, a feeble, narrow rim of light, comprehending within its imperfect circle the darkened orb of the old. A great cycle has yet to run, before it will attain its full round of brightness.

"The priests ostensibly professing Christianity, seem determined to make it subservient to the recovery of that supremacy which their class possessed under the ancient religion. Constantine is dead, and they have brought his body in a golden coffin to the city; it lies exposed to view in the great hall of the palace, and is treated with all the marks of adoration which were paid to him by his officers and the court when he was alive. This, however, they say, was the ancient custom with which the bodies of the emperors, after death, were reverenced; and which they have only revived.

"They have buried him in the church dedicated to the Apostles, near the palace, and pretend it was at his own request; in order that he may partake of the prayers offered there by the faithful, in honour of the holy Apos-

---

* Gibbon.

tles.* They affect also to consider his body as something sacred, and entrusted to their particular charge; for Constantine, his son and successor, not being yet baptized, was obliged, after attending the funeral, to withdraw from the church, while they performed the final ceremonies. There is much of the spirit of temporal aggrandisement in all this; and, it is the first step towards the revival of the ancient ritual of Apotheosis."

In the sequel, we shall have occasion to notice, how well-founded these anticipations of Hareach were; in the meantime, the following anecdote of Eusebia, the wife of Constantius, will serve to show, how soon, after the public establishment of the church, the priests showed their determination to assert their pretensions to superiority.

"Leontius, bishop of Tripoli, in Lydia, has been some time in the city; he gives himself airs of great importance, and is mightily offended with the clergy, because, in his opinion, they have degraded their order, by considering themselves as bound to respect the etiquettes of society. The man has been the first personage in a small town, and does not understand the gradations of rank above his own degree.

"Last night the empress sent for him, for he has the reputation of great sanctity; but he returned this insolent message, that he would not go near her, because she had not been in the practice of receiving the bishops in a proper manner: and he requested the messenger to inform her majesty, that, unless she promised to descend from her throne as soon as he appeared; to meet him near the door; to receive his blessing in a humble posture; and stand till he had taken his place, and given her leave to sit down; he would not approach the imperial residence."

---

* Eusebius.

CHAPTER IV.

Anecdotes of Julian the Apostate.

[A.D. 361–363.]

ALTHOUGH Christianity was established by law, and openly professed by the members of government, it was far from being yet the universal religion of the empire; indeed, the teachers found themselves so often thwarted by the professors of the abrogated mythology, that they fancied the gods of the Pantheon were not mere idols, but so many evil demons at war with the saints and angels for the souls of men;—a notion strengthened by no circumstance more than by the apostacy of the emperor Julian.

This prince was the nephew of Constantine the Great, and was educated with his brother Gallus, by the orders of his cousin, Constantius, with great care. At the age of seven, he was placed under the charge of Mardonius, a eunuch who inspired him with an aversion to ignoble pursuits, and taught him the most important of all knowledge,—the art of self-government; he was subsequently committed to the care of Eusebius, bishop of Nicomedia, a professor of the Arian opinions, but a man highly esteemed and respected. At the age of fourteen, he was removed, along with his brother, to Cæsaria in Cappadocia, where they had a royal palace for their habitation, a splendid establishment, and the best masters to instruct them in every science; and, having remained their about six years, they were brought to Constantinople to complete their education.

Nature had endowed Julian with extraordinary capacity, and education rendered him the most accomplished prince of his time. He wrote with distinguished elegance; spoke with great ease and grace; and, although his countenance wore an unpleasant expression, he possessed the charm of conciliating all who approached him. In his unstudied answers, he displayed an uncommon penetration, vivacity, and presence of mind; and, in the greatest dangers, undaunted courage and intrepidity. His stature was low, but his limbs were well formed, and he was singularly expert and active: he was naturally of a mild temper, had a strong thirst after glory, was greatly attached to his own opinion, which he frequently preferred to the advice of his wisest counsellors, and addicted to satirical raillery, which sometimes offended his friends. But, with all these high, various, and rare qualities, he was naturally superstitious; and to that cause we must ascribe the singular act of his apostacy from Christianity to Paganism. Our author's account of the causes that led to it is interesting.

"His cousin the emperor, being alarmed at the popularity which he had acquired by his insinuating manners, sent him from Constantinople to Nicomedia, strictly enjoining him not to frequent the lectures of Libanius, a Pagan sophist, who, having been banished from Constantinople, had opened a school in that city. Julian, however, only kept the letter of his promise; for, holding that orator in great esteem, he purchased his books, and studied them with care.

"While he was thus employed in his exile at Nicomedia, he became acquainted with Maximus of Ephesus, another Pagan philosopher of great celebrity, much addicted to magic and astrology, and who flattered him with the prediction that he was destined to ascend the imperial throne. The pretensions and doctrines of this impostor, were calculated to awaken the superstitious enthusiasm of Julian's character; and, while he affected to initiate him in the mysteries of magic, he inspired him with a hatred for the Christian religion, which condemns that vain and unhallowed art.

"Julian, however, was not entirely persuaded of the truth of what Maximus taught, and his Christian principles were for a long time only shaken, not subverted; indeed, he appears at first to have clung to them with a degree of passion and fervour, as if to save himself from the grasps of the evil genius that assailed him by the means of Maximus. He shaved his head, imitated the dress and manners of an anchoret, and read and prayed fervently during the day in the principal church of Nicomedia; but still, in the evening, he returned to the study of magical rites. A sacrilegious curiosity to know his destiny, prevailed over every other circumstance; and he at length worshipped in secret the Pagan deities, as demons that ruled the elements, and possessed dominion over men."

We should here observe, that, although it is not improbable, that Julian was influenced by a superstitious bias, yet, as his views were early and covetously turned to the imperial dignity, he may only have employed Paganism as the means of attaining the object of his ambition; for, when he soon after visited Athens, we are informed that he cultivated the acquaintance of the most zealous advocates for Paganism, and the persons best versed in magic, expressing to them, in confidence, his concern for the downfal of the old religion, and his desire and intention of restoring it to its former lustre, should he ever become possessed of the power:*—thereby insinuating a motive for them to espouse his cause. We shall now resume our extracts.

"His election to the empire confirmed the prediction of Maximus; and, by working on his superstition, settled the preference which he had secretly cherished for the old religion. But, it was not till after the feast of the Epiphany, in the year immediately following his promotion, that he threw off the mask, and opened again the temples of the heathen deities, exhorting all persons to follow his example, and restore the religion of their ancestors to its former lustre.

"If Julian was not sincere in his conversion, he was the most artful of men, and most uselessly so; for he only gained the odium of the greatest number of his subjects. It reflects however little credit on the kind of Christianity now taught, that it should appear to the con-

---

* Universal History.

viction of so virtuous a man, and so enlightened a prince, as inferior to the worship of such gods as Jupiter, and such powers as the Sun and Moon.

"The Christains, offended at his apostacy, accuse him of the most unheard of crimes, and say, that the river Orontes at Antioch was, during his residence there, choaked up with the bodies of such as had been murdered by his orders, and that all the ditches, caves, wells, and ponds, in the neighbourhood of that city, were filled with the remains of the young virgins and children whom he had inhumanly sacrificed, hoping to discover future events in their entrails. It is to be regretted, for their integrity, that the relations of these numerous victims make no complaint of their loss. It may be true, that the rites of magic require human sacrifices, but the religion that Julian professes does not; and there is no authority in the Roman law, by which a professor of magic may with impunity commit murder.

"Julian, though earnest in the restoration of the old religion, and though, by changing the priesthood, displacing the Christian, and recalling the Pagan, he acts with even more severity and oppression towards individuals, than Constantine did, when he prohibited idolatry, yet his own conduct is not that of a bigot. As he was approaching Berææa with his army, on their route to Persia, a young man presented himself before him, and implored his protection, informing him that he had renounced Christianity for Paganism, which his father, a zealous Christian, so highly resented, that he had turned him out of doors.

"The emperor, pitying his condition, bade him take courage, and be under no concern; for he would himself undertake to appease the old man, and procure his restoration to favour. Mindful of his promise, he invited the chief citizens to sup with him, and placed the father and son near himself; the father being at the head of the council of the magistracy.—'I do not think it reasonable, (said the emperor,) to use any violence in point of religion. Allow your son to profess a religion different from your's, as I allow you to profess one different from mine, though I might easily oblige you to renounce it.—What! (exclaimed the old man,) are you speaking in favour of an impious wretch, abhorred by heaven, who has preferred falsehood to truth, and renounced the worship of the true God, to fall down before idols.'—Injuries and invectives, (replied Julian,) interrupting him, are foreign to our purpose; and therefore I beg you would repress them.'—Then turning to the son, he said, it is incumbent upon me to take care of you, since your father is deaf to my prayers and entreaties in your behalf."*

The conduct of Julian in this instance was truly liberal, for he had himself committed the same fault that the old man blamed in his son; and the reproaches of the father applied with emphatic poignancy to his own apostacy. But, the Christianity of that age was not the doctrine of Christ; on the contrary, it was darkly embued with those errors, which it has been the great object of the learned and pious, since the Reformation, to expunge.

CHAPTER V.

The City of Paris in the Fourth Century.

AMONG other places of comparatively little note, it appears that Hareach, our author, visited Lutitia, during the time that Julian resided there, in the reign of Constantius; and that this was no other than what is now the famous city of Paris, the capital of France.

"It was," said he, "early in the spring when we approached Lutitia, which Julian had chosen for his retreat in that inclement season. It stands on an island, in the river which bathes the foot of the walls, and supplies the inhabitants with salubrious water. A forest of venerable trees overspreads the northern banks of the stream, but the southern are cleared and adorned with a palace and baths, and a field of Mars, for the exercise of the Roman soldiers.*

"The climate is remarkably mild, although occasionally the winter reigns with distressing rigour; and the inhabitants are singularly disposed to be kind and obliging to strangers. Separated from the rest of the world, to which they have access only by two wooden bridges, their social affections are as it were concentrated; and they are at more pains, perhaps owing to their sequestered situation, to be on a happy and friendly footing with one another, than any other people in the whole extent of the empire.

"Their clear and beautiful river, their rural and cheerful little town, derive an additional charm from the amenity of their manners; and their endeavours to please and amuse, are perhaps the more remarkable, as they have no theatres among them, nor any of those places of recreation, which absolve, as it were, the inhabitants of other cities from the obligations of hospitality.

"The most remarkable peculiarity about the agreeable foibles of this amiable and uncorrupted people, is their innocent conceit of their own superiority. Circumscribed to their little islet, and only seeing strangers, whose business it is, to conciliate their favour as an official duty, or, who are pleased with its delightful situation, in the midst of a crystal river, overhung with beautiful trees, and fringed with vineyards and gardens, they fancy it is the finest town in the world; and, while they acknowledge that Rome herself may be more magnificent, they are persuaded that no other place is half so desirable to live in. This charming simplicity can only, however, be justly appreciated by travellers; but, such is the happy self-complacency of these good citizens, that when they see you smiling at their harmless vanity, they interpret your looks into an assent to the truth of their amusing hyperboles.

Gibbon.

"Whether they ever were religious, is not easy to be ascertained; but Julian seems to have taken pains to eradicate their Christian prejudices. They were never much addicted to the Roman gods, and, I imagine, but little also to the teachers of Christianity; and he has encouraged them to make processions and festivals, which, although nominally of a religious character, are really but cheerful holidays, and apologies for indulging in frolic and diversion. If they are not apostates in their hearts, they will think it no great sin at any time to be so; and when they change, it will be in a spirit of gaiety, that must acquit them of any necessity to be austerely sincere.

"These festivals, which he has so encouraged, and to which they really seem by nature themselves much prone, has given them a curious taste for finery of apparel, and a love of ornament to such a degree, that they seem always dressed for an entertainment. Their grotesque gaudiness might be taken for frivolity, were it not so much their customary habit, that it interferes no more with their serious pursuits, than if they were as invariable in their garb and manners as the descendants of Ishmael in the deserts of Arabia and Petrææ; much, indeed, of the pleasure enjoyed among them, is owing to this apparent frivolity; for, one is continually surprised at the good sense and intellectual refinement, combined with so little propriety of appearance; perhaps it is the more striking on that account."

CHAPTER VI.

Hareach at Daphne.

"At a short distance from Antioch, the Macedonian kings of Syria had consecrated to Apollo one of the most elegant places of devotion in the Pagan world. A magnificent temple containing a colossal statue, enriched with many ornaments of Grecian art, almost filled the sanctuary. The god was represented in a bending attitude, with a cup in his hand, pouring out a libation on the earth, as if he supplicated the venerable mother to give to his arms the cold and beauteous Daphne. The perpetual resort of pilgrims and spectators, insensibly formed, in the neighbourhood of the temple, the stately and populous village of Daphne, which emulated the splendour of a city.

"The temple and the village were embosomed in a thick grove of laurels and cypresses, which reached as far as a circumference of ten miles, and formed, in the most sultry summers, a cool and impenetrable shade. A thousand streams of the purest water, issuing from every hill, preserved the verdure of the earth, and the temperature of the air; the senses were gratified with harmonious sounds and delicious odours, and the grove was consecrated to health and joy, and luxury and love. The soldier* and the philosopher wisely avoided the temptations of this sensual paradise, where Pleasure assuming the character of religion, imperceptibly dissolved the firmness of manly virtue. But the groves of Daphne continued to enjoy for many ages the veneration of natives and strangers; the privileges of the holy ground were enlarged by the munificence of succeeding emperors; and every generation added new ornaments to the splendors of the temple.

"When Julian, on the day of the annual festival, hastened to adore the Apollo of Daphne, his devotion was raised to the highest pitch of eagerness and impatience. His lively imagination anticipated the grateful pomp of victims, of libations, and of incense; a long procession of youths and virgins, clothed in white robes, the symbols of their innocence; and the tumultuous concourse of an innumerable people. But the zeal of Antioch was diverted, since the reign of Christianity, into a

---

* Cassius dismissed or punished every soldier who was seen at Daphne.

different channel. Instead of hecatombs of fat oxen, sacrificed by the tribes of a wealthy city to their tutelar deity, the emperor found only a single goose, provided at the expense of a priest, the pale and solitary inhabitant of the decayed temple. The altar was deserted, the oracle had been reduced to silence, and the consecrated ground was profaned by the introduction of Christian and funeral rites.

"After Babylas (a bishop of Antioch, who died in prison in the persecution of Decius) had rested near a century in his grave, his body, by the order of Cæsar Gallus, was transported into the midst of the grove of Daphne. A magnificent church was erected over his remains; a portion of the sacred lands was usurped for the maintenance of the clergy, and for the burial of the Christians at Antioch who were ambitious of lying at the feet of their bishop; and the priests of Apollo retired, with their affrighted and indignant votaries."

We have taken the description of this voluptuous region from the eloquent volumes of Gibbon, as a prelude to the following incident, from the Manuscript of Hareach.

"The Apostate was so disappointed at the sacrifice of the goose to Apollo, instead of the whole hecatombs and the splendid processions he had anticipated, that at first he looked exceedingly out of countenance. In a short time, however, he recovered his wonted good-humour; and, with his habitual loquacity, rallied the poor old priest on his ludicrous offering: telling him, however, that he might assure the god of his determination to restore the ancient rites; and, on returning to Antioch, he gave orders, the same day, that the church over the relics of Babylas should be thrown down, and the bodies which profaned the sacred grove disinterred and removed.

"This was done accordingly; but permission was given to the ministers of the church to convey the remains of St. Babylas to their former shrine, within the walls of Antioch. The modest behaviour, which might have assuaged the jealousy of an hostile government, was, however, neglected by them on this occasion.

"A lofty car was prepared for the bones of the martyred bishop, and they were transported to the city amidst songs of triumph, and psalms expressive of contempt for idols, chanted by an innumerable multitude. The emperor felt this indiscreet zeal as an insult, and exerted his pride to dissemble his resentment. But, during the night of this fanatical ceremony, the temple was in flames, the statue of Apollo destroyed, and the walls of the edifice left a naked monument of ruin.

"The Christians asserted that St. Babylas had pointed the lightnings of heaven against the devoted roof: but Julian, with some probability, accused them of being themselves the incendiaries; and ordered the doors to be shut, and the treasures of the cathedral of Antioch to be confiscated."

CHAPTER VII.

The Attempt to Rebuild the Temple of Jerusalem.

[A. D. 363.]

THE mixed character of Julian the Apostate renders it difficult to discriminate the motives of his conduct. Having restored the Pagan worship without exactly proscribing the Christian religion, he determined to rebuild the Temple of Jerusalem, and to renew the rites and sacrifices that had been formerly used there, although nothing could be more different in its object and principles than the worship of the Omnipotent Creator and that of Jupiter and Apollo. The probability is, that Julian, being averse to the faith he had deserted, and desirous perhaps of an apology for his own apostacy, that it should be brought into contempt, determined to rebuild the temple,—to prove to the Christians, that the everlasting sentence of destruction, which they believed to have been pronounced against the whole fabric of the Mosaical law, was a fallacy that he could demonstrate. If this was his motive, he was undoubtedly convicted of error by the result. It does not however become us to examine the circumstances attending this transaction, nor indeed do the means exist by which the true facts might be ascertained. One thing however is clear,—that the temple was not rebuilt; and, whether the attempt was prevented by supernatural fires, or by ordinary casualties, does not affect the nature of this truth. We know not how it happens, that a notion is cherished among mankind, that the interferences of Divine providence, in the affairs of the world, are always attended with circumstances that affect the imagination. If the end is attained, what signifies the means? Simple are the oracles of divine wisdom, and the world sees not the mighty hand that has been at work in its affairs, till the result surprises by its completeness. Without therefore entering into the controversial points of this remarkable transaction, we shall extract our author's account of it; for he appears, like all the rest of his nation, to have taken a deep interest in the event, and to have anticipated in the success of the design, the end of his own companionless wandering.

" Alypius, the friend of Julian, was appointed to superintend the restoration of Jerusalem. He was a man well qualified for the task, possessing that elegance of taste, which was requisite to do justice to the magnificent designs of the emperor, with that manly fortitude and love of justice, so essential to the administration of public trusts. His first act was to make known to the governor of Palestine the intentions of Julian, and by him notice was given to the scattered of Israel over all the country. The tidings were received as the deliverance from Babylon was of old.

" From all parts and provinces of the empire we assembled on the holy mountain. It was a scene such as can never take place again, till the resurrection of the dead: we embraced each other as friends that had been long separated,—for we were all kindred. Every one brought with him the earnings of his industry, and there was a prodigious treasure. Some had provided spades and pickaxes of silver, to assist in clearing the rubbish from the consecrated scite of the holies, and others gave their mantles of silk and purple to carry it away.

"My heart however misgave when I saw all this; for I reflected, that the undertaking was at the command of a prince who disbelieved our religion, and was not dictated by any reverence for the true God: and I remembered the spirit of ancient prophecy, that the restoration of the Jews was to be effected by a king of our own race. I retired to the Mount of Olives, and looked down on the thousands that swarmed and clustered among the ruins and the rocks below; and my heart swelled with painful emotions, when I saw, amidst the tombs in the valley of Jehosaphat, numerous groups of the old and young, searching for the sepulchres of their ancestors.

"At day-break on the morning appointed for the commencement of the work, the whole multitude assembled round the ruins of the temple; and the area was soon so entirely cleared, that not a trace of where it had stood appeared. A pause then ensued, and preparations were made to clear the foundation,—when a panic fell upon the crowd, and a cry arose that the earth was sinking. In the same moment, a heavy black cloud, which hung over the heights of the Mount of Olives, discharged terrible flashes of lightning, and peals of the most tremendous thunder rattled through all the firmament. The multitude fled; and, on looking back towards the scite of the temple, it seemed as if the darkness and the thunder were concentrated on the spot, and the launched fires cast forth from that throne of clouds, to blast the builders, and prohibit the work. The storm raged all day, and the consternation of the people was scarcely less appalling. Alypius himself was smitten with religious dread. The Christians, in their church built over the tomb of Jesus, continued in fervent prayer till midnight, and baptized many of the Jews converted by the miracle.

"Next morning, Alypius, and the governor of Palestine, left Jerusalem, without giving any orders to the workmen; and it being considered that the undertaking was abandoned, the Jews also began to scatter, and go away. I also departed,—to return there no more, until my solitary destiny is fulfilled."

CHAPTER VIII.

The Misopogon.

THE life of the emperor Julian affords a curious view of human nature; and, if he was not the greatest of the Roman potentates, he was certainly the most singular of princes. Compared with the conduct of some of his predecessors whom we have had occasion to notice, he was an illustrious and liberal character; and the whole of his deportment, in the imperial station, affords a favourable example of the amended morals of the world, while it was certainly scarcely less at variance with our modern notions of dignity, than some of the other extravagances that our author has so strongly condemned. The following is perhaps one of the most pleasing, and yet undignified, transactions of his reign.

"He had rendered himself obnoxious to the Syrian Greeks, by interfering with their monopolies in grain; and they made no scruple of lampooning his appearance, and deriding his religion, and even his beard, in their songs. Having himself a strong sense of the ridiculous, he was exceedingly provoked at this malicious wit; but, although possessed of absolute power, he refused himself the gratification of a revenge, such as even an Adrian would not have scrupled to indulge. He might have proscribed without distinction the lives and fortunes of the citizens of Antioch; and his courtiers, perhaps many of his subjects, would have applauded an act of justice, which vindicated the dignity of the supreme magistrate. But, instead of abusing or exerting the authority of the state to revenge the personal levity with which he had been treated, he pays the Syrians in their own coin. He has composed a satire called the Misopogon, or the Enemy of the Beard, which has been this morning exposed at the gates of the palace; and, in an ironical confession of his own faults, has severely chastised the licentious and effeminate manners of Antioch.

"It is a singular thing to see a prince retaliating in this manner the raillery of his subjects. They laugh at him only the more, but confess the superiority of his talent. Those however who know him best, allege, that he will not be content with only expressing his ridicule. Perhaps they are right;—but he is a strange man."

CHAPTER IX.

The Death of Julian the Apostate.

MANY incidents in the life of Julian afford ground to think, that, in apostatizing from the Christian religion, he was not very sincere in embracing the Pagan polytheism; at least, the account which our author gives of his death, and it is historically true, warrants this opinion.

"The legions, on their return from the Persian expedition, suffered exceedingly from the climate and the harassing pursuit of the enemy. Their provisions failed, and the most gloomy apprehensions began to rise among them that they must all perish, either by famine, or the sword of the barbarians. Julian, however, still wore a serene and confident countenance, sharing the fatigues of the veterans with undaunted fortitude, and faring as meanly and as sparingly as the private soldier. But this resolution, which was so well calculated to support the courage of the men, was dissolved by the influence of sleep; and his slumbers were disturbed with ominous visions. On the evening before the battle in which he received his wound, he dreamt that the genius of the empire appeared before him, covered with a funeral veil his head and his horn of abundance, and then slowly retired from his presence. Starting from his couch, and stepping forth to refresh his wearied spirits with the coolness of the midnight air, he beheld a fiery meteor, which shot athwart the sky, and vanished suddenly. Convinced that this apparition was no other than the god of war, and that he had seen him with a menacing countenance, he summoned the Haruspices, (expounders of omens,) whom he had always in his court; and they unanimously pronounced that he should abstain from battle. But necessity rendered this impracticable. The salvation of the legions depended on the celerity of their march; and the enemy awaited them in a valley, through which they were forced to pass.

"Julian was wounded in the side by a javelin, which he endeavoured himself to draw out, but his fingers were cut by the sharpness of the edge, and he fell senseless from his horse. The report of his fall spread from rank to rank. The courage of the army was inflamed with revenge. The barbarians were routed. The first words that the emperor uttered, after recovering from his fainting-fit, were expressive of his martial spirit. He called for a horse and arms, and was impatient to rush into the battle, but his strength was exhausted; and the surgeons who examined his wound, discovered the symptoms of approaching death. He perceived his situation by their looks, and, having advised the philosophers who had accompanied him in this fatal expedition, to assemble with his officers round his couch, he addressed them as follows:

" ' Friends and fellow-soldiers: The seasonable period of my departure is now arrived, and I discharge, with the cheerfulness of a ready debtor, the demands of nature. I have learned from philosophy how much the soul is more excellent than the body; and that the separation of the noblest substance should be the subject of joy rather than of affliction. I have learned from religion, that an early death has often been the reward of piety; and I accept, as a favour of the gods, the mortal stroke that secures me from the danger of disgracing a character which has hitherto been supported by virtue and fortitude. I die without remorse, as I have lived without guilt. I am pleased to reflect on the innocence of my private life; and I can affirm, with confidence, that the supreme authority,— that emanation of the Divine power,—has been preserved in my hands pure and immaculate. Detesting the corrupt and destructive maxims of despotism, I have considered the people as the end of government. Submitting my actions to the laws of prudence, of justice, and of moderation, I have trusted the event to the care of Providence. Peace was the object of my counsels, as long as peace was consistent with the public welfare;—but when the imperious voice of my country summoned me to arms, I exposed my person to the dangers of war, with the clear foreknowledge (which I had acquired from the art of divination) that I was destined to fall by the sword. I now offer my tribute of gratitude to the Eternal Being, who has not suffered me to perish by the cruelty of a tyrant, by the secret dagger of conspiracy, or by the slow tortures of lingering disease. He has given me, in the midst of an honourable career, a splendid and glorious departure from this world; and I hold it equally absurd, equally base, to solicit, or to decline, the stroke of fate.——Thus much I have attempted to say; but my strength fails me, and I feel the approach of death. I shall cautiously refrain from any word that may tend to influence your suffrages in the election of an emperor. My choice might be imprudent or injudicious; and, if it should not be ratified by the consent of the army, it might be fatal to the person whom I should recommend. I shall only, as a good citizen, express my hopes that the Romans may be blessed with the government of a virtuous sovereign.'

"After this oration, which was delivered in a firm and persuasive tone of voice, he distributed, by a verbal testament, (such as the laws allow to soldiers upon actual service,) the remains of his private fortune, and reproved the grief to which some of the spectators had given way, conjuring them not to disgrace, by unmanly tears, the fate of a prince, who, in a few minutes, would be united with heaven and the stars. He then entered into a metaphysical argument with the philosophers Priscus and Maximus on the nature of the soul; but his wounds, excited by his exertions, began to bleed with fresh violence, and his breathing became difficult. Having called for a draught of cold water, he drank it, and expired without pain. Such was the end of Julian the Apostate, in the thirty-second year of his age, after a reign of only twenty months; but which, from the variety and interest of the events, appears longer in the retrospect than many of more years."

CHAPTER X.

Restoration of the Church.

[A. D. 363.]

The death of Julian was an important event in the history of the church; for he was succeeded by Jovian, a zealous Christian, if it is not improper to apply that epithet to any of those virulent sectarians who, by their contentious disputes for temporal power, under the pretext of purity of doctrine, brought odium on the religion and the name. "The Christians," in fact, at this time, as their adversary Gibbon has remarked, "had forgotten the spirit of the gospel; and the Pagans had imbibed the spirit of the church." Jovian unfurled the banner of the cross, the Labarum of Constantinople, at the head of the legions, and the Christians applauded his piety. But they were ignorant what creed he professed, or would choose for the standard of orthodoxy. Hareach gives the following description of the first effect of his edict in favour of the churches.

"The news produced a great sensation throughout the empire, and stirred, as it were, from the bottom, into furious fermentation, all the conflicting opinions that had simmered so long in the bosoms of the opposite religious factions. The Pagan priesthood, with their adherents, were smitten with a deadly dismay. They recollected, in the dread of retribution, with what zeal they had compelled the Christians, during the reign of Julian, to make full and ample satisfaction for the temples which they had destroyed. They were oppressed with terror, when they remembered in what manner they had pulled down the churches erected on the lands formerly appropriated to their idols, and, in the triumph and exultation of their adversaries, they anticipated, because they deserved, a tremendous retaliation. Nor was the conduct of the church, at this restoration, distinguished by that temperance, which the peaceful precepts of the religion ought to have dictated. The leaders of the contending sects into which the Christian family had been long already divided, convinced, from experience, how much their fate depended on who should make the earliest impression on the mind of an untutored soldier like Jovian, hastened to meet him. The highways of the East were crowded with Homoousian, and Arian, and Semiarian, and Eunomian, bishops, struggling with heel and hand in the holy race. The apartments of the palace resounded with their clamours; the emperor was astonished and deafened by their metaphysical arguments and virulent invectives. They rushed before him with books in their hands; and, when one attempted to state in what consisted the superiority of his own creed, his eloquence was drowned by the vociferation of the other hydra-heads of the ecclesiastical dragon. Jovian entreated them to be calm, recommended concord and charity, confessed his inability to determine their dispute, and begged them to await the sentence of a future council of the church, which should be summoned to allay the ferment.

"This frantic theology disgusted the emperor; and he summoned before him Athanasius, declaring his preference for the Nicene creed by the epithet of *celestial*, which he bestowed on the virtues of that intrepid veteran of the faith.

"Athanasius was at this time in the seventieth year of his age: his figure, which rose to the majestic, was rendered strikingly venerable by his flowing hoary hair and beard, the serene fortitude of his countenance, and the mildness of his demeanour,—the impression of which was strengthened on the mind of the spectator by an eloquence at once dignified and insinuating.

"The conduct of Jovian, after his conference with Athanasius, was exemplary. He published an indulgent edict of toleration, in which he declared that his subjects might exercise with freedom and safety the ceremonies of the ancient worship, but that the sacrilegious rites of magic would be punished with the utmost rigour. The effect of this wise and moderate course allayed the apprehensions of the Pagans; and few of the temples that were shut, on his first elevation of the cross, were afterwards opened. The philosophers, as the advocates of polytheism were called, who had abused the transient favour which they derived from the apostacy of Julian, shaved their beards, and assumed the demeanour of moderation; and the Christian zealots, discountenanced in their unchristian thirst of revenge by the liberality of the imperial edict, boasted of their forbearance."

CHAPTER XI.

Anecdotes of St. Athanasius.

St. Athanasius, to whom no inconsiderable portion of the merit which Jovian acquired by his judicious restoration of the church may be ascribed, affords an admirable example of what obstacles may be surmounted by the force of a persevering mind, when it is inflexibly applied to the pursuit of a single object. The first public demonstration of his talents was at the council of Nice, in which he opposed the Arian doctrines with so much eloquence and effect, that, in the course of five months after his return to Alexandria, he was elected by the clergy of Egypt to fill the archiepiscopal throne, which had then become vacant. It is only since the Reformation, that seculars and princes have assumed the authority of interfering with the concerns of the church. This eminent station he occupied above forty-six years, during the whole of which he waged indefatigable war with the errors of Arianism. Five times he was expelled from his throne; twenty years he passed as an exile or a fugitive; and almost every province of the Roman empire was a witness to his merit and his suffering in the great controversy to which he had devoted his life. But, although he has always been esteemed one of the most accurate masters of the Christian theology, it has been alleged, that he was addicted to the art of divination by magic. Our author gives the following account of his third expulsion from the archiepiscopal throne, which is strikingly illustrative of the courage and fortitude of the saint.

" It is strange, that a doctrine which enjoins peace and good-will towards all men, should, by a difference of opinion respecting the meaning of verbal expressions, give rise to the most bitter animosities. The purpose of

Christianity is lost in the contentions of the priesthood. The theology of Athanasius having been condemned by the councils of Arles and Milan, his adversaries demand his expulsion from the pastoral chair of Egypt, but the affection in which he is held by his flock, prevents the arm of the civil power from being exerted against him. It is said, that the resolute prelate refuses to submit to the sentence, and considers the requisition which has come from Constantinople, for his resignation, as not sufficiently authentic. He performs his ecclesiastical duties, and acts in all respects as if he were in the undisputed possession of his dignity and office. It is even remarked, that he seems more ostentatious in the exercise of his functions, since the order for his expulsion was received ——— * * *

"A terrible sacrilege fills Alexandria with consternation and crimes. Syrianus,* at the head of five thousand men, entered the city last night. The archbishop was convinced they were come to overawe his friends, and to force his abdication; but their arrival did not make the slightest change in his deportment. He performed all the business that he had previously arranged for the day, and attended divine service in the evening, as if totally unconscious of any impending danger. At midnight, according to his wonted custom, he also went to church, and a great number of his faithful flock, in apprehension of some treachery, also attended. I was among the number. The service began as usual; but an extraordinary expression of anxiety was vivid in every eye,—and the psalms were chanted with a tone of high enthusiasm. In the pauses of the worship an awful silence prevailed, and the slightest noise startled the whole congregation. Athanasius sat on the archiepiscopal throne with a sublime serenity of countenance. His eye never wandered from the book before him, and towards him every eye was turned with earnestness and solicitude.

"About the end of the second prayer the sound of a

---

* He was duke or governor of Egypt at this time.

distant tumult was heard, and the noise and clamour rolled nearer and nearer. The officiating priest became agitated; the service was suspended; and the congregation was moved as by a sudden panic. In this moment of confusion, Athanasius rose, and, with a firm and commanding voice, requested them to join him in the cxxxvth Psalm, which he immediately began himself. A glorious shout of religious confidence burst at once from them all; and, in the same moment, the blaspheming soldiers thundered at the doors. The noise for a time was lost in the triumphant chorus of devotion, but at length the doors were burst open. A cloud of arrows announced the entrance of the military: the people fled, bursting from the church by the windows, as the soldiers rushed in with drawn swords. The dreadful gleam of arms was reflected from the holy lamps of the sanctuary; but the lamps were soon extinguished in the confusion, and Athanasius, folded up as it were in the darkness, escaped —— * * *

"Syrianus, enraged at losing his victim, whose head he deemed would be the most acceptable present he could send to Constantinople, has abandoned the town to the licentious soldiery. The churches have been plundered; the faithful have been slain; the houses have been entered with violence; and lust, and rapine, and avarice, and resentment, with all the other fiends that instigate the crimes of mankind, are now rioting throughout the city."

CHAPTER XII.

Adventures of St. Athanasius.

WE shall now extract an account of some of the adventures of the Saint, after his escape from the church of St. Theonas.

"Counts, prefects, tribunes, and whole armies, were successively employed in pursuit of the fugitive. The vigilance of the civil and military powers was awakened by the imperial edicts; rewards were offered to the man who should produce the primate, dead or alive, and dreadful penalties denounced against those who should harbour or protect him. But the disciples of St. Anthony, a race of wild yet submissive fanatics, who preferred the commands of their abbot to the laws of their sovereign, received him in the deserts of Thebais. They admired his patience and humility, collected the sentences that dropped from his lips as the maxims of inspired wisdom; and they persuaded themselves, that even their prayers, their fasts, and their vigils, were less meritorious than the dangers which they braved in the defence of the holy man.

"Their monasteries are situated in lonely and desolate places on the summits of the mountains, and in the islands of the Nile. When their retreats were invaded by a military force, which it was impossible to resist, they submitted to the executioner; and proved, by their fortitude, that they were of that true Egyptian race, from whom tortures would never wrest the confession of a secret which they were resolved not to disclose. On these occasions, Athanasius, for whose safety they devoted their lives, was swiftly removed from one place of concealment to another, till he was placed in security, amidst the secret recesses of the great desert. With these faithful and incorruptible fanatics he spent several years, during which, his zeal in the cause of orthodox theology suffered no abatement. By their assistance he opened a correspondence with his friends; and by their means he was often enabled, in disguise, to visit Alexandria.

"On one occasion, when he was secreted in a dry cistern, in the city, a female slave happened to discover him, and betrayed him by her terror. But, before her screams brought any one to the spot, he escaped. At another time, when he was pursued, he obtained an asylum in the house of a virgin, only twenty years of age, who was celebrated for her exquisite beauty. At the hour of midnight, in a loose dress, as he had fled from his couch, he entered her apartment, and conjured her to afford him protection; and she concealed him in her most secret chamber, and watched over his safety, with the tenderness of a friend and the assiduity of a servant. She supplied him with books and provisions, washed his feet, managed his correspondence, and dexterously concealed from the eye of suspicion their solitary intercourse —— * * *"

About six years after this adventure, Athanasius was recalled to the archiepiscopal dignity,—from which he was again expelled by Julian the Apostate, after whose death he was restored by Jovian, his successor. In his old age, his unwearied persecutors, the adherents of the Arian dereliction, a fifth time attempted his overthrow. But the zeal of his flock, who instantly flew to arms, intimidated the prefect from carrying the design into effect; and the venerable prelate, after a reign of forty-seven years, distinguished by the most courageous defence and promulgation of his religious sentiments, was permitted to end his days in peace.

The death of this distinguished champion of the faith, having completed one of the most interesting periods in the history of the church, connected with the fate of the Roman republic, we shall now turn our attention to the falling fortunes of that once mighty and superb state. The barbarians, on all sides, were pressing towards the heart of the empire; the armies were divided; and a shattered and uncertain policy in the government, indicated the tottering inability of old age.

CHAPTER XIII.

The Inroad of the Barbarians.

In every age, the immense plains of Scythia or Tartary have been inhabited by pastoral tribes, who refuse to cultivate the earth, and disdain the confinement of a sedentary life. From time immemorial they have been renowned for their courage and their conquests. Pekin and Paris have alike been visited by their victorious arms; and the narratives of antiquity are justified by the experience of modern times. The following extracts, respecting some of the barbarous nations which now began their inroads on the Roman empire, will enable the reader to comprehend how ineffectual the opposition of the degenerated legions must have been to these iron hordes, who, in personal strength and daring, were perhaps superior even to the hardy original founders of the military republic.

"The Scythians are necessarily cruel, by the simplicity of their roving life. The ox or the sheep are slaughtered by the same hand from which they were fed, and the bleeding limbs of the lamb that was caressed by their children, are served, with very little preparation, to their children for food. Thus, those horrid objects, which are disguised by the refinement of Roman manners, are exposed in their most disgusting form in the tents of these rude shepherds; and the innate sympathy of compassion is weakened by the practice of domestic cruelty.

"Their march is unincumbered with baggage, and the lines of it uncertain; for they require no preparation of magazines of provisions like the legions. They come, accompanied with their flocks and herds, and their patience and abstinence require little more than what these supply. Horse-flesh, which is proscribed among the Romans, is with them a luxury; and the field of battle, when their cavalry suffers, often furnishes their banquets. When the forage round their camp is almost consumed, they slaughter the greatest part of their cattle, and preserve the flesh, either smoked, or dried in the sun. On sudden emergencies, they provide themselves with balls of hard curds, which they dissolve in water; and, on this unsubstantial diet, they will endure the fatigue of many days.

"Their houses are tents, and their cities encampments, which they remove as often as the surrounding forage is consumed; and the necessary order in which this must be done, to prevent confusion, inures them to the warlike habits of order and obedience. The choice of their foraging stations is regulated by the difference of the season. In the summer, they spread themselves over the pastures of the north; and, in winter, they seek the sheltered valleys, and the sunny side of the southern hills.

"This wandering life makes them unacquainted with local attachments. They have no country, but only personal friends; and, in the most distant marches from the spot of his birth and childhood, the Scythian is still surrounded by the objects which are dear, or valuable, or familiar, to his eyes. A severe winter often drives them like overflowing waters upon countries that they had not visited before; and, when they have once tasted the wines and luxuries of these new regions, they seldom return to their former haunts, but leave their other tribes behind. Conquest with them is colonization.

"Compared with the labour of agriculture, and the industry of manufactures, their pastoral life is a life of idleness; but they are strangers to the delight of indolence. The Scythian plains are traversed by bands of strong and spirited horses; and the training of these for hunting and war, is the pastime of these bold and adventurous shepherds. They excel in the dexterous management of the lance; they draw the bow with a nervous arm, and direct their weighty arrows with unerring aim and irresistible force.

"Such are the barbarians who now are pouring from their eastern regions; and incredible tales are related of their deformity and passions. Incapable of relishing the beauties of art and the embellishments of life, they set no value on what is ornamental; and the sacred temple, and the shed of the artizan, are indiscriminately converted to the use of their cattle. The harvest-field and the vineyard are burnt down, as impediments in their progress.*

"The Gothic nations have already begun to fly before them, and have solicited the permission of the emperor Valens to allow them an asylum on this side of the Danube:—thus abandoning their native soil to these eastern hordes, and bringing down among the Roman subjects new customs, new superstitions, and new manners, at a time when the whole empire is in a state of dissolution. The effect of this will do more towards the obliteration of the ancient Roman character, than all the changes that have yet taken place —— * * *

"The emperor having granted the request of the Goths, they are now settled within the Roman territory. A bridge, formed of boats and vessels, was constructed across the Danube; and the Gothic myriads, from all parts of the country, rushed towards it like the tributary streams of the river. Night and day, without intermission, the crowd continued to pass. The Roman officers for a time endeavoured to keep an account of their numbers, but soon desisted, with amazement and dismay, from the prosecution of the endless and impracticable task.

"It was a magnificent act of Roman generosity, to afford an asylum within the bosom of the empire to a whole people; but the terms on which it was granted destroyed its virtue. Before passing the river, the Goths were required to deliver up their arms. It was likewise stipulated that their children should also be given up, and dispersed through the provinces of Asia, where they might be civilized by the arts of education, and serve as hostages for the fidelity of their parents.

---

* The western emigration of these multitudes was probably occasioned by the building of the great wall of China.

Distress alone could extort from the indignant Goths these harsh conditions!

"The children of the nobility were separated from the multitude, and conducted without delay to the distant places assigned for their residence; and, as these numerous hostages, victims of remorseless policy, passed through the cities, their gay apparel, their innocent wonder, and the martial and robust appearance of their attendants, moved the Roman subjects with alternate emotions of admiration and pity."

CHAPTER XIV.

The Insurrection of the Goths.

ALATHEUS and Saphrax, the leaders of the Ostrogoths, having heard of the success which attended the supplication of the Visigoths, also applied to Valens to receive their nation likewise. But his decided refusal showed that the imperial council already repented of their generosity.

In the meantime, the emigrants had, according to the arrangements previously made, spread themselves over the uncultivated plains between the ridges of Mount Hæmus and the Danube. As their numbers greatly exceeded what were expected, the stock of provisions began to fail. The spirit of discontent arose among them; but, the means of relief and revenge they had surrendered with their arms, which were in the hands of the Romans. They felt the instigations of that keen resentment which is always the consequence of fraudulent favours; but famine clung around them closer and closer. When their property was all exhausted, the lofty freedom which they had cherished, was humiliated to the earth by the distresses of their families, and they sold themselves as slaves, to preserve a miserable existence. But this low submission of the broken heart, to which many of them yielded, had its limit; and the clamours of a hungry multitude announced their determination to obtain relief.

In these circumstances, Alatheus and Saphrax, who still lingered with their countrymen along the northern banks of the Danube, opened a correspondence with Alavivus and Fritigern, the leaders of the emigrants; and a union of their nations was concerted among them. We shall now quote our author's account of the incident which gave rise to their united war against the empire.

"Lupicinus, the Roman commander, invited the Gothic chiefs to a splendid entertainment at Marcianopolis; and their attendants, who, on this occasion of ceremony, were permitted to wear their arms, remained on the outside of the palace. The gates of the city were strictly guarded. No preparation being made for the entertainment of the train of Alavivus and Fritigern, they applied to the townsmen for provisions, and their application was rejected with derision. Altercation led to reproaches;—a sword was hastily drawn, and a tumult ensued. Lupicinus, already inflamed with wine, was privately informed by one of his officers that several of his men were slain, and rashly ordered that their death should be instantly revenged by the massacre of the guards of Fritigern and Alavivus.

"The shouts and dying groans apprised the chiefs of their danger; and Fritigern saw, with the intrepid spirit of a hero, that he was lost, if he allowed a moment of deliberation to the man who had so deeply injured himself and his whole nation. 'A trifling dispute,' said he aloud at the banquet, with a firm and unembarrassed manner, 'appears to have arisen between the two nations; but it may be productive of the most dangerous consequences, unless the tumult is appeased by the assurance of our safety, and the authority of our presence.' At these words, Fritigern and his companions drew their swords, rushed through the unresisting crowd of Romans, who filled the palace, the streets, and the gates, and, mounting their horses, were, to the astonishment of Lupicinus, beyond the reach of his power.

"Meanwhile, Alatheus and Saphrax, watching a favourable opportunity to bring their army across the river, availed themselves of the neglected state in which the Romans had left the fortifications and vessels which constituted the defences of the Danube; and, by the help of such rafts and boats as could be hastily procured, transported their troops without opposition, and fixed an independent camp on the territories of the empire. To this camp Fritigern and his companions repaired, and were received with full and joyful acclamations. War was resolved on. The banners of the nations were unfurled, and the air resounded with their mournful but sublime music.

"Lupicinus marched against Fritigern; and, at the distance of about nine miles from Marcianopolis, was defeated with great disgrace. From that day, the distress of the Goths, and the security of the Romans, ended. The strangers, renouncing their precarious condition, assumed the character of citizens and masters, claimed dominion over the possessors of the land, and held, in their own right, the provinces of the empire which are bounded by the Danube.

"Not content with victory, the exasperated Goths gratified their revenge. Having been deprived of the common benefits of nature, and the fair intercourse of social life, they retaliated these wrongs with a stern heart and an unsparing sword. In the course of these depredations, a great number of their children, who had been sold into captivity, were restored to their embraces; but these tender interviews, which might have softened their natures to compassionate the sufferings of other parents, tended only to inflame their native fierceness. They listened with eagerness to the complaints of their children, who had suffered the most cruel indignities from the lustful or angry passions of their masters; and the same cruelties, the same indignities, were severely retaliated on the sons and daughters of the Romans."*

---

* Gibbon.

CHAPTER XV.

The Defeat and Death of Valens.

The army of the Gothic association passed the ridges of Hæmus; and, descending on the plains of Thrace, advanced towards Hadrianople. The emperor Valens was then in that city at the head of his army; and, on hearing of their approach, went out to give them battle. The following is our author's account of the conflict and its consequences.

" The Goths were encamped at the distance of about twelves miles from the city. By some accidental misconception of the orders, the right wing of the imperial army arrived in sight of the enemy, whilst the left was still far behind. This error might have been rectified by the decision of an abler general; for the Gothic cavalry were scattered over the neighbouring country in foraging parties. The address of Fritigern on this occasion deserves immortal renown. He observed that the Romans were embarrassed by the rapid advance of their right wing, and that, while waiting till their left could be brought up, they several times fell into confusion; but he was not in a condition to attack them. To gain time, however, for the arrival of his cavalry, he sent messengers of peace, and made overtures for a negociation with the emperor. Valens, desirous of ending the war, sent an ambassador to treat; but, before this minister had advanced half way between the two armies, he was recalled by the alarms of battle. An imprudent attack was made by one of the Roman officers with a detachment of archers and targetiers. In the same moment, the flying squadrons of Alatheus and Saphrax, hastily recalled from their foraging, invested like a whirlwind the flanks of the imperial army, and added new terrors to the tumultuous but irresistible onset of the Barbarians. The Romans fled; their cavalry was scattered, and their infantry dispersed, like chaff in the tempest. Valens was wounded, and carried by a party of his guards to a neighbouring cottage. But scarcely had they entered, when the house was surrounded by the enemy, who knew not who had sought an asylum within. They tried to force the doors:—the guards defended them. Provoked by a discharge of arrows from the roof, they set fire to a pile of faggots, and consumed the cottage, and the Roman emperor, with his train. A youth, who dropped from the window, alone escaped, to attest the tragical tale, and to inform the Goths of the inestimable prize that they had lost by their own rashness.

" When the news of this disastrous engagement reached Constantinople, the whole city was overwhelmed with alarm and fear. The streets were filled as by enchantment with an incredible multitude. The youth prepared to man the walls. The women clamoured with grief. Fugitives, from the scattered legions, from time to time arrived, and were overwhelmed, sometimes with execrations for their cowardice, and sometimes welcomed with mournful salutations. A rushing at one moment from the streets towards the gates of the palace raised a cry that the emperor had escaped; but, in a moment, the billows rolled back, and the murmurings of despondency succeeded. All night there was an unusual light seen over the city; for few went to bed, and the windows of the houses were open. Nothing was heard but lamentation, and the occasional stir of ineffectual preparation.

" In the midst of this universal consternation, I could not but remember with what indifference, in the days of their glory, this once haughty people, now so tremblingly anxious for themselves, regarded the sufferings of others: and, when I heard them declaiming, in the impotence of despair, on the violence of the Barbarians, I recollected with what cold elegance Cæsar relates, in the Commentaries of the Gallic War, that he put to death the senate of the Veneti, who had yielded to his mercy, and laboured to extirpate the whole nation;* and that his soldiers spared neither age nor sex: and I could not withhold from my conviction, that the flood of barbaric rapacity that was now wasting the country to the gates of the capital, was but the reaction of those triumphant cruelties, which had pushed the frontiers so far into the regions of other independent states."

CHAPTER XVI.

The Massacre of the Gothic Youth.

WITHOUT preface, we shall extract the following account of the Massacre of the Gothic Youth, who had been distributed through the Asiatic provinces, to be educated as Romans, according to the articles of the treaty, by which the nation had been admitted into the bosom of the empire.

" It was impossible to conceal from the Gothic youth the events of the war, nor force their bold and warlike spirit, to repress their exultation. They assembled together in the evenings, when the tasks of their education were over, and sung with heroic enthusiasm the odes which recounted the valour and achievements of their ancestors. It was therefore not altogether without reason, that this intripid demeanour was seen with apprehension by the Romans. Reports of their daring indiscretion were transmitted to Constantinople; and the senate of the city was consulted on the subject by Julius,

---

* Cæsar Comment.

who, during the vacancy of the throne, held the important trust of Master-General of the troops. This pusillanimous body, the worthy inheritors of the degeneracy of Rome, advised him to assume the power of acting as he should judge most expedient for the common good; and, upon this authority, he concerted with his officers the necessary measures for a bloody design. An order was promulgated, that, on a stated day, the Gothic youth should assemble in the capital cities of the respective provinces among which they had been scattered; and a report was instantaneously circulated, that they were summoned to receive gifts of money and land. On the appointed day, the unarmed multitude of these friendless young men was carefully collected together in the forum. The streets were occupied with troops, the houses were adorned as on a holiday, but on the roofs were stationed archers and slingers. At the same hour, in all the cities of the East, the signal was given; and the Gothic youth were all slaughtered.

"This attrocious act of policy secured for a time the Asiatic provinces; but it has kindled an implacable revenge in the breasts of the Goths, and their genius is evidently acquiring the ascendancy. No longer able to encounter them in open war, the Romans have recourse to craft, and the artifices of intrigue and cunning; the weapons of the vindictive and the weak are employed, instead of that frank arrogance of arms, which distinguished the prosperous epochs of the republic. In the meantime the empire is broken in on all sides; and the population of the provinces has strangely diminished, while the swarming herds of the North seem to increase in an equal proportion.

"In the territories where the Barbarians have settled, the original inhabitants have almost disappeared; and the country begins to assume a new and ruder character. Cultivation is neglected for pasturage; the inclosures are in a state of decay; the hamlets have fallen into ruin; and every thing indicates the relapse of the world into barbarism. The villas of the nobles on the skirts of the cities, are fenced, and provided with armed domestics against sudden assaults; distrust between man and man has dissolved the ties of society; and the laws are but feebly administered. Justice has become so expensive, that the injured often submit in silence to great wrongs, rather than pay the price; and fraud walks with impunity openly abroad. Every thing demonstrates the approach of some great consummation: religion, departing entirely from its practical character, is resolved into ceremonies and speculative dogmas. The Christian priests have even dared to exult at the altar over the slaughter of the innocent Gothic youth, and to consider their mournful fate as an equitable judgment of Divine vengeance, for the disrespect with which their fathers and kindred treated the churches of Thrace. They ascribe to Omnipotence their own sordid passions, and see a wicked providence in the crimes of the age, acting according to their own iniquitous desires.

"I am sick of Constantinople, and will for a time bid it adieu."

CHAPTER XVII.

The Destruction of the Temple of Serapis

[A. D. 389.]

HARBACH wandered from place to place, recording from time to time his observations, but in such abrupt and detached sentences, that we cannot string them into any thing like a connected narrative. After the penal edicts of the emperor Theodosius against the sacrifice and worship of the Pagan superstition, he describes the Christians as actuated by fanatic fury, demolishing the temples, and destroying the idols and archives of the old religion in all parts of the empire. To this intolerant zeal we may ascribe the loss of many rich collections of literature, and that darknes of the mind which now involves so many eastern nations, once the most enlightened and flourishing portions of the Roman world; at least, his account of the destruction of the temple of Serapis at Alexandria, warrants this supposition.

"It was the noblest building in the city. A magnificent quadrangular portico enclosed a spacious square, and in the middle, on a lofty platform, to which the ascent was by a hundred steps, stood the temple. In the interior of the substructure were numerous vaulted chambers, filled with the accumulated treasures of the votive offerings; and the surrounding edifices, consisting of stately halls, adorned with exquisite statues, and the most beautiful productions of art, contained the famous library, to the formation of which Mark Antony gave two hundred thousand volumes to Cleopatra, when she resolved to replace the collection of the Ptolemies, destroyed in the Alexandrian war of Julius Cæsar.

"Theophilus,* a man of turbulent spirit, had long seen with indignation, that, notwithstanding the imperial edicts, sacrifices were still offered to Serapis, and that the rites were respected by even his own flock, from a superstitious notion that they had some influence on the periodical inundations of the Nile. An incident in itself trifling roused his anger to the utmost, and he resolved to root out this last weed of idolatry. The votaries of Serapis flew to arms, determined to die in defence of their god; the temple was converted into a fortress, and resisted the Christian zealots with success. In the meantime the archbishop wrote to Constantinople, representing what had happened; and a truce was mediated by the magistrates, until the answer of Theodosius should arrive. When this was received, the two parties assembled without arms, in the principal square, and the imperial report was publicly read. It contained the sentence of destruction on Serapis; and the Christians, on hearing it, set up a shout of joy and exultation, whilst the Pagans overwhelmed with alarm, retired with hasty steps from the

---

* At this period archbishop of Alexandria.

derision of their triumphant enemies, who immediately proceeded, in a tumultuous manner, to carry the sentence into execution. The vaulted treasures were pillaged; the images and vases of gold and silver were borne to the archiepiscopal residence, and melted; and the books of the library, the gathered treasures of ancient wisdom, were scattered in the streets, and torn to pieces by the multitude. The temple was constructed with great strength and massy materials, and the doors, being of solid brass, resisted for a very long time the fury of the assailants; in the end, however, they were burst open, and the colossal statue of Serapis disclosed to full view. It was an extraordinary achievement of art; and the magnitude of the figure, and the majesty of his aspect, for a moment overawed the assailants. He was seated on a throne, and seemed to fill the whole temple; in his left hand he held a sceptre, and in his right a symbolic monster, of which I could obtain no explanation. It consisted of the head and body of a serpent branching into three tails, which were again terminated by the triple heads of a dog, a lion, and a wolf. It was believed by many in the crowd, that, if any impious hand dared to insult the god, the heavens and the earth would instantly return to their original chaos. This, with the sublime greatness of the statue, and the awful obscurity in which he was throned within the spacious edifice, had for some time the effect of restraining their impetuosity. But a zealous soldier at last ventured into the sanctuary, armed with a weighty battle-axe;—a profound silenced ensued, as if every one expected some terrific event. The soldier, however, was undaunted, and struck the statue on the cheek with so much vigour, that the plate of metal of which it consisted started off from the wood to which it was fastened and fell to the ground, with a clang that echoed throughout the building. The multitude shouted; the victorious soldier repeated his blows; he had soon companions in the work; and, in the course of a few minutes, the huge idol was overthrown. The metal plates were torn off, and the broken limbs, dragged through the streets, were burnt in the amphitheatre."

CHAPTER XVIII.

The Revival of Polytheism.

THE destruction of Serapis at Alexandria, ended the Pagan idolatry; but it was not long till the manifold superstition, which had been imbided from the ancient polytheism, showed itself in a new form, and not in a much better character. To suffer with patience for the sake of their religion, was an illustrious duty, which the early Christians gloried in performing; and the splendid example of constancy which many of them displayed, was calculated to excite the admiration of the pious. In the indulgence of this feeling, one of the most amiable of our nature, memorials of distinguished martyrs were sought for, and preserved with affection and reverence. A trade in them was the consequence; and, so long as it was confined to the innocent fraud, if the expression may be used, of selling fictitious relics, it was perhaps not particularly deserving of animadversion. But it did not remain for any length of time in this mercantile state; corrupt priests, perceiving the lucrative advantages of the votive offerings which the Pagans were in the practice of making to shrines of their deities, devised the artifice of ascribing miraculous influence to the relics of the saints and martyrs, in order to reap a portion of this profitable harvest. At what time the imposition was first practised in the church, or by whom invented, cannot be ascertained; but, about the close of the fourth century, it was in full operation; and so much were the minds of men engrossed with the fictions of relics and of saintly legends, that the sublime and simple theology of the primitive Christians was totally neglected.

The transition was easy, from believing in the miraculous virtues of relics, to believe also that the souls of departed saints stooped from their beatitude, and took an interest in the affairs of this world. Nor was it difficult to persuade the credulous pilgrim, as he offered his oraisons at the shrine of his favourite martyr, that the spirit of the dead possessed an influence in heaven, and was worthy of being solicited to mediate for him there. Thus, from the feeling of affection, that leads us to wish for memorials of those whom we love or admire, the trade in relics originated. Artifice converted it into a miraculous system of fraud, out of which grew that apotheosis of the pious, so contrary to the sublime simplicity of the Christian religion.

The polytheism of what may be called the mythology of the saints, was soon followed by other imitations of the Pagan ritual. The holy rags and bones which performed so many miracles deserved precious caskets to hold them, in the ornamenting of which the ingenuity of art was exhausted. It was also natural in the pilgrims, to long for a sight of the face and form of their saint; and the monks could do no less than try to procure their portraits and statues. But, it is time to return to our author.

CHAPTER XIX.

State of the Roman Nobility.

[A.D. 408.]

AFTER lingering some time at Alexandria, Hareach appears to have passed over again to Italy, and to have been at Rome, when Alaric advanced to that capital. But, before entering upon the incidents of that eventful period, we must indulge our readers with an extract from an elaborate character of the Roman nobles, with which he opens this portion of his narrative.

"The greatness of Rome was founded on the rare alliance of virtue and of fortune: her infancy was employed in a laborious struggle against the tribes of Italy. In the strength of youth she sustained the storms of war, carried her victorious arms beyond the seas and mountains, and gathered honours from every quarter of the globe. At length, verging towards old age, and still great by the terror of her name, she sought the blessings of ease and tranquillity. A secure and profound peace succeeded to the tumults of the republic, but this happiness was degraded by the conduct of her nobles; who, unmindful of their own dignity and that of their country, assumed an unbounded license of vice and folly.

"They contend with each other in the empty vanity of titles and surnames, and curiously select or invent the most sonorous appellations, to impress the vulgar with respect. From a vain ambition of perpetuating their memory, they multiply their likeness, in statues of bronze and marble. Their chariots are often of solid silver, embossed and carved with great art, and the trappings of their mules and horses adorned with buckles and ornaments of gold. Their long robes of silk and purple float in the wind, and, as they are agitated by art or accident, they occasionally discover the under garments embroidered according to the taste of the wearer, sometimes with wolves, lions, woods, hunting-matches, and flowers, and sometimes with legends and figures of the saints. They never go abroad without a numerous retinue of servants, and their carriages are driven along the streets with a tearing velocity: when they visit the public places, they talk aloud with audacious arrogance, and act as if none else were present but themselves. Sometimes they undertake the arduous enterprises of hunting on their estates by the aid of servile hands; and sometimes, on smooth seas, they risk the bold adventure of sailing along the sunny shores in their gilded galleys, and speak of their exploits afterwards, as if they beggared the achievements of Cæsar and Alexander. In travelling to their villas, the whole body of their household marches with the master; and, from afar, the approach of a great man may be distinguished on the highways, by the cloud of dust in which he moves. Their baggage and wardrobe set forward first, and to these succeed a multitude of inferior domestics. The main body is composed of a promiscuous crowd of slaves, accidental guests, and the members of the family; and the rear is closed by their eunuchs, arranged according to their respective trusts and seniority.

"In the exercise of their domestic jurisdiction, they express an exquisite sensibility for any personal injury, and a contemptuous indifference for the rest of the human species. When a slave has been tardy in the performance of any of their orders, he is immediately chastised with merciless rigour. Hospitality was once numbered among their virtues; but now, if a stranger is introduced to any of these pompous personages, he is received with such warm professions and polite inquiries, that he retires enchanted with their affability. Secure of a favourable reception, he repeats his visits next day, and is mortified to find that his person, name, and country, are forgotten. To this there are no doubt exceptions, and the stranger may occasionally meet with friendly entertainments, until it is understood that he has proclaimed their hospitality; then he is noticed no more; but his place filled up by some other, who, in his turn, receives the same courtesy, and the same tacit dismissal. Their only favourites are needy parasites, who minister to their vanity and vices by the grosest adulation and servility, and who live, by pillaging the wealthy simpletons invited to the honour of gambling at their parties. They have libraries in their houses, in which the volumes are magnificently disposed for show, but rarely opened, and not then for reading, but only to be looked at on account of the beauty of the ornaments and the penmanship. Their only passion, besides the love of pleasure, is avarice; and it is exhibited among them in the most degrading aspect. Relations, through the medium of money-lenders, traffic with the necessities of each other; and, while they are respectively using all the means of overreaching, by their agents, they seemingly live on terms of the most cordial intimacy. They do nothing from the dictates of their own judgment, or the promptings of the heart, but employ lawyers even in the acts of their ostentatious benevolence; by which the whole effective power of the state has become merged in the hands of that cold and artificial class. It it thus that reformation is stifled and corruption grows; for the lawyers are too deeply interested in preserving the forms of existing practices, to regard the essentials of engagements. The affairs of life are no longer regulated by what is right, but by what is legal; and law, the edicts of the emperors, and the decrees of the senate, are deemed superior to justice."*

To this humiliating account of the Roman nobles, we must add our author's description of several things, that tend to illustrate the general character of the populace at the same period; and which throw some light on what may be considered as the Roman system of providing for the poor.

"The distribution of provisions has a fatal effect on the manners of the plebeians; it weakens their industry, and makes them trust to the public for the means of that support, which they should owe to their own exertions. The monthly rations of corn have been converted into a daily allowance of bread. At an appointed hour, each citizen who has obtained a ticket from the overseers of his district, goes to the place of distribution, and, according to his circumstances, as expressed in the ticket, receives a certain quantity of bread, either at a cheap rate, or in charity. The forests of Lucania, whose acorns fattened numerous droves of wild hogs, afforded a plentiful supply of wholesome meat; of which, during five months of the year, about four millions of pounds are distributed among the poor. Oil is also given to them in a too liberal measure; and wine has likewise become a necessary part of this questionable system of public benevolence.

---

* This description of the degenerate nobility of Rome, is chiefly taken from Ammianus Marcellinus.

"But the liberality of the state is not limited to the necessaries of life; sumptuous baths are provided for the populace, of which those of Caracalla and Dioclesian are still the most magnificent. In the former, the accommodation are sufficient for sixteen hundred persons, and no less than three thousand may enjoy the luxury of the latter at the same time. The walls of the lofty apartments in these gorgeous edifices, are encrusted with marble and beautiful mosaics, which imitate the art of the pencil; and perpetual streams of hot water are poured into capacious basins, through sculptured mouths of bright and massy silver. Swarms of ragged plebeians, without shoes, and without a mantle;—a vast and dangerous class, who loiter their time in the streets or forum, to hear news and hold disputes, who have dissipated in extravagance the miserable pittance of their wives and children, and spent the hours of the night in obscure taverns and brothels, in the indulgence of gross and vulgar sensuality,—are constantly seen hovering round these baths, of which it might almost be said they are the constant inmates, were they the same individuals; but their number is so great, that, though always changing, they are never the same.

"The theatres, and public spectacles, are other institutions dependant on the government, and which the people enjoy with equal freedom. But, except in the splendour of decorations, and in this respect they are also greatly inferior to what they were in the days of Adrian and Trajan, they have no pretensions to admiration; for the diversions of the amphitheatre and the circus have lost much of their interest, since the mortal combats of the gladiators have been prohibited; and licentious farces, effeminate music, gorgeous pageants, and gaudy pantomimes, now occupy the stage. Above three thousand female dancers, and as many singers, belong at this time to the theatres of Rome.

"It is these things which have engendered that disease in the heart of the state, by which the vigour of the body is so much impaired, that the Barbarians insult and trample it in all directions.

CHAPTER XX.

The Invasion of Alaric, and first Gothic Siege of Rome.

[A.D. 409.]

ALARIC the Goth, as we have already mentioned, was marching towards Rome about the time that our author arrived in Italy. It has been commonly alleged, by the cotemporary historians, that this enterprise was undertaken at the suggestion of the imperial minister Stilicho, but no credible motive has ever been assigned for such a traitorous act on his part. On the contrary, he had often defeated the Goths in battle; and the general purity of his conduct, ought to have exempted him from an imputation, which seems to have had no other foundation than that of his having advocated in the senate the payment of a sum of money, which Alaric had demanded as due to him. Considering how much it had grown into a custom, in the policy of the declining empire, to purchase the forbearance of the Barbarians, it is highly probable that some contract of this nature had been concluded with Alaric subsequent to the drawn battle of Pollentia; and that, to enforce the fulfilment of the conditions, the Gothic king had again taken up arms.

Stilicho, however, on the suspicion of being in correspondence with Alaric, and of having instigated the invasion, was put to death, and his estates confiscated, after having given, in his daughters, two empresses to Rome, and commanded the Roman armies with honour for the space of twenty-three years.

The alleged perfidy of their commander excited a great ferment among the troops; and the garrisons, in the different cities of Italy, simultaneously flew to arms, out of hatred to Stilicho, and inhumanly slaughtered the wives and children of the Goths, whom he had taken into the public service, and whom, on that account, they considered as participators in his guilt. Exasperated by this dreadful transaction, these unfortunate men, who by no forbearance could ever conciliate the Romans, immediately quitted the service of Honorius the emperor, to the number of thirty thousand, and joined the standards of their countrymen under Alaric. With this formidable reinforcement that warlike prince advanced to the walls of the capital; and, by a skilful disposition of his numerous forces, who impatiently watched the moment of assault, he commanded the twelve principal gates of the city, which intercepted all communication with the adjacent country, and guarded the navigation of the Tyber, from which the Romans derived their surest and most plentiful supply of provisions. The first emotions of the nobles and people on this occasion were those of surprise and indignation, that a Barbarian should dare to insult the capital of the world; but their arrogance was soon humbled, and their unmanly rage, instead of being directed against an enemy in arms, was meanly exercised on a defenceless and innocent victim. We shall now quote our author's account of their proceedings.

"They expected that Alaric would have invested Ravenna, where the emperor and the court then were, and did not credit the messengers who brought the news of his advancing directly on Rome. In the course of the day, bands of families, flying before the van of the Barbarians, came to the gates for refuge; but still neither the senate or the people imagined it possible that Alaric would dare to approach their sacred city; and made no provision for the event.

"In the afternoon, the populace ascended the walls, and clustered on the roofs of the houses. The whole country seemed alive. The roads were thronged with fugitives coming to the town,—terrified mothers dragging their children, and wretched old men invigorated only by their fears. As the sun was setting, the glancing of the Gothic spears were seen flickering through the clouds of dust, under which they were advancing, like the lightnings that precede the storm. A shriek of horror from the walls, echoed from the houses, announced the tremendous discovery to the whole city. The gates were instantly closed, and strengthened within with heaps of rubbish. The senators flew to the capital. The name of Stilicho was pronounced with execrations. Serena, his widow, in the first paroxysm of this panic, was accused of being in correspondence with Alaric, and ordered to be strangled. But still the Barbarians advanced; and, while the senators, in their frantic deliberation, thus showed how far they had degenerated from that equanimity which their ancestors displayed when the Gauls before attacked the city, and Hannibal menaced their gates, the army of Alaric surrounded the walls.

"In the course of a few days, an alarm of famine began to spread; the daily allowance of bread to the poor was reduced to half its quantity; but the price of every article of life rose, till there was no longer any supply. Expedients of the most absurd kind,—magic and spells were gravely discussed in the senate,—among the means of getting rid of the enemy. Still the horrors of want made frightful progress; and it was fearfully rumoured that some desperate wretches fed on the bodies of their fellow-creatures; and that even mothers, yielding in the horrid conflict between starvation and affection, laid desperate hands on their infants, and furiously seized on their flesh. Thousands of the inhabitants expired in their houses and in the streets; and, as the public sepulchres were in the possession of the besiegers, the stench which arose from the unburied carcasses infected the air, and a pestilence, that was augmented by its own ravages, was the consequence.

"Humbled to the earth by these afflicting circumstances, the senate determined to open a negociation with Alaric; and two ambassadors for this purpose were sent to his camp. The conduct of these men strongly illustrated the pride and fallen greatness of Rome. When introduced into the presence of the Gothic king, they affected supreme dignity, and began the conference by declaring that the Romans were determined to maintain their superiority either in war or peace; and that, if he refused them a fair and honourable capitulation, he might sound his trumpets, and prepare to give battle to an innumerable people, exercised in arms, and animated by despair. Alaric listened to this harangue in contemptuous silence; and at the conclusion said, with an insulting laugh, 'The thicker the hay, the easier it is mowed:' adding, 'the terms on which I will spare Rome from destruction, are—ALL the gold and silver in the city, whether the property of the state or of individuals;—ALL the rich and precious movables;—and ALL the slaves who can prove their title to the name of Barbarians.' The Roman deputies, thunderstruck at the magnitude of these demands, and dismayed with the reflection that the means of resisting them did not exist, said, in a suppliant tone, 'If such, O, king! are your demands, what do you intend to leave us?' Alaric for a moment examined them from head to foot with a look of ineffable scorn, and said, 'YOUR LIVES!' They trembled and retired. But, as they were departing from his tent, he called them back, and, relaxing from his sternness, invited them to sit down and discuss the affair calmly; admonishing them of the absurdity of the haughty demeanour which they had assumed at their introduction. A negociation was then temperately opened; and Alaric consented to raise the siege and withdraw his army, on receiving five thousand pounds of gold, thirty thousand of silver, four thousand robes of silk, three thousand pieces of fine scarlet, and three thousand weight of pepper.

"But the public treasury is exhausted; and the fulfilment of these terms, which are more liberal than might have been expected, occasions great embarrassment to the senate. Avarice withholds the private hoards of individuals, and claims the sacrifice of the utensils that were formerly employed in the service of the temples. The golden statue of Valour is ordered to be melted; and the common people lament it, as an omen fatal to the military renown of Rome."

CHAPTER XXI.

The Second Gothic Siege of Rome.

WE shall now continue our author's account of this interesting period.

"The discipline in the Gothic camp is strikingly contrasted with the insubordination of the Roman populace. Until the terms are fulfilled, Alaric has consented that several of the gates should be opened, and a supply of provisions admitted. Prices having fallen, the citizens have again become insolent, and talk of resisting the Barbarians. This is not unknown to the Goth,—but it makes no change on his firmness ——— * * *

"A party of his soldiers insulted some Roman travellers on the road to Ostia,—and he has punished the offenders with death ——— * * *

"The treaty has been ratified by Honorius at Ravenna. The ransom is paid, and the victorious Barbarians are retiring with their booty.

"The moderation which Alaric has shown surprises every body, now that the city is relieved from the terrors of his presence, and the horrors of the siege; and the senate, grovelling in its dotage, imagines, that had they stood out a little longer, the Goths must, from some secret cause, which they have not been able to discover,—some consciousness of weakness,—have been obliged to retire of their own accord.

"The exultation has not lasted long. Alaric has halted his army in Hetruria, and the Goths through all Italy have shaken off their servile fetters, and are flocking to his standard;—but this makes no alteration in his prudence. He declares himself anxious to be considered as the friend of peace and of the Romans; and, at his request, the senate have sent three of their own body, to urge the emperor to exchange hostages with him, for the faithful observance of the conditions of the treaty.

"Honorius has refused the wise proposals of the Goth, and Alaric is again returning to the siege. How different is the conduct of the inhabitants now to what it was on the former occasion! Every one is busy laying-up stores of provisions, and fear and consternation is in every face. They expect no mercy; and they are conscious of no strength. The Roman valour is indeed melted down,— and for ever.

"The senate have sent a second deputation to the emperor, imploring him to exchange the hostages, and to execute without delay all the conditions of the treaty, which he had himself ratified. The moderation of Alaric acquires the dignity of greatness. He feels himself master of the Romans, and refrains from making them more sensible of his authority than what they provoke by their own behaviour.

"The emperor has rejected again the advice of the senate. Jovius, the prefect of Italy, who has been appointed minister by the secret cabal of the court, was with Alaric in his tent when the letters came announcing this decision. He was desirous of arranging the terms of a satisfactory treaty before joining Honorius; and, not doubting that the answer was favourable, read the letters aloud. The Gothic king, incensed at the language in which the haughty perfidy of the emperor was couched, instantly rose from his seat, and ordered his army to advance, and again lay siege to the imperial city. He is now under the walls —— * * *

"Still the magnanimity of Alaric puts the Romans to shame. He has sent himself the bishops of the neighbouring towns to Ravenna, to entreat Honorius not to suffer the metropolis, which has for so many ages been revered by all nations as the mistress of the world, to become a prey to her enemies —— * * *

"The answer of the emperor marks his own infatuation, and the doom of the Roman state. He has rejected the generous entreaties of the conqueror, and declares that he has sworn never to enter into truce or treaty with the Barbarian. The senate and the people are in despair. A terrible movement is seen in the Gothic camp. They are dragging their engines; and a vast detachment is marching towards Ostia. Alaric himself is at the head of this division —— * * *

"He has made himself master of Ostia, and of all the public granaries, on which the subsistence of the capital depends: there is no hope —— * * *

"He has summoned the senate to surrender the city at discretion; and, recounting to them the treachery and obstinacy of Honorius, exhorts them to consult their own safety and that of the Romans by throwing off their allegiance. The senate seem still disposed to hold out,— misled by a fallacy which his former moderation has inspired. But he is firm to his purpose; and his answer to their refusal is, that unless they submit all to him, he will destroy the granaries, and put it equally out of his own power, as it is already out of theirs, to prevent the capital from being devoured by famine —— * * *

"The clamours of the people, and the menaces of Alaric, have prevailed. The senate has surrendered —— * * *

"Alaric, attended by a few of his guards, has been admitted. As he passed under the arches of the Roman triumphs, in his way to the senate, he was observed to smile. This was the only indication of any consciousness on his part of the vastness of the conquest which he had achieved. On entering the capitol, he paused for a moment, and ordered his guards to halt on the stairs that ascend to the portal. In this crisis of humiliation to the former masters of the world, an involuntary act, on their part, threw a gleam of splendour, almost like the lustre of virtue, on their deportment. Conscious of their abject state, they affected no pride, but rose, at his entrance, and received him as the sovereign of their fate.

"This unexpected homage did not disturb the heroic self-possession of the magnanimous Barbarian. He stepped forward, with a reverential air, seemingly indeed affected by the sight of so many old and venerable men, the descendants of those illustrious warriors who had, with a heroism not inferior to his own, reduced so many nations to a servitude baser than that which he meditated for Rome; and, advancing towards Attalus, the prefect of the city, saluted him with the title of emperor. This sublime act of moderation astonished the senators; for they expected that he would himself have ascended the throne, and punished them for the resistance which they had opposed to his demands."

CHAPTER XXII.

The Sack of Rome by the Goths.

The conduct of Attalus in the imperial dignity soon forfeited the confidence of Alaric; and he resolved to suffer his misrule no longer. But we must give our author's account of this transaction.

"Alaric was at this time in the neighbourhood of Rimini. Attalus was with him, conferring on the subject of an expedition which it was resolved should be sent to Africa, to insure a more regular supply of corn to the capital than had for some time been furnished from the African provinces. Alaric, who had but little confidence in the Roman troops, and aware of the renown of the Gothic soldiers, insisted that five hundred of them should be embarked with the expedition. This Attalus refused. Sharp words were exchanged. The Gothic king reproached the Roman emperor, whom he had himself created, with incapacity. In the same moment he ordered the army under arms, and directed Attalus to be taken to the middle of the camp, where, in the presence of the imperial guards and the Barbarians, he, with his own hands, took the diadem from his brow, and despoiled him of the purple, which he immediately sent to Honorius, as the pledge of his sincerity in offering to renew the negociations which that ill-advised monarch had so often before rejected. Honorius listened to this proposal, but required that the usurper, as he called Attalus, with his son Ampalius, must be delivered up. To this however the noble-minded Goth, without noticing the request, replied, by declaring that, as he considered himself responsible for what Attalus had done, the first article of the treaty must be his unconditional pardon. This was acceded to;—and Alaric advanced within three miles of Ravenna, to complete the negociation. But the members of a dissolute court were incapable of comprehending the noble nature, and the lofty motives, by which the generous Barbarian was actuated; and the imperial ministers, attributing his conduct to some change in his fortune, resumed their wonted insolence towards him. Sarus, a rival chieftain, who happened to arrive at this time at Ravenna, was welcomed by them with open arms; and they had the perfidy, while treating with Alaric, to allow him to sally from the gates, with three hundred men, to attempt the seizure of the Gothic king. The enterprise was nearly successful. Sarus cut in pieces a considerable body of the Goths, and re-entered the city in triumph. This petty exploit intoxicated the imperial ministers with more madness than wine; and next day they sent a herald to Alaric, to declare that he was for ever excluded from the friendship and alliance of Honorius.

"The astonishment with which Alaric at first listened to this audacious guilt was quickly succeeded by a tempest of passion. The thought of the forbearance and moderation which he had hitherto shown, was to his rage like oil thrown upon fire; and his resentment, partaking of the generosity of his spirit, flamed up into the sublime wrath of a divine avenger. He exclaimed against the crimes of Rome, her treachery, and her aggressions; and, grasping his sword with terrific fierceness, drew it from the scabbard, never to be sheathed till he had punished the iniquities which he had too long spared. In the same moment he mounted his horse, and joined the main body of his army, which was then encamped under the walls of the capital, on the meadows of the Tyber. The cause of his sudden return was soon known: the soldiers flew to arms; the camp echoed with shouts, that filled the city with consternation; the gates were hastily shut; the senators rushed to the capitol; and Alaric, without dismounting from his horse, declared to his troops, that he was now resolved to wreak a terrible vengeance on the guilty city. 'All the wealth that it contains,' he exclaimed, with vehemence, 'you have twice before won, and it is yours again; therefore seize it freely: but shed not the blood of those who make no resistance, nor profane the sanctuaries to which the weak and the fearful may fly from you for refuge, especially the churches of the Apostles St. Peter and St. Paul, in which, from their magnitude, the greater numbers will be found. Let us show that we respect religion, and that we have drawn the sword not for conquest, but in the holy cause of avenging justice.' A proclamation to the same effect was afterwards published; and the remainder of the day was spent by the Barbarians in making preparations for the assault.

"In the meantime the dismay within the walls amounted to despair. The senators sat till the evening in the capitol, expecting some communication from the avenger; but the sentence was pronounced, and the interval was but that phantasma of horror between doom and execution. I felt myself in this terrible crisis under the influence of an awful spirit; my soul was troubled with a strange emotion; my heart swelled, and sudden tears often gushed from my eyes. I walked the streets, and saw every one actuated by the same terrible thought; alarm was in every eye, and hurry in all their steps. No one stopped to speak; all hastened on their respective purposes. Business was at an end; the shops were shut, but every door was open; and the slaves stood in bands, with fierce and treacherous aspects. An audacious familiarity was in the looks of the felons employed in the street, and they suspended their abject tasks, and shook their chains with hideous exultation. The churches were thronged; and many a Pagan temple, that had been closed for years, was filled with votaries that had long been esteemed exemplary Christians. It was the day of vengeance, and no one had courage to practice his wonted hypocrisy.

"The sun at last set, but still no messenger came from Alaric; the senators, hoping that he would yet respite the city, went to their respective palaces; and an apparent confidence seemed to be restored, when it was understood that they had retired home; but it was like the unblest repose procured by medicine,—the slightest disturbance was calculated to raise it into fury. The slaves, particularly those of Gothic origin, whose demeanour had been distinguished by an ill-restrained insolence during the day, kept possession of the streets, disobeyed the summons of their masters, and, as the citizens gradually retired to rest, their bands, as if brought together by some occult sympathy, coalesced into formidable bodies. About the hour of midnight one of these bands opened the Salarian gate. The avenger entered; and, in the same moment, a tremendous blast of the Gothic trumpets startled the sleepers. The mutinous slaves answered the sound with shouts from all quarters; and the enemy pouring in, the work of revenge, of punishment, and destruction, commenced.

"The orders of Alaric were for sometime faithfully obeyed; and the horrors of the sack were, on the part of the well-disciplined Goths, unstained with any excesses.

"While they roamed through the city in quest of prey, one of them forced open the humble dwelling of an aged virgin, who had devoted her life to the service of the ——, and demanded all the gold and silver in her possession. She made no reply; but immediately conducted —— a splendid hoard of massy plate, of the richest —— and the most curious workmanship. The Barbarian viewed with wonder and delight this valuable acquisition, till he was interrupted by a serious admonition. 'These,' said the venerable sister, 'are consecrated vessels belonging to St. Peter; if you presume to touch them, the sacrilegious deed will remain on your conscience; for my part, I dare not keep what I am unable to defend.' The Goth was struck with awe, and dispatched a messenger to inform the king of the treasure which he had discovered. Alaric instantly ordered that all the consecrated plate and ornaments should be transported without damage or delay to the church of the Apostle. A numerous detachment of soldiers protected a procession of their devout companions, who bore aloft on their heads the sacred vessels of gold and silver; and the martial shouts were mingled with the sound of religious psalmody, as they marched along from the Quirinal-hill to the Vatican.

"But this moderation did not last long: the citizens sometimes defended their treasures with arms. Resistance provoked retaliation; and the orders of Alaric were forgotten in the moment of fury. Slaughter ensued: the slaves indulged in their private revenge; and the tragedy of rapine, sensuality, and blood, grew more dark and busy.

"The matrons and virgins were exposed to injuries more dreadful in the apprehension of chastity than death itself; but even in these offences, the simplicity of the Gothic character, as contrasted with the licentiousness of the Roman slaves, was eminently distinguished. A lady of singular beauty had excited the impatient desires of a young Goth. Provoked by her obstinate resistance, he drew his sword; and, with the anger of a lover, slightly wounded her neck. The bleeding heroine still continued to brave his resentment, and to repel his passion, till the ravisher, subdued by her entreaties or awed by her virtue, at length desisted, and respectfully conducted her to the sanctuary of St. Peter's church, where he gave six pieces of gold to the guards, on condition that they should restore her inviolate to the arms of her husband.

"In the meantime a furious conflagration was gradually spreading. The Goths, at their entrance through the Salarian gate, fired some of the adjacent houses, to guide them in the dreadful business of the night, and the flames being neglected in the general confusion, rose to such a height, that the horrible work of sack and havoc was obliged to be suspended before their progress was arrested. Many public and private buildings of great magnificence were destroyed. At the same time, a tremendous thunder-storm came on; the wrath of heaven, in peal after peal, was mingled with the shouts of the avengers; and the proud Forum, adorned with the statues of so many gods and heroes, was, in this final night, levelled by the lightning into dust. I could not but see with stern satisfaction the fiery right arm of Jehovah stretched from the cloud, and crushing the monuments of that military dominion which had overwhelmed so many nations. I remembered the destruction of Jerusalem by Titus, and contemplated the spreading volumes of the flames that involved these stately edifices, as the retribution due for the calamities which the Romans, in their pride of power, lavished on the house of Israel.

"On this night the sceptre was wrested from Rome, and the sword for ever taken from her. She has been—and is no more. The ruins of her greatness fill the world; and the story of the Consuls and the Cæsars is ended."

CHAPTER XXIII.

Summary of Events from the Sack of Rome by the Goths, till the Plundering of it by Vandals.

THE victorious Goths evacuated Rome on the sixth day after their conquest; and our author accompanied them in their expedition to the southward. Their intrepid leader led his army, encumbered with spoil, along the Appian Way, destroying whatever dared to oppose his passage. Whether fame, conquest, or riches, were the object of Alaric, he pursued that object with an indefatigable ardour, which could neither be quelled by adversity nor satiated by success. No sooner had he reached the shores of Calabria than he was attracted by the neighbouring prospect of Sicily, whose fertile and romantic coast invited his ambition. But, even the possession of that delightful island, he considered only as an intermediate step to an expedition which he already meditated against the continent of Africa. This design, however, was frustrated by his death; and our author, in allusion to his funeral, says, " It displayed the ferocious character of the Barbarians. By the labour of a captive multitude, they diverted the course of the river Busentinus; and, in the depths of the vacant bed, constructed a grave, in which they deposited the remains of their hero, with some of the most splendid of the trophies brought from Rome, and then restored the waters to their natural channel. The better to conceal the secret spot, they inhumanly massacred all the prisoners who had been employed to execute the work."

Among the captives whom the conquerors carried from Rome, was Placida, the sister of the emperor, with whom Adolphus, the successor of Alaric, became enamoured, and was desirous of marrying. He made proposals accordingly to the ministers of Honorius, but they rejected his offer with scorn, and demanded the restitution of the princess, as the preliminary condition of entering into any treaty with the Goths. Placida herself, however, was not so haughty to her young and valiant conqueror: she consented to his wishes; and their wedding was celebrated with a degree of pomp, that constitutes it one of the most remarkable banquets recorded in history.

The bride, attired and adorned like a Roman empress, was placed on a throne of state; and the king of the Goths, who assumed on this occasion the Roman habit, contented himself with a less honourable seat by her side. The table was adorned with the richest spoils of Rome, consisting of chalices of gold, enriched with exquisite carvings ornamented with jewels, and of plates of entire pieces of emerald encircled with pearls. Fifty beautiful youths, in silken robes, carrying a bason in each hand, filled with pieces of gold and precious stones, presented to Placida a nuptial present, according to the custom of the Goths;—but it was drawn from the plunder of her country. She was observed to sigh as it was offered; but, in the same moment, she took the hand of Adolphus, and pressed it to her heart.

By the intercession of Placida, an arrangement took place, under which the Goths consented to retire from Italy; and they were led by Adolphus into Gaul. Here an opportunity presented itself of avenging the treacherous sally of Sarus on Alaric at Ravenna. In an unguarded moment, Adolphus attacked that chieftain and put him to death. But his fall was in turn not long unrevenged. The Goths having entered Spain, were lying at Barcelona, when their queen was delivered of a son, who did not long survive his birth. While her tears were yet flowing for his loss, one of the followers of Sarus, whom Adolphus had imprudently taken into his service, irritated by some observations on his own diminutive person, assassinated the king; and Singeric, a stranger to the royal race, the brother of Sarus, was raised to the throne. The first act of his reign, was the murder of the six children of Adolphus, the issue of a former marriage, whom he tore, without pity, from the feeble arms of an aged bishop, to whose care they had been entrusted. The unfortunate Placida, instead of the compassion due to her situation and birth, was treated with wanton cruelty, and obliged to march on foot above twelve miles, confounded among a crowd of vulgar captives, before the horse of the assassin of her husband.

These notes are necessary, to connect the Narrative of our author; for his memoranda, respecting his residence with Adolphus and Placida, are confused, abrupt, and imperfect.

CHAPTER XXIV.

The Revolt of Bonifacius in Africa—His Union with Genseric the Vandal—Their Rupture—Rome plundered by the Vandals.

[A. D. 415—435—476.]

As far as we can make out the matter distinctly, Hareach, on the elevation of Singeric to the Gothic throne, passed suddenly over into Africa; for the notes which immediately follow the account of the ignominious treatment of Placida, relate to transactions in that country: and we know, from history, that Singeric was only permitted to reign seven days. These notes are not in themselves interesting. They describe the remains of the Roman armies as still waging an ineffectual war with the Vandals, who overran the African provinces much in the same manner as the Goths laid waste those of Europe; and we find the same precarious loyalty and insubordinate spirit actuating the commanders who received their appointments from the emperor. We cannot however omit to notice what our author says respecting Bonifacius, the imperial general; and his description of Genseric, the king of the Vandals.

"Sigisvult the Goth, who was sent by the court of Ravenna to subdue Bonifacius, continues to make head against the revolt. He has taken Carthage and Hippo. Bonifacius, alarmed at this, has entered into a treaty with Genseric the Vandal, and they have agreed to unite their forces against the imperials, and divide the sovereignty of Africa between them —— ***

"In consequence of this treaty, the Vandals, with their wives and children, have left Spain; and, crossing the sea at the straits of Hercules, are now in the country. The situation of Bonifacius is extremely perplexing. It appears that the injuries which induced him to revolt, were owing to misrepresentations of Aetius; so that he is as anxious to get rid of the Vandals, as he was before desirous of their assistance —— ***

"Genseric considers himself as allured into a snare by the Roman, and is exceedingly indignant. He has requested to see Bonifacius; and the latter, distrusting his integrity, has appointed the place of meeting at some distance from their armies, and has gone to it with a guard —— ***

"The appearance of Genseric is not calculated to inspire confidence; his demeanour is vulgar and unprepossessing. He seems always rapt in profound thought, and says little; but his sentences are pregnant with reflection. Notwithstanding his mean deportment, there is much of the element of heroic greatness in his character: an enemy to intemperance of every kind, he is abstemious and severe to himself. His manners are marked with firmness and rectitude, by which the affections of his people are knit to his fortunes; even his enemies respect his declarations; and, if two different accounts of the same affair give more credit to his statements than those of their own officers, his courage is also the theme of the soldiers' admiration, whether in his own or in the ranks of his adversaries. But these qualities, which, mingled with benevolence, would have been virtues, are rendered odious by his merciless cruelty. At the death of the late king Garderic, his brother, he put the widow to death, and ordered all her children to be slaughtered, that his possession of the throne might not be endangered by the claims of any lawful competitor —— * * *

"The interview has terminated as might have been expected. Bonifacius offered the Vandal a large sum of money to retire from Africa, and try his fortunes again in Spain. Genseric returned a contemptuous answer; high words arose; swords were drawn; and their respective guards took this as a signal for conflict. The Vandals proving superior to the Romans, nearly cut the whole of them to pieces; and Bonifacius with difficulty has escaped to Hippo.

"Carthage, Hippo, and Cirtha, are now the only places in all Africa that obey the laws and mandates of the Roman emperor —— * * *

"Carthage is taken by Genseric, after having remained subject to Rome five hundred and eighty-five years —— * * *

"Genseric, the conqueror of Carthage, is actually preparing to invade Italy.

"He has made himself master of Rome; and the Vandals are now plundering that degraded and devoted city. He has taken possession of the palace, and has sent Eudoxia the empress, and her two daughters aboard his ship, as captives. The gilded brass from the roof of the capitol he has torn off; and the sacred vessels that belonged to the temple of Jerusalem,—the spoils of Titus,—that Alaric on account of their holiness refrained from touching, are among his trophies —— * * *

"We are again in Carthage. The vessels dedicated to the service of the temple, are saved from profanation.

A storm was sent from heaven to preserve them; and they are now safely deposited in the treasury of the ocean ——— * * *

"Genseric has married his eldest son Hunneric to one of the imperial daughters ——— * * *

"There is no end to the enterprises of this ambitious and indefatigable man. He has sent an expedition against the Greek Islands ——— * * *

"How unstable is the fortune that is erected on the ruins of war! Disaster after disaster withers the power of Genseric. The Romans have made wonderful exertions; and he considers his situation so desperate, that it is reported he intends to abandon Carthage ——— * * *

"The destiny of Genseric is still triumphant. He has made incredible exertions; and the Roman fleet that menaced him with an utter overthrow, has been put to flight" ——— * * *

These extracts comprehend the most remarkable incidents mentioned by our author during the time that he was in Africa, or connected with the Vandals. It would seem that, soon after the dispersion of the Roman fleet, he went back to Italy; for a number of obscure hints, and imperfect sentences, tend to show that he must have been in that country when Odoacer abolished the nominal sovereignty of Rome, and in the city, when that conqueror ordered himself to be proclaimed king of Italy. We shall extract his account of the ceremonies.

CHAPTER XXV.

The Last Day of the Roman Sovereignty.

" ODOACER has acted with more moderation than was expected from the fierceness of his character. He has spared the life of Augustulus, the young emperor; but has confined him for the present to the castle of Lucullanum, after however stripping him of all the imperial insignia.

" He entered the city last night, and has taken possession of the palace. A vague rumour is abroad this morning, that he intends to assume the imperial dignity himself, and will re-assemble the senate. But some doubt the truth of this opinion; alleging, how can he wear the purple but as commander of the Roman armies?

" Many of the senators have been to the palace, and were received by him with respectful civility; but his conversation related to indifferent topics, and he did not recognise them as possessing any other rank than the common herd of the nobility. This has damped their expectation exceedingly; and they begin to fear that he entertains some undivulged project, fatal to their ancient dignity.

" A great sensation has been excited throughout the city. The heralds of Odoacer, in their garbs of ceremony, attended by a sumptuous retinue of his guards, have gone towards the capitol. The whole population of Rome is pushing in that direction. It is a fearful crowd; the high-born and the ignoble, the freeman and the slave, all who have part or interest in the fate of the universal city,—are animated by one sentiment, and press forward to hear the proclamation of Odoacer.

"I obtained by accident a favourable place, on the pedestal of a broken statue, for hearing the heralds. The soldiers lined the stairs ascending to the portico, and they made a gay and glittering appearance; the skies were overcast with masses of black clouds, but a splendid burst of sunshine fell on them, and they shone as it were in glorious contrast to the Romans, who were obscured with the shadows. The assembled crowd was prodigious. The whole space around the foot of the hill, and as far as the eye could reach along the streets in every direction, was a mosaic of human faces. It was an appalling sight to look on such a multitude. It was, as when the waters are out, and the landmarks are flooded, and a wide deluge overspreads the wonted bounds of the river. The slightest simultaneous action of so many thousands seemed, by its own physical mass, capable of treading into dust the conqueror and all his armies; but nothing could more effectually demonstrate the entire extinction of the Roman spirit, than the mercurial fluidity of this enormous multitude.

"Some little time passed before the chief herald was in readiness to read the proclamation. He at first ascended to the portico of the building, seemingly with the intention of reading it there; but, on some observations from the officer who commanded the guard, he returned between the ranks of the soldiers, about half way down the steps. At this moment a loud rushing sound rose from the crowd; and, when he had taken his station, the trumpets sounded a solemn flourish. My eye involuntarily turned towards the capitol, where, for so many ages, the oracle of the Roman people had proclaimed slavery and degradation to the kingdoms of the earth. It was in ruins. The roof, which had not been repaired since it was stripped of its golden covering by Genseric, had fallen in in several places.

"The trumpets ceased; there was a profound silence; and the herald, with a loud voice, proclaimed Odoacer king of Italy, without even mentioning the Roman name. An awful response rose from the multitude. It was not a sigh, nor a murmur, nor a sound like any thing I had ever before heard; but a deep and dreadful sob, as if some mighty life had in that ultimate crisis expired. It subdued the soldiers of Odoacer; and I saw them look at one another and grow pale, as if chilled with supernatural fear. The very flesh crawled on my own bones; and it was with difficulty that my faultering knees sustained me where I stood.

"But this sublime paroxysm did not last long. The soldiers soon recovered their wonted self-possession, and cried out 'Long live Odoacer king of Italy!' to which the crowd, as if suddenly transmuted from the Roman into another character, answered, with a magnificent shout, that reverberated through the empty halls of the capitol, 'Odoacer king of Italy!' Thus was the very name of Rome expunged from the sovereignties of the world; and all her glory, her greatness, and her crimes, reduced to an epitaph."

We should here mention, that this great event happened in the four hundred and seventy-sixth year of the Christian era; five hundred and seventy years after the battle of Actium, when the imperial monarchy was first established; and one thousand three hundred and twenty-four, from the foundation of the city.

CHAPTER XXVI.

Establishment of the Salique Law in France.

[A. D. 486.]

HAVING followed the wanderings of our mysterious author, in the interesting transactions that completed the secular history of Rome, we have now to trace his movements among the first rudiments of a nation, which, in our own time, has emulated the pride, pomp, and circumstance of the Romans, in the periods of their highest prosperity. After the proclamation of Odoacer, Hareach appears to have crossed the Alps; but we are furnished with no clue to the motive which induced him to undertake this journey, nor indeed of the exact time when it was performed; for his narrative is very illegibly written, and damp, in many places, has destroyed the ink. But he was certainly at Soissons when Clovis, the first of the French kings, established the salic law; that celebrated law, which declares that "in respect to salic land, no part of it shall ever be inherited by a woman; but, being acquired by the males, males only shall be capable of the succession,—is still admitted as the fundamental law of the French monarchy. Before proceeding with the narrative of Hareach, it may be proper to give some account of the probable origin of this law, and the few authentic particulars that are known respecting its history.

The Franks, before their irruption into Gaul, inhabited a part of Germany which, in the old geographical tables, is from thence denominated Francia; and by some authors it is called Old France, and by others the Germanic France, to distinguish it from the country that now bears the same name. The Franks were composed of several tribes, each having its particular chief. Thus, at the same time that Clovis was king of the Salians, Sigebert reigned in the same quality over the Repuarians, and other princes over other tribes. Each of these tribes had their particular customs, which, being collected and reduced to writing, form the code of their laws; and hence it is most probable, that what is styled the Salique law, received that name from being the code of the customs that prevailed among the Salians. What now exists is not, strictly speaking, the Salique law, because it is not the entire code, but an abstract of it. There are two editions: the first was printed by John Basil, a herald in 1557, from a manuscript which, before the revolution, was in the abbey of Fulde; and the other later, as comprehending the alterations and additions made by several kings: but they agree very well in the main, and show clearly that they were the customs which prevailed amongst a barbarous and warlike people, in order to prevent them from raising the sword at every turn against each other.

This abstract is divided into seventy-one heads, penned in vile Latin, full of barbarous word borrowed from different languages. They prescribe punishment for murder, theft, injuries, and all the various kinds of violence to which the subjects of such fierce and rude nations were addicted. But it is remarkable, that they do not contain one single word respecting priests, sacrifices, or religion.

It is not easy to fix their origin; some attribute them to Pharamond, others believe them still more ancient. It seems however to be generally agreed, that Clovis published them in their present state, or rather gave his sanction to that code from which the abstract alluded to has been made. They are now become chiefly famous, for the few lines in the sixty-second head, which we have quoted, and by which it has been contended, that this law disabled the daughters from inheriting the crown of France; in which, if there is any truth, it must be by construction.

The Salians, as we have observed, were only one tribe

of the Franks. When they were fixed in their conquests, the king rewarded eminent services by grants of lands subject to military aid. These lands thus granted, were the lands mentioned in the law, and such an estate was styled Salique ground, or land held according to this Salique custom. These estates were opposed to another kind of estates which were styled allodial, and might be acquired by descent, by marriage, or by purchase. Of the six articles which constitute the sixty-second head of the code, five relate to the succession of allodial property, in which the females are fully as much favoured as the males.

But it is time that we should leave this legal disquisition, and return to the descriptive anecdotes of our author; before doing so, however, we may extract his reflections respecting the Salique law.

"Clovis, by declaring the customs of his warlike tribe the laws of his kingdom, is laying the foundations of a military nation. This principle of giving lands to his officers, on the condition that they shall always be prepared to attend him in war, is constituting the nucleus of a force, very different in its nature from the organized bodies of the departed Roman empire. The citizens will become soldiers, and the soldiers citizens;—all the institutions of the nation must necessarily therefore partake of a military character, and military ambition be the primary object of the government: since renown in arms cannot, by such an order of things, fail to be the darling passion of the people. The establishment of this military relationship, combined with civil ties, indicates a new modification of society. There will be more stability of government than formerly, the military will be less licentious in the use of power, being thus identified with property; and the exercise of the sovereign authority is less likely to be disturbed by the audacity or ambition of adventurers."

CHAPTER XXVII.

The Foundation of the French Monarchy.

[A.D 510.]

"CLOVIS," observes our author, "is without doubt a sagacious monarch; but he is one of the sternest of all the Barbarian princes that have seated themselves within the bounds of the ancient empire.

"The sovereign of Constantinople has sent him a purple robe and a diadem, which he has accepted, and affects to be honoured by the gift; but, from the pomp with which he directed himself to be invested, it is evident that there is more of policy than of gratitude in his feeling.

"I have not been mistaken. Clovis makes it known, that he considers himself as deserving some superiority of power from the Eastern emperor by those gifts of royalty; and his craft is busily at work, to subvert the chieftainships of the other tribes of Franks, that he may have the whole nation under the dominion of his own posterity ——— * * *

"His hint to Chloderic, the son of Sigibert, the king of Cologne, that his father had spun the thread of life too long, was not without effect. Chloderic committed parricide; and Clovis, affecting great indignation at the crime, bribed one of his attendants to stab him while he was in the act of taking possession of the old man's treasure.

"His treatment of Chararic king of Cambray, and his son, has been no less unprincipled: he caused them both to be shaved, and to become priests. The prince having indignantly said that the locks of Samson grew again, he has struck off both their heads.

"In the perpetration of this bloody policy he is as audacious as he is unjust. Having seduced the ministers of Ragnacharius to deliver him and his brother Richarius into his hands, he reproached the unfortunate princes for suffering themselves to be chained; and, bursting into a great passion, he cleft them down on the spot with his battle-axe. Their perfidious ministers, discovering that he had paid the hire of their guilt in gilded copper, complained of the fraud, and he bluntly replied, 'I always pay traitors in that coin.'

"An incident has occurred inconceivably ridiculous. Clovis is dead; and the monks and ecclesiastics, are talking of placing his name among the list of the saints. What will posterity think of this? or will history be so falsified, that he will actually be regarded as such by posterity? His dominions have been divided among his four sons —— * * *

"The state of Clovis, founded in blood and treachery, is rapidly advancing in crime. Thieri, Clodimir, Childebert, and Clotaire, his four sons, under the influence of Queen Clotildis, a woman of extraordinary prudence, were preserved for several years in amity. But Clodimir being slain in battle, and leaving three sons, his brothers have taken possession of his dominions, under the pretext of being guardians of the children.

"Thieri seems resolved to possess himself of the territories of Clotaire. On a late occasion he invited him to a banquet; but Clotaire, on entering the hall, saw the feet of armed men behind the tapestry, and suspecting his brother's intentions, beckoned on his attendants to come forward. This disconcerted Thieri, and he endeavoured to treat him with unusual complaisance —— * * *

"Clotildis, their mother, being at Paris, with her three grandchildren,—the sons of their brother Clodimir,—she pressed Childebert to do justice to the orphans; and he, seeming to acquiesce in her demand, sent for Clotaire, to arrange the method of putting them in possession of their dominions. On his arrival the young princes were sent for; and the queen, confiding in their affection, delivered them to the messengers. But her fears were soon awakened, when informed by some of her domestics that they were placed under a guard. At this moment

Arcadius, the minister of Childebert, entered her apartment, with a sword in one hand, and a pair of scissars in the other, and informed her that he was desired by the brother-kings to enquire which she would prefer for the children. She was filled with horror; for, by the signs, she perceived that the choice was between putting them to death and making them priests. In a fit of despair, she exclaimed—'Rather let the orphans die than become monks.' On this being repeated to the two kings, Clotaire immediately stabbed the eldest boy, who was about ten years old, with his dagger. The second, about seven, embraced the knees of his uncle Childebert, by which he was so much moved, that he implored Clotaire to spare the child; but the ferocious Frank cried out ' It was at your instigation that I engaged in this bloody work;—die yourself, or let me finish what you have begun.' Childebert affrighted, stepped out of his way, and he instantly dispatched the crying child. During this short dispute, the feelings of his domestics were overcome by this hideous tragedy; and they contrived to convey the last of the orphans to a monastery, the sanctuary of which the royal ruffians did not dare to violate.

"As Thieri had no hand in this massacre, it might have been expected that he would have made it a pretext to raise a war against his brothers, whose portion of their father's dominions he was as desirous of obtaining as they were to keep possession of the birth-right of Clodimir's children. But, either he has not found himself in a condition to do so with any success, or he is contented with the share that they have offered,—for he is reconciled to them" —— * * *

The affairs of these fickle, ambitious, and deceitful, Franks, are more remarkable than interesting; and the observations which our author makes on them do not possess that picturesque distinctness which we find in some other passages of his book. The history, however, of Fredegonde, the mistress of Chilpercic, the son of Clotaire, and who succeeded his father as king of Soissons, is an exception, and is worthy of a separate Chapter.

CHAPTER XXVIII.

The Story of Chilperic and Fredigonde.

"Fredigonde was the daughter of a peasant, and Chilperic, when they were both very young, took her for his concubine. She was endowed with the most exquisite beauty, and possessed a mind rich in many fascinating qualities, but without principle or virtue. After they had lived together several years, he became enamoured of Andovera, the daughter of a neighbour prince, and made her his queen.

"This event was naturally calculated to excite into activity all the latent bad passions of the peasant's daughter; but she disguised her malice; and, with infinite address and affected humility and tenderness, obtained permission to remain at court in the capacity of an attendant on Andovera. In this situation, she not only gained the confidence of her royal mistress, but acquired an ascendancy over the mind of Chilperic,—such as she had not before aspired to. Her object was not only to effect the divorce of the queen, but to raise herself into the throne. For this purpose, she laboured with a degree of skill and perseverance, that rendered her conduct a model of intrigue; and she so far succeeded, that Andovera was, on the slight pretence of a religious scruple, imprisoned in a monastery.

"The ambition however of Fredigonde, was for this time frustrated. Sigebert, the brother of Chilperic, having married Brunchaut, a Spanish princess, with whom he received a vast treasure as a dower, the approbation with which this match was received by his subjects, induced the mutable Chilperic to resolve on asking the hand of her sister Galswintha. Fredigonde was, in consequence, on the very day that she anticipated her elevation to the throne, dismissed from the court.

"The proposal to Galswintha being accepted, she was conducted with great pomp to Soissons, and the marriage celebrated amidst the acclamations of the satisfied people. But this joy was not of long continuance. Chilperic found Galswintha less beautiful than he was taught to expect; and he soon treated her with indifference; which Fredigonde learning from some of her friends, was induced to throw herself again in the king's way. This she accomplished by falling in with him, as it were by accident, while he was hunting. Their intercourse was renewed, and her wonted ascendancy restored.

"The queen, on learning this, requested permission to return to her own country; but Chilperic refused his consent, while with Fredigonde he planned and executed a design which covers his name with indelible infamy. He pretended to soothe Galswintha with the appearance of much contrition for his infidelity; and finally succeeded in lulling her jealousy, and in convincing his people that they lived in perfect conjugal felicity. While this impression was strongest, he strangled her in bed, and gave it out to the public, with all the ostentation of profound and inconsolable sorrow, that she had died of a fit in his arms.

"The story was believed for a few days; and perhaps, had he acted with more caution, and Fredigonde been less distrustful of his unstable character, the crime might have sunk into oblivion, among the other undivulged offences of secret criminals. Might, did I say?—It was murder: and the blood of the murdered ever cries to heaven till the deed is expiated.

"On the third day after the death of the unfortunate Galswintha, Fredigonde came privately to court, and refused to quit Chilperic until he had openly raised her to the royal dignity. Cajoled by her blandishments, he complied with her requests; and the preparations for their nuptials, and the funeral of the queen, went forward at the same time together.

"This awakened suspicions; and Brunchaut, the wife of Sigebert, in affliction for the loss of her sister, urged him to revenge the guilt of her murder, and the insult which the criminals had committed to her memory so soon after her death. Sigebert, sympathising with the indignation of his queen, not only immediately put his forces in motion against Chilperic, but obtaining also the aid of Gontran king of Orleans, invaded the territory of Soissons, and besieged the city, while the guilty pair were enjoying the empoisoned revelries of their marriage-feast. The event overwhelmed them with consternation. Chilperic, in the panic of the moment, betrayed the cowardly apprehensions of his conscience. But Fredigonde, with more than masculine self-possession, rose like a stirred-up flame in the alarm, and displayed a courage and fortitude that would have done honour to molested virtue. Inspirited by her example, the soldiers flew to arms, the walls were manned, and the avengers repulsed, and forced to raise the siege. But they soon rallied; and Sigebert returning to the assault, the army of Chilperic was defeated, and he was glad to purchase a hasty peace, by the surrender of several of his most important towns. The success of Sigebert was soon however resented in a manner worthy of Fredigonde. She prevailed on two desperate men to murder him; and who, under the pretext of having matter of great importance to communicate only to his own ear, obtained access to his tent, and buried their daggers in his bowels.

"As soon as this perfidious tragedy was performed, Fredigonde seized the widow, children, and treasures, of Sigebert, and sent them prisoners to Rouen. Meroreus, the eldest son of Chilperic by Andovera, having been much struck with the beauty of Brunchaut, visited her privately, and, in the end, persuaded her to marry him. This exceedingly exasperated Fredigonde, who attributed all the troubles of her royal condition to that princess; and, after many complex and guilty artifices, succeeded in separating Meroreus from his wife, and having imprisoned him in a fortress, ordered him to be secretly put to death.

"In the meantime, this she-wolf had formed an attachment for one of her officers of the name of Landry. Chilperic by accident discovered it, and vowed revenge;

but, before he could take any steps to arrest her and her paramour, he was assassinated by one of his own domestics. Her situation, however, was not greatly improved by this new crime. She had offended the bad by her pride, and the good by her vices; and, when she was no longer supported by the authority of the king, even the abject ventured to resent her inordinate arrogance; for she had all that presumption of the ignoble, elevated out of their sphere not by merit but fortune, by which their prosperity is ever rendered obnoxious to those around them.

"I was at Rouen when the sacrilege was committed on Pretextatus the bishop, who had married her step-son Meroreus to Brunchaut. As the prelate was assisting in the wonted service at the altar, a stranger entered the church, and, without pausing to perform the customary homage of worship, walked directly up towards the bishop. This singular circumstance occasioned the whole congregation to turn their eyes towards him; for, being in armour, the sound of his approach resounded through the cathedral; and they saw, with an emotion of surprise and dread, a naked dagger in his hand. He never halted, but walked straight on; and, on reaching Pretextatus, stabbed him in the side. Having executed this mysterious act of vengeance, he turned round, and, with the same resounding step, grasping his bloody instrument, walked to the door, and disappeared. The congregation, entranced with horror and astonishment, were deprived of the power of action; and it was not until the wounded bishop himself called for assistance, that any one thought of pursuing the assassin.

" Fredigonde, who was then in the city, affected to be greatly shocked at the sacrilege, and went to visit the bishop at his residence. She told him how happy she should be to see the criminal apprehended and punished.—' The criminal,' said the bishop with emphasis, ' is no other than the same person who has filled the kingdom with crimes, who has murdered kings, and shed rivers of innocent blood." She pretended not to understand him; but, with a soothing, kindly manner, offered her own physicians to attend him; an insult which so provoked the dying man, that he told her with indignation, 'You are yourself the criminal—you caused me to be assassinated. It is you alone who has practised so many hideous crimes, and who, universally execrated in this world, will be everlastingly punished in the next:' and, in uttering these words, he expired."

Our author takes no farther notice of this atrocious female. Indeed, he appears about this time to have left Rouen for the South, and to have embarked at Marseilles for Constantinople; and therefore we may mention here, before proceeding with our extracts, that, notwithstanding her manifold iniquities, this intrepid delinquent, after having governed the kingdom of her husband and son for nearly thirty years, was allowed to die in peace, and in the possession of the royal dignity. But she was not unpunished; for her life was one continued conflict of vicissitudes; and, although she sustained them with Promethean fortitude, she was so constantly pushed to the brink of ignominious ruin, that she had no taste of rational enjoyment. Her offences were so great, that it might almost be said that heaven had no other mode of punishing her.

CHAPTER XXIX.

State of the Eastern Church in the Age of Mahomet.

In his voyage from Marseilles to Constantinople our author met with no adventures; and, on his arrival at the Eastern capital, where he remained but a short time, we find only a few detached reflections on the state of the city, not tending to afford us any satisfactory information.

From Constantinople he passed to Nicomedia by water; and he describes that city as being in a state of great decay. An earthquake had many years before shaken the imperial residence into ruins; and pestilence, at different periods, had thinned the inhabitants.

From Nicomedia he travelled to Antioch, which he describes as still more declined from its ancient greatness. The groves of Daphne were laid waste, and a convent built on the scite of the temple. In the course of his journey, he speaks of Christian churches being erected everywhere on the spots where he had formerly seen temples; but, in entering them, he says, " I seek in vain for the Christian religion. An unmeaning chant of prayers has been substituted for those sublime exhortations to benevolence, and the reciprocities of kindness, which constituted the sermons of the early preachers. Where there are no idols there are pictures, and the name of Jesus is confounded in a list of saints, respecting whom few of the worshippers know more than the name.

" It seems to me that the Pagan religion is in a great measure restored, but in a more fanatical and irrational form; for the ancient Pagans, in their worship, believed in gods suited to the different occasions for which they required celestial aid. In their love, they addressed themselves to Cupid and Venus; in their vengeance, to Jove; in their voyages, to Neptune and Æolus; and, in their wars and resentments, to Mars. But, to the human deities of these new idolaters, a universal influence is ascribed; and the saint is preferred, according to the fancy of the suppliant, without regard to any particular power which he may be supposed to possess. Independent of all this, the Pagan mythology was much more cheerful, and the deference paid to the priests was of a more grateful kind than the reverence exacted by the priests of the Christian mythology. I must call it by that name; for they do still use the name of Christ, and profess to be Christians.

" The religious ceremonies, in honour of the ancient gods, were celebrated in a spirit of festivity. They were so many joyous expressions of gratitude for favour conferred, and of confidence in their protection; and the heart of the votary was in consequence gay, his steps light, and his voice musical. But now, the days of celebration are solemn, and the rites morose; for they commemorate tortures and oppression. It would seem, that the objects of the new apotheosis acquire their title to reverence and adoration, by the degree of corporeal anguish to which they were subjected in their lives, without any great respect to the rectitude and virtue of their moral conduct; and it is to this cause that I would attribute the gloom and heaviness that weighs upon the heart at their festivals.

"Under the Pagan system, the priests were respected on account of the communion which it was supposed they occasionally held with their respective gods; but these Christian priests do not pretend to this high intercourse. They however affect to have received a power to acquit the confessing sinner of his sins; and they dispense this power with the natural corruption of man. The consequence is, that they are regarded with emotions of dread by the conscious offender; and, as it is a part of their system to inculcate that all have offended, their influence is only limited by the number of their votaries. Pretending thus to hold the keys of heaven and hell, they have acquired a degree of power to which the Pagan priests never laid any claim; for, under the old religion, immortality after death did not depend on the favour of the heavenly powers; nor was it ever very clearly understood by the Pagans, that their gods had any authority over man when he had once crossed the Styx in Charon's ferry-boat —— * * *

"How long this eclipse of the human understanding is to last, is impossible to be conjectured; but it is evident that, when once a man can submit to allow his reason to be bound in fetters to the opinions of another, there is nothing too gross for him to credit. On the first preaching of Christianity, a visible improvement in morals and manners took place; and it was held that, to be a Christian, it was necessary to be more pure, blameless, and holy, than other men. But this is no longer the case;—it is only necessary to submit entirely to the dictation of the priesthood, who, by their usurpation of the power of dispensing pardon for sins, have acquired an interest in promoting sin. Much of their emolument is derived from the gifts and fines which they obtain from their offending flock; they have therefore a motive to permit sins to take place, in order that they may reap the benefit of the penalty. They however affect to be greatly scandalised at this imputation; but, if the case is not so, how has it happened, that now when Christianity, as they call it, is universally established over all the regions of the gods of Greece and Rome, the morals and manners of mankind have become, in every respect, as licentious as they were under the old religion! It cannot be said that this is owing to the Christian doctrines; it must therefore be ascribed to some radical defect in the administration of the priesthood."

Our author having in this manner settled, apparently to his own satisfaction, that, although the Christian name was still used throughout the Eastern empire, the religion itself was at least in a dormant state, proceeds to regret the occultation of the Jewish institutions, and the extinguished fires of the sacrifice in the Temple of Jerusalem. But, as our business is not so much with his opinions, as with his account of the events at which he happened to be present, or acquired a knowledge of from cotemporaries, we shall follow him no further in these reflections. They serve, however, as a very proper introduction to his account of Mahomet, who, soon after this period, began his career, and of whom it appears that Hareach had some personal acquaintance. But, on so important a topic, we must quote his own words.

CHAPTER XXX.

Some Account of Mahomet before he assumed the Mission of a Prophet.

"THERE is at present in Mecca a very extraordinary young man of the name of Mohamed, or Mahomet. He is descended, according to the traditions of the Arabs, in a direct line from Ishmael, the son of Abraham and Hagar; and his ancestors, for four generations, have been the guardians of the sacred black stone called the Caaba, an ancient altar, probably consecrated to the service of the true God from the days of the Patriarch. He is the handsomest and best made man of all the Arabs; speaks with great grace and eloquence; and his deportment is singularly distinguished for propriety, and a wisdom beyond his years. There is a strong presentiment in the minds of all who know him, that he will prove a very eminent character; and this persuasion gathers strength as he advances in life. Indeed, he derives his name from this presentiment; for, in the language of the country, it signifies *the glorified*: and no other has before borne it.

"It is reported, that his birth was attended with some remarkable circumstances, which probably have excited that expectation of his future greatness so generally entertained.

"His father having died before he was born, when he was only seven days old, his grandfather Abd'al Motalleb made a feast, to which he invited all the principal men of their tribe, who, after the repast, desired him to name the infant whom he had invited them to see. The old man replied, 'Then I call him Mohamed.' They were surprised at this answer, and enquired why he did not rather give him a name which had belonged to the tribe. But he only invoked a blessing on the glorious child.

"His mother having died when he was still young, his grandfather took him under his protection, and in many respects preferred him to his own children,* often repeating 'We must take particular care of this boy.' At the death of Abd'al Motalleb, Mahomet was affectionately entertained in the family of his uncle Abu Taleb, who instructed him in the business of a merchant; and while he was yet only in his thirteenth year, took him with him into Syria, having occasion to go there himself on affairs of commerce.

"On entering Bosra, an ancient city in that country, they fell in with a Nestorian monk surnamed Boheira, who, on looking at the boy, was greatly struck with his appearance, and declared that he saw a luminous halo around his head, and other bright indications of his being endowed with the prophetic character. 'Depart,' he exclaimed to Abu Taleb, 'with this child, and take great care of him; for he will one day become a very extraordinary person.'† When Abu Taleb returned to Mecca, he mentioned this singular prediction;—and it had the effect of rendering young Mahomet an object of great interest to all the people.

"Soon after their return, a circumstance occurred which tended to impress the prediction of Boheira very deeply on the public mind. The Koreish tribe, to which Mahomet belonged, and who were the special guardians of the Caaba, having resolved to enlarge the temple in which that sacred stone was deposited, could not agree among themselves about the person who should have the honour of removing it to the new situation which they prepared. They, however, came at last to a resolution to refer the decision of the dispute to the person who should next approach the holy place; and it happened to be Ma-

---

* Universal History.
† Hareach does not report this correctly; he suppresses an allusion which the monk made to the Jews. According to the Mahomedan writers, the words were, "Take care that he does not fall into the hands of the Jews; for your nephew will one day become a very wonderful man."

homet. At his direction, the stone was raised on a carpet by one man of every tribe to the height of its intended place, in which it was fixed by the youth himself; and it was regarded by all as an instance of great sagacity, that he should have procured so remarkable an honour for himself, without giving offence to any one.

"Mahomet is at present in the condition of a factor to Khadijah, a noble and rich widow, who being left by her late husband, a merchant, involved in many intricate mercantile transactions, has committed the management of them to this young man; and he is preparing to set out on a journey to Bosra in Syria ——

"Mahomet has returned, and some remarkable stories are circulated respecting him. He has acquitted himself so well in the business of his mistress, that she has offered to marry him; and, although he is fifteen years younger, it is said he has accepted her hand. This renders him more than ever the topic of conversation; for the modest and chaste life of the widow prevents the insinuations of calumny; and the integrity of the young man would also frustrate detraction, were there any disposition to impute the match to improper passion on the one side, or avarice on the other. It is said that, during his stay at Bosra, he was frequently with Boheira, the Nestorian monk, who was so much interested in his appearance when he visited that city with his uncle; and that he has been instructed by him in the Christian religion ——

"Since his marriage, Mahomet has conducted himself with great propriety. His mercantile affairs have flourished exceedingly, and his exemplary attentions to his wife, to whom he is mainly indebted for his prosperity, has procured him the respect of the whole city. In the course of the last fourteen years, he has made many journies into different parts of Asia, as well as to Egypt and Syria; and his conversation, which was always remarkable for sagacity and shrewdness, has become peculiarly interesting. He has certainly acquired a deep insight of the mysteries of human nature; and he speaks with great contempt of the state of religion throughout the countries he has visited, considering as equally absurd and idolatrous the worship in vogue among the Jews, the Christians, and the Arabs; declaring that it has no resemblance to the religion inculcated by Adam, Noah, Abraham, Moses, Jesus, and the Prophets,—which he knows, or pretends to know, better than the priests. But what renders his critical strictures the more remarkable is, that no one controverts them. He has been so long considered as a man destined to attain greatness, that whatever he does is well received, even in matters of religion."

CHAPTER XXXI.

The Mission of Mahomet.

[A. D. 609.]

"THE character of Mahomet begins to develop itself. Last year he closed his accounts as a merchant; and has, since that time, led a sequestered life of great simplicity and intense study. He retired, for the purpose of meditation, to a cave in Mount Hara, where he remained thirty days, and where, it is reported, he was visited by an angel, and commanded to reform the state of religion throughout the world. Few of his friends are now admitted to see him. He is spoken of as constantly at prayer; and all his domestics have become singularly solemn in their deportment, conscious as it were of some new virtue acquired by their intercourse with so chosen a minister. Waraka, the cousin of his wife, a person of eminent erudition, declares that he is certainly endowed with a divine spirit, and appointed to accomplish some great purpose in the world.

"Mahomet perseveres in his design. Last night there was a numerous assemblage of his relations and admirers at his house, when he exhorted them to adopt the worship of the one only living and true God, eschew the degradation of idolatry, and espouse the holy cause of religious reformation. 'I know not a man,' he said, 'in the whole peninsula of Arabia, who can propose to his friends any thing more excellent than what I now do to you: I offer you the felicity both of this world and that which is to come. God Almighty hath commanded me to call you to him; who, therefore, among you will be my assistant, and also become my brother and vicegerent.' Ali, his cousin, seeing them hesitate, rose, and vehemently declared, that he would not only assist him, but resist all that opposed him. 'I,' he exclaimed, 'O prophet of God, will be thy minister; I myself will beat out the teeth, pull out the eyes, rip open the bellies, and cut off the legs, of all who shall dare to oppose thee.' Mahomet, upon this declaration, embraced Ali with great demonstrations of affection, and desired all present to harken and obey him as his deputy. 'This,' said he, 'is my brother, my deputy, and my vicar; therefore, show yourselves submissive and obedient to him.' But all the guests broke out into laughter, telling Abu Taleb, who was present, that he must now pay obedience and submission to his own son.

"Mahomet was not, however, to be deterred by such a repulse. This morning he has been openly preaching to the people against idolatry, and the corruptions of religion, and was listened to with respectful attention; some of them, at the conclusion of his discourse, indeed, embraced his doctrines.

The affair has produced a great sensation. The principal chiefs of the Koreishites have waited on Abu Taleb, and requested him to persuade his nephew to desist, but the old man is himself almost a proselyte; he has, however, been with Mahomet, and represented that he, and all his followers, run a great risk of being ill-treated, if he continued to persevere as a reformer. 'Tell those that sent you, Abu Taleb,' replied the preacher, 'that were my enemies to set the sun against me on the right, and the moon against me on the left, I will not give up my holy undertaking."*

"The reformer calls his doctrines a new version of the religion of Abraham, and his followers lay claim for him to the sanctity and miraculous powers of a prophet; but this only provokes the enmity of the worshippers of the Caaba. If his religion be that of Abraham, it is, like the teacher himself, of bastard descent; yet, compared with the Christianity of the church, in these parts, it is rational and sublime. Prayer, fasting, and alms, are the duties inculcated by the new sect. Prayer, they say, will carry a man half-way to God, fasting will take him to the door of his palace, and alms will gain him admittance. Five times a-day must the faithful address themselves in prayer; and as every spot on earth is, in their opinion, fit for the service of God, they indifferently pray in their chamber, in the streets, and on the highways. As a distinction from the Jews and Christians, Friday in each week is set apart for religious exercise; and priests and sacrifices are proscribed; and monks are declared alike abhorrent to nature and religion.

"Temperance is the mother of the virtues, in the opinions of this extraordinary man; and his followers are not only exhorted to practice it on all occasions, but are denied without any reservation the use of wine, or any intoxicating liquor. Temperance is inculcated as the first duty towards ourselves, and charity as the first towards others. The faithful are ordered to give the tenth part of their income to the assistance of the indigent and unfortunate; and, if his conscience accuses him of fraud or extortion, he is to repair the wrong by giving the fifth. In this, the obligation to act justly is implied, since we are forbid to injure those whom we are bound to aid.

"The creed of the Mahomedans, for so I may denominate his followers, is brief and simple, consisting but of two articles,—THAT THERE IS A GOD; AND THAT

---

* Universal History.

MAHOMET IS HIS PROPHET: and their practical duties are all comprehended in prayer, temperance, cleanliness, and charity.

"I know not why it is supposed that Mahomet himself is not sincere in what he professes to teach. Surely, it is no new thing for a man to persuade himself that he is a chosen instrument in the hands of Providence. But his sincerity proves nothing; and it is but an equivocal expression to say, that what he does is done by divine authority; for the destinies of all mankind are also of divine authority; although it is not divulged to us, in our earthly state, for what reason evil, that shadow of good, is permitted to spread so darkly over the scene of life.

"The whole tribe of the Koreish are divided and agitated by the new doctrine; and the preacher is indefatigable. The conduct of Abu Taleb, his uncle, in this crisis, affords a fine example of toleration. Anxious to preserve the old worship, he calls on the pilgrims and strangers who frequent the sermons of Mahomet, not to listen to his heresies, and impious novelties, but to stand fast in the faith of their fathers, while his heart, free from bigotry, compassionates the errors of his beloved nephew with the tears of affection. This amiable behaviour of the old man subdues the fierceness of the elders; and, while they, from time to time, threaten to punish the apostate,* his intercession turns aside their anger, and softens them to gentleness and forbearance. But the believers in Mahomet increase, and this indulgence will not last long; for rancour begins to grow up between the old and the new worshippers, and fathers no longer permit their children to intermarry with the apostates."

---

* Gibbon.

CHAPTER XXXII.

The Flight of Mahomet from Mecca, and his Reception at Medina.

"The death of Abu Taleb has removed the only restraint that kept the Koreishites from proceeding to acts of violence against Mahomet. The most helpless and timid of his disciples have fled to Ethiopia, and he has been himself obliged to seek an asylum in the country.

"Abu Sophian, a mortal foe of the line of Hashem, the family of Mahomet, and a zealous votary of idolatry, is nominated chief magistrate. He has convened a meeting of the Koreish tribe, and their allies, to determine what ought to be done with the reformer. This is establishing his doctrines, organizing his followers into a body, and making them feel their own consequence.

"It is determined that Mahomet shall be put to death; and, to divide the responsibility of this deed, and to cement themselves by the bond of guilt, in order to be able to resist the vengeance of his friends, they have resolved, that a sword from each tribe shall be buried in his heart.

"Mahomet has been informed of their conspiracy, and has again fled the city; accompanied by his friend Abubeker: he escaped in silence from his house at the dead of night.

"Three days the fugitives were concealed in the caves of Thor; and, in the close of each evening, they received from the son and daughter of Abubeker a secret supply of intelligence and food. The scouts of their enemies explored every haunt in the neighbourhood of the city. On the third morning, they arrived at the entrance of the cavern, and their approach was seen by the prophet and his companion, who sat secluded in the darkness within. 'What shall we do,' said the trembling Abubeker; 'it is in vain to attack them: for we are but two?'—'There is a third with us,' said Mahomet, calmly,—'God himself.'

"The pursuers by this time had reached the mouth of the cave; but a pigeon's nest on the rocks, which the fugitives had left untouched, and a spider's-web, which had been woven in the course of the night, made the place appear so solitary and inviolated, that they deemed it unnecessary to proceed further.

"When the pursuit abated, the fugitives issued from the rock, mounted their camels, and sought the road to Yathreb. They were overtaken by the emissaries of Abu Sophian, but redeemed themselves with prayers and promises from their hands.

"Some of the citizens of Yathreb, in their pilgrimages to the Caaba, had heard the sermons of Mahomet, and embraced his doctrines. Foreseeing that he would certainly soon be persecuted, they held several meetings, at which he was present, and, binding themselves by a mutual oath of fidelity, promised, in the name of their city, that if he should be banished from Mecca, they would receive him as a confederate, obey him as a leader, and defend him to the last extremity, like their wives and children. 'But,' said they, 'if you are recalled by your country, will you abandon your new allies?'—'All things', replied the prophet, 'are now common between us: your blood is as my blood, your ruin as my ruin: we are bound to each other by the ties of honour and interest; I am your friend, and the enemy of your foes.'—'But, if we are killed in your cause,' enquired his disciples, 'what will be our reward?'—'PARADISE,' replied the prophet. 'Stretch forth thy hand,' they exclaimed, with one voice; and he did so: and they reiterated the oath of allegiance.

"On their return home, this party, which consisted of seventy-three men and two women, communicated to the other Mahomedans at Yathreb what they had done; and their engagement was ratified by the whole sect. It was in consequence of this arrangement, that Mahomet and Abubeker directed their flight towards that city.

"After a perilous journey along the coast of the Red Sea, they halted at Koba, two miles distant from Yathreb; and sixteen days after his escape from Mecca, he verified the proverb, that a prophet is rarely respected in his own country; for he was welcomed into the city by a vast concourse of spectators and disciples.

"I was led, by the fame of this reception, to follow him to Yathreb; for the news came with many exaggerations, and it was asserted, that he had assumed a regal character; and that the name of the city was changed to Medina.

"The city of Yathreb or Medina, as it must now be called, before the arrival of Mahomet, was divided between the tribes of the Charegites and the Awsites, who had each of them numerous adherents of the scattered remnants of Israel, by whom they were instructed in a knowledge of the true religion of Abraham; a circumstance that prepared them for a more ready acceptance of the Mahomedan doctrines, than if they had been either Christian or Pagan idolators. To eradicate the seeds of jealousy between the two rival tribes, Mahomet judiciously enjoined his followers to forego all particular aims, prejudices, and partialities, and knit themselves together in the holy union of brotherhood; the consequence of which was, that the two parties vied with each other in a generous emulation of fidelity and devotion to the prophet: so that the report of his having assumed the regal dignity was virtually true; for undoubtedly, by the voluntary submission of the leaders of the Charegites and Awsites, he became invested with supreme authority among them, and it was deemed impious to appeal from a judge, whose decrees were considered as inspired by divine wisdom.

"The conduct of Mahomet in his new situation has undergone no change,—a strong proof that he really believes himself selected to improve the religion of mankind. His demeanor is marked by the same simplicity and gracefulness which rendered him so distinguished in his youth; but time has crowned him with more dignity. On the Fridays he preaches in the fields under the shade of a palm-tree. I have seen the Cæsar of Rome; but never did I behold a king among his subjects, like Mahomet among his auditors. They listen to him with an impassioned eagerness; and they collect the water of his lustrations, and even his spittle, from the ground, as if they participated in some degree of the holiness which they ascribe to himself.

CHAPTER XXXIII.

Mahomet acts as a Conqueror.

[A. D. 623.]

"Success has intoxicated the spirit of Mahomet, and the fine fervour of his enthusiasm is smothered in the fumes of ambition. Persecution has inflamed his resentment, and his sermons against idolatry are sharpened with rancour, at the recollection of his expulsion from Mecca. His new revelations are in a fiercer and more sanguinary tone; he lays less stress than formerly on the virtues of prayer, temperance, cleanliness, and charity, but justifies the drawing of the sword against idolators, appealing to the example of Moses. To subdue, but not to extirpate, he inculcates as a duty; making the distinction evidently less for the propagation of the truth, if his religion were true, than for the acquisition of temporal power. But last Friday he declared that he was instructed by the angel Gabriel to inform the faithful, 'that the sword is the key of heaven and of hell: a drop of blood shed in the cause of God,—a night spent in arms,—is of more avail than two months of fasting and prayer; whosoever falls in battle, his sins are forgiven: at the day of judgment, his wounds shall be resplendent as vermilion, and odoriferous as musk; and the loss of his limbs shall be supplied by the wings of angels and cherubim.'

"In these warlike sentiments, he evidently consults the heroic spirit of the Arabs; and he has kindled in his followers a fanatic thirst for blood.

"The opportunity has not been long wanting, to indulge the ardour of his disciples. His adversary, Abu Sophian, with a rich caravan from Egypt of a thousand camels, is approaching the vicinity of Medina, on his way to Mecca; and he has resolved to attack the idolator. For this purpose he has sent out a party of the most experienced warriors of the city, to reconnoitre the movements of the enemy.

"Abu Sophian, suspecting the enmity of Mahomet, and knowing his power, has sent to Mecca for additional guards. Mahomet and Abubeker have gone out, with upwards of three hundred men, to meet him.

"In the valley of Beder, the prophet was informed by his scouts that the caravan was approaching on the one side, and one hundred horse and eight hundred and fifty foot, from Mecca, were coming to its protection on the other. After a short consultation, in which some of his officers were desirous that the caravan, on account of its riches, should be the main object, religion and revenge prevailed; and it was determined, that, against the great body of idolators, the sword should be drawn.

"As the numbers of the Koreishites were seen descending into the valley, he exclaimed, looking at his followers: 'O God, if these are destroyed, by whom wilt thou be worshipped on the earth? Courage, my children; close your ranks; discharge your arrows, and the day is your own.' At these words, he mounted the pulpit, which was brought with him for the purpose of preaching from, and demanded from heaven the succour of Gabriel and three thousand angels;—the caravan passed on unmolested;—the Koreishites advanced;—the Mussulmans were pressed and alarmed. In that decisive moment Mahomet leaped from the pulpit, mounted his horse, and cast a handful of sand in the air, crying, ' Let their faces be covered with confusion!' Both armies heard the thunder of his voice: and in their fancy beheld the angelic warriors. The Koreishites trembled and fled: seventy of their bravest were slain, and seventy captives fell into the hands of Mahomet. The bodies of the dead were stripped by the faithful; two of the most obnoxious of the prisoners were put to death, and the ransom demanded for the others, indemnified the Mussulmans for the loss of the caravan.

"The battle of Beder has whetted the sword of Mahomet, and the bloody cup of victory, which he tasted on that day, has inflamed him with the thirst for conquest. Abu Sophian is preparing to revenge the discomfiture that the Meccanites suffered; and Mahomet is no less active in strengthening himself for further achievements.

"The rivals have met: Mahomet has been wounded in the conflict, and the faithful almost dispersed; but they rallied and routed the idolators.

"Abu Sophian is only roused to greater exertions by these defeats. He has advanced with augmented numbers, and threatens the city with a siege.

"He invested Medina with an army of ten thousand men; but a furious tempest of hail and rain has scattered his tents, and dispersed his confederates.

"The crafty character of Mahomet is now no longer questionable; or rather the new circumstances in which he has been called to act, have drawn forth qualities, which, but for them, would perhaps have never been, even by his enemies, imputed to his nature. He affected at first great respect for our ancient nation; and indeed the Kebla point to which he directed his followers to turn in prayer, was Jerusalem; but to-day he has given notice, that all the Jews in Medina must either embrace his religion, or prepare to contend with him in battle."

CHAPTER XXIV.

The Conquest of Mecca, and the Destruction of the Idols in the Caaba.

THE demand which Mahomet made on the Jews, seems to have occasioned our author to quit Medina, and return to Mecca. And we must suppose, that it was the sense of his own singular destiny that alone prevented Hareach from taking arms along with his brethren, in the resistance to which they had but only the alternative of apostatising from their religion; for doubtless, his high moral feeling and fraternal spirit, would have induced him to share their triumph or their martyrdom. It is however certain, that about this period, seven hundred Jews, on account of their adherence to the faith of their fathers, perhaps also for trafficking a little during the war with the idolatrous Abu Sophian, were dragged to the market-place of Medina, and compelled, in the presence of the warlike Prophet, to descend into a pit which had been prepared for their execution and burial. But it is not our object to relate the history of Mahomet; only to give what our author has noted down concerning him.

Hareach, it appears, left Medina on the occasion referred to, and he was certainly at Mecca when Mahomet approached that city in the character of a pilgrim. His account is as follows.

"Having by treaty obtained permission to perform the sacred visitation to the Caaba, he came with a great retinue, and seventy camels designed for sacrifice. The Koreishites, agreeably to what had been stipulated, retired to the mountains, and left the city free to his entrance.

"He was mounted on a camel, and surrounded on all sides by his most devoted disciples: Ald Allah Ebn Rawaka marched before him, leading the camel by the bridle. On his arrival at the temple, when he came to the corner where THE BLACK STONE is fixed, he kissed it with great devotion; from thence, followed by his companions, he seven times encompassed the holy edifice; and, as often as they passed THE BLACK STONE, they either kissed it, after the example of their prophet,* or touched it with their hand, and kissed that. The seven circuits round the Caaba being finished, Mahomet ordered his crier, Belâl, to give notice of the time of prayer; which being likewise done, the Prophet mounted his camel, and ran seven times between the mountains of Saffa and Merwa, partly with a slow and partly with an accelerated pace. Lastly, he sacrificed the camels brought for that purpose; and the Mussulmans having shaved their heads, Mahomet, after remaining four days at Mecca, retired to Shorf.

"The Koreishites, although gratified by the religious homage which Mahomet had thus paid to the immemorial sanctity of the Caaba, violated the treaty in virtue of some of the stipulations of which he had been permitted his pilgrimage, and, in consequence, he resolved to attack the Meccanites, and advanced against the city with ten thousand men. The haughty Abu Sophian saw that resistance was vain to this devoted army of enthusiasts, and presented the keys of Mecca to the fugitive whom he had forced to abscond from that persecution which had contributed so much to his extraordinary elevation.

"The conqueror made his public entry into the town exactly at the time the sun appeared upon the horizon. He was mounted on his camel Al Kaswa, having on his right hand Abubeker, on his left hand Osaid Ebn Hodhair, followed by Osama Ebn Zeid; and, as he rode towards the Caaba, he sung aloud "*The Victory.*"*

"Having reached the Caaba, he alighted, and walked seven times, as in his pilgrimage round it, touching THE BLACK STONE with his truncheon as often as he passed. He then entered the temple; and, beholding the statues of Abraham and Ishmael, with the arrows of divination in their hands, he ordered them to be destroyed. He also broke to pieces himself with his sword a wooden pigeon, that had long been held in great veneration by the idolatrous Koreishites. Afterwards, entering the most holy place of the interior, he prayed, turning to all parts of the temple; and, from between the two pillars, said to those around him, 'This henceforth is your Kebla, the place towards which you are to turn your faces in prayer.'

"Besides the idols which I have mentioned, three hundred and sixty more, the representatives of the days of the Arabian year, obtained the worship due to the true God in the Caaba; and Mahomet ordered them all to be broken, and the pieces cast out. When he had thus removed these abominations, he published a law, declaring

---

* The forty-eighth chapter of the Koran.

that no unbeliever should, on pain of death, dare to set his foot within the territory of the holy city.

"Thus has this extraordinary man verified the presentiment that was entertained of him from his childhood, and not only purged his native city of idolatry, but raised himself into the throne of Arabia; for, by the conquest of Mecca, many of the tribes that hesitated in their religious faith, have now professed themselves his disciples."

CHAPTER XXXV.

The Final Abolition of Idolatry in Arabia.

MUCH of the opprobrium that we are all in the habit of attaching to the name of Mahomet, is owing to two distinct, and very different, causes. The one is, that inherited hatred which arose in consequence of his relentless persecution of every species of idolatrous worship, and which involved alike the corruptions of the Christian church and the rites of the Pagan temple. In consequence of his declared determination to root out the worship of idols, his proselytes and successors found themselves warranted to persecute the Christians who would not receive what they considered the gospel of the Koran; and this persecution, of which it may justly be said that it is continued by the Mahomedans to the present day, occasioned that abhorrence with which traditionally we regard the memory of Mahomet. The other cause is, our contempt for his imposture, and for the absurd series of miracles and visions by which his pretended advent was supported; perhaps also something should be taken into the account, in consideration of his having employed the sword to establish his doctrines. But, could we divest ourselves of the just indignation that must always be cherished against imposture, it would not be difficult to rid our minds of the hereditary prejudice, and we should in that case be forced to admit that Mahomet was one of the most illustrious characters that ever figured on the stage of nations. The object of his ambition,—the reformation of religion, had it been simply assumed as a human undertaking, was the greatest that any conqueror ever adopted; and the sincerity with which he pursued it, and the magnanimity which he often displayed in the pursuit, present a singular contrast to the hypocrisy of his prophetic pretensions, and to the baseness of the frauds which, it is alleged, he practised on the credulity of his disciples. Hitherto we have seen him, by the extracts of our author, in the character of a religious apostle, led on by the natural progress of human affairs to the possession of wide dominion and regal authority. We have now to contemplate him in the simple light of an enthusiastic warrior, believing, or affecting to believe, that he is favoured of Heaven; and it will not be easy, from the records of ancient heroism, to surpass the examples that may be quoted from his life, of true greatness of mind. These, no doubt, contributed to his success; and doubtless, in like manner, the magnanimity of Alexander and Cæsar contributed to their renown: why, therefore, should we withhold from Mahomet the praise we bestow on them? The reformed Christianity of our own country, and the history of the Protestant religion in general, should teach us to appreciate his undertaking more correctly, than to repeat the calumnies of those nominal Christians who were proscribed among the idolators, against whom he more particularly unfurled the hostile banner; and, when we condemn the blood-thirsty conduct of the Mahomedans throughout the world, we should recollect that much of the feeling with which we are on such occasions actuated, is owing to the exaggerated reports of the crusaders, and is derived from the bravery and constancy with which the Saracens, and the other infidels, as they were called, resisted the fanatic warriors who, for an object far less rational than that of Mahomet, so long maintained the ineffectual conflicts of THE

HOLY WAR. But it is time that we should return to our author; for the events which he relates subsequent to the conquest of Mecca, and the purification of the Caaba, bring, as it were, immediately before us the train of circumstances which have tended to impress the inhabitants of modern Europe with that unfair and partial opinion of the religious conqueror, to which we have, in these observations, called the attention of our readers.

"The conquest of Mecca," says Hareach, "determined the faith and obedience of the Arabian tribes; who, according to the vicissitudes of fortune, had obeyed or disregarded the eloquence or the arms of the Prophet. Yet an obstinate remnant still adhered to the religion and liberty of their ancestors, and the war of the Honains derived a proper appellation from the idols which Mahomet had vowed to destroy, and which the confederates of Tayef had sworn to defend. Four thousand Pagans advanced with secrecy and speed to surprise the conqueror: they dispersed the Koreish tribes, for the tameness of their submission; but they probably calculated on their assistance. Not believing that submission sincere, or that a religion dictated by the victor who had destroyed their gods could be ought else among them than an external profession, Mahomet anticipated their approach; and twelve thousand Mussulmans, under his banner, glorying in the persuasion of invincible strength, without precaution, descended into the valley of Honain. The heights and rocks in the meantime were occupied by the archers and slingers of the Pagans, and the army of the Prophet, assailed on all sides by their missiles, fell into confusion. Mahomet, on his white mule, was encompassed by the enemy, and attempted to rush on their spears in search of an heroic death. Ten of his faithful companions interposed their shields and their bosoms, and three fell dead at his feet. His despair was banished by this courageous devotion; his conduct and example restored order; and he animated his troops to inflict a merciless revenge on the authors of their shame.

"From the field of Honain he marched to Tayef; but, after laying siege to it for twenty days, he sounded a retreat, from some motive of policy never explained; for he was soon after followed by deputies from the city. 'Grant,' they cried, as they prostrated themselves before him; 'Grant us, O! apostle of God, a truce for three years, with the toleration of our ancient worship.' —'Not a month, not an hour;' was his stern answer.— 'Excuse us, at least,' they implored, 'from the obligation of prayer.'—'Without prayer,' said he, 'the profession of religion is of no avail.' They submitted in silence; their temples were demolished; and the same sentence of destruction was executed on all the idols of Arabia. The nation submitted to God and the sceptre of Mahomet; the opprobrious name of tribute was abolished from among the tribes; the oblations of alms and tithes were applied to the public service, as the contributions of religious allegiance; and, in the last pilgrimage of Mahomet to his native city, one hundred and fourteen thousand devout zealots to his doctrines attended him to the Caaba."*

CHAPTER XXXVI.

The first War between the Christians and the Mahomedans, and the Death of Mahomet.

WHEN Heraclius, the emperor of Constantinople, was returning from his victorious campaign against the Persians, he was visited at Emessa by one of the ambassadors whom Mahomet had sent to invite the princes of the earth to the profession of his religion. It is even said,

---

* Gibbon.

that an interview took place between the Prophet and the inheritor of the titles of the Cæsars; but our author gives no account of any such circumstance. On the contrary, he mentions, that about this time, in consequence of the murder of a Mahomedan envoy by some of the imperials, Mahomet directed three thousand Saracen soldiers to invade Palestine. But we shall now resume our extracts.

"The holy banner was entrusted to Zeid: on the event of his decease, Jaafar and Abdallah were appointed successively to succeed. In the battle of Muta, the first military action between the Mahomedans and a Christian power, the three leaders were slain. Zeid fell like a soldier in the foremost ranks. The death of Jaafar was still more heroic: he lost his right hand, shifted the standard to his left; the left was severed from his body; he embraced the standard with his bleeding stumps, and held it erect till he was transfixed to the ground with fifty honourable wounds. 'Advance!' cried Abdallah, as he stepped into the vacant place: 'Mussulmans advance: either victory or paradise is our own!' The lance of an imperial warrior decided the alternative; but the falling standard was rescued by Caleb, and his valour withstood and repulsed the Christians. His skilful evolutions, on the ensuing day, secured a victorious retreat to the Saracens. Mahomet saluted Caleb with the honourable epithet of the *Sword of God*, and described with prophetic rapture, from the pulpit, the crowns of glory that had been conferred on the martyrs. In the evening he visited the daughter of Zeid, and, in conversing with her on the merits of her father, he burst into tears. 'What do I see?' exclaimed the astonished maid.—'A man,' replied the Prophet, 'deploring the loss of his most faithful friend.'

"War being thus commenced between Mahomet and the emperor of Constantinople, he made vast preparations to prosecute it with vigour; but Heraclius opposed no resistance, and the conqueror displayed his banner at the head of ten thousand horse and twenty thousand foot, as far into the territories of the empire as half way between Medina and Damascus; and the Christians were glad to submit to his dominion on a more liberal capitulation than might have been expected from his ostensible purpose —— * * *

"The career of this wonderful man is finished. A fever of fourteen days, which deprived him by intervals of the use of reason, on abating, left no hopes of his recovery. He called around him his friends, his household, and many of his disciples. 'If there be any man,' said he, 'whom I have unjustly scourged, I submit my own back to the lash of retaliation. Have I aspersed the reputation of a Mussulman? Let him proclaim my faults in the face of the congregation. Has any one been despoiled of his goods? The little that I possess shall compensate the principal and interest of the debt.'—'Yes', replied a voice from the crowd, 'I am entitled to three drachms of silver.' Mahomet heard the complaint, satisfied the demand, and said to his creditor, 'I thank thee for accusing me at this time, rather than at the day of judgment.' He then emancipated his slaves, seventeen men and eleven women, minutely directed the order of his funeral, and comforted his weeping friends. 'The angel of death,' said he, 'is now standing near me, but will not take my spirit till I have given him permission. Take it, and bear me hence.' In uttering these words he reclined his head on the lap of Ayesha, the best beloved of all his wives, and fainted away. In a short time he recovered, and with a steady look, though in a faultering voice, he articulated, 'O God—pardon my sins—Yes—I come among my fellow-citizens on high:' and thus peacefully expired.

"For a moment after the departure of his spirit a solemn silence prevailed, but it was soon broken by a universal wail and lament from all present. The city became a scene of clamorous sorrow. 'How can he be dead,' was the cry; 'our witness, our intercessor, our mediator with God? He is not dead: like Moses, and Jesus, he is wrapt in a holy trance, and will speedily return to his faithful people.' The evidence of sense was disregarded; and Omar, unsheathing his scymetar, threatened to strike off the heads of the infidels, who should dare to affirm that the Prophet was no more. The tumult was appeased by Abubeker. 'Is it Mahomet,' said he to Omar and the multitude, ' or the God of Mahomet, whom you worship? The God of Mahomet liveth for ever, but the apostle was a mortal, like ourselves; and, according to his prediction, he has experienced the common fate of mortality.'

"A grave was dug where he expired, in which the tree, according to his own directions, was laid where it fell, without ostentation, and a simple tomb raised on the spot.

"After the funeral, Abubeker, the friend of Mahomet, was declared the first Caliph or Commander of the Faithful."

CHAPTER XXXVII.

The Conquest of Alexandria by the Mahomedans; and some account of the Library destroyed by the command of Omar the Caliph.

[A.D. 639.]

It is impossible, within our narrow limits, to trace the victorious progress of the religion and successors of Mahomet. One hundred years after his flight from Mecca, the dominions of the Caliph extended from India to the Atlantic Ocean. We shall therefore, without any particular reference to the history of the Saracenic empire, as the theocratic conquests of the Arabian fanatics may be called, select only such extracts from our author, as tend to illustrate some of those events of which posterity confesses the influence, by still feeling an interest in the record of their circumstances. The first that presents itself, is his account of the destruction of the Alexandrian library. The reader will recollect, that Hareach was present in Alexandria when the temple of Serapis was destroyed; and that he gave some account of the dispersion of the great collection of books which, in that edifice, had been formed by Mark Antony and Cleopatra. We beg attention particularly to this point; because, in his account of the conquest of the capital of Egypt by Amrou, in the caliphat of Omar, the successor of Abubeker, he differs materially from almost every historian,[*] and particularly in what respects the library.

"After a siege of fourteen months, Alexandria received the conqueror, and the standard of Mahomet waved on the towers where the eagles of Rome had so long perched. The Saracens were astonished at the magnificence of the city. In the exultation of the moment, Amrou magnified to the caliph the splendour of the conquest; and adding, 'the town having been subdued by force of arms, without treaty or capitulation, the Moslems are impatient to seize the fruit of their victories.'[†] Omar rejected with firmness the idea of pillage, and directed Amrou to reserve the public wealth and revenue for the propagation of the faith.

"Had these simple sons of the mountain and the desert beheld the city in her glory, such as it was in the days of Adrian, or even in the decline of her fortunes, when the last of her idols was overthrown, what must have been their emotion, when they express so much admiration in the days of her ruin. The blast that has laid in the earth the laurels of Greece and Rome, withered the palm-trees of Egypt, and Alexandria has long pined in irremediable decay.

"In the palace of the governor the relics of the ancient library have been collected; and a prodigious

---

[*] Mr. Gibbon is among the first that has decidedly called in question the fact of the destruction of the Alexandrian library by the order of Omar. The probability is, that the real dispersion of that great depository took place long before, and by the Christians, when they destroyed the temple of Serapis.

[†] Eutychius Annal.

mass of Arian and Monophysite controversy added to the collection. Some of the learned, particularly John, the disciple of Ammonius, who, on account of his grammatical studies and philosophy, has obtained the surname of Philoponus, have solicited Amrou to preserve the library for the use of the public; and he has submitted their request to the caliph, representing to him that the collection consists chiefly of commentaries on the religion of Jesus and the Bible.

"The answer of Omar has excited some regret; for it has been literally interpreted to apply to the whole library, although it obviously refers only to the controversial writings. 'If these books,' says the caliph, 'agree with the book of God, they are useless, and need not be preserved: if they disagree, they are pernicious, and ought to be destroyed.'—Amrou cannot enter into any controversy with the Commander of the Faithful; and he has ordered the whole collection to be distributed among the public baths for destruction. The world will be well rid of so large a mass of human presumption; but, no doubt, among so great a number of volumes, there were many treatises which merit preservation. However, of all the best books, a sufficient number of copies still exist, to continue their light to the world."

CHAPTER XXXVIII.

The Death of Hosein.

[A. D. 680.]

THE introduction of a new religion among the Arabians, did not change the heroic simplicity of their character; and perhaps, with the exception of the story of Leonides, the records of classic antiquity present no incident more affecting than the death of Hosein, the grandson of Mahomet. Whether our author was present at the event, or heard the particulars from some eye-witness, cannot be gathered from his notes. We are however inclined to be of the latter opinion, as it will appear from the extract, that he has brought several things together in a historical form, which he could not have done, had he written under the immediate impression of the circumstances.

"Yezid had not been long proclaimed caliph at Damascus, till a list was secretly transmitted to Hosein at Medina of one hundred and forty thousand Moslems, who were desirous to invest him with that dignity to which he possessed the better claim of hereditary descent from the Prophet; and this list was accompanied with a declaration of their eagerness to draw their swords in his cause as soon as he should appear on the banks of the Euphrates. Against the wisest advice, he determined to embrace the invitation, and traversed the desert with a few faithful friends, and a timorous retinue of women and children. As he approached the confines of Irak, he was alarmed by the solitary or hostile appearance of the country, and suspected either the defection or ruin of his party. His fears were well-founded. The insurrection was extinguished; and Hosein, with his followers, was encompassed in the plain of Kerbela by a body of five thousand horse. He might still have escaped to a fortress in the desert, that had defied the power of the Roman Cæsars and Persian Chosroes, and confided in the fidelity of the tribe of Tai, which would have armed ten thousand warriors in defence of the grandson of the Prophet. But, in a conference with the chief of the enemy, he proposed the option of three honourable conditions; that he should be allowed to return to Medina, or be stationed in a frontier garrison against the Turks, or safely conducted to the presence of Yezid. He was however told that he must either submit as a captive and a criminal to the arms of the caliph, or expect the consequences of his rebellion. ' Do you think,' replied he, ' to terrify me with death?' and, during the short space of a night that he was allowed to determine, he prepared, with calm and solemn resignation, to encounter his fate. He checked the lamentations of his sister Fatima, who deplored the impending ruin of their house. 'Our trust,' said Hosein, 'is in God alone. All things, both in heaven and earth, must perish, and return to their creator. My brother, my father, my mother, were better than me; and every Mussulman has an example in the Prophet.' He pressed his friends to consult their safety, by a timely flight; but they unanimously refused to desert or survive their beloved master.

"On the following morning he mounted his horse, with his sword in one hand and the Koran in the other: his generous band of martyrs consisted only of thirty-two horse and forty foot, but their flanks and rear were secured by their tent-ropes, and by a trench which they had filled with burning faggots.

"The enemy advanced with reluctance; and one of their chiefs deserted, with thirty followers, to claim the partnership of inevitable death. In every close onset, or single combat, the despair of the devoted was invincible; but the surrounding multitudes galled them from a distance with showers of arrows; and horses and men were successively slain: a truce was allowed on both sides for the hour of prayer; and the battle at length expired, by the death of the last of the companions of Hosein. Alone, weary, and wounded, his horse being killed under him, he seated himself at the door of his tent. As he tasted a drop of water he was pierced in the mouth with a dart; and his son and nephew, two beautiful boys, were killed in his arms. He lifted his hands to heaven; they were full of blood; and he uttered a funeral prayer for the living and the dead. In a transport of despair, his sister issued from the tent, and abjured Shamer, the commander of the enemy, not to suffer Hosein to be murdered before his eyes: and the boldest of the assailants fell back on every side, as the dying hero threw himself among them. The remorseless Shamer reproached their pusillanimity; and the grandson of the Prophet was slain with three-and-thirty strokes of lances and swords. After they had trampled on the body, they carried the head to the castle of Cufa, and Obeidollah struck him on the mouth with a cane. 'Alas!' exclaimed an aged Mussulman among his attendants; 'on those lips I have seen the lips of the apostle of God.'

"When the family of Hosein were taken in chains to Damascus, the caliph was advised to extirpate the enmity of a popular race, whom he had injured by this tragical transaction beyond the hope of reconciliation. But Yezid preferred the councils of mercy; and the mourners were honourably sent back, to mingle their tears with their kindred at Medina.*

CHAPTER XXXIX.

The first Mahomedan Siege of Constantinople, with some Account of the cause of the Disappearance of the Greek and Roman Coinage, and the Introduction of our Arithmetical Cyphers.

WHILE the caliphs extended the conquest of the Faithful to the Indus on the east, and over Africa and Spain to the Pyrenees on the west, they also advanced towards the north, animated by a traditional saying, ascribed to the Prophet, that, to the first army which besieged Constantinople, their sins would be forgiven. Accordingly, forty-six years after the flight of Mahomet from Mecca, his disciples appeared in arms around the city of the Cæsars. But, after many ineffectual assaults, they were compelled to raise the siege. This happened some years before the death of Hosein; and, as Yezib had, in a subsequent treaty with the imperial ambassadors, engaged to pay an annual tribute of fifty horses of a noble breed,

---

* Gibbon.

fifty slaves, and three thousand pieces of gold, to the Greek emperor, it is probable that the shade which this treaty threw on the glory of the faithful, was the chief cause which had moved the malcontents of Damascus to apply to the unfortunate Hosein.

From the first siege of Constantinople down to the close of the seventh century, we meet with nothing particularly deserving of notice; nor does it very clearly appear in what part of the world Hareach was during that period. The inference, however, that we should draw from his notes, is, that he resided at Damascus: for he mentions, that "the caliph Abdalmalek has established a mint for a coinage of gold and silver, by which all the beautiful varieties of money, the lasting memorials of Grecian art and Roman valour, are daily disappearing from the circulation;" and, a little farther on, we find a still more curious memorandum.

"Many of the officers in the service of the caliph Waled, being natives of distant parts of the world, he has abolished, for the general convenience, the use of local numerals; and adopted in their stead new characters, in which all matters relative to numbers are in future ordered to be noted."

It would thus appear, that an official regulation has promoted the most important discoveries of arithmetic, algebra, and the mathematical sciences; for we need not inform our readers, that the universal cyphers to which our author here refers, are those which are now in use throughout the world. The use of the Roman method of notation had indeed been found inconvenient before this time, in the transactions between the citizens and the Barbarians; and there is some reason to believe that a character, resembling the distribution of the spots on our playing-cards, was in use among them: at least, marks of this kind, on several ancient books and manuscripts, have been ascertained to signify their date.

With the exception of these two notes, there is nothing interesting in the Volume of Hareach, till he describes the second Mahomedan siege of Constantinople, at which, it appears, he was present, and in the city. Indeed, it would seem that he had been resident there some time before; for he mentions, in a cursory manner, that " the senate have shown greater wisdom than might have been expected from them, in choosing the emperor's secretary to succeed him in the imperial dignity." This was Artemius, the secretary of Philippicus, and who, on being raised to the throne, assumed the name of Anastasius the Second. He proved a wise and courageous sovereign; and, three years after his elevation, prepared for the defence of the city with great resolution, in the second siege of which we shall extract our author's account.

CHAPTER XL.

Second Siege of Constantinople by the Mahomedans.

[A.D. 718.]

" THE expected messengers have returned from Damascus. Soliman has not only refused to pay the tribute any longer, but threatens to indemnify himself a thousand-fold for all that has been paid since the days of Yezid. His preparations, both by sea and land, are described as transcending all belief —— * * *

" The precautions of Anastasius are suitable to the emergency. He has ordered all families, not provided with the means of subsistence for three years, to leave the city. He fills the public granaries, replenishes the arsenals, and re-fortifies the walls —— * * *

" A fleet, sent to destroy the cedars hewn from Mount Lebanon, and which were piled along the Phœnician shore for the service of the enemy's navy fitting-out at Alexandria, has mutinied, and proclaimed Theodosius emperor —— * * *

"Theodosius, in his turn, has been deposed; and Leo, an Isaurian, the general of the oriental armies, has been chosen emperor. It is said that he was originally a pedlar, who drove an ass with paltry merchandize to the neighbouring fairs; and that he one day happened to meet a fortune-teller, who predicted that he would attain the imperial dignity. His first service was in the guards of Justinian; and, having gradually raised himself by the force of his talents to distinction, he was appointed by Anastasius to the command of the Asiatic legions ――― * * *

"Moslemah, the brother of Soliman the caliph, at the head of a hundred and twenty thousand Saracenic troops, the greater part mounted on horses and camels, after taking Tyana, Amorium, and Pergamus, are approaching the shores of the Hellespont.—He has crossed the waters at Abydos; and, without pausing to take possession of the cities on the coast of the Propontis, is now forming his camp under the walls of the city. Prepared for this invasion, his arrival has produced comparatively but little effect. It is expected that he will be induced to raise the siege, by the offer of a sum of money ――― * * *

"A considerable alarm has spread throughout the city, in consequence of Moslemah refusing the offer of a piece of gold for every inhabitant, as the ransom of the city. He says that he will enter into no conditions, and only waits the arrival of the ships of Egypt and Syria ――― * * *

"The hostile fleet is in sight: like a thunder-cloud in the heavens, it darkens the bright face of the Propontis, and threatens the religion and empire of the Christians with an utter overthrow. The courage of Leo rises to the danger: a marvellous spirit of confidence is felt by all his soldiers, and the inhabitants dread not the enemy ――― * * *

"I have been with the crowd to see the fire-ships prepared to resist the hostile navies of the enemy. They were vessels formerly employed in the recreations of the imperial court. The prows of these vessels being adorned with marine monsters—tubes of brass, filled with the secret combustibles, project from their mouths; and the engineers tell us, that, when they approach the enemy, they will vomit flames, like the chimera of the poets. The composition of this liquid fire is unknown; and water, instead of extinguishing, only exasperates its fury. It was a discovery of Callinicus, a native of Heliopolis; and the knowledge of the ingredients is preserved as the most precious secret of the imperial court —— * * *

"The ramparts are crowded with spectators;—the emperor has ordered the fire-ships to be launched. The sun is setting; and, by the movements in the camp of Moslemah, it is supposed that he intends an assault, as the fleet approaches the harbour, into which Leo decoys them, by withdrawing the chain that defended the entrance —— * * *

"How beautiful is the stillness of the heavens in this cloudless night! The winds are asleep; and the rising moon, as she dawns over the eastern hills, shows the roofs and walls of the city covered with anxious spectators, silently watching the progress of the hostile fleet. The din of preparation in the enemy's camp breaks softly from a distance on the ear; and the sound of the oars in the fire-vessels, as they move towards the fleet, echoes the beating heart of the city —— * * *

"A crash and outcry burst from the land and the sea. The engines of Moslemah thunder on the gates, and the ships of Leo grasp with their flames the vessels of the Saracens. The shouts of the assembled inhabitants rise above the noise of war; and the burning navy of the enemy sheds a red and troubled light on the camp, the city, and the sea —— * * *

"The returning daylight shows the success of the fortitude and preparations of Leo. The fleet, on which Moslemah placed so much reliance, is reduced to fragments of charcoal and smoking wrecks, that only darken the shores of the Propontis; and his assault on the walls has only wearied his men * * *

"The Saracens still continue the siege; but they are not destined to succeed at this time. The stars in their courses fight against them. The winter has set in with uncommon rigour. The snow is seen on the tops of hills that the oldest alive do not remember to have ever beheld so covered. Ice was this morning found in the basons of the public fountains, and the atmosphere is charged with a foul grey vapour. The snow has commenced;—all night it fell,—and the tents of the natives of the sultry climes of Egypt and Arabia are covered with a load, that would benumb the hardy sons of Germany, and the frozen regions beyond the Danube —— * * *

"After a siege of thirteen months, the hopeless Moslemah has struck his tent. This morning his army was seen at break-of-day defiling along the shores of the Propontis. The Mahomedans have reaped only disgrace by this expedition. The vigour of the Greek empire is decayed, but it still enjoys a healthy state of repose. It can no longer engage in distant enterprises, but it has strength enough to defend itself."

CHAPTER XLI.

The first Decisive Indication of the Independence of the Papal Government.

[A. D. 726.]

THE return of Hareach to Constantinople revives his attention to the history of the church; and for a short time we may be allowed to indulge ourselves with a few extracts from his observations on ecclesiastical affairs.

"As the worship of images never was established by any general law, its progress had been retarded or accelerated by the differences of men and manners, the degrees of local refinement, and the personal character of the bishops. After the Saracens abandoned the siege of the capital, the prejudice which had been for some time gathering the strength of reason against the ecclesiastical corruption, burst forth with great vehemence; and the emperor himself encouraged it on several accounts. His early habits, and his intercourse with the remains of our nation, as well as the Mahomedan doctrines, of which he had acquired some knowledge during his campaigns as a soldier, had taught him to despise idolatry. In a council, at which several senators and bishops assisted, it was enacted, that all statues should be removed from the sanctuary and altars of the churches; and he subsequently ordered the pictures to be defaced, and the images of Christ, the Virgin, and the saints, demolished. His first hostilities were directed against a lofty effigy of Jesus above the gate of the palace. A ladder was raised to take it down: a mob of frantic women and furious fanatics rushed to the spot. They seized the ladder;—they shook down the workmen;—and, with insane transports of religious passion, shouted as they beheld the ministers of what they deemed sacrilege, tumbling from on high, and dashed against the pavement. Leo was exceedingly provoked at this outrage; and many of the leaders of the tumult, being seized by the guard, were afterwards punished with death as rebels: but they gloried in their suffering for righteousness-sake, as they were pleased to consider their folly; and the honours of the ancient martyrs of the faith were prostituted to these rebellious champions of idolatry

* * *

"This interdict of the Christian idolatry has excited the alarm of Gregory, the head of the Roman church, and who, in his see, is a potentate of greater authority than the patriarch of Constantinople. He has written a letter to the emperor, distinguished for its insolence. "During ten years," says the pontiff of Rome, "we have tasted the annual comfort of your royal letters, subscribed in purple ink, with your own hand, the sacred pledges of your attachment to the orthodox creed of our fathers. How deplorable is the change!—how awful the scandal! You now accuse the Catholics of idolatry; and, by the accusation, you betray your own impiety and ignorance. To this ignorance we are compelled to adapt our style and arguments: the first elements of holy letters are sufficient for your confusion; and, were you to enter a grammar-school, and avow yourself the enemy of our worship, the simple and pious children would be provoked to cast their horn-books at your head.' Such was the salutation with which the pope affected to discriminate the difference between the idols of antiquity and the Christian images; and he concluded by asserting the bold falsehood,—no doubt grounded on his belief of Leo's ignorance,—that images had been in constant use in the church from the Apostolic age. He then recommends peace, silence, and implicit obedience to his spiritual guides, and defines the several jurisdictions of the civil and ecclesiastical power. To the former, he appropriates the body; to the latter, the soul: the sword of justice is in the hands of the magistrate; the more formidable weapon of excommunication, is entrusted to the priest.' 'Your assault,' said the holy father; 'your assault is, O, tyrant! with a carnal and military hand: unarmed and naked, we can only implore Christ, the Prince of the heavenly host, to send unto you a devil to destroy your body, in order to save your soul. You declare, with foolish arrogance, I will dispatch my orders to Rome: I will break in pieces the image of St. Peter; and Gregory shall be transported in chains to the foot of the imperial throne. But, may the fate of Constans serve as a warning to the persecuters of the church. After his condemnation by the bishops of Sicily, the tyrant was cut-off, in the fulness of his sins, by a domestic servant. Incapable as you are of defending your Roman subjects, the maritime situation of their city may perhaps expose it to your depredations; but we can remove to the first fortress of the Lombards, and then you may pursue the winds! Are you ignorant that the popes are the bond of union, the mediator between the East and the West? The eyes of the nations are fixed on our humility; and they revere, as a god upon earth, the apostle St. Peter, whose images you threaten to destroy. The remote and interior kingdoms of the West present their homage to Christ and his vicegerent; and we now prepare to visit one of their most powerful monarchs, who desires to receive from our hands the sacrament of baptism. The Barbarians have submitted to the gospel, and you alone are deaf to the voice of the shepherd. These pious Barbarians are kindled into rage: they threaten to avenge the persecution of the East. Abandon your rash and fatal undertaking; reflect, tremble, and repent. If you persist, we are innocent of the blood that will be spilt in the contest:——May it fall on your own head.'

"Gregory, not content with this insolent letter, has actually set the power of the emperor at defiance; and every thing portends the re-establishment of an ecclesiastical empire in the ancient capital of the world."

CHAPTER XLII.

The Progress of the Mahomedan Religion arrested by Charles Martel, in France.

[A.D. 732.]

FROM the flight of Mahomet, the conquests of the Faithful, as his followers called themselves, had continued unabated. From Africa the Saracens passed into Spain; and, having subdued all that Peninsula, crossed the Pyrenees, and entered Gaul. No power seemed capable of resisting their force; and all that is now known by the name of Christendom, was threatened with subjection to the dominion and religion of the Arabians.

Hareach, during the quarrel between the pope and the emperor of Constantinople, respecting the use of images in the churches, appears to have wandered westward. But we meet with no remarks particularly deserving of notice, till we find him at the court of Pepin king of France. The descendants of Clovis had lost the inheritance of his martial and ferocious spirit; and their misfortune or demerit has affixed the epithet of "lazy" to the last kings of the Merovingian race. A country-palace, in the neighbourhood of Compeigne, was their residence and prison; but, each year, in the month of May,* a general assembly of the chiefs of the Franks was held, to which the king was conducted in a waggon drawn by oxen, to give audience to foreign ambassadors, and to ratify the acts of his minister, who, under the title of "Mayor of the Palace," exercised the whole royal authority. Things were in this state when Eudes duke of Aquitain, assumed the title and authority of king. In his time, the Saracens, or Moors, as they have since been more properly denominated, being the converts to Mahomedanism, who, from Morocco, had possessed themselves of Spain, passed the Pyrenees, and were defeated by him at Thoulouse. But this repulse only sharpened their ambition; and, in a new inroad, a Moslem colony was established in Languedoc; and the vineyards of Gascony, and the city of Bourdeaux, confessed obedience to the sovereign of Damascus, who comprehended beneath the sway of his scymitar, a wider portion of the globe than had obeyed the mandates of the Roman Cæsars.

But it was the enjoined duty of the Mahomedans to spread their religion over the whole earth; and Abderame, who had been appointed by the caliph to the command of the Faithful in Spain, determined to gratify his impatient soldiers by extending their conquests to the utmost regions of the north. Accordingly, he crossed the Pyrenees with a prodigious army, some time before our desultory author appears to have arrived at the court of Pepin; for we find him referring to the siege of Arles, and the defeat of Eudes, in which it was said so many Christians fell that God

---

* This is the origin of the Champ de Mai, which Bonaparte, on his return from Elba, affected to revive.

alone could reckon the number of the slain, as to events already passed. But we must return to his Volume.

"Charles the Bastard, who by his father was appointed Mayor of the Palace, is a very extraordinary character; with a prudence which no emergency shakes, he possesses such undaunted courage, and a strength of arm so uncommon, that the soldiers, on account of the force with which he strikes down his enemies, call him Martel or the Hammer. Abderame continues his victorious career, and still the Hammer remains idle,—but idle only in appearance.

"The duke of Aquitain has implored his assistance, and the voice of the whole country calls on him to resist the invader; but, firm to his purpose, he still replies, 'Interrupt not their march: they are like a torrent, which it is dangerous to stem in its rage: the thirst of riches, and the consciousness of success, redouble their valour. Be patient, till they have loaded themselves with the weight of their spoil: the possession of wealth will divide their councils, and ensure you victory,——* * *

"The policy of Charles is now developed. The progress of the Saracens having convinced the divided Franks that only a cordial union can save them from ruin, they are concentrating from all quarters around his standard.

"In the centre of the country he has found the adversary. Six days of desultory combat mingled the blood of the natives of Asia, Africa, and Europe, on the plains of Gaul. In the closer onset of the seventh, Abderame was killed; but the Saracens, without defeat or victory, retired to their tents in the evening. They had, however, felt the iron hands of the German allies of the Franks; and the armies disagreeing in the choice of a successor to Abderame, each consulted his own safety by a hasty and separate retreat. Charles pursued them to the Pyrenees, and has purged the land of them all. But, although by his prudence and heroism he has thus saved his country, and the Christian religion in this part of the world, the monks and priests have raised a loud clamour against him, because he has been obliged to apply the riches and revenues of the church to defray the expences of the war; and the ungrateful priesthood, that he has saved from entire destruction, threaten him with eternal perdition. His patriotism, his heroism, and all his great public merits, are forgotten; the acts of his necessity are alone remembered, and are stigmatised to the abhorrence of the pious by the epithet of sacrilege."

The cotemporary animadversions on this illustrious hero were, however, excelled by the audacity of later priests. In a letter addressed by the bishops and abbots of the provinces of Rheims and Rouen to Louis the Germanic, the grandson of Charlemagne, about the middle of the ninth century, they declare that his ancestor was damned; that, on the opening of his tomb, the spectators were affrighted by a smell of fire, and the aspect of a horrid dragon; and that a holy man had been comforted in his sleep with the pleasant vision of the soul and body of Charles Martel "burning to all eternity in the abyss of hell." They forgot to say whether the saint was informed that this punishment was for melting the golden images of the churches, or for preventing the purer theology of Mahomet from being substituted for the idolatrous jargon which the monks had established under the name of Christianity.

CHAPTER XLIII.

The Magnificence of the Caliphs, and their Encouragement of Learning.

Soon after the death of Charles Martel, our author appears to have travelled into Spain, and embarked with a party of Saracens at Barcelona, who were bound on a pilgrimage to Mecca. By a storm, the vessel was compelled to take shelter in the river of Ephesus; and we find him deploring the desolation which had overspread the rich and fertile valleys of Asia Minor, by the terrible pestilence that depopulated so many countries in the reign of the emperor Justinian. Among other cities, Ephesus had suffered to so great degree, that many of the inhabitants, abandoning their houses, had built for themselves a new town on a promontory at some distance; where, from the wholesome breezes of the sea, they hoped to avoid the infection exhaled from the marshes around their native city. He speaks indeed of the old town as being almost entirely deserted. "Earthquakes have shaken down the temples, and broken the arches of the aqueducts, and the water which formerly supplied the wants of a hundred thousand inhabitants, stands in fetid pools, over which the demons of desolation are continually inhaling the vapour of disease, to breathe it out on the squalid and miserable survivors."

Having remained a few days at this place, he sailed with his companions for Egypt; landed at Alexandria, ascended the Nile, and crossed the desert with them, to the shores of the Red Sea, where they embarked for the nearest port in Arabia. Here they left him for Mecca, and he joined a numerous caravan that was bound from Medina to Damascus. But he did not long remain in that city; for Almansor the caliph, having some years before founded the city of Bagdad, Hareach was led by curiosity, excited by the fame of his magnificence, to visit the new metropolis, in order to see how far the report was true that in pomp and splendour Almansor excelled the Cæsars of Rome, or the emperors of Constantinople. We extract his observations.

"The walls of Babylon having been long in a state of irreparable decay, and the air of the city having become exceedingly insalubrious, by the stagnant waters amidst the ruins, Almansor formed the design of building the new town, to which he removed the inhabitants.

"But when I beheld the grandeur of the caliph, his innumerable guards in radiant armour; the gorgeous officers around his throne; the thousands of slaves and eunuchs covered with cloth of gold and purple studded with gems; the gilded barges, that in the sunshine, on the glossy surface of the Tigris, moved like so many floating fires; the palace of thirty thousand chambers, adorned with tapestry and the rich products of the Persian looms; the hundred lions, brought forth, with their keepers, as the emblems of his power; the golden fountains, replenished, not with water, but quicksilver; and that hall of audience, where the eye was so dazzled with the lustre of jewels and the exquisite productions of art, that the golden floor was justly said to be scarcely splendid enough for the glory of the walls and ceiling,*—I felt myself inspired as it were with the gift of prophecy, and could not refrain from exclaiming, 'This, too, is but a passing meteor; a few years, and it will be extinguished, like the lustre of Babylon.'— In that moment, the frugal household of Mahomet, to whom all the inordinate magnificence of the caliphs owed its origin, seemed to be renewed before me. I thought I again saw him spreading the carpet of repose for the stranger, and assisting to kindle the evening fire to prepare his supper. With his own hands he mended his shoes and woollen garments; and, disdaining the penance and merit of an hermit, observed, without ostentation, the abstemious diet of an Arab and a soldier. On solemn occasions, when he feasted the chiefs of his tribe, it was with rustic hospitality; but weeks passed in the domestic life of the founder of the greatest empire ever established and preserved by the genius of one man, during which the culinary fire was not lighted on his hearth."

But our author does not do justice to the caliphs of Bagdad, in speaking only of their "barbaric pearl and gold." They were a race of great princes; and, under their protection, the muses found an asylum, when banished from Greece and Rome by the bigottry of a daring priesthood. Almansor, the founder of Bagdad, gave encouragement to every species of learning, and was himself not only profoundly skilled in the knowledge of the Ma-

---

* Gibbon.

hometan law, but an eminent proficient in the study of astronomy. His grandson Almamon may, without prejudice, be deservedly ranked, for his patronage of literature, above Augustus, or Cardinal Wolsey, or Louis the XIVth of France. His ambassadors at Constantinople, his agents in Armenia, Syria, and Egypt, collected the volumes of Grecian science: at his command they were carefully translated into Arabic; and he himself assisted with pleasure and modesty at the assemblies and disputations of the learned. His visier consecrated a sum of two hundred thousand pieces of gold to the foundation of a college at Bagdad, in which instruction was communicated to six thousand disciples of every degree, from the son of the noble to that of the mechanic. The munificent example of the caliph was imitated through all his dominions. In every city the productions of Arabic literature were copied and collected by the curiosity of the studious, and the vanity of the rich. The Arabian tales, that still surpass in ingenuity and fancy the richest fictions of Europe, are often but poetical and allegorical celebrations of real events, which took place during the reign of the successors of Almansor. In the story of Sinbad the Sailor, we have an amusing exaggeration of a real voyage to Ceylon;* and in that of Aladdin, perhaps, an account of a chymist, who was supposed to have discovered the philosopher's stone; for the science of chymistry owes its origin and improvements to the subjects of the caliphs. They first invented and named the alembic for distillation, analysed substances, tried the distinction and affinities of alkalies and acids, and converted the poisonous minerals into mild and salutary medicines, in their search for the convertive element of the transmutation of metals, and the elixir of immortal health.†

We have thought it necessary to make these observations, as our author, in noting down his reflections, seems to have had no particular object in view; in consequence,

---

* My friend, Mons. Langles, the erudite Parisian orientalist, in his beautiful Arabic version of the tale, has shown this.

† Gibbon.

his extracts, taken without some qualification of this kind, would appear not merely detached facts and circumstances, but tend to inculcate opinions at variance with historical truth.

CHAPTER XLIV.

The History of the Caliph Montasser

Hareach remained many years at Bagdad; indeed, it does not appear that he quitted the environs of that city till the Turkish guards, first introduced by the caliph Motassem, renewed, in their insolence towards their sovereigns, the audacity of the prætorians of Rome. In a brief account of one of their insurrections, we meet with an affecting anecdote, which it would be improper, after so many dry details, not to transcribe.

"Molawakkel, a jealous and cruel tyrant, had rendered himself so odious to his subjects, that the chief officers of the palace waited on Montasser, his son, and represented to him, that the public could no longer endure his tyranny and crimes. The prince was much moved, and implored them to spare the life of his father; but they told him that his own life, and the continuation of the caliphate in his family, depended on his acquiescence in their design; and that it was not only necessary he should consent to the deed, but ensure their pardon, after it was committed, by heading the conspiracy himself. Montasser was not possessed of sufficient fortitude to withstand their promises and menaces, and the pusillanimity of personal safety, palliated to himself by considerations of public duty, induced him to sanction the stern justice of the conspirators.

"At midnight they assembled in the hall adjoining the night-chambers of the caliph, and the presence of Montasser excused to the guards their unusual appearance. He commanded the soldiers to withdraw; and when they had retired to the outside of the palace, the doors were bolted, and the conspirators burst into the room where Molawakkel lay asleep. Montasser, overpowered by his feelings, remained behind, and heard with indescribable horror the cry of his father for assistance, the imprecation of the avengers, the clash of arms, and the dying groans of the victim.

"Having satisfied the awful claims of public justice, the conspirators returned; and, with their swords still reeking with the blood of his father, tendered to the pale and trembling prince their homage and allegiance. The guards were then admitted, and told that the tyrant was dead, and Montasser the caliph.

"These guards consisted of robust barbarians, whom Motassem first introduced into the capital, as being likely to prove more faithful adherents to the sovereign than the armed citizens, to whom the successors of Mahomet had previously trusted their safety and government. This event was to them a tremendous lesson; for, to ensure their obedience to the new caliph, the conspirators bribed them with a large sum of money: thus at once informing them of the importance attached to their power, and furnishing them with a motive to depose the sovereign as often as rage or avarice instigated them to rebellion.

"On the following morning, preparations were made for Montasser to receive the public homage of his officers and subjects. The hall of audience, in which the throne was placed, was hung with tapestry representing various historical scenes. Among others, it exhibited, with appalling effect, a picture of the crime and punishment of the son of Chosroes, the Persian monarch, for his parricide.

"I was present before Montasser appeared. A vast crowd filled the floor, leaving an open space from the entrance to the foot of the throne, around which the great officers of state stood assembled. By some strange sympathy, the eyes of all were turned to the picture; and every one, without uttering a word, evidently applied it to the occasion of the ceremony which we had come to witness. At this moment, a flourish of trumpets announced the approach of the caliph; and a splendid succession of the eunuchs and officers of the palace entered; and, walking up to the throne, and returning down each side of the open space, formed an avenue for the commander of the Faithful to advance and ascend the throne. When they had taken their places, he came in alone. His step was unsteady; his eye alarmed; but, having wound himself up for the pompous servitude in which he was engaged, his deportment had still an air of dignity, and there was something touching in the mild expression of his youthful melancholy. He, however, mounted the steps of the throne with sufficient firmness, and the ceremony of receiving the homage commenced. Nothing particular happened for some time; and his attention was occupied by the successive approach of the different persons who came to prostrate themselves before him. But a pause of a few seconds took place, in consequence of one of the principal officers, an old man, being lame, and requiring more time than the others to reach the foot of the throne. In this interval, Montasser raised his eyes, and, glancing them with a look of complacency on the respectful multitude before him, the picture of the fate of the son of Chosroes met his view, and appalled him like a spectre. His eyelids dropped; the colour of his complexion fled; his lips became pale; and, turning his head aside, and shaking his averted hands, he burst into tears: and, in an agony of remorse, exclaimed, 'I have lost both this world, and that which is to come!'

"This extraordinary incident excited a prodigious alarm;—the spectators fled, in dread of some horrible catastrophe;—the conspirators present were scarcely less appalled;—the whole city was thrown into tumults of confusion;—and a panic, which no one could resist, agitated every bosom. The unhappy Montasser sank under the upbraidings of his conscience. He did nothing for many days but sit weeping before the picture; and, when his strength could no longer withstand the pangs of remorse, he expired with howls of despair, believing himself doomed to everlasting perdition."

CHAPTER XLV.

Hareach among the Ruins of Babylon.

Soon after the death of Montasser Hareach left Bagdad; and visiting several parts of the country, which he describes as in the bloom and foliage of the summer of prosperity, he wandered towards the ruins of Babylon.

"In the afternoon," says he, "I reached the cottage of a peasant, distant about two hours walk from the city. It was the nearest habitation to the deserted region; and it stood among the ruins of a large pile of building, which, when Babylon was inhabited, had served as a caravansera. Here I took some refreshment, and rested for a short time.

"On telling my host that I intended to visit the ruins, he endeavoured to dissuade me, by representing that, during day-light, they were infested with robbers, and that at night the fearful voices of demons, and other unholy spirits, were often heard howling among them. I was not, however, to be deterred by the fables of credulity and superstition. It was possible that, during the day, men might be led by avarice to search the fallen palaces for buried treasures; and the beasts of prey, which, according to the sentence so long pronounced, had no doubt taken posssesion of the chambers of Nebuchadnezzar, sufficiently accounted for the nocturnal cries:—besides, what had I to fear?

"About an hour before sun-set I left the cottage, and walked leisurely along what had been one of the great highways to this once proud capital. The boundaries of the road on each side were in many places obliterated, still however the lines were easily traced; but what had been the carriage-way was thickly knotted with weeds and brambles; indeed, the vegetation along the track of the road was considerably more vigorous than in the adjacent fields.

"It was truly a solitary walk. As I approached the shapeless mounds into which the walls had subsided, I passed the ruins of several villas and gardens. I only however knew them to be such by the regular distribution of the trees, and the variety of the shrubs; for the buildings had long sunk, and only a tumulus, covered with withered grass, showed where they had stood. I endeavoured in vain to discover some object, to satisfy me that I had been along the same road before; but every thing had so hastened into oblivion, that I could find no memorial even of the days of Trajan.

"I could only account for this rapid disappearance of the grandeur of Babylon to the edifices having been constructed with brick, and covered with stucco. They were not only crushed beneath the foot of time, but pulverized into dust by the weather.

"As the sun was setting I came within sight of the walls, but they no longer retained the form of building: they had fallen into broken masses, which in many places had melted, if I may use the expression, into the common level of the earth; and the Tower,* which, with its airy superstructures, pierced so far into the heavens, barely retained the outline of its form. I could trace in it none even of that faded splendour which it still retained in the time of Trajan. It was, in fact, almost become a mound,— the heap over a sepulchre.

"The extreme stillness that reigned around, made me almost wish I had not determined to come alone: for the sun was now set, and the twilight fast closing.

"I however quickened my pace, and reached the gate to which the road led before the darkness was complete; but what I imagined to be the gate, was only a hollow in the shapeless chain of mounds, that marked where the walls had been.

"On entering within the scite of the city, I was at first surprised at the luxuriant grass that had grown up in the streets, and shuddered to go forward, in apprehension of

---

* Riche's Account of the Ruins of Babylon.

treading on the snakes, that delight to inhabit such rank herbage. But, in a short time I recovered resolution, and advanced towards the banks of the river; which, with a hoarse and continued murmur, seemed to deplore the doom of his gorgeous bride.

"I sat down on a mass of earth by the side of the stream, and the spectre of ages passed before me. A feeling, to which no language can give utterance, rose in my heart. I was as a being placed between the world that is, and the world to be. The region of man seemed as at an immeasurable distance. The events of yesterday, even of the day that had passed, were mingled with the earliest impressions of my memory, and the traditions of the most remote antiquity; constituting, as it were, all the past into one dark, ponderous, and oppressive thought. The rushing of the river, as it rolled along, sounded in my ear like the passing of those mighty spirits, which are continually going forth, without intermission, from the throne of heaven, to perform the tasks of Providence, and in giving being to the events of time.

"While I sat absorbed in these solemn reflections, the lunar morning began to dawn; and I heard at a distance the cry of some beast of prey, that seemed to be approaching towards me, and hastily quitted my station. I had trusted to find among the ruins some place of shelter for the night, otherwise I should have remained at the peasant's cottage till the next day; but I wandered in quest of a broken vault, or tenantless habitation, for upwards of two hours by the rising moon, and met with nothing that bore any trace of man. All had perished:—temple and dwelling were alike crumbled into dust, and the grass growing where they had once been.

"Wearied with the fatigue I had undergone, I again sat down. By this time the moon was considerably advanced in her wonted journey. The black shadows which her light threw from the heaps and mounds of ruin were greatly shortened, and that visionary phenomenon, which the inequalities of the ground present to her rising light, had gradually disappeared. The vapours of my imagination had also vanished; and, after I had been seated some time, I felt myself in a state of unusual tranquillity: my emotion had entirely subsided; and I looked upon the earth, and the heavens, and the silent majesty of the silver planet floating in the blue abyss of the air. In this situation, I saw a person coming towards me, as it were from the river. He appeared taller than the sons of man, and his hair, in the moon-light, hoary and flowing. He drew near; and, on looking at him again, my spirit was moved by the awful expression of his countenance: it exhibited the fixed and dismal solemnity of the dead, and his eyes possessed no light of intelligence, but only glittered in the moonshine"—— * * *

Our author does not mention the particulars of what passed with this mysterious and apparitional personage. Leaving, however, a break in the page, he says, "after this I raised my eyes, but he was not there; and, on looking again, the morning light dazzled me; and I then found I had fallen asleep, and that the stranger with whom I held this long communion, was but the spirit of a dream."

CHAPTER XLVI.

Zingis Khan of Tartary, and the Conquest of China.

AFTER his solitary visit to the ruins of Babylon, our author, as if weary of the conflicts of ambition and religion, avoided the busy haunts of men; and for many years we find him wandering among the pastoral tribes of Tartary, and the mountains of Thibet. The modern map furnishes no clue to his aberrations; nor indeed have many of the places which he visited in those remote eastern regions been described by any geographer. His notes are brief and unsatisfactory. They either relate to scenes which no European traveller has yet visited, or to persons whose exploits and crimes were too insignificant to be heard, amidst the convulsions that rent the empire of Constantinople into pieces, and occasioned the fanatic uproar of the crusades and holy war. But, after a long series of these uninteresting memoranda, we find ourselves in the midst of great and striking events. Having passed this desert, we reach a populous city, full of cares, intrigues, and tumults; and are compelled to take a part, by our sympathy, in a new series of transactions, that, no less than the preaching of Mahomet, changed the condition of a large portion of the world.

The ancient seats of the Barbarians, whose emigrations westward drove in the Gothic nations on the Roman empire, were still occupied by many pastoral tribes of the same origin and character; and among them arose the famous Zingis Khan, the conqueror of Asia, the founder of the Mogul empire. The original name of this oriental Alexander was Temugin; and we have no doubt that the youth described in the following note, under that appellation, is the same person.

"The father of Temugin left him heir and chief of thirteen hordes, consisting of about forty thousand families. He was then a beardless stripling;—but the darling of the old, on account of his firmness of character, and the admiration of the young, for his boldness and dexterity. Some of the distant tribes that had obeyed the command of his father, when they heard of the old man's death, and the green years of Temugin, refused to pay the wonted tythes and obedience. The intrepid boy resolved to chastise their insubordination; and, by the bravery of his premature manhood, induced the elders entrusted with the care of his education, to indulge him with an attack on his enemies. The numbers of the rebels greatly exceeded his force, and he was compelled to fly; but not far: for the genius that ruled his destiny was awakened; and, with an energy to which the beauty of youth gave the persuasion of inspired heroism, he rallied his flying friends, and exhibited an example of prudence to the oldest warriors of the tribe. 'These infidels,' he exclaimed, 'that have driven us back with this disgrace, have only been permitted to do so, for the purpose of provoking our courage to punish them with a more complete vengeance. Go, three of you, to their tents, and tell them, that, unless they submit immediately, and bring to us in the morning the tribute that we claim, not one of them shall be spared, to relate their offence to posterity!

"The singular boldness of this resolution, after having sustained a defeat, surprised and animated his adherents; and when the three elders whom he directed to carry his message arrived among the rebels, the demand had such an effect on them, that many immediately submitted. Reinforced by their numbers, he pursued those who, in their desertion, had retired across the plain; and, having reduced them to submission, he placed seventy cauldrons on the fire, and seventy of the most guilty rebels were cast headlong into the boiling water.

"Having thus overcome, with extraordinary spirit, the adversaries of his youth, this strong and dauntless warrior, as he rose to manhood, became still more courageous: his fame was extended, his conquests increased, and his followers augmented in numbers.

"Inspired by his own genius, or taught by the example of Mahomet in legislating for his subjects, he employed the influence of superstition, and pretended that a naked prophet, who could ascend into heaven on a white horse, had bestowed on him the title of Zingis, or the *Most Great*, and endowed him with a divine right to the conquest of the whole earth.

"The arms of Zingis and his lieutenants successively reduced the tribes of the desert who traversed with their herds and flocks the wide expanse of territory between the wall of China and the Volga; and he became, by alliance and victory, the lord of many millions of shepherds and soldiers, impatient to rush on the mild and luxurious climates of the south. The act of alliance with this monarch of the pastoral world, was ratified with rites suitable to the vigorous simplicity of his powers: a horse was sacrificed on the banks of a river, and the running stream tasted by the allies.

"His ancestors had been tributaries to China, but he determined to remain so no more; on the contrary, to exact tribute from that enormous nation. The court of Pekin was astonished at the demand, and endeavoured to disguise their dread of the audacious vassal by an haughty answer. This was expected by Zingis; and his innumerable squadrons soon pierced the feeble rampart of the great wall,—that stupendous monument of political precaution, which beggars all the labours of the Egyptians, the Greeks, and the Romans. It incloses the frontiers of the empire; and, stretching over mountains and valleys, forms a line on the map of the earth, making itself a part of the world, even to the eye that can comprehend the whole. In this expedition, the Chinese consented to the demands of Zingis. A daughter of the emperor was bestowed on him in marriage; and the tribute of slaves and riches which he extorted, was disguised under the propitiatory epithet of her dower.

"It was in his second expedition that I accompanied the most great Khan into the bosom of the Chinese empire. The army pierced the great wall in a wide and spacious valley, which it crossed diagonally. The long array of towers after towers, stretching beyond the reach of vision over the tops of the hills, and the flourishing cultivated appearance of the country within this mighty enclosure, contrasted with the wild and desert aspect of the Tartar regions without, made me shudder, when I beheld the barbaric hordes of the conqueror spreading themselves like locusts amidst the beautiful bowers and gardens of civilization. The Chinese at first had resolved to defend the wall; but, when they saw the innumerable multitude of the Tartars, pouring like torrents from the hills, they retreated into the interior; and Zingis, unmolested, penetrated as far as Pekin, to which he laid siege.

"In the course of the march, I had frequent occasion to lament his barbarian career. The monuments of his former expedition were the ruins of ninety great cities, and of spacious canals, that had supplied their inhabitants with the luxuries of commerce, and the necessaries of life.

"The inhabitants of Pekin defended their city with a courage and fortitude never surpassed in the western world, save only at the siege of Jerusalem. They sacrificed their furniture, their temples, and all but their gods, to supply their engines; and, when they had nothing less precious or effectual, they discharged against the besiegers ingots of gold and silver. Horrible famine raged among them, but it did not impair their patriotism. Determined to withstand the conqueror to the last extremity, they decimated their fellow-citizens, and fed upon them, when all the other means of subsistence failed. This unexampled resolution was, however, of no avail. Zingis had, in the meantime, ordered a mine to be formed under the walls into the heart of the city; into which, when completed, he ordered his men during the night to enter. At the dawn of day, the helpless Chinese looked from their watch-towers, and beheld the camp of the enemy deserted. Believing his patience had been overcome, and that he had retired from the siege, they shouted with joy and exultation, and were answered by a terrible sound from the town. The conqueror and the Tartars were there; and volumes of smoke, rising from the imperial palace, showed that the vengeance of Zingis had commenced."

CHAPTER XLVIII.

Notes respecting the History of the Turks.

How long our author remained in China we have no means of ascertaining; for there is a considerable portion of the Volume so defaced by damp, that it was impossible to read it; but the next legible passage that we meet with is curious.

"The mountains to the south of the Caspian Sea were inhabited by an odious race called the "Assassins," who blended with the fanaticism of the Koran the Indian doctrine of the transmigration of souls, and the visions of prophets among themselves. Their chief priest was called the Old Man of the Mountain, but his abode was unknown; and they deemed it their first duty to devote their souls and bodies in blind obedience to his service. In this the daggers of their missionaries were felt both in the East and West; and their national name has become the peculiar title of the secret murderer throughout the world."

A little further on, we are informed that the descendants of Zingis conquered Bagdad, put to death the caliph Motassun, the last of the temporal successors of Mahomet, whose noble kinsmen had reigned above five hundred years; and, after penetrating as far as Aleppo and Damascus, were forced to retire to the eastward of the Euphrates by the Mamalukes, a military power that had grown up from slavery in Egypt to the possession of that kingdom.

"Since this retreat," says Hareach, "the dominion of the descendants of Zingis have declined; and different petty chiefs and adventurers, the worms that live in the carcasses of fallen empires, begin to revel in blood
* * *

"Among others, who have formed little principalities for themselves, I should notice Othman, the chief of a small tribe of four hundred tents of Turkmans. He seems resolved to wage a holy war against the Greek empire, now declined into the last stage of inactivity and decay. Through the now unguarded passes of the Bithynian Olympus he makes bold incursions, and almost with impunity, on the narrow relics of that empire, whose vast eastern provinces induced the first Constantine to remove the imperial government from Rome to Byzantium
* * *

"Orchan, the son of Othman, is laying the foundations of a state; and his army, now swelled to thousands, although still called the Turks or Ottomans, consists of many soldiers that once acknowledged the emperor of Constantinople as their sovereign.

"Nice and Nicomedia have submitted to the Turks. Andronicus the emperor has been defeated by the son of Othman, who has thus achieved the conquest of Bithynia ——— * * *

"Constantinople is hastening to her doom. Orchan has obtained in marriage the daughter of the emperor, and the privilege to sell his captives in the market of that city: these captives were all subjects of that emperor ——— * * *

"Amurath, the son of Orchan, has succeeded his father. He has subdued, without resistance, all that portion of the empire between the Hellespont and Mount Hæmus, and fixed the seat of his government at Adrianople. His dominions may be said to reach to the walls of Constantinople. The emperor and his sons have visited him in his camp: for this homage he has respited the city." ——— * * *

By various scattered fragments of this kind, interspersed among a number of broken sentences and hints for recollection, we are thus led on to form some idea of the establishment of the Ottoman empire, and prepared for the final conquest of Constantinople, at which Hareach appears to have been present; and with his account of which we shall conclude the second Part of our compilation from his Volume.

CHAPTER XLIX.

The last Siege and Fall of Constantinople; with the final Extinction of all the Military and Imperial Institutions that originated with the Roman People.

[A. D. 1453.]

"In all my wanderings," says Hareach, "I have not met with a man who has revived in my bosom so many of the dormant feelings of human nature as the emperor Constantine Palæologus. He is awake to his inevitable doom; but a noble sense of duty adds the energy of heroism to his piety. No task that virtue may claim has been neglected. He has implored the aid of heaven; but, in the signs of the times, he sees that aid denied. He has addressed himself to all the Christian powers, but their hearts are seared against him; and, in the midst of his empire, now circumscribed to the walls of the capital, he stands as a martyr fastened to the stake, — a martyr to his dignity and his country.

"The armies of the sultan extend on the right and left from the Propontis to the harbour. The suburb of Galata, on the other side of the harbour, is also surrounded by a subordinate army. The whole force of the enemy exceeds two hundred and fifty thousand men, many of whom are but little skilled in the exercises of war, but all are instigated to enterprise by the keen motives of religious fanaticism and baser passions.

"The population of the city might still furnish a hundred thousand men; but Phranza, the imperial minister, has diligently enquired who among them were still brave enough to risk their lives in defence of their families and property, and only four thousand nine hundred and seventy have enrolled their names. The lists were collected in different parts of the city, so that none of the subordinate officers know the result; but Phranza* himself has told me the number; and that the emperor had deemed it prudent to withhold the disclosure of this comfortless secret.

"It is remarked, that the emperor begins to look pale, that his eyes have become unusually quick and penetrating, and his voice clear, piercing, and yet exceedingly pathetic. His commands are delivered with sufficient firmness; but they strike upon the ear with the tone of solicitation.

"Justiniani, a noble Genoese merchant, is the last and only ally of the inheritor of all that remains of the victorious achievements of the Roman consuls and the Cæsars. He has embodied and collected two thousand men in Galata, with which he defends that suburb.

"Of the triangle which composes the figure of Constantinople, the two sides along the sea are inaccessible to the enemy; and the third, the land side, is protected by a double wall, with many lofty towers, and a deep ditch more than a hundred feet in width. Against this line of fortifications the Turks are embattled, occupying, from the waters of the sea to those of the harbour, a front of about four miles in extent.†

"The sultan employs the ancient and modern engines of war. A deserter, from Constantinople, has cast for him cannon of prodigious calibre. Sixty oxen, and between four and five hundred men, were required to bring only one of them from Adrianople; and two months were spent in the laborious journey. The bullet and the bat-

---

* Phranza has written an account of the siege.
† Phranza says six miles; but we have used an English estimate, having walked the space in little more than an hour: we have also substituted width for depth in the dimensions given of the ditch, being satisfied, from actual inspection, that Gibbon has in this committed an error.

tering-ram thunder against the same walls, but hitherto without effect.

"I have to-day beheld a magnificent spectacle. The Turkish fleet, in the form of a crescent, was drawn up at the mouth of the Bosphorus, to resist the approach of five vessels with reinforcements and supplies of provisions to the city. The breeze was fair and brisk;—the five stately vessels came gallantly on with all their canvas spread;— the Turkish galleys were as so many clusters of warriors;— the ramparts, the camp, and the coasts of Europe and Asia, were lined with spectators;—and the sultan sat on horseback on the beach, and encouraged his men by his voice and his gestures. The headmost of the succours bore the imperial flag; and she advanced with a rapid and majestic motion. As she approached the Turkish line, a fearful sensation shook the multitude on the ramparts,— and they were all silent,—but the Turks shouted with exultation. In the same moment her artillery vomited the liquid fire; but the enemy, none dismayed, almost overpowered her. In this crisis, her companions reached the scene of conflict. The fire was lavished on all sides;— the open row-galleys were crushed beneath their prows, and hundreds of the Turks perished;—the spectators on the walls rent the air with acclamations;—the rage of the besiegers rose louder and fiercer;—the sultan madly spurred his charger into the sea, and was hoarse with his reproaches: but the intrepid squadron still steadily steered towards the port; and, while the three hundred galleys of the enemy fled in disorder to the shores of Asia and Europe, they securely anchored within the chain that defends the entrance to the harbour.

"Mahomet the sultan, sensible, unless a double attack can be made from the harbour and the land, that the reduction of the city, while she can so receive assistance by sea, must be hopeless, has executed a bold and difficult undertaking. He has drawn galleys across the land behind Galata from the Bosphorus, and launched them in the harbour.* In one night he has accomplished this decisive measure, and the fate of Constantinople can be no longer averted. The garrison is diminished and exhausted;—the fortifications are dismantled on all sides;— many breaches are open in the walls;—and four of the towers at the gate of St. Romanus are levelled with the ground. There is a talk of negociation and a truce; but the sultan has declared that he will either find a throne or a grave at Constantinople; and the emperor has determined to abide the last extremities of war.

"This is the last night of the empire. It is understood that, at two o'clock, the sultan, emboldened by astrological predictions, has resolved on a general assault. The Turkish camp resounds with shouts of defiance; and the sea and land, from Galata to the castle of the Seven Towers, are illuminated by the blaze of their innumerable fires. The city exhibits the extravagance and folly of devoted dotage. The inhabitants deplore their sins;— they carry the image of the Virgin Mary from place to place;—they accuse the emperor of obstinacy for refusing to surrender:—and, while they deplore the horrors of their fate, they sigh for the ignominious repose of Turkish servitude.

"I accompanied Phranza to the palace, where, about two hours after sun-set, the noblest of the citizens and the bravest officers assembled. It was the sublimest scene that the vicissitudes of fortune, and the instability of human grandeur, ever exhibited. The hall in which the meeting was held, was the great audience-chamber of the palace. Every one was silent; each, as he entered, saluted his neighbour with the solemnity observed at funerals. The servants had prepared for the occasion;

---

* Gibbon, with his usual acuteness, questions the alleged distance of ten miles. It is not, however, more than two. The track which was taken, we conceive, from personal inspection, to have been on the north side of the rising ground on which the palace of the British ambassador stands. It is occupied by pleasure-gardens and burying-grounds.

and the gorgeous lamps, and massy old domestic ornaments, were lighted and set out. After some time, the interchange of a few whispers begot a little confidence; and when we had waited about half an hour, there was a buz, approaching to conversation. But, when the emperor entered, a dead silence ensued. I was struck with his appearance. His countenance wore a serene, I would almost say, a celestial expression of resignation. He said a few words, so pregnant with meaning, that several who were present, interpreting by their own feelings, represented them as an oration: but his eye spoke more than his tongue; and his calmness was more eloquent than his exhortations to courage. He then addressed himself to each of his officers with an assumed cheerfulness, that was so truly pathetic, that many of the stoutest-hearted burst into tears. For himself the flood-gates of sorrow seemed to be closed; and he was either rendered incapable, or raised above the weakness, of weeping.

"We attended him to the church of St. Sophia, while the officers generally went to their posts on the wall. Here he received the sacrament; and, in the moment that the priest pronounced the words over the broken bread, in allusion to the broken body, the imperial martyr heaved a deep and awful sigh, and a tear trickled down his cheek. When this final ceremony was over, he walked back to the palace; and, without undressing, threw himself on a couch, and fell, or seemed to fall, asleep. Having thus rested about three hours, he rose, ordered the domestics to be assembled, and solicited them by name to pardon him, if he had ever done them any wilful wrong: but they could only answer him with their lamentations. Soon after midnight he left the palace, to return no more.

"The image of this noble victim is so constantly before me, that I in vain attempt to recollect the series of incidents that passed between his departure from the palace and his fall. A terrible chaos of things rise upon my imagination. I see the dawn of the morning breaking in the east;—phalanx after phalanx led to the assault;—

engines thundering with destruction and bursting fires;— while a wild dissonance of cries and shouts appal my hearing. In the midst of the smoke, the havoc, and the fury, the grim figure of the sultan, grasping an iron mace, passes swiftly before me—the demon of the hurricane. From the lines, the galleys, and the platforms, the artillery rages on all sides.

"Justiniani received a wound. It was not in itself dangerous, but he saw that all effort was in vain; and, with a prudence that, by its baseness, deserves to be held up to perpetual scorn, he quitted his post. Palæologus saw him retiring, ran to him, and seized him by the arm. The Genoese, without speaking, showed him his wound.—' It is slight,' exclaimed the emperor; ' the danger is pressing: and whither will you retire?'—' By the same road which God has opened to the Turks',—was the sullen answer. The emperor dropped his hold, and for a moment drooped his head; but, when he saw this pusillanimous ally retiring through one of the breaches, he looked towards the heavens with an awful glance of remonstrance and despair.

"In this terrible moment, the Turks had, not far from the spot, scaled the broken walls. The emperor had still retained the purple robe; and he was surrounded by his few faithful nobles, who fought till their last breath. ' Cannot,' he cried, as he saw them falling; ' cannot a Christian be found to cut off my head?'—for his only fear was of falling alive into the hands of the infidels. In saying these words, he tore the imperial mantle from his shoulders; and, grasping his sword with the boundless energy of despair, rushed towards the breach, through which the enemy was pouring like a torrent, and fell by an unknown hand —— * * *

"I saw no more: the crowd, pressing towards the spot where I stood, forced me to change my station; and I bore in my mind such an awful impression of the last look and despair of the emperor, that the interest of every other object was absorbed by the intensity of the single feeling which he had awakened." —— * * *

The death of Constantine Palæologus closes the history

of all the military and imperial institutions that originated with the Roman people; and the conquest of Constantinople forms one of the most important epochs of history; for it is not only memorable, on account of the many high and various associations of the mind connected with the history of the place, but also remarkable, as fixing a period to the progress of Mahomedan fanaticism and of Christian bigotry. Since the Turks acquired this city, the religion of Mahomet has ceased to spread; and the contests of the Greek and Roman churches have been superseded by the reformation of Christianity. The dogmas and dictation of individuals have lost their power; and the pretensions of piety, and the pretexts of policy, are alike subjected to the jurisdiction of reason and the standard of utility.

END OF PART II.

PART III.

CHAPTER I.

The Retreat and Character of a Hermit in the Island of Samos.

IMMEDIATELY after the conquest of Constantinople, our desultory traveller embarked with a party of other fugitives in a Venetian vessel for the island of Chios, which was then in the hands of the Genoese; and, immediately on landing there, took his passage in another ship bound for Naples. But they had not left the harbour many hours, when a strong gale of northerly wind drove them with great violence into a port in the island of Samos. Here he remained several days; and seemed disposed, if we may so infer from some of his notes, to change his route, and again return towards the regions of the East: but a desire prevailed to see the change that had taken place in the scenes and countries he had formerly visited in the West; and he resolved to continue his voyage with the vessel in which he had come from Chios. In the meantime, however, he had rambled into the interior of the island; and, the wind becoming favourable during his absence, the vessel sailed without him. Being thus constrained to remain until another opportunity presented itself, he wandered round the shores of Vathi, as the inlet where he had disembarked was called, and ascended the stupendous mountains which overlook and shelter that admirable natural harbour. These mountains he describes as covered with a forest of stately trees, and containing within their interesting valleys many beautiful sequestered recesses, inhabited by a race of hardy and independent shepherds. "The energy of the Greek character," he says, " is unimpaired among this bold and primitive race; but, wanting the controul of a superior greater than the leading men among themselves, they indulge in a freedom of action destructive of real liberty, by removing its only true bulwark,—security."

In one of his excursions among the mountains of Samos, he fell in with a hermit, with whom he remained several days. His account of the retreat and character of this anchorite, form an agreeable episode to the general strain of his personal narrative; and, as it throws some light on the manners of the age, we extract it with the less scruple.

" I was descending from the hill along a path that followed a ravine, in which a small summer stream, by its pleasing gurgling, might be said to be performing a musical imitation of the wild and headlong fury of the winter's torrent. The sea below was as smooth as glass, and the heavens above were as calm and azure as the sea. About half-way down the mountain, the path which I had hitherto traced on the skirts of the ravine suddenly sloped towards the bottom, and passed under a lofty precipice overhung by several pines, which stooped from their natural erectness in a beautiful and fantastic manner. In following this track, I came to the edge of a rock, over which the water fell; and I paused,—at a loss to conceive for what purpose the road could have been trodden so near to the brink of the cataract. While in this situation, and almost dizzy with looking down the precipice, I observed the trunk of a long slender pine leaning against the side-rocks within reach; and, as the bark on the stumps of the branches had the appearance of being worn off, it occurred to me that it was used as a ladder by the persons who frequented the path. I went towards it; and, having examined how far the footing was firm, I descended. It did not, however, reach to the bottom, but only to a ledge of the rock about half-way down; and I was now still more perplexed than before.

"As I stood ruminating in doubt what to do, a voice from below said, 'Stranger, what do you seek here?'—I could not see from whom the voice proceeded, for the speaker was under a projection of the rock on which I stood; but I answered, 'Having been at the top of the mountain, I have followed the footpath in my descent; and I am at a loss how to proceed farther.'—'Are you alone?' enquired the voice: and, when I had replied in the affirmative, the speaker stepped out from his concealment, and threw a piece of wood, to which a cord was fastened, over the trunk of the pine. To the other end of the cord a rope was tied; and the end to which the wood was attached having dropped within reach of the hermit's hand, he pulled the rope over the pine, and doubled it.—'By this,' said he, 'you can slide down.'

"I readily accepted the invitation, and found myself in one of the most beautiful recesses of solitude. On all sides but the south it was surrounded by cliffs and lofty precipices, crowned with pines and tapestried with ivy. A spacious and profound bason, in which the falling waters, thrown like a curve of crystal from the corner of the rock almost to the middle of the pool, occupied the centre of this delicious valley; and the margin was covered with a close-felted grass of the freshest verdure, embroidered with the brightest flowers.

"While I stood gazing with delight at the secluded paradise into which I had been so suddenly transported, my hands still glowing with the effects of the friction of the cord in my descent, the genius of the place, for as such I can alone properly designate the sole inhabitant, having redrawn the rope, came towards me. He was past the prime of life, but his hair and beard were only slightly sprinkled with hoariness. He wore a loose brown mantle of shagged hair cloth, tied by a cord round the waist, to which a string of beads suspending a little cross was affixed. His feet were bare, but his tread was firm and lordly; and his whole figure, notwithstanding the singular poverty of his dress, was at once courteous and commanding.—'Stranger,' said he, 'you cannot be otherwise than fatigued by your walk;—the day has been unusually warm, and repose and refreshment must be acceptable. I have little within my cell to offer you, but, such as it is, I shall be honoured by your partaking.' Without waiting for a reply he walked forward; and, having advanced a few paces, turned round, and said, ' through the cavern in which I have taken up my abode is the only outlet by which you can pass from this place.' I followed him; and he conducted me into a hollow in the rocks, the sides of which, gradually leaning over as we went forward, formed, at last, the entrance to a cave, through which a cold wind came rushing with considerable violence. 'This wind,' said he, 'is always strongest during the heat of the day, and in proportion to the hotness of the weather; but my cell is not comfortless: and he led me into a branch of the cave, which gradually expanded into a chamber of agreeable proportions, lighted by an opening in the rocks, which commanded, at a great height, a view of the sea towards the west as far as the Black Mountains of Eubea on the one hand, and the islands of Naxia, Paros, and Mycone, on the other.

"The furniture of this apartment corresponded with the simplicity and appearance of my host. On the one side was a rude sofa covered with sheep-skins. The root of a tree, which stood near it, was the only table I could discover: attached to the opposite wall was a shelf, on which a few books, a lamp, a piece of bread, and several melons, were placed; and a gourd bottle hung from a peg, stuck into a cleft in the rock, over the aperture that served for the window. A pitcher, covered with a shell, and which stood in a corner, completed the inventory.

"When I was seated on the couch, he placed the bread and one of the melons on the table, with a sheathed knife, that I had not before noticed, and which he wore in his belt. He took down the gourd, and placed it at my feet, while he brought the pitcher and the shell within my reach. 'I do not indulge myself in wine,' said the hermit; ' but a worthy peasant, one of my neighbours, brought me this bottle yesterday; and it seems to have been a well-suggested gift, since it enables me to entertain you better than I could otherwise have done.'

"After I had tasted his bread and fruit, and taken some of the wine mixed with the delicious cool water, he enquired, without asking any questions respecting myself, if I had heard any news respecting the progress of the siege of Constantinople; and, when I told him of the success of the Turks, and the fate of the emperor, he appeared, for a short time, overwhelmed with a profound internal sense of sorrow.—' Palæologus merited a better fortune,' was his observation; ' but it is the will of Heaven to visit the offences of the parents on the children to the third and fourth generation; at least, we can no otherwise account for the adversity and afflictions with which the good and worthy are so often visited. What an awful obligation does the knowledge of this divine truth impose upon man! But it is calculated also to make the stubborn heart repine at its destiny. How long in vain have I contended with mine!'

"These words seemed to escape from the hermit as if he only thought aloud; for they were uttered in that low and inward tone with which a man, in the agitated moods of the mind, converses with himself. In the course of a few minutes our conversation took a more general direction; and he showed himself singularly, I would almost say splendidly, acquainted with the state of Christendom. The turn of his reflections were those of one accustomed to view the affairs of the world from the vantage ground of high trusts, and to contemplate things in the general mass with reference to their general consequences."

CHAPTER II.

A general View of the State of Christendom about the Middle of the Fifteenth Century.

"'All Christendom at this time,' said the hermit, 'although subdivided into a number of secular kingdoms and principalities, is yet but one great theocratic empire, of which the pope of Rome is the head and sovereign. I reckon the Greek church, now that the imperial government is utterly subverted at Constantinople, as beyond the pale of Christendom; and, if not so already, nearly in a state of vassalage to the Mahomedan authority.

"'Italy, once the most powerful division of the Roman empire, is the weakest, in a collective sense, of all the provinces of the Papacy; owing to the multitude of little states, by which the political institutions of the country are prevented from being brought into simultaneous action. There is no one peculiar arm sufficiently strong to command or direct the energies of the whole; and the government of the pope takes too comprehensive a sweep, to regard the detail of Italian affairs otherwise than as provincial or parochial concerns, which are safe enough in the hands of the local magistrates. Italy, however, is still the greatest country in Europe, the most flourishing, the most populous, and the most enlightened; and, as the authority of a king is always weakest in his own court and capital, that of the pope is less respected in Italy than in the rest of Christendom.

"'In France, the Gaul of the Romans, there is a bold and ambitious spirit abroad, but altogether of a military character. A strange thirst of warlike fame actuates the people; but, while they pay all due respect to the spiritual dominion of the pope, they do not allow it to interfere with their political predilections; and these are all of the heroic kind. They have constantly aspired to the empire of Europe; but, forgetting that tolerant spirit with which the Romans conciliated, as well as conquered, they carry their own peculiar manners along with them, and cannot imagine a conquest achieved, unless they have converted the conquered people into Frenchmen. Thus they make themselves, in time, hated wherever they carry their arms, and are often repulsed with infamy from places where they were received with acclamation; particularly from Italy, towards which, at this moment, they are again looking with covetous and longing eyes.

"' Next to France, England must be regarded as the second great province of the empire of Christendom: perhaps it would have been the first, but for a series of civil wars between the York and Lancaster branches of the Royal family, or the factions of the Red and White Rose, —wars which, whether considered with reference to the virulence of spirit displayed in them, or the alternate changes of fortune to the parties, are the most remarkable in the annals of any nation. But for these terrible civil wars, it is probable that the crowns of France and England would have been united on the brow of the same monarch; for a succession of able and politic princes, supported by a wonderful race of wise and indefatigable warriors, have twice enabled the English, in less than a hundred years, to assert with success the claims of birth, by the force of arms, to the inheritance of the French throne. This has given to the genius of the nation a decided ascendancy over that of France.

"' Adjoining to England, part of the same island, is another spirited state, called Scotland, attached by policy and ancient intercourse to France, as a counterpoise against the English. The people of that country live in a constant alarm for their independence; by which their wits, animosities, and courage, are surprisingly sharpened. The nation itself seems, however, barred by nature from all chance of extending its dominion; for, although it bravely sets the power of the greater state of England at defiance, it has not the means of extending its sway over any portion of the English territories. A union of England and Scotland, by consolidating the whole British power into one compact state, would form a fulcrum for an engine, sufficient, indeed, to shake and raise the whole earth. But how that is to be accomplished, unless by an accident arising out of some matrimonial alliance, is not easily to be conjectured; for it will never be the effect of any negociation of political expediency.

"'At this time Germany, however, ought perhaps to be naturally the first secular state; for, under the same language, and governed by the same monarch, it comprehends a much greater extent of territory and population, than either England or France. The sovereign is dignified with the title of Emperor, but it is a dignity without any precise power, except what is enjoyed by the person possessing it from his own hereditary dominions;—for the empire consists, like Italy, of a number of petty states, each pursuing, with all its little means of intrigue, its own separate interests. Still, however, in the hands of a great man, endowed with a popular genius, the German empire would be a formidable adversary to the other members of the Christian confederation. But heroes of that stamp are not indigenous to the country.

"'In the peninsula beyond the Pyrences, the Moors still possess Granada, one of the finest kingdoms; and different jealous governments, though leagued respectively with the kings of Castile and Arragon, maintain a warlike independence of each other. From them, however, I should except Portugal, a state which possesses energy enough, properly directed, to reduce the whole peninsula into one monarchy. Of the kingdoms beyond Germany I know little; but an association of free commercial cities, known by the name of the Hanse Towns, are reported to rival, in enterprise and wealth, the republics of Venice, Florence, and Genoa.

"'Such is the present state of Christendom, over which the pope of Rome waves the crosier with more necromantic influence than ever the greatest of the Cæsars did the imperial sceptre. His will reaches the ear of every individual subject beneath the scope of that mysterious dominion, and a whisper, conveyed by his agents, is sufficient to blast, in the pride of victory, the proudest monarchs, and to change the destiny of nations. Theory never contemplated so perfect a model of its kind as the practical government of the Papacy; for though, like all other frames of government, it rules its subjects by the medium of their fears, yet it does not, as most others do, allow them, in any case, a plausible semblance of exercising their reason, but exacts a degree of implicit obedience, such as no other ever aspired to attain.

"' By the oracle, as it may be called, of auricular confession, it has acquired the mastery of the thoughts, the passions, and the actions of its subjects. In the form of penance or indulgence, it makes its will felt with the potency of a charm, that compels the patient to execute purposes of which he is insensible of the issue, and produces a simultaneous effect over the whole extent of the empire, that has all the energy and enthusiasm of spontaneous resolution. It is reported by historians, that, when the council of the pope determined on the holy war for the recovery of Palestine, in the same night the decision was known throughout Christendom. Can it be doubted, that the determination had been really previously arranged in secret, and communicated to the different immediate agents of the conclave, to be divulged on the day appointed for the ceremony of the public deliberation? By the means of this awful and occult power, the secular authorities are forced to yield obedience to the pope as to a God; but the moment that the dogmas are questioned by which he has possessed himself of this irrational and amazing supremacy, it will pass away like the shadow of the cloud which darkens the landscape, and saddens the vital spirit.'

" While the hermit was thus speaking," says Hareach, " I could not but several times question the veracity of my sight,—his appearance and abode were so much at variance with the words that impressed my hearing. His garb, and frugal table, his venerable look, and solitary abstemious seclusion, formed a strange contrast to the magnificence of his political views,—and I felt myself involuntarily constrained to express my surprise, that a man so habituated to contemplate the affairs of the world with the eye of a politician, should, with so little religious enthusiasm, have devoted himself to the sterile duties of an anchorite. 'Were you acquainted with my story, you would cease to wonder;' said he: 'I have not assumed this habit, nor retired to this cave, from any devotional sentiment.

"In saying this, his countenance appeared somewhat overcast; and he evidently struggled against the emotion of some strong and painful recollection. But, soon recovering his self-possession, he added, 'But my story is not long; and, while you are resting, it may serve to pass the time.'"

CHAPTER III.

The Story of the Hermit of Samos.

"'It is unnecessary,' said the hermit, ' to inform you of my name or country,—but my birth was noble, and my inheritance such as befitted the heir of an ancient and distinguished race. In the court of my sovereign I was early favoured; and I had scarcely arrived at manhood, when, by his partiality, I was honoured with important trusts. At this time I married a lady, celebrated for her wit and beauty; and the prospect of domestic felicity before me was bright and promising, when the king was pleased to request me to visit the pope, on a confidential business, in which his happiness was tenderly concerned. I shall not trouble you with any account of what took place in parting from my wife. It is enough to say, that the sorrow I suffered was sincere, and that the tears which she so profusely shed, I thought the faithful witnesses of unfeigned affection. I hastened on my journey, and my only anxiety was on her account. When I was sometime at Rome, and dispatched the commission with which I had been entrusted, the carnival commenced. I was a young man of cheerful spirits, and I entered into the amusements of that jocund festival with the wonted ardour of my character.

"'One evening, finding myself overcome with fatigue, and tired with the bustle and dissipation, I went into a tavern for some refreshment. I was alone; and, according to the custom of the time, in masque. The house I entered was one much frequented by the lower class, by servants, and persons of their condition. As I was sitting in the corner of the room, one of my own servants, accompanied by another masque, entered. I recognised the one by his voice; and their conversation, which was carried on in my native language, soon informed me who was the other,—a nobleman of whom I had but a slight acquaintance, although nearly related to my wife. His reputation was not good; in a word, he was a prodigal libertine, who had spent fortunes, and destroyed the happiness and honour of many families.

"'By his conversation with my domestic, I found they were on terms of great equality, but that their meeting had been accidental. I was averse to listen, and did not choose to disclose myself; but there was something in this circumstance which fixed me to the spot. After the first mutual enquiries of a sudden meeting were over, the servant told him, in an accent that made my whole frame thrill, that he was in my service, and that I had lately married. I cannot repeat what he said of my wife; but it withered my heart. I still, however, possessed sufficient self-command to remain concealed, and listened to them now with greedy ears, that drank-in horror and poison to my existence. I cannot detail to you what passed; only a confused recollection flashes across my memory, like lightning over the waves of a tempestuous sea. I only heard by my feelings, and remember by the anguish which the sensation has still left. It is enough, that I was satisfied my wife, before her marriage, had submitted to the embraces of her cousin, and that my domestic was in the confidence of the guilty lovers. At first I was stunned, and sat listening, unconscious of any power of action; but when the first impression abated, my emotion became so extreme, that I was forced to quit the house, to prevent myself from being discovered.

"'I hurried to my lodgings, breathing murder and revenge, till a flood of tears relieved me. I then sat down to consider what I ought to do. My determination was, to conceal carefully what I had learnt, and to hasten home, and institute a course of vigilance, to detect the guilty and deceitful woman in her crime. I gave orders the same night to prepare for my immediate return; and next morning I was on the road. I had not, however, proceeded far, when I began to reflect more at leisure, and it seemed to me that my happiness was entirely wrecked. —Of what avail was the punishment of the adultress to me? I turned my horse's head, and changed my route towards Naples, where I remained some time, abandoned to the pleasures of that licentious city. I strove to fly from my own thoughts; but they pursued me like demons, and forced me into the most wild and frantic courses. In this state letters came to me from my friends, expressing astonishment at my altered conduct; and, among others, one from my wife, couched in the tenderest phrases of affectionate solicitation and remonstrance. This fresh instance of duplicity roused my vengeance anew. I hired a vessel to transport me immediately to Marseilles, and the same day embarked.

"'The wind was favourable when we sailed; but, in the course of two hours afterwards, the heavens were overcast, and the omens of a storm were seen in the clouds, and heard in the wind. At sun-set, the blasts came out at intervals with violent gusts: the sea became of a dark leaden colour, and the swell of the waves, which but seldom burst, rolled heavier and more abrupt. The mariners were alarmed, and stood away before the wind for the coast of Sicily. About midnight the fury of the storm abated, but the gale still blew from the same quarter; and we had no alternative but to continue our course.

"'I was so entranced with my own moody meditations, that I paid no attention to what was going forward in the vessel, till I was awakened from my abstraction by one of my domestics, who informed me that there was no one on-board acquainted with the Sicilian coast, or in what part of it to find a harbour. This intelligence, so frightful to them, was comfort to me. My life was bitter, but my religion would not permit me to cast it away; and I thought that Providence, by placing us in so much danger, was about to loosen me from the vulture that devoured my heart.

"'At day-break we were fast driving towards the coast; and, about two hours afterwards, the vessel struck on a rock, not far from the shore, and in a few minutes was forced by the waves on her beam-ends. The sailors and servants exerted themselves to reach the shore, and I also plunged into the raging surf, but soon found myself incapable of contending with it. In this situation I was rescued by the fellow that had so ministered to my dishonour. Saved by the wretch against whom I cherished the most implacable revenge! It was a pang of which language has no terms to describe the anguish.

"'The wreck of the vessel attracted the peasants from the interior of the country, and they treated us with all the hospitality in their power. I was conducted to a monastery, in a village about two miles distant from the scene of our disaster; where the turbulence of my mind, with the cold and fatigue of my struggling in the waves, brought on a severe fit of indisposition, during which my preserver, who seemed to be possessed of much natural kindness of disposition, attended me with the most exemplary solicitude.

"'In the course of a few days the fever subsided, but left me very weak; and, as I lay on my couch, I had leisure to reflect on my peculiar fate. I am not of an enthusiastic temperament, though I have felt acutely; and therefore, when I inform you that I resolved to assign my property to the church, and become what you now see me, you must not suppose that it was dictated by religious devotion, although the circumstance of my escape from shipwreck furnished a pretext of that kind, had I chosen to have had recourse to any such subterfuge.

"'I will not trouble you farther with details. My resolution was carried into effect. I dismissed my servants; rewarded the one that saved me, as if I was unconscious of his crime; and, having completed the necessary papers for the appropriation of my estates, I embarked at Messina on a pilgrimage to the Holy Sepulchre. On the evening of our departure, I wrote my wife a circumstantial account of the circumstances that had come to my knowledge.

"' In the course of our voyage we happened to touch at this island; and, being detained by contrary winds, I rambled, like yourself, among the mountains. Accident brought me to this cave. I entered: and the beautiful recess under the waterfall seemed an asylum,—a cloister prepared for one who had, like me, no longer any part or interest in the affairs of this world. From that time I have led a solitary life—I know not how many years, for I keep no reckoning of time; but a peasant boy, one of my earliest visitors, has, in the interim, grown up into manhood, is married, and the father of several children, to whom I am occasionally indebted for the luxuries of wine and fruit."'

CHAPTER IV.

The Brother of the Sultan a Prisoner at Rome.—Pope Alexander VI.

[A.D. 1489—1503.]

Our author makes no comment on the hermit's story; indeed, a considerable time intervenes between the date of his excursion to the mountains of Samos, and that of his next memorandum. We are therefore led to conjecture, that, after leaving Samos, he embarked for Italy, and that nothing occurred during the voyage worthy of being recorded. Rome appears always to have offered peculiar attractions to him; for we find him again resident there, where he must have remained many years. All his observations for a long period relate to occurrences which took place in that metropolis, and which, however interesting at the time, have long ceased to be so with posterity. We find, however, one little story, which we shall extract.

"Peter Daubusson* has mightily obliged the pope, by allowing his prisoner, Zizim, the brother of the Grand Signor, to be removed from Paris to Rome. Daubusson, in the pride of his heart, had sent the captive, guarded by a party of the knights of Rhodes, to the court of his native country; but, when the wonder there at beholding so formidable a Turk had subsided, he consented that he should be brought to Rome,—the Pope being regarded as the head of the cause against the infidels. The ceremony of introducing the Ottoman prince to his Holiness was singularly ridiculous. He was presented to him in a public consistory by the French ambassador; but, notwithstanding the entreaties and threats of all present, the stubborn Turk would not kneel before the pope, nor consent to kiss his foot.

"It now appears, that the bringing of Zizim to Rome was not a matter of mere ceremony, but in consequence of a determination, on the part of the Papal court, to form a crusade against Bajazet the sultan. A wonderful noise of preparation is sounding far and wide through Christendom; and it is even reported that Zizim is to be employed in the holy war against his brother.

"The crusade has ended in smoke. It seems to have been a shrewd scheme, on the part of the Papal court, to replenish the treasury by the contributions of the pious from all parts of Christendom; for the dreadful Bajazet,

---

* He was Grand Master of the Knights of Rhodes; the same order that, when Rhodes was taken, transferred their residence to Malta.

against whom all the fulminations of the Vatican were directed, has sent an ambassador, offering an annual subsidy for the subsistence of his brother, whom he wishes the Pope still to retain; and, since the arrival of this embassy, nothing more is said about the crusade. * * *

"It seems to me that Rome, under the popes, differs very little in its morality from what it was under the emperors, and that personal purity is but lightly considered by these flagrant usurpers of divine authority. Innocent the Eighth is dead, and Cardinal Borgia has been elected his successor under the name of Alexander VI. This man would have reflected dishonour on any situation in life: what then must be the moral sensibility of those who have chosen him to the highest earthly dignity? When a very young man he was created a cardinal by his uncle, Calixtus III. but his life was so infamous, that Pius II. would not at last allow him to enter his presence. He kept in his house the wife of Vanocia, a Roman, by whom he had four sons and one daughter.

"Pope Alexander is, without question, a man of great endowments; and he possesses, in a very eminent degree, the powers of address and persuasion: but his vices are still more remarkable. His fearless licentiousness, his insincerity, his impudence, and cruelty, are each of them more than a sufficient counterpoise to all his virtues. * * *

"There has been to-day a strange rumour abroad respecting the new world which the Spaniards have discovered. It is said that the pope has issued a bull, granting to Ferdinand and Isabella, the king and queen of Spain, and to their heirs, all the islands and continents discovered, or to be discovered, on the west side of a meridian line to be computed at a certain distance from the Azores. On what pretext has his Holiness assumed the power of thus granting these unknown territories?

"There is no limit to the audacity of this man. Among others, he has promoted his son, Cæsar Borgia, to the rank of cardinal, in contempt of the whole sacred college, by procuring false witnesses to swear that he was the legitimate son of another person,—bastards being ineligible to the cardinaline dignity. So much for the infallibility of the popes, and their authority to pardon sins! —— * * *

"The French, in their designs on Naples, have entered Rome, not exactly however as conquerors, but evidently as masters, under the command of their king, Charles VIII. in person. The pope, and two of the cardinals, have taken refuge in the castle of St. Angelo. The other cardinals have waited on the French king, and solicited him to depose the pope, as unworthy longer to reign. —— * * *

"The bold and subtle Alexander has been more dexterous than his enemies; and has concluded a treaty with the king, in virtue of which he has left the castle, and returned to his palace; and preparations are now making in the church of St. Peter to receive Charles with all due ecclesiastical pomp, and to confer on the French arms the Papal benediction,—the blessing of pope Alexander.

"A very horrid tale is openly repeated. The Ottoman prince Zizim lately died suddenly at Capua; and it is said that his death was procured by the head of the church. What renders this dreadful accusation not improbable, is a letter which is said to have been received some time ago from the sultan Bajazet, wherein he advises the pope to hasten the death of his brother,—an event which, at any rate, must happen in the course of nature; and promises him three hundred thousand crowns, if he would send his corpse to any port in the Turkish dominions. Can the system endure, of which such things are but spoken?

"The murder of the Ottoman prince has been followed by a terrible retribution on the Pope,—one of his sons has assassinated the other in the streets. The cause of this fratricide is too hideous to be repeated.* Is it the air and climate of Rome that engender these monstrous offences? The pope himself is struck with remorse; and, it is said, has deplored with tears in the consistory his own flagitious life, which he has resolved to amend.

"The gorgeous papal harlot has drained the cup of her

---

* Guicciardini.

abominations to the dregs. Savonarola, a Dominican friar of great authority at Florence, openly preaches against the corruption of the church; and has written, it is said, to the emperor, and to the kings of France, England, Spain, and Portugal, exhorting them to concur, by the authority of a general council, in reforming the state of religion. The pope is much disturbed at this new light; but is determined, it would seem, to preserve the existing mass of corruption, as if such a thing could be preserved.

"The spirit of reformation is abroad. One of the Roman bishops, accused of preaching new doctrines at variance with the worship of idols, and the other gross corruptions of the church, has been degraded, and imprisoned for heresy and Mahomedanism.

"Savonarola has been burnt at Florence for heresy,—the first martyr of a new cause."

By these brief notices it would appear, that the attention of Hareach was directed to the moral change which the enormities of the pope had rendered inevitable. The reformation of Christianity was ushered in by a species of necessity, seemingly independant of the doctrines called in question by the reformers.

The personal conduct of the members of the Papal government emulated the licentiousness of the ancient imperial courts; and the world seemed to be sensible, that it was requisite to subject them to the tribunal of human opinion. It is impossible to conceive a state of society in which vice was enthroned with more dominion than in the apostolic chair of the Papacy under pope Alexander. His pontificate was the very midnight of the Christian religion; and, from that epoch, the dawn of the new day began to break upon the moral world. But, before concluding this chapter, we should mention what our author has noted respecting his death.

"I am not satisfied with this story about the poisoning of the pope and his son Cæsar Borgia. It is too great a crime to be credited; and yet improbability in crime is often a species of proof. The report is, that the holy father and his son formed a scheme to poison all the rich cardinals, and to seize their revenues and estates; that the party were invited to sup in the gardens of cardinal Corneto; and that Borgia sent a present of some flasks of poisoned wine to the entertainment, with instructions, that, as it was very rare and valuable, it should only be given to the cardinals. The pope, soon after the arrival of the wine, happened to come before supper was ready; and, calling for wine, the servant who had charge of the poisoned flasks, thinking the prohibition could not extend to the holy father, poured him out some. Borgia also arriving while his father was drinking, likewise requested a little wine diluted with water; and both were poisoned. The pope died next day. Borgia is still ill, though likely to recover, although his skin and hair have fallen off. Considering the detestation in which both the pope and his son were held, I think it is quite as probable that the poisoned wine was intended for them by some of their enemies, as that they intended to destroy all the rich cardinals."

CHAPTER V.

State of Rome in the Fifteenth Century; with Reflexions on the Causes that have contributed to the Destruction of her ancient Edifices.

THE description which our author gives of the state of Rome, after his long absence, is too interesting to be omitted; we shall therefore, before proceeding with the progress of the Reformation, extract the passage.

"I ascended the Capitoline hill alone, and sat down amidst the ruins of columns and temples, to contemplate the wide and various prospect of desolation around. The place and the objects taught a solemn lesson of the vicissitudes of fortune, which spares neither man nor the proudest of his works, and which buries cities and empires in a common grave. In proportion to her former greatness, the fall of Rome is the more awful and mournful. Her primeval state, such as she might appear in a remote age, when Evander entertained the stranger of Troy, has been delineated by the fancy of Virgil. The Tarpeian rock was then a savage and solitary thicket. In the days of the poet, it was crowned with the golden roofs of a temple. The temple is overthrown;—the gold has been pillaged;—the wheel of fortune has accomplished her revolution;—and the hallowed ground is again disfigured with thorns and brambles. This hill of the capitol was formerly the head of the Roman empire,—the citadel of the earth,—the terror of kings: illustrated by the footsteps of so many triumphs,—enriched with the spoils and tribute of so many nations! This glory of the world, how is it faded,—how changed! The path of victory is obliterated by vines;—the benches of the senators are concealed by a dunghill. My eye ranges over the Palatine hill, and seeks, among the shapeless and enormous fragments, the marble theatre, the obelisks, the colossal statues, and the porticoes of the palace built by Nero; and, on all sides around me, the vacant space is intercepted only by ruins and gardens.

"The forum of the Roman people, where they assembled to enact their laws and elect their magistrates, is now inclosed for the cultivation of pot-herbs, or thrown open for the reception of cattle. The public and private edifices, that were founded for eternity, lie prostrate, naked, and broken, like the limbs of a mighty giant; and the ruin is the more striking, from the stupendous relics that have survived the injuries of time and fortune.*

"Of the remains of the first age of the republic, I discern a bridge, an arch, a sepulchre, and the pyramid of Cestius. Of countless temples, I trace but the wreck of eleven. The Pantheon is still entire. Three arches and one marble column of that edifice, which I saw so resplendent with the spoils of Jerusalem, are all that mark the

---

* Gibbon.

TRIUMPHAL ARCH
in the Sixteenth Century.

TEMPLE OF PEACE
in the Sixteenth Century.

place where the temple of Peace erected by Vespasian once stood. The baths of Dioclesian and Antoninus Caracalla still retain the names of their founders, and astonish the modern spectator by their solidity and extent, the variety of marbles, the size and multitude of the columns;—but, like the traditions of history, they only serve to furnish an imperfect idea of the outline. Of the triumphal arches, those of Titus, Severus, and Constantine, only, are entire. A fragment is all that remains of Trajan's; but his column is still erect, as well as that of Antoninus. The Egyptian obelisks are buried in the dust. The multitude of gods and heroes, that might be called a people of statues, are reduced to one equestrian figure of bronze and five of marble. The mausoleum of Augustus is a heap of earth; and Adrian's, stripped of its columns and ornaments, is the great tower of the castle of St. Angelo. The Colosseum alone can furnish the wandering traveller of these latter times with any index to the ancient grandeur of Rome.

"The art of man is able to construct monuments far more permanent than the narrow span of his own existence: yet these monuments, like himself, are perishable and frail; and, in the boundless annals of time, his life and his labours must equally be measured as a fleeting moment. As wonders of ancient days, the Pyramids attracted the curiosity of the ancients:* an hundred generations—the leaves of autumn,—have dropt into the grave; and, after the fall of the Pharoahs, and the Ptolemies, the Cæsars, and the Caliphs, the same fabrics still stand sublime and unshaken above the floods of the Nile. The lofty turrets of Rome have tottered from their foundations—but the Seven hills still remain; nor has the city been exposed to the convulsions of nature, which have crumbled the walls of ages into dust at

---

* This is true even with respect to Hareach. Diodorus Siculus is unable to decide whether they were constructed 1000 or 3400 years before the 180th olympiad. Sir John Marsham's contracted scale of the Egyptian Dynasties would fix them above 2000 years before Christ.

Antioch and Nicomedia. Fires and inundations, however, have been busy with her destruction. By the former, the domestic habitations of the people were reduced to walls, which the latter undermined and swept away. The hands of the Barbarians, the Goth, and the Vandal, spared the solid piles of antiquity, and but removed their ornamental decorations:—to the papal religion must be ascribed that wide desolation, so much more awful than the remotest solitudes of nature. The statues, altars, and mansions, of the gods, or demons, as they were supposed after the abolition of Paganism, were abominations in the eyes of the Roman Christians; and the demolition of the temples in the East was an example that they doubtless deemed it pious to imitate. Yet their abhorrence was confined to the monuments of heathen superstition; and the several structures which were dedicated to the business and pleasure of society, might have been preserved without injury or scandal. But even over these the influence of the new religion was exerted. The theatres were neglected, in which the sufferings and the heroism of ancient virtue were exhibited; and those admirable compositions, in which the partialities of the gods were mingled with the passions and affections of man, were in them represented no more. Poverty also consumed the means of procuring pleasures. The streams of wealth, which had flowed for so many ages into the Roman treasury, have been long stopped at the fountain-head; and the meagre revenue, arising from the impositions of the clergy, affords but a stinted substitute for the tides of affluence that poured from the victorious legions. It is religion and poverty, more than any other agents, that have accomplished the ruin of this vast city. The Barbarian conquerors usurped in a moment the toil and treasure of successive ages. They viewed without desire all that could not be removed in their fleets or waggons. Gold and silver were the first objects of their avarice; as, in every country, and in the smallest compass, they represent the most ample command of the industry and possessions of mankind. A vase or a statue of those precious metals might tempt the vanity of some Barbarian chief; but the grosser multitude, regardless of the form, were tenacious only of the substance: and the melted ingots might be readily divided and stamped into current coin. The less active or less fortunate robbers, were reduced to the baser plunder of brass, lead, and copper. The edifices of Rome were a vast and various mine. The first labour of extracting the materials was already performed;—the metals were purified and cast;—the marbles were hewn and polished;—and, after foreign and domestic rapine had been satiated, the remains of the city were still venal. The monuments of antiquity had been left naked of their precious ornaments; but the degenerate Romans would demolish with their own hands the arches and walls, if the hope of profit could surpass the cost of the labour and transportation. A fragment, a ruin, however mangled or profaned, may be viewed with pleasure and regret; but the greater part of those ancient marbles have probably been deprived of substance, as well as of place and proportion, and burnt to lime, for the purpose of cement.

"For a period of five hundred years, Rome has been afflicted by the sanguinary quarrels of the nobles and the people,—the Guelphs and Ghibeline, the Colonna and Ursini, factions. Every quarrel was decided by the sword; and none could trust their lives and properties to the impotence of the law. The powerful citizens were armed for safety or defence against the domestic enemies whom they feared or hated. The nobles fortified their houses, and erected strong towers, capable of resisting sudden attacks. The city was thus filled with hostile edifices; and the works of antiquity were demolished, to supply the materials employed in the construction. The temples and arches afforded a broad and solid basis for these new structures; and towers for defence are still attached to the monuments of Julius Cæsar, Titus, and the Antonines. After the death of pope Nicholas the Fourth, Rome, for a period of six months, was abandoned to the fury of a civil war. The houses were crushed by the weight and velocity of enormous stones; the walls broken by the strokes of the battering-ram; and the towers involved in fire and smoke.*

"But why should I thus dwell on the dilapidation of ages?—All in nature suffers, no less than Rome, the influence of decay:—it is the common fate of things. The soul of man is alone imperishable upon earth. When its mortal residence falls into dust, which, with the sentenced globe, shall return into the elements, it ascends on high, where it awaits the general vanishing of all things; and will behold its frailties pass away with the transitory dross and vapour of the world!"

CHAPTER VI.

The Beginning of the Reformation.

[A. D. 1503.]

THE variety and number of our author's notes during the busy period of the Reformation, leave us in doubt whether we ought to pursue the plan hitherto followed in the selection of the extracts, or attempt the construction of a regular historical narrative. The latter is certainly the best calculated to show in what respects his observations differ from the statements of other historians; but, as his materials, though abundant, and in correct chronological order, only refer to what passed within the sphere of his own knowledge, the work as a history would probably be greatly defective: it may therefore be as well to adhere to our original arrangement, supplying, from time to time, such historical illustrations as may be requisite. With this view, it seems necessary, before having recourse

---

* Gibbon.

to the Volume, that we should give some account of the character and conduct of the popes in whose time the Reformation took its rise.

On the death of Alexander the Sixth, the Cardinal Picolomini was chosen his successor, and assumed the name of Pius III. He was a prudent and learned man, and was supposed to have had the reformation of the church much at heart, having declared, immediately after his election, that there was no occasion for arms to uphold the cause of religion,—but only piety and good works. His reign, however, was very short; for he died, or was poisoned, on the twenty-sixth day after his election, and Cardinal Julian de la Rovere chosen in his stead. This is the famous Julius the Second, the most turbulent and warlike of all the pontiffs that filled the theocratic throne of Rome. He was of a bold and impetuous spirit, and had spent many years of his life in travelling. His taste was magnificent, his liberality judicious; and, being accounted faithful to his word, he had many friends. The cathedral of St. Peter, the noblest and most stupendous fabric erected by the moderns, is the monument of his genius. The character of the priest, however, was absorbed in that of the warrior; and he actually took upon himself the command of an army. His impetuosity in the field, as well as in council, often reduced him to extremity; for he was one of those characters who make for themselves great reverses,—who, by the earnestness with which they engage in their undertakings, lose the recollection of the value of the things which they consider as impediments to their designs—destroying them as such. It is not easy now to discover the particular object of Julius's policy; for it seems to have been as much dictated by personal feeling, as by any comprehensible principle. But it had the effect of bringing the papal authority still more into question than even the conduct of Alexander, insomuch as it was of a more public nature. In this point of view, we may therefore regard it as contributing in no small degree to that state of public opinion, which rendered the doctrines of Luther so popular during the pontificate of his successor, Leo X.

Few men, in what respects reputation, have been more fortunate than pope Leo X. and not many have less deserved, in any degree, so much celebrity as attaches to his name. The son of Lorenzo de Medici, a man of great talent and influence, he was in his boyhood created a cardinal; and, at the early age of thirty-seven, elected to the supreme dignity of the Papacy. Throughout the whole of his career he evinced the possession of no eminent ability; but the suavity of his manners, and his taste for the elegancies of art and of literature, conciliated the goodwill of all who approached him: and the gratitude of the artists and authors whom he patronised, have drawn a veil of splendid flattery over the grossness of his personal vices.

The flagitious life of Alexander VI. opened the eyes of the Christian world to the corruptions of the Papal government; the warlike and indecorous bravery of Julius the Second exasperated the secular princes against the temporal power of the popes; and the attempt of Leo X. to levy money under the form of indulgences, completed, by the indiscretion of his agents, all that was requisite to render a reformation necessary.

Indulgences were originally exemptions from taxes, granted by the emperors and governors to provinces that had been harassed by enemies, earthquakes, unfruitful seasons, and other calamities. The popes, who had gradually usurped or revived as much as they possibly could of the ancient imperial power, applied the indulgences to spiritual matters, and granted them to the crusaders. They dispensed them likewise to those who, instead of marching personally against the infidels, contributed to the expense of the expedition. Afterwards indulgences and pardons became more common; but Leo X. prostituted them to a greater degree than they had ever been before:* for, instead of being, as anciently, exemptions from church-dues, they were issued by him literally as indulgences to sin,— the persons obtaining them paying, in fact, a price which exempted them in their transgressions from the ordinary penances.

---

* Universal History.

Auricular confession was one of the great secrets by which the church attained and preserved her exorbitant domination; and it had been rendered completely effectual by the episcopal appointment of confessors, who were usually selected from priests unfeignedly devoted to the ecclesiastical cause. Sinners often felt the hardship of this regulation, and trembled to reveal the instigations of young desire, and the levities of youthful blood, to austere and sanctimonious old men. Leo, in devising his fiscal expedient of the indulgences, thought that freedom in the choice of confessors would be a great comfort to sinners;* and licences to choose them were accordingly included in the list of dispensations for sale. Those who framed these infamous licenses of ecclesiastical fraud, endeavoured to sell them as quickly as possible. Powers for delivering souls from purgatory were accordingly openly sold; and pardon for uncommitted crimes of every description might be purchased in taverns and bagnios. It was therefore not surprising, that the conscientious, as well as the discontented, members of the apostolic flock, should openly complain of the abuses of the papal government. The advocates of the existing practices exposed in vain the turbulent self-sufficiency of the reformers; and recalled to remembrance with what constancy of virtue their ancestors had reared and supported that venerable frame of things, which a reprobate generation, actuated by a strange frenzy, was rushing to destroy. But the misconduct of its advocates never can impair the principles of a cause. Institutions are only improved by the pressure of external circumstances. Reformations may be ascribed to the wisdom of particular individuals; but they are always the effects of remote causes, and extorted by the force of public opinion, if not by the constraint of arms. The ecclesiastical machine was decayed in all its parts. It could no longer perform its wonted functions; and a new one, suited to the improved knowledge of the age, was indispensable. Among the reformers were many virtuous characters,—haters of

---

* Galt's Life of Cardinal Wolsey.

corruption for its own sake, and sincere professors of Christianity for a recompence not of this world: nor can it be denied, that the church of Rome contained, in the number of her firmest adherents, many members of consciences equally irreproachable; but the plunderers of shrines, and the burners of heretics, were not of this description.

In the sale of the indulgences, the agents of the pope's sister employed the Dominican friars, who acted with great indiscretion, by printing inflated accounts of the power and efficacy of the articles which they had to sell. This mightily offended the Augustines; and John Stanpitz, vicar-general of that order, preached loudly against the abuse at Wittemberg, where he was assisted by Martin Luther, a monk of the same order, and a professor in that university.

Luther was a native of Islebe, in the county of Mansfield, in Upper Saxony. His father intended him for the profession of the law; but, when he had finished his course of philosophy, one day, while he was walking in the fields, he was terrified by a clap of thunder which killed his companion; and he made a vow of becoming a monk,—a vow which he performed two years afterwards at Erfurd, in the twenty-second year of his age. He was soon after appointed to a professor's chair in the university which Frederick the Wise duke of Saxony had a few years before established at Wittemberg; and distinguished himself by his active genius, great memory and natural eloquence. In 1516 he began to study the Greek and Hebrew; and published several theses concerning free-will, the merit of good works, and human traditions contrary to the opinions entertained by the scholastic divines, for whom he entertained the greatest contempt.

In his private conduct, Luther was, according to his own confession, far from being either pure or blameless; but he was a shrewd and intrepid preacher, and his spirit rose to the circumstances in which he was called to act.

The pope at first paid little attention to his doctrines; but the bold tone of his controversial writings made at length so great a noise, that Leo was constrained, by the general outcry of the church, to notice them. From that moment, Luther became necessarily, as it were, the champion not only of all those who complained of the corruptions of the church, but an oracle of instruction to those who were dissatisfied with her doctrines.

CHAPTER VII.

Hareach accompanies Cardinal Campeggio to England.— The public Entry of the Cardinal into London, and what happened on that Occasion; with Remarks on the League of London.

Having thus prepared the reader for the state of the public mind throughout Christendom, we must now take up again the desultory Volume of our indefatigable traveller. It appears, that when Cardinal Campeggio was sent as a legate to London by Leo X. in order to induce the government of Henry VIII. to engage in a great crusade against sultan Selim, Hareach went in his suite. We shall extract his account of the reception of the cardinal in London.

"We were obliged to remain some time at Calais, Cardinal Wolsey not choosing that any churchman should appear in England greater than himself. The obstacle, however, was soon removed by the pope joining him in the legantine commission. Campeggio was naturally a modest character, and not inclined to ostentation; but Wolsey was not only proud and arrogant, but one of those statesmen who deemed magnificence of appearance essential even to moral dignity. The consequence of this occasioned great inconvenience, for Campeggio was not prepared to make any splendid show; but the English cardinal, to impress the nation with the importance of his mission, insisted that he should make a grand public entry into London. Accordingly, on our landing at Dover, we were necessitated to put every thing in the best state, and Wolsey sent us a plentiful supply of scarlet cloth to cover our trunks and packages, and other mean baggage. Orders were also given to the magistrates and churchmen in every town through which we had to pass, in our way to the metropolis, to receive the legate with all possible ceremony and respect. On Blackheath we were met by a sumptuous assemblage of the nobility, prelates, and gentlemen. The clergy of London received us in the Borough of Southwark with all their processional paraphernalia; the freemen of London lined the streets through which we passed; the Lord Mayor and Aldermen humiliated themselves before the astonished legate; and Sir Thomas More, in the name of the city, welcomed him in a fine Latin oration. The Italians were so amazed at these wonderful testimonies of veneration, that they could scarcely credit the evidence of their senses. But, alas! their exaltation was not of long duration. As the procession moved along Cheapside, the principal street of the city, one of the mules became restive, and threw the whole pageantry into confusion.

"The trunks and coffers, covered with the scarlet gifts of Wolsey, and which the people gazed at as arks filled with treasure and indulgences, were thrown down, and some of them bursting open, disclosed a ludicrous collection of the crumbs and scraps of beggary,—such as old shoes, ragged garments, and broken meat. This unfortunate occurrence turned the whole solemnity of the day into derision; for the populace laughed and shouted, and treated the whole spectacle as a ridiculous imposition. Campeggio is excessively mortified; but Wolsey makes light of the accident: and perhaps it is a matter in itself not deserving of much serious consideration; but the precarious state of public opinion renders the impression most unfavourable to the interests of the Papacy in England."

Campeggio did not remain long in England; but our author took up his abode for several years in London, and seems to have entered with more than common interest into the public transactions of that great epoch of British history,—the administration of Cardinal Wolsey. In speaking of the English people he expresses himself with unusual warmth; and even applauds the government of Henry the Eighth, when he has occasion to notice any of the different measures which political circumstances called forth.

" Compared with Italy, and the withered regions of the East, this is a land of green freshness and flourishing vigour. Here the spirit of man is so nerved with innate courage, that he is necessarily free. No form of government, no excess of power, no modification of law, can change this indestructible quality,—for it is the inspiration of the climate. It is the very nature of the soil to nurse a haughty temperament: even the dog of England is a creature of singular fierceness and jealousy. The horse partakes of the insolent character of the groom; and man, congenial with the oak of the country, is firm, stern, and muscular. This is, indeed, the land of untamed men: rude as their jealous dogs to the approach of strangers, but faithful to those who trust them, this nation must be ruled generously, not indulgently. With a strong hand and a tight rein, a sharp spur, and a bold rider, who shall set limits to its career, or outstrip it in its course? The greatest fault of this people is the very basis of their virtue. Prone to sift their rights, rather than forego any one of their old usages, they will defend it with the implacable resentment of revenge, and fight even for the forms of ancient customs up to the shoulders in blood. But, when satisfied in their claims, or believing that it is right to submit, they are capable of enduring such a pressure, that tyranny itself will first relent,—admiring their generous patience. Their strong feeling of individual right, and of national superiority, are pledges which Providence has given to them of a glorious destiny; and their indefatigable activity, is a lever of greater power than the force of numbers, in their national undertakings."

This eulogium serves as an introduction to some account of an important treaty which Cardinal Wolsey concluded with the French government, and which our author justly considers as changing the whole relations of Christendom, by uniting the secular princes into one general confederation, independent altogether of the papal authority. "The object of this league (says he) is to preserve the relative state of the different nations; but it is chiefly worthy of notice, as being an alteration in the constitution of Christendom: for the Pope is admitted as a party to it only on the same footing as the secular princes; and he foregoes his supremacy, and subjects himself to the penalties and forfeitures provided to give it stability and effect. It may be regarded as the great compact of the Christian nations; for it embraces all the allies respectively of France and England. It declares, if the dominions of any of the contracting powers are at any time invaded by another, the aggressor shall be required to desist, and make reparation; which if he refuse to do within the space of a month from the date of the admonition, the confederates bind themselves to declare war against him. If rebellions happen to arise in any of their respective states, none of the confederates are to interfere, unless a foreign prince has been the cause, and then their forces are to be united against him. It is also declared, that none of the confederates shall suffer their subjects to bear arms against those of the other;—nor retain foreign troops in their service; and that all persons accused of high treason, shall not be allowed to remain more than twenty days within the territories of any of the confederates, after having been warned to depart. The object of this grand confederation is ostensibly to anticipate the consequence of the preponderance of power that may fall into the hands of Charles king of Spain, should he, in preference to Francis king of France, be elected Emperor of Germany. But it is the foundation-stone of a great superstructure of public law for the community of the European nations."

CHAPTER VIII.

The Meeting of the French and English Courts in the Field of the Cloth of Gold.—The Reformation in England.—Anecdote of the English House of Commons. —Tax on Income.

In tracing our author's observations on the course of events in England, it would seem that he was present at the meeting of the French and English courts on the Field of Gold Cloth. We shall extract his brief note.

"This meeting is the most gorgeous event in the records of magnificent spectacles. The two kings are in the flower of life, their attendants have been selected from the most renowned of the high-born of the rival nations, and the profusion of wealth and riches emulously exhibited, surpass all computation. Temporary palaces, transcending in magnificence the regular abodes of the English monarch, have been prepared in parts, and sent from England. The walls of the apartments are hung with costly arras and tapestry, and the chapel is adorned with everything that can augment the ritual of worship. The genius of the French nation is evident in the taste of the retinue and equipage of their king. Francis dwells in pavilions of golden tissue, lined with blue velvet, embroidered with the lilies of France, and fastened with cords of silk twisted with cyprian gold.—— * * *

"Kings by their greatness cannot long continue together. Fourteen days have exhausted all the means of pleasure which the wealth and genius of France and England could procure or invent. The sovereigns have separated,—the tents of grandeur are struck,—and the costly pile of the English palace is broken up, and the materials sold for fire-wood."

The next note which we shall extract, relates to the state of the public mind during the great Italian wars between Francis and Charles, while the doctrines of the Reformation were spreading with the violence and destructive power of fire throughout the ecclesiastical edifice.

"The wisdom of Cardinal Wolsey, both as a churchman and a statesman, appears with amazing lustre, contrasted with the policy which Leo X. pursues at this time. The Cardinal, in virtue of his legantine authority, and as minister of the secular government, has adopted a system of vigorous reformation in the manners and mansions of the priesthood. By using the power of the crown to carry into effect his ecclesiastical resolutions, he saves the nation from popular outrages against the monasteries,—outrages which distract other countries, and endanger the stability of their governments. But Leo, instead of amending the errors and vices of the church, punishes those who complain of them. The flames of persecution, however, aid the light of truth; and still more awfully illuminate the atheistical atrocities of the Vatican. Luther has been cited to Rome, suspended from preaching, and excommunicated. The clergy, by their continual outcry against him, inflame the curiosity of the public; and, by endeavouring to refute his truths, make their own fallacies the more evident. The spirit of controversy has, in consequence, seized on all ranks, ages, and sexes; strange aspects are observed by the astrologers in the courses of the stars; and the shrines of idolatry, in all parts of the world, are shaken and overthrown. On the grim idols of Mexico, besmeared with human blood, and the Hindoo emblems of Brahma and Vishnu, the phials of wrath are now pouring and the mantle of the destroying angel sweeps away in his career the no less ignominious monuments of human folly, that a crafty and ambitious priesthood have reared under the name of saints and martyrs, in the churches of Europe."

In speaking of the war, Hareach relates an interesting anecdote of Henry VIII. Wolsey, and the House of

Commons, which serves to illustrate how much, in fact, the spirit of English liberty depends on the genius of the people, rather than on any principles recognized in the charters or statutes. The Cardinal had obtained from the clergy a grant of ten per cent. on their incomes, to enable the king to carry on the war in which he was at this period engaged. But, on applying to Parliament for a similar grant, he was not so successful. The circumstances, as related by our author, are as follow.

"When the customary ceremonies at opening a new Parliament were over, Cardinal Wolsey, attended by several prelates and peers, members of the king's council, entered the House with a verbal message from the king, and addressed the Speaker on the expediency of granting supplies adequate to the vigorous prosecution of the war. When he had retired a long debate ensued, which terminated in a resolution to grant only half the sum requested. One of the members, of the name of Montague,* who had taken a decided part with the Opposition, being at court in the evening, went, according to custom, to present himself to the king, and knelt as usual to kiss his majesty's hands, but the king took him by the ear abruptly, and said aloud, in a half serious half jocular manner, 'Ho! will ye not suffer my bill to pass. If it is not passed to-morrow, I'll take off this head of yours.' Some affected to consider this as a violent breach of the privileges of the Commons; but the story, on being reported abroad, only excited the laughter of the people, who are well acquainted with the humour of the king: he has, indeed, much of the national character about him, and is exceedingly popular with all ranks. But the stinted grant of the Commons greatly disturbed Cardinal Wolsey; and next day he went again to the House, and begged to hear the reasons of those who opposed and who limited the supply. The Speaker however told him, that it was a standing order of the House to hear, but not to reason,

---

* The maternal ancestor of the present Dukes of Marlborough and Buccleugh.

—except among themselves. The Cardinal was disconcerted by this firmness; but, with his usual self-possession, he again urged the arguments which he had before stated. The Commons, however, remained settled in their purpose; and, affecting to make a distinction between a war of policy and one in revenge for injuries received, or dangers actually manifest, restricted the grant to five per cent. on income,—the half of what the government had applied for, and what the clergy had been induced to give.

"Even this was loudly complained of; and the people universally repined that their means and properties should be subject to the investigation of the collectors of the tax. Deputations from the merchants of London waited on the Cardinal, and begged him, for God's sake, to consider that the richest merchants were often bare of money in war; and they entreated that they might not be sworn as to the value of their property,—for the valuation was necessarily doubtful, and many an honest man's credit was better than his capital. 'To make us swear, (said they,) will expose us to the temptation to commit perjury.'—'The fear of committing perjury, (replied the Cardinal drily,) is at least a sign of grace; but you should give the king some proof of your loyalty. I will send a person into the city to receive the estimates of your means; and let such of you as have more credit than property come privately to me, and I will take care that he shall not be injured.'*

"According to his menace, the Cardinal sent his secretary yesterday into the city; and the merchants came very quietly with their statements to him. It is not supposed that any will apply for indulgence to the Cardinal, as it might become known, and so injure their credit."

---

* Galt's Life of Wolsey.

CHAPTER IX.

Anecdote of Wolsey respecting a Riot and Insurrection in the County of Suffolk.

WHILE the English government, restricted in its exertions by the limited grant of the income-tax, and somewhat dissatisfied with the conduct of the Emperor Charles V. for whose cause the war had at first been undertaken, hesitated respecting a change of policy, the tidings arrived in London of the defeat and captivity of Francis the First at Pavia. The conduct of Charles, on being thus put in possession of his rival, exceedingly disgusted Henry VIII. who determined that he should either deliver Francis up to him, according to the terms of a treaty which they had previously concluded, or feel the weight of his vengeance. For this purpose, the preparations which had been made to co-operate with him in the war were redoubled, to force him to fulfil his engagements. This sudden change of policy was extremely unpopular; and the Cardinal, having made an attempt to raise money under the name of a benevolence or voluntary contribution, without the concurrence of Parliament, rendered his government particularly odious: and great discontent, and open insurrection, was manifested in different parts of the country. In the county of Suffolk, where the wealthy manufacturers and traders were persuaded to comply with the wishes of the crown, at a public meeting convened to take their opinion on the subject, the common people assembled in crowds, and riotously attacked them. The constables were, in consequence, directed to seize all arms in private houses: which enraged the people still more. The alarm-bells were rung, and upwards of four thousand men appeared in arms, and threatened with death all those who had consented to grant the benevolence. The Duke of Suffolk, brother-in-law to the king, hastily summoned the gentlemen of the county to assist in suppressing the insurrection; and, by the prudent measures of forbearance and firmness adopted by him, the insurgents were prevailed on to deliver up their leaders and disperse; under an assurance, however, that the grievance of which they complained should be considered by the king. The leaders being taken to London, were carried before the court of the Star Chamber, in which Wolsey presided. Our author appears to have been present on that occasion; and his account of what took place, is finely characteristic of the bold and frank spirit of that intrepid age.

"The Duke of Norfolk sat beside the Cardinal, and almost the whole of the king's council were also present. On the delinquents confessing their guilt, and imploring pardon, the Cardinal, who never lost an opportunity of indulging himself in speaking, of which he was a great master, rebuked them in very high and haughty terms; pointing out the mischief that their imprudence had occasioned to many innocent persons, and the ruin it had brought on themselves. 'But (said he) the king, in consideration of your ignorance, is graciously pleased to pardon you for this time, provided that you can give satisfactory security for your future good behaviour.' The prisoners replied, that they were poor men, and all their friends were poor; and they had no sureties to offer. 'Indeed, (said the Cardinal,) then my Lord of Norfolk here will be one for you; and, as you are my countrymen, I will be the other.'* This unexpected turn produced a great sensation on all present: the magnanimity of the Cardinal was greatly applauded, and the Duke of Norfolk appeared delighted with his dexterity, saying, that it would do more to conciliate the goodwill of the people than the remission of all the taxes. Nor has his Grace, in this respect, been mistaken; for the Cardinal, in returning from the Star Chamber to his own residence, was

---

* The Cardinal was born at Ipswich, in Suffolk.

loudly cheered by the people,—by the same multitude who, in his way to the court, loaded him with all manner of odious reproaches."

After this singular incident, we do not find anything particularly interesting for several pages.

CHAPTER X.

The Exchange of Francis the First for his Children.

In the midst of a long series of uninteresting political reflections, we meet with a lively description of one of the most important events in the history of that time, namely, the liberation of Francis the First in exchange for his children, who were delivered as hostages for the fulfilment of the treaty by which Charles had consented to restore him to liberty. How our author happened to be present we are not informed, but we shall extract his account of that affecting scene.

"The Dauphin and the Duke of Orleans, the children of Francis, and who were to be delivered as the hostages, were brought to Bayonne by the Regent of France, their grandmother, attended by the great officers of the French court; and the king was at the same time conveyed to Fonterabia, a small town on the sea-coast, between the province of Biscay, and the duchy of Guyen. Accompanied by two persons of high rank, and surrounded by cavalry, he was conducted to the river which divides the frontiers of France and Spain. The young princes were already on the opposite side. The banks were crowded with a vast number of spectators. In the middle of the stream lay a vessel at anchor. No person was permitted to be aboard. Francis, with the two imperial officers, and eight men armed with short swords, entered a barge, and were rowed towards the vessel. At the same moment the hostages, similarly attended, also embarked. The spectators were all hushed. The boats reached the vessel. The king and the princes were put on-board. The children passed across the deck, without speaking, to the boat which their father had left, and were received into the arms of the officers who had attended him. Francis only looked at them as he also passed hastily, and sighing deeply, leaped into the boat; and, being rapidly conveyed to the shores of his own kingdom, was welcomed by his subjects and his soldiers with the loudest acclamations of joy. He, however, took no notice of their shouts, but hurried up the bank to where a fleet Arabian horse stood ready saddled, and, vaulting upon his back, waved his hand triumphantly to the crowd, and exclaiming 'I am again a king!' clapped spurs to the horse, and, followed by his officers, who had at the same time also mounted, was soon out of sight."

CHAPTER XI.

The Trial of Henry VIII. and Queen Catharine.

WE do not meet with any anecdote particularly interesting till the second visit of Cardinal Campeggio to England, when he was sent by the Pope, to try, in conjunction with Cardinal Wolsey, the validity of the marriage of Henry the Eighth with Catharine of Arragon. On what particular occasion Hareach had left England is not mentioned; and it is only by an incidental expression that we learn he returned with Campeggio. Before giving his description of the trial, we must notice the historical account of the circumstances that gave rise to that extraordinary event,—an event which tends to show, more than any other in the history of this country, how much the English, above every people, are distinguished for their love of justice, and the open administration of the law.

Catharine, the queen of Henry, had been formerly married to his brother, Arthur prince of Wales. Arthur was then only in his sixteenth year; and they lived together as man and wife upwards of four months. In consequence of this, when he died, Henry was not created prince of Wales until it was ascertained that the widow was not with child. The political motives which led originally to the union of Arthur and Catharine did not terminate with his life; and Henry the Seventh, his father, in order to keep her great dowry, was induced by his avarice to devise the plan of marrying her to his second son, her husband's brother, then in his boyhood. Against this incestuous match archbishop Warham openly protested; but a bull, procured from Pope Julius the Second, silenced all objections.

Soon after the union of Henry and Catharine, which was solemnized under the authority of this infamous bull, the old tyrant began to doubt the rectitude of what he committed, and his conscience grew unquiet and reproachable, insomuch that when the prince attained the age of fourteen, at which period the heirs of the English crown are allowed to exercise the rights of independent judgment, he implored him to protest that, being under age, he had been married without his consent, and that he did not now confirm that marriage; but, on the contrary, intended, in due form of law, to make it void. Not satisfied with merely obtaining this avowal of an intention, the king, on his death-bed, again earnestly exhorted his son to break the incestuous union. Accordingly, one of the first questions which, after his death, engaged the attention of the council, was, whether the marriage should be annulled or consummated. The opinion in favour of the moral offence prevailed with the pliant consciences of the politicians; and Henry the Eighth, by the determination of his council, was publicly married to his brother's widow. For many years the connexion remained undisputed; but of several children, which were the issue, Mary, afterwards queen, alone survived.

Catharine having fallen into ill heath, Henry had for several years deserted her bed; and, seeing no likelihood of her giving him a male heir to the throne, he became restless, and thought with regret of the equivocal ground on which his marriage had been concluded; but he did not think of dissolving it, until, in the progress of a negociation for marrying his daughter to the Duke of Orleans, the son of Francis the First, the French ambassador questioned the legitimacy of the princess, urging that the marriage, of which she was the fruit, had been contracted in violation of a divine law, which no human authority could impair.*

From all these circumstances, the king became uneasy on the subject, and disclosed his apprehensions and anxieties to his confessor. The attachment which he formed in the meantime for Ann Boleyn, no doubt, also contributed to make him desirous for the dissolution of the marriage; but it certainly was not the primary cause which induced him to institute the enquiry into the validity of his union with his brother's widow. Such were the circumstances that led to this famous trial, of which we shall now extract our author's account.

"The monarch of a great kingdom, under no apprehensions from any foreign power, submitting to be cited before a tribunal erected within his own capital, for the purpose of determining a cause in which his own honour and happiness were so deeply involved, was a spectacle equally singular and interesting, and calculated to attract the eyes of all descriptions of men. The hall of the Blackfriars' convent, in London, was prepared for the occasion. At the upper end was a throne and canopy, where the king sat. The queen was seated at some distance, a little lower. In front of the king, but three steps beneath him, and so placed that the one appeared on his right hand, and the other on his left, the two cardinals were placed; and at their feet several clerks and officers

---

* Bishop Burnet.

of the court; before whom, and within the bar, were the prelates of the realm. Without the bar, on one side, stood the advocates and proctors of the king; and, on the other, those appointed for the queen. The sides of the hall were occupied with successive tiers of benches, which were thronged with all the most illustrious and noble persons of the kingdom.

"Silence being proclaimed, and the commission of the legates read, an officer rose, and cried aloud, 'Henry king of England, come into court.'* The king answered, 'Here I am.' The queen was then also summoned; but she made no reply. Rising from her chair, she descended to the floor, and walked round the court. Not a breathing was heard. When she came opposite to the king, she knelt down, and addressed him to the following effect: 'I humbly beseech your majesty to extend to me your wonted clemency. I am a helpless woman and a stranger, born out of your dominions, and destitute of friends and counsel. I cannot plead for myself, and I know not whom to employ. Those that are retained for me, are only such as you have been pleased to appoint. They are your own subjects; and who can believe that they shall be able to withstand your will and pleasure? Alas! sir, in what have I offended, that after twenty years,

---

* Bishop Burnet affirms, that the king did not appear personally, but by proxy; and that the queen withdrew, after reading a protest against the competency of her judges: " and from this it is clear," says the Bishop, "that the speeches that the historians have made for them are all plain falsities." But it must be observed, that the testimony for the personal appearance of the king before the cardinals is surprisingly powerful; even though we do not go beyond Cavendish and the other ordinary historians; for, in addition to these, reference may be made to the authority of William Thomas, clerk of the council in the reign of Edward VI. and a well-informed writer, who, in a professed apology for Henry VIII. extant in manuscript in the Lambeth and some other libraries, speaking of this affair, affirms, "that the cardinal (Campegius) caused the king, as a private partye, in person to appeare before him, and the ladie Katharine both." Page 31.

spent in peaceable wedlock, and having borne to you so many children, you should think of putting me away? I was, I confess, the widow of your brother, if she can be accounted a widow whom her husband never knew; for I take Almighty God to witness, that I came to your bed an unblemished virgin. How I have behaved myself, I am willing to appeal even to those who wish me the least good. Certainly, whatever their verdict may be, you have always found me a most faithful servant. I may rather say than wife, having never to my knowledge opposed, even in appearance, your will. I always loved, without regard to their merits, those whom you favoured. I so anxiously contributed to your happiness, that I fear I have offended God in studying your inclinations too much, and not by neglecting any duty. By my fidelity, if ever you thought it worthy of regard,—by our common issue, and by the memory of your father, which you sometimes held dear,—I implore you to defer the proceedings of this cause, until I have consulted my friends in Spain. If then, in justice, it shall be thought meet to send me from you, a part of whom I have so long been, (and the apprehension is more terrible than death,) I will continue my long-observed obedience, and submit. But when I reflect on the reputation of our fathers, by whose endeavours our union was formed, I hope confidently of my cause. Your father, for his admirable wisdom, was accounted a second Solomon: nor can Spain, throughout the whole succession of the sovereigns of all her kingdoms, produce any one to parallel mine. What kind of counsellors must we think those princes had, that all should, as it were, conspire to hurl us into incestuous sin. No question was then made of the lawfulness of our marriage; and yet those times afforded learned men, who, in holiness and love of truth, far surpassed the flatterers of these in which we now live.'—She then rose, and, making obeisance to the king, hastened out of the court. She had not, however, proceeded far, when the king commanded the apparitor to call her back. Without attending to the summons, she still went forward. A gentleman, on whose arm she leaned, observed, that she was called. 'I hear it very well,' she replied, 'but on,—on,—go you on. Let them proceed against me as they please: I am resolved not to stay.'

"'In the queen's absence,' said Henry, addressing himself to the audience, 'I will freely declare to you all, that she has been uniformly as true, as obedient, and as dutiful a wife, as I could wish or desire. She has all the virtues that ought to be in a woman of her dignity, or in any other of inferior condition. Her birth is indeed not more noble than her qualities.' Wolsey, conceiving that some of Catharine's insinuations were directed towards him, entreated the king to declare, whether he had either been the first or the chief mover in the business, as suspicions to that effect were entertained. 'My lord Cardinal,' answered Henry, 'I can well excuse you: so far from being a mover, you have been rather against me. The first cause was the disturbance produced in my mind by the doubts entertained of the legitimacy of my daughter. These doubts engendered such scruples in my bosom, that I became greatly perplexed. I began to think myself in danger of God's indignation, which appeared already manifest; for all the sons that my wife brought to me were cut off immediately after they came into the world. Being thus tossed on the waves of doubtful thought, and despairing of having any other issue by the queen, it became my duty to consider the state of the kingdom, and the calamities of a disputed succession. I therefore conceived it to be good, for the ease of my conscience, and also for the security of the nation, to ascertain, in the event of my marriage proving unlawful, whether I might take another wife: and it is this point which we are about to try, by the learning and wisdom of you, the prelates and pastors of the kingdom. To you I have committed the judgment, and to your decision I am willing to submit. My lord of Lincoln,' said he, addressing the bishop of that see, 'it was first to you in confession that I communicated my scruples; and, as you were yourself in doubt, you advised me to consult all these my lords; upon which I moved you, my lord of Canterbury, as metropolitan, to put the question to the bishops; and all your opinions, granted under your respective seals, are here to be exhibited. It is now almost twenty years since we began our reign; in the course of which we have, by the assistance of Providence, so behaved ourself, that we hope you, our subjects, have no cause to complain, nor our enemies to glory. No foreign power has attempted to injure you with impunity;—nor have we employed our arms without victory. Whether you regard the fruits of peace or the trophies of war, we dare boldly aver, that we have shewn ourself not unworthy of our ancestors. But, when we reflect on the end of frail life, we are surprised by fear, lest the miseries of future times obscure the splendour and memory of our present felicity. We see here many who, by their age, may have been witnesses of the late civil wars, which, for eighty years together, so dreadfully afflicted this kingdom. No man knew whom to acknowledge for his sovereign, until the happy union of our parents removed the cause of this doubt. Consider then whether, after our death, you may hope for better days than when the factions of York and Lancaster distracted the nation? We have a daughter, whom we the more affectionately love because she is our only child. But it is proper to inform you, that, treating with the French king concerning a match with her and our godson Henry Duke of Orleans, one of his privy-counsellors obected to the legitimacy of the princess, her mother having been married to our deceased brother; alleging, at the same time, that the marriage with our queen could not be deemed otherwise than incestuous. How much this allegation afflicted us, God, the searcher of hearts, only knows; for the question affected not only our consort and daughter, but implied the danger of eternal punishment to our souls, if, after being admonished of such horrible incest, we did not endeavour to amend. For your parts, you cannot but foresee the evils with which this matter is pregnant to you and your posterity. Desirous of being resolved on a point so important, we first conferred with our friends, and then with men the most learned in human and divine laws; but they gave no satisfaction, and only left us more perplexed. We then had recourse to the Pope, and procured the venerable legate who has lately arrived from Rome to investigate the case. For the queen, whatever may be the detractions of women and tatlers, we willingly and openly profess, that, in nobleness of mind, she far transcends the greatness of her birth,—in mildness, prudence, sanctity, and conversation, she is not to be paralleled. But we were given to the world for other ends than the pursuit of our own pleasure. We therefore prefer the hazard of uncertain trial, rather than commit impiety against heaven and ingratitude against our country, the weal and safety of which every man should prefer before his life and fortune.'—The king having delivered this address, retired, and the court adjourned."

CHAPTER XII.

Anecdotes of Cardinal Wolsey; with an Account of his House, and manner of entertaining Strangers.

WE shall continue, with as few interruptions as possible, the narrative of our author's notes respecting the transactions of the English court during his residence at this time in London.

"While the trial was proceeding, but adjourned from week to week, Cardinal Campeggio, and his principal gentlemen, frequently dined with Cardinal Wolsey; and on one of these occasions, when a number of learned men and foreign scholars were to be there, I was also invited.

"The house which he inhabited belonged to the archbishopric of York; but he had enlarged and adorned it with many superb works of art. The chambers were less lofty and magnificent than those of the Italian palaces; but the furniture was more rare and curious than I had ever seen in the palaces of the greatest modern princes. The walls of the chambers and galleries were hung with the most gorgeous tapestry, representing different events in the history of revealed religion, designed with admirable skill, and coloured with amazing beauty, so as to surpass in effect the liveliest paintings. In the great gallery, the whole history of Nebuchadnezzar was represented with surpassing art, and bordered with devices, which showed that the tapestry had been prepared at the express desire of the Cardinal himself,—the ornaments being interspersed with his arms and the ensigns of his dignity.*

"These woven pictures are, no doubt, the work of Italian artists, and executed from designs by the great masters who reflect so much lustre on the ecclesiastical government.

"But his household was still more magnificent than his apartments. A prodigious number of servants and retainers, not less I conceive than seven or eight hundred, were arranged, according to their degrees, in different rows, through which we were conducted to the apartment where the Cardinal himself sat to receive his guests, attended by several young noblemen as pages. These pages, although they wore his livery and badges, performed no menial office, being sent to be educated in his house,—an ancient custom, taking its origin from the learning of the priesthood, and not peculiar to the English nation.

"In his person this famous Cardinal is tall and corpulent; he dresses with great care and splendour, and his shoes, of scarlet velvet, were adorned with precious stones. His manners are affable, and tinctured with a little sarcastic humour; but the guarded decorum of his deport-

---

* There is a catalogue of the pictures of his tapestry in the British Museum.

ment represses the least approach to familiarity.* No doubt, his surprising good fortune has inflated him with a high opinion of his own talents; but he is undoubtedly a man of the first class of men; and, if he has been ambitious to amass wealth and acquire power, he dispenses the gifts of fortune with a munificent, and generally with a judicious, hand. The greatest subject in the world, his undertakings would reflect honour on the greatest kings; and, were he not a churchman, he would probably be one of the most popular ministers that the nation ever possessed,—as he is one of the ablest and most successful.

"On the different guests being announced, he received them with the shrewdest discrimination. To those who were grave and formal he was solemn and dignified,—but, with the gay or facetious, he varied his manner. Sir Thomas More was of the party; and, although his pleasant temper is calculated to diffuse cheerfulness, I thought the Cardinal under some degree of restraint with him: for Sir Thomas being of an easy and familiar turn, took liberties which his host did not seem entirely to relish.

"When dinner was announced, we were conducted with great state to the banquet-room,—the heralds carefully arranging the company according to their different

---

* The following description of the Cardinal's person is given by a cotemporary poet:

> A great carl he is and fat;
> Wearing on his head a red hat,
>   Procured with angel's subsidy;
> And, as they say, in time of rain,
> Four of his gentlemen are fain
>   To hold o'er it a canopy.
> Besides this, to tell thee more news,
> He hath a pair of costly shoes,
>   Which seldom touch the ground;
> They are so goodly and curious,
> All of gold and stones precious,
>   Costing many a thousand pound.
> And who did for these shoes pay?
> Truly many a rich abbey,
>   To be eased of his visitation."

degrees of rank and seniority. During the intervals between bringing-in the successive dishes, the Cardinal exerted himself with great effect for the entertainment of his guests; and, had he confined himself to the general topics or anecdotes of the day, we should have left him in high admiration of his conversational powers, which, unquestionably, are very extraordinary. But, unfortunately, he had that day delivered an important decision in the Court of Chancery; and, as was usual with him on such occasions, he had made a long oration on the merits and the law of the case. Many of the guests having been in the court, he was evidently anxious to know what they thought of his speech; and, after various endeavours to draw forth an opinion, he at last bluntly asked the question. The effect was somewhat ludicrous; for it particularly overawed the churchmen present, who, having great expectations from his favour, were solicitous to give the most agreeable criticism possible. The Cardinal perceived the embarrassment which he had produced, but extricated himself and the party with much address, by saying, in a jocular manner, 'I must have all your opinions separately and circumstantially:'—thus converting the object of his vanity into a topic of entertainment. Those who had heard the oration then delivered their sentences, each according to his rank as they were placed at table; as if it was a matter of the commonweal discussed in solemn council. The person who sat highest, and who summed up the several opinions, was a learned doctor, and a great beneficed man. It was astonishing to see what pains he took to ingratiate himself with his patron, and to display his own abilities. How he did mark every word, and sift its fitness; and the more fit and proper it was, the less he seemed to like it. The man even became warm with the labour of his task, and was fain to wipe his face. During the whole of this effort, the Cardinal listened with profound attention, and some degree of satisfaction; but, it was evident that the sycophant, by offending the modesty of nature, sank in the opinion of his Eminence; and, if his flattery pleased, I much suspect it did no good to himself."

CHAPTER XIII.

The Issue of the Trial of Henry VIII. and his Queen.

THE trial of the marriage did not proceed with that celerity which suited the impatient temper of the king; and he began to repine at the frequent adjournments of the court. He treated Cardinal Wolsey, in consequence, with less cordiality than formerly; and the enemies of that statesman, observing the altered affection of the king, also changed in their demeanour towards him. One day, returning in his barge from the trial at Blackfriars to his residence in Westminster, the Bishop of Carlisle, who accompanied him, happened to complain of the excessive heat of the weather.—' If you were so chafed, my lord, as I have been to-day, you would be warm indeed,' said the Cardinal, alluding to a conversation which he had immediately before held with the king.

As soon as he entered his house, he undressed, and went to bed, oppressed with fatigue and a boding dejection of the spirits. He had not however long lain down, when the father of Ann Boleyn came to him from the king, requesting that he and Campeggio would repair immediately to the queen, and exhort her to retire to some religious house, rather than undergo the disgrace of a public divorce.—' You, and other lords of the counsel,' exclaimed Wolsey with indignation, ' have put fancies into the king's head, which would trouble the nation; and for which, in the end, you will reap but little recompense.' We shall now quote our author's account of the sequel.

" Campeggio received a message from Wolsey to come to him with as little delay as possible, which surprised him exceedingly; but he lost no time in going to the

English cardinal. He was absent several hours; and, when he returned, he appeared very sad and thoughtful; and, at supper, he informed his secretary that he had been with Wolsey to see Queen Catharine.—' When we were shown into her presence,' said he, ' we found her sitting among her gentlewomen, embroidering, with a skein of thread hanging about her neck.' She rose as we entered the room; and, in some degree of agitation, requested to know on what business we had come. Wolsey addressed her in Latin, being reluctant to let the women know the object of our visit. But she interrupted him in a sharp and reproachful tone, and said, ' Speak to me in English, that these witnesses may know what you say.' The Cardinal, however, was not disconcerted; but replied, in the most respectful manner, ' If it please you, madam, we come to know, from yourself, how you are really disposed to act in the business between you and the king, and to offer our opinion and advice.'—' As for your good-will,' said the queen proudly, ' I thank you; and I am willing to hear your advice;—but the business on which you come is of such importance, that it requires much deliberation, and the help of a mind superior to feminine infirmities. You see my employment. It is thus that my time is spent among my women, who are not the wisest counsellors; and yet, I have no other in England; and Spain, where my only friends are, God knows! is far off. Still, I am content to hear what you have to say, and will give you an answer when I can conveniently.' She then conducted us into an inner apartment, where, having attentively listened to our advice that she should retire to a nunnery, and end this unhappy trial, instead of giving any reply, she addressed Wolsey with great vehemence, accused him of being the author of all her misfortunes, animadverted with acrimony on his arrogance and luxurious life; nor would she permit him to say a word, but dismissed him with marked displeasure, while she affected to treat me with the utmost courtesy."

" Campeggio, (continues Hareach,) was much distressed at this new turn which the business had taken.

He had been aware from the first, that the divorce was what the king desired more than to ascertain the validity of the marriage; and, perhaps, as the queen is in declining health, it was concerted between him and Wolsey, to procrastinate the trial till her death, which, in all probability, cannot, I understand, be far distant. But the determination of the king to procure a sentence of divorce, at all hazards, has frustrated this policy.

"'England,' resumed the Cardinal, 'is lost for ever to the Papacy by this trial; and the error that Pope Julius committed, in granting the bull to allow of the incestuous union, will be visited with a terrible retribution. But it is my duty to procure delay. To-morrow the consistory adjourns at Rome; and, as the legatine court here sits as a part of the consistory, I will adjourn it likewise, whatever the consequence may be. Things have now come to that state between the Papacy and England, that the Church must no farther compromise her dignity, by compliance with the arbitrary humours of the English king.'

"Accordingly, next day, he did adjourn the court, declaring he would not give judgment without the express authority of the Pope, to whom the whole proceedings must be previously communicated.—'The affair,' said he, 'is itself too high for us to deliver a hasty decision, considering the dignity of the persons to whom it relates, the doubtful occasion of it, the nature of our commission, and the authority by which we act. It is therefore requisite that we should consult our proper head and lord. I am not to please, for favour, fee, or reward, any man alive, be he king or subject; and the queen will make no answer to our summons, but has appealed to the Pope. I am an old man, sickly and infirm, looking every day for death. What will it avail me, to put my eternal soul in danger, for the favour of any potentate of this transitory world?' He then rose, and left the hall. Cardinal Wolsey also rose; but, instead of going as usual immediately to his barge, he retired into an inner apartment, where some sharp words passed between him and the Duke of Suffolk respecting the adjournment.

"Campeggio, on returning to his lodgings, made hasty preparations for his departure; and it was reported that Cardinal Wolsey also intended to leave the kingdom,—it being generally understood that the king was determined to break entirely with the Pope, and declare himself the head of the church of England. But Wolsey, although well informed of all these things, affected not to know them. He continued as usual to exercise his ministerial functions, as if unconscious of any impending change in his fortune; nor abated in the slightest degree any of his wonted ostentation. When Campeggio took leave of him, he evidently felt deeply; and there was more sincere sorrow at their parting than usually takes place at the separation of statesmen. Their parting was the separation of England from the papal authority,—the English from the Roman church."

As our author accompanied Campeggio out of the kingdom, we find no farther notice of what afterwards befel Cardinal Wolsey; we shall therefore, for the satisfaction of the reader, supply, in the next chapter, a few interesting particulars concerning his fall and death.

CHAPTER XIV.

The Fall and Death of Cardinal Wolsey.

CARDINAL WOLSEY opened the Michaelmas term at Westminster Hall with all his wonted pomp and ceremony. In the course of the same evening, it is supposed that he received private information that his dismissal from office was determined; for the next day he remained at home, but no messenger came from the king. On the following morning, however, the dukes of Norfolk and Suffolk arrived, and demanded the great seal to be delivered to them; but, with this requisition he refused to comply, alleging, that, as it had been given to him by the king himself, to be holden with the chancellorship for life, with letters-patent to that effect, it was necessary that they should produce their commission before he could lawfully part with it. A warm altercation ensued; but the Cardinal was firm: and they were obliged to depart without their object. Next day, however, they returned sufficiently empowered; and the seal was delivered. In the meantime, the Cardinal ordered inventories to be made of his furniture, wealth, and plate, which he directed his treasurer to hold at the disposal of the king; and immediately prepared to retire to a house at Ashur, which belonged to him as bishop of Winchester.

It was reported in the city that the king intended to send him to the Tower; and a vast crowd of the common people assembled at the Privy-garden stairs, where his barge lay. But, to their surprise, he came from his residence attended by his usual gentlemen and yeomen. The generosity of the people was awakened for the fallen man; and they made way for him to embark in respectful silence.

The barge was rowed to Putney, where he landed, and mounted his mule. The servants followed on foot; but they had not advanced far, when a horseman was discovered coming down the hill. It was a messenger from the king, sent to assure him of his majesty's unaltered esteem and friendship; and to say that the severity with which he acted towards him, was dictated more by political consideration than by motives of anger or resentment. Wolsey, on receiving this comfortable intelligence, alighted; and, kneeling on the spot, returned thanks to Heaven, and rewarded the bearer with a chain of gold from his own neck: and, as a proof to the king of the pleasure which his message had afforded, he sent him a jester from among his train, with whose fooleries his majesty had been often diverted. But the fool was reluctant to go; and could only be parted by force from the fallen fortune of his master.

Ruin is doubtless the same to men of all conditions; but persons in elevated stations, as they fall from a greater height than men of an ordinary rank, perhaps, suffer under a more overwhelming sense of calamity. Disgrace also is more acutely felt as it is more generally known; and the interest of a whole people adds an ideal weight to the misfortunes of fallen greatness. Wolsey now stood forth to view confessedly a ruined man. Sudden adversity had blasted all his blushing honours; and, as a sure prognostic of approaching decay, the ephemeral swarms which had lived in his shade disappeared, and left him in solitude. Of all afflictions which assail the human heart, ingratitude has ever given the severest blow; and men, who have lost the possession of extensive power, are peculiarly exposed to the evil. The official dependants of the Cardinal manifested the common baseness of political adherents; and none but his immediate domestics, who partook in the overthrow of his fortunes, remained to console their deserted master. Bodily suffering would have been relief to his proud and fervent mind; but, to be left alone to brood over his disgrace,—to feel the coldness of deliberate neglect,—to be conscious of the insolent triumph of his enemies;—and, with so liberal a spirit, to be deprived of the means of rewarding the faithful attachment of his servants, was a punishment, as he observed himself, far worse than death. The agitations of suspense gradually subsided into despondency; and he was seized with that sickness of spirit which is more fatal to the powers of life than the sharpest sorrow. Had he been sent to the scaffold, he would in all probability have met death with firmness; but the course which the king pursued, though dictated, no doubt, by some remains of esteem, was that of all others against which he was least able to bear himself with fortitude.*

Articles of impeachment were drawn up against him, and presented to the House of Commons, but were so manfully opposed by his secretary, Thomas Cromwell, that the House threw out the bill. His enemies, however,

---

* Galt's Life of Cardinal Wolsey.

indicted him on an old law, for having exercised his legatine authority within the realm without the king's authority,—an accusation manifestly absurd. To one of the judges who was sent to him at Ashur, where he at this time resided, his answer to this accusation was proud and melancholy.—' I am,' said he, ' now sixty years old, and the best of my days have been spent in his majesty's service, in which my whole endeavour was to please him: and is this that heinous offence for which I am deprived in old age of my all, and driven as it were to beg my bread? I expected some higher charge; not that I am guilty, but because his majesty knows how ill it becomes the magnanimity of a king to condemn without a hearing a servant who was greatest in his favour; and to inflict, for a slight fault, a punishment more cruel than death. What man is he that would not die, rather than witness those whose faithful service he has long experienced, starving around him? But, since so little can be alleged against me, I hope that this machination of combined envy will be as easily broken as my impeachment was thrown out of the parliament. It is well known to the king, that I would not have presumed to exercise my legatine commission without his royal assent. All my property, as you know, is under sequestration; I cannot therefore at present produce his letters: neither, indeed, if I could, would I: for, why should I contend with the king? Go, therefore, and tell him, that I acknowledge all that I have, (but of what do I speak?—for I have nothing left,) or whatsoever I had, to be the gifts of his royal bounty; and it is but just, that he should revoke his favours, if he think me unworthy of them. I remit my cause to him, to be at his pleasure either condemned or pardoned. If you will have me acknowledge myself guilty, be it so; but the king knows my innocence, and neither my own confession, nor the detractions of my enemies, can deceive him."* The judge then requested him to resign York-place,† the archiepiscopal residence in Westminster. The Cardinal, not considering it as his property, was surprised

---

* Godwin's Annals, p. 62.   † Whitehall.

at the request, and said to the judge, 'Sir, I know that the king possesses a royal spirit, not requiring more by law than what is reasonable; therefore I advise you, and all his council, to put no more into his head than may stand with his conscience. The council of a king ought to respect equity more than law;—for it is more honourable to do what is just than lawful. The king, for his own dignity, should mitigate the rigour of the laws; and it is for this purpose that he has appointed a chancellor, with power to appease and restrain the severity with which, in some cases, they might operate. And now, sir, can I give away that which belongs as much to those who shall succeed me as to myself? I pray you, show me whether it be consistent with law or equity?' The judge was perplexed by these observations, and knew not well what answer to give.—"In truth," said he, "there is little equity in the matter; but the king's great power is sufficient to recompense the see of York with double the value of the place."—'That I know,' replied the Cardinal, 'but there is no such condition in the proposal. You require of me a full and entire surrender of the rights of others with which I have been entrusted. If every bishop were to comply with such a request, what would become of the patrimony of the church? But I must submit to the king's power. I charge you, however, to exonerate me from the guilt of this act; and to tell his majesty to remember, that there is both a heaven and a hell.' With this answer the judge returned to London.

Cromwell, who in the House of Commons had so ably defended him, being on a visit of consolation to him at Ashur, he one day took occasion to mention that no provision had been made for several of the servants who had proved themselves very faithful, and had never forsaken him.—'Alas!' replied the Cardinal, 'you know that I have nothing to give them, nor to reward you.' Cromwell then proposed that the Cardinal's chaplains, who had been preferred to rich benefices by his influence, should, with himself, contribute a little money for the support of the domestics; and it was agreed that, as the return of the king's favour was uncertain, it was necessary to reduce their number. The servants were therefore summoned into the hall, at the upper end of which stood Wolsey in his pontifical robes, attended by the chaplains and officers of his household, with whom he continued in conversation till the whole were assembled. Turning to address them, he paused for a moment. The sight of so many faithful though humble friends powerfully touched his feelings, and for some time he was unable to speak. The tears started into his eyes, and the servants, perceiving his emotion, gave way to their own sorrows. When he had recovered from his agitation, and silence was restored, he spoke to them in the following manner: 'Most faithful gentlemen, and true-hearted yeomen, I lament that in my prosperity I did not so much for you as I might have done, nor what was then in my power. I considered, indeed, that if I promoted you, to the exclusion of the king's servants, I should have been exposed to their malice, and to the slander of the world. But now my power is gone. It has pleased the king to take away all that I had, and I have nothing left but my robe and my integrity. My punishment, however, far exceeds my offence; and I trust to be soon restored to his majesty's favour, when I shall remember the treasure I possessed in you, the value of which I knew not before. Whatever may then be the surplus of my income, it shall be divided among you; for I will never consider the riches of this world as given for any other end than for the maintenance of that condition to which Providence calls me. Should the king not soon replace me in his confidence, I will recommend you to himself, or to some nobleman; and I trust that the king, or any nobleman, will yet respect my recommendation.' He concluded by advising them to repair to their families; and Cromwell and the chaplains having raised a sum of money for their relief, it was immediately distributed, and many of them departed to their respective homes.

Soon after, he was regularly pardoned, and replaced in the see of York, with a pension of a thousand marks per annum from the bishopric of Winchester; and the king restored to him plate and effects to the value of more than six thousand pounds. These unexpected testimonies of affection essentially contributed to his recovery; and he ventured to solicit leave to remove from Ashur to the more cheerful air and scenery of Richmond, which was readily granted. But his enemies, fearing that, if he was permitted to reside long so near the court, the king might be induced to visit or recal him, recommended that, as he was not now detained by the duties of the Chancery, he should be sent to the government of his diocese; and he was accordingly banished to York.

Sometime previous to his departure, the domestics observed an interesting change in his demeanour. Like many other great men in adversity, his mind took a superstitious turn, and seemed to discover, in accidents certainly trivial, an ominous and fatal meaning. He grew pensive, wore a shirt of hair-cloth, and held frequent conferences with a venerable old man belonging to the brotherhood of the Charter-house at Richmond.

He commenced his journey towards York about the end of Lent. His train consisted of a hundred and sixty horses, and seventy-two waggons, loaded with the relics of his furniture. Having stopped at Peterborough to celebrate the festival of Easter, on Palm Sunday, he walked in the procession of the monks to the cathedral; and, on the following Thursday, kept Maundy, according to the practice of the church, washing the feet of the poor, and bestowing alms and blessings. From Peterborough he proceeded slowly, exercising his pastoral functions by the way, and halted at Stoby, where he resided till Michaelmas, preaching in the churches of the adjacent parishes, interposing to reconcile the variance of neighbours, relieving the necessitous, and performing many other exemplary acts of piety and benevolence. He then went forward to Caywood Castle, one of the residences of the archbishop of York, distant from the city about twelve miles. A great conflux of people, drawn together by curiosity, waited to see him arrive; among whom were the clergy of the diocese, who welcomed him with the reverence due to his pontifical dignity. The castle having been long untenanted, required extensive repairs, which the Cardinal immediately commenced. The short period of his residence in this ancient mansion, was, perhaps, the happiest of his life. He appeared delighted with the composure of rural affairs; and, by the equity of his demeanour, and a mild condescension, which belied the reports of his haughtiness, he won the hearts of his diocesans. He professed himself a convert from ambition; and, having suffered the perils and terrors of shipwreck, he was thankful that at length he had cast anchor in a calm and pleasant haven, with the expectation of safety and rest.

As he had never been installed in the archiepiscopal see, he gave orders to prepare the cathedral for the ceremony; and a day was appointed for the celebration. On this occasion the arrangements were unusually simple; but, as the day approached, incredible quantities of provisions were sent to him by the neighbouring gentry and clergy, in order that he might maintain the customary hospitalities in a style suitable to his character and dignity.

The Monday after All-souls-day was fixed for the installation; but, on the preceding Friday, as he was sitting at dinner, the earl of Northumberland, who, while lord Percy, had been educated in his house as one of his pages, accompanied by a privy-counsellor, and a large retinue, arrived at the castle. He was received with a paternal and a cheerful welcome, and conducted by Wolsey into his own apartments; where they had not, however, exchanged many words, when the earl became agitated, and, in a low and troubled voice, arrested him for high treason. Astonished by a charge so unexpected, Wolsey for some time was unable to speak; but, recovering his spirits, he requested Northumberland to show him the warrant, protesting that, otherwise, he would not surrender himself; for, as a member of the college of Cardinals, he was exempted from the jurisdiction of all secular princes. At this moment the privy-counsellor entered the room. Wolsey, on seeing him, observed, that, as a counsellor of the king, he was sufficiently commissioned to take him into custody, and immediately intimated that he was their prisoner.—' I fear not,' added he, ' the cruelty of my enemies, nor the scrutiny of my allegiance; and I take heaven to witness, that neither in word or deed have I injured the king, and will maintain my innocence face to face with any man alive.'

When it was known in the neighbourhood that he was to be conveyed to London, a great crowd assembled round the castle; and, as he came out on his mule, guarded, the people began to exclaim, ' God save your Grace, and foul evil overtake them that have taken you from us.' With these, and other testimonies of popular affection, he was followed to a considerable distance. Northumberland conducted him to Sheffield-park, and delivered him to the custody of the earl of Shrewsbury, with whom he resided for about a fortnight, until the king's further pleasure was known. Shrewsbury entertained him with the respect that became his own honour, and assured him, that though the king could not satisfy the council without sending him to trial, still he believed him guiltless, and that his enemies dreaded his restoration to favour more than he ought to do their malice. But the Cardinal could no longer be cheered. He considered his destruction as irrevocably fixed, and resigned himself to the comfortless thoughts which that gloomy notion inspired. His constitution, impaired by age, and by the vicissitudes of hope and fear, suddenly gave way. One day, at dinner, he complained of a coldness in his stomach, and was soon after seized with a violent flux, which greatly drained his strength. In this situation he was found by sir William Kingston, constable of the Tower, who, with twenty yeomen of the guard, that had formerly been in his own service, came to convey him to London. Sir William, on being taken to his presence, knelt down, and assured him, in the king's name, of his majesty's unbroken friendship; adding, that it was not necessary for him to make more haste in the journey than suited his health and convenience. The Cardinal, however, thought that delay might be regarded as evidence of conscious guilt; and, declineing the indulgence, anxiously proceeded forward.

Although he travelled slowly, his illness was increased by fatigue, and he grew weak and feverish. On the evening of the third day after leaving Sheffield-park, he approached Leicester. The appearance of nature accorded with the condition of the prisoner. The end of the year was drawing nigh,—and he beheld for the last time the falling leaf and the setting sun.

When the cavalcade had reached the monastery, the day was shut in; and the abbot and friars, apprised of his coming, waited, with torches, at the gate, to receive him. But the honours of this world had ceased to afford him pleasure; and, as he passed towards the bottom of the stairs, he said, 'I am come to lay my bones among you.' Being supported into a chamber, he immediately went to bed, and languished, with increasing signs of dissolution, all the next day. The following morning, Cavendish, his usher, and afterwards historian, as he was watching near him, thought that he perceived the symptoms of death. The Cardinal noticing him, inquired the hour, and was told eight o'clock: 'That cannot be,' he replied, 'for at eight o'clock you shall lose your master. My time is at hand, and I must depart this world.' His confessor, who was standing near, requested Cavendish to enquire if he would be confessed. 'What have you to do with that?' answered he, angrily; but was pacified by the interference of the confessor. Continuing to grow weaker and weaker, he frequently fainted during the course of the day. About four o'clock of the following morning he asked for some refreshment; which having received, and made confession, sir William Kingston entered his room, and inquired how he felt himself.—'Sir,' said Wolsey, 'I tarry but the pleasure of God, to render up my poor soul into his hands;' and, after a few other words between them, he resumed: 'I have now been eight days together troubled with a continual flux and fever, a species of disease, which, if it do not remit its violence within that period, never fails to terminate in death. I pray you commend me humbly to the king; and beseech him, in my behalf, to call to his princely remembrance all matters that have passed between him and me, particularly in what respects the business of the queen, and then he must know whether I have given him any offence. He is a prince of a most royal nature; but rather than want any part of his pleasure, he will endanger the half of his kingdom. Often have I knelt before him for three hours together, endeavouring to persuade him from his will and appetite, and could not prevail. Had I served God as diligently as I have done the king, he would not have given me over in my grey hairs.'* He then continued for a short time to give sir William some advice, in case he should ever be called to the privy-council; and, adding a few general observations on the revolutionary temper of the times, concluded by saying, Farewell, I wish all good things to have success. My time draws fast on. I may not tarry with you. Forget not what I have said; and, when I am gone, call it often to mind.' Towards the conclusion he began to falter and linger in the articulation of his words. At the end, his eyes became motionless, and his sight failed. The abbot was summoned to administer the extreme unction; and the yeomen of the guard were called in to see him die. As the clock struck eight he expired."

Such was the end of this famous Cardinal, of whose character we cannot give a better summary than in the words of Campion, an historian of Ireland in the reign of Queen Elizabeth.

"He was a man undoubtedly born to honour. I think some prince's bastard, no butcher's son: exceeding wise, fair spoken, high-minded, full of revenge, vicious of his body, lofty to his enemies, were they never so big; to those who accepted and sought his friendship, wonderful courteous; a ripe schoolman, thrall to affections; brought-a-bed with flattery; insatiable to get, most princelike in bestowing, (as appeareth by his two colleges at

---

* This sentiment seems to be common to fallen ministers. When Samrah, the governor of Busorah, was deposed by Maoujyah, the sixth caliph, he is reported to have said, 'If I had served God so well as I served him, he would not have condemned me:' and Antonio Perez, the favourite of Philip II. of Spain, made a similar complaint.

Ipswich and at Oxford; the one suppressed at his fall, the other unfinished; and yet, as it lieth, a house of students incomparable throughout Christendom:) a great preferer of his servants; advancer of learning; stout in every quarrel, never happy till his overthrow: therein he showed such moderation, and ended so patiently, that the hour of his death did him more honour than all the pomp of his life."

CHAPTER XV.

Notes respecting Francis I. and the State of the Protestant Religion in France when Mary Queen of Scots was married to the French King.

We cannot follow, with any degree of satisfaction to ourselves, the train of incidents, during a period of more than fifty years, interspersed among the reflections of our author, after his departure from England with Cardinal Campeggio. The Cardinal went forward to Rome, but Hareach remained in France; and his observations, which chiefly relate to transactions at Paris, are brief, abrupt, and inconclusive. We may, however, extract those in which he speaks of the personal appearance and character of Francis I. one of the most celebrated modern kings, not only on account of his adventures and accomplishments, but for his patronage of learned men and of artists. It is indeed, perhaps, to the personal predilections of this great monarch, that the French nation owe that taste for literature and the fine arts, in which they are so honourably distinguished.

"Francis," says our author, "bears a very striking resemblance to his friend, Henry the Eighth of England, although he is much less corpulent. The resemblance, however, is less in particular features than in their general air, voice, and manners. Henry is of a bolder humour, and somewhat boisterous in his temper; he is perhaps also more generous, and less discriminative; but it is surprising to perceive how much these two kings are in their deportment, pursuits, pleasures, and dispositions, alike. In respect to natural abilities, I think Francis the superior; his taste is more cultivated, his information more extensive, and his accomplishments more elegant: had he not, indeed, been so much harassed with the concerns of state, he would probably have distinguished himself as a poet. Henry also has written verses as well as divinity; but, although very respectable effusions for a king, all respectable poetry is very bad. The little pieces of Francis are, however, touched with an agreeable spirit, and enriched with the fruit of his extensive erudition: for, at all his meals, and his leisure time before going to sleep, a person regularly attends to read to him, by which he has gained a general acquaintance with the literature of the age, and a considerable acquaintance with the merits of the learned. He has done much to augment the magnificence of the French kings; but, although his seats and palaces are still far inferior to those of the English sovereign, he has adorned them with a more correct and refined taste; and his liberality to literary men, shows that he has a just notion of the true method of securing an honourable place in the esteem of posterity."

In the year 1557 we meet with a short note respecting the unfortunate Mary Queen of Scots, not unworthy of being added to the list of "the criminal mysteries attached to the fame of the modern Helen."

"The marriage of the Dauphin with the beautiful Queen of Scotland was celebrated a few days ago; but the ambassadors sent from the states of her kingdom, having refused to acknowledge him as their king, alledging the usage and laws of their country, the Lorraine faction are grievously disconcerted. It is thought, however, that they will leave no stone unturned that may help them to attain this object. The constable of France, however, regards the marriage as very impolitic, considering the state of religion at present in Scotland, where the Reformation is making a ravaging progress, and predicts that it will be a source of great unhappiness to both countries, especially as it is proposed to assert the claims of the Queen of Scotland to the English throne. In the minds of all good Catholics, it must certainly be allowed that these claims are well founded; for queen Elizabeth is the fruit of a marriage which they do not recognize as lawful. But the English nation have recognized it, and will not permit the French to tell them that they have done wrong."

"A very hideous transaction obtrudes itself on the suspicious of the world. Four of the Scottish deputies have died suddenly. They were stout-hearted men, and full of nationality. It is to be hoped that the Cardinal Lorraine and his faction have had no hand in their death. But the thing does not look well. It is said that the greater part of the Scottish nation are infected, as it is called, with the heresies of the reformation in religion, and that the deputies were heretics; and there can be no doubt, that at this time, the court of France is actuated by the furor of bigotry against all the professors of the new opinions.

"A strange fatality is interwoven with the fortune of the young queen of Scotland. The House of Guise, not content with the absolute direction of the two kingdoms of France and Scotland, aspire to a like dominion over that of England, and still persist in the claim for their niece of the throne of that kingdom, although it is filled by Elizabeth, one of the most popular sovereigns of the age, and whose government is necessarily energetic; having embraced the reformed religion, and, of course, necessitated to be on the alert, and prepared against the vengeance of the Papal adherents.

"A terrible conspiracy has been discovered, having religion for its motive. Some time ago, the Protestants, seeing the determined hostility of the Court against their religion, held a meeting at Nantes. One hundred and fifty deputies from the reformed in all the different provinces of France were present, and it was resolved to take the only measure left for their own defence,—that of putting themselves in arms. With this view, the Prince of Condé was chosen the secret chief of the association, and Renaudie the ostensible. This gentleman was a person of great parts and determined resolution; but, it is said that, in his youth, he was guilty of some irregularities, which might have been fatal to him but for the favour of the Duke of Guise. Subordinate chiefs were likewise chosen, to direct the intended armament among the reformed. Renaudie went to England to solicit the countenance and pecuniary assistance of Queen Elizabeth; and she received him favourably, and assured him of her aid. The association being informed of this, and also of the favourable disposition of some of the German Protestant princes, determined to surprise the court at Blois,—to secure the person of the king,—to rid themselves of the members of the insolent House of Guise, and oblige the king to declare the Prince of Condé lieutenant-general of the kingdom: in a word, to change the whole face of affairs.* The fifteenth day of March was fixed for this enterprise; and it was arranged, that their forces to carry it into execution should defile with all possible secrecy in small parties towards the scene of action, under chiefs appointed from every quarter. The conspiracy was brought to maturity with such profound secrecy, that the court had not the least intelligence of it, till Renaudie, having communicated the whole to Peter Annelles, an advocate of Paris with whom he lodged, this man, either through fear, or from some other motive, betrayed the design to the court, where the thing at first appeared so amazing, that it was scarcely credited; but, upon more consideration, it was thought prudent to lose no time in providing for the king's security as well as that of the Guises: and, for this purpose, the Court suddenly removed from the castle of Amboise. Of this removal the conspirators

---

* Universal History.

were apprised; but, being so far advanced in their design, they resolved still to proceed.

"The duke of Guise perceived that respect to the king's name, and the influence of his own authority as lieutenant-general of the kingdom, would enable him to assemble troops enough to disappoint at least the leaders, embarked in this meditated attack; and, by his resolution, dilligence, and military skill, it ended as he anticipated. The count de Sancerre defeated the troops from Bearn; the duke de Nemours surprised the baron de Castelneau, and made him prisoner, with the greatest part of his officers; Pardaillan fell upon Renaudie in a wood, defeated the troops that still remained with him, and, in a personal engagement, ran him twice through the body: his page also wounded him with a harquebuss, notwithstanding which he killed the page. His body was exposed upon a gibbet, and afterwards quartered. Three of the chiefs, who surrendered, were tortured, and put to death, in the presence of the queen-dowager and the ladies of her court. Pagan antiquity affords no blacker example of female turpitude than this: and yet these ladies were actuated by religious motives, and a religion which they call Christian! But an incident occurred at the execution, that left an awful impression on all the spectators. One of the victims, whose name was Villemonge, before submitting to the executioner, dipped his hands in the blood of his companions, and cried out, in a voice that knelled like the voice of prophecy to every heart, "Lord avenge our cause!"

"Of the unfortunate or imprudent men engaged in this fanatic conspiracy twelve hundred were hanged, beheaded, or drowned in the river; and the streets of Amboise literally swam with blood. The chancellor Olivier, a good old man, who did all he could to arrest the crushing grasps of cruelty, died of grief and horror at the sight of these atrocities."*

The notes which follow are not particularly interesting; but it is singular, that Francis the Second, in whose time

---

* L'Histoire du Tumulte d'Amboise.

this horrible massacre, according to law, took place, is styled, in the French histories, the king without vice,— so entirely were the whole affairs of the kingdom managed by his mother, Catherine de Medici, and the audacious brothers of the House of Guise.

CHAPTER XVI.

The Massacre of the Protestants in France on the Eve of St. Bartholomew.

[A. D. 1571.]

We have now to extract the particulars of a transaction, which excels in guilt all the conspiracies of antiquity, and has only been equalled, not surpassed, by the atrocities of the French revolution. The queen-dowager, Catherine of Medici, unable to resist the progress which the Reformation was making in France during the reign of her son Charles XI. who succeeded Francis II. held a cabinet council on the 22d of August, to fix the execution of a design which she had meditated for many years, as the only effectual mode of suppressing the Protestants. We shall particularize the members of this council; for it is fit and proper, that the names of such men should be held up to everlasting execration. Public opinion is the only check on the bad passions of statesmen; and it is the duty of history to make them know, that, although they may escape actual punishment during life, they shall for ever stand accursed by posterity. For this reason, in all cases of aggression against the people, it is the imperious duty of historians to record with minute fidelity the names of the parties; it is even desirable that medals and monuments should be employed, to perpetuate their infamy. The incarnated demons that met CATHERINE DE MEDICI on the evening of the day alluded to, bore the Christian appellations of HENRY duke of Anjou, afterwards king of Poland and of France; GONZAGUA duke of Nevers; HENRY of Angouleme, grand prior of France, and bastard-brother of the king; and ALBERT DE GONDI, with the Marshal de RHETZ: and they determined, that the Protestants in general, throughout France, should be massacred. It was with some difficulty that the duke de Nevers and Marshal Tavannes persuaded them to spare the king of Navarre and the prince of Condé, together with the marshals Montmorenci and Damville, who were at first with the rest doomed to slaughter. The direction of the whole bloody business was confided to the duke of Guise. We shall now extract our author's account of the details.

" I had that evening remained abroad late after supper, and was returning along the quay between the Louvre and the river. There was something in the state of the air, that disposed the mind to be peculiarly sensitive and easily alarmed. The night was very dark, and a strange torpor seemed to affect the very twinkling of the stars. The murmuring of the river had a low and preternatural sound; and it seemed to me as if there were an unusual number of lights to be seen in the city. As I passed along, this circumstance struck my fancy, and I fell into a train of reflections, in which the objects that presented themselves to my imagination were persons lying on their death-bed, attended by their friends, and doctors busily visiting the couches of the sick.

" While these things were passing in my mind, my attention was roused by an unusual bustle among the guards at the gate of the Palace. I felt a strange emotion of alarm, without any assignable cause, and hastened home. I had not however proceeded far, when I observed, by the faint light of a lamp burning before an image of Christ, a great appearance of soldiers moving towards the Hotel de Ville. I involuntarily stepped aside into a narrow passage which led to the street where the Admiral Coligni resided, intending to go by that way to my lodgings. I had not however proceeded far, when a dreadful sound startled me, and I stood still. It was not the cries of the human voice, nor the neighing of horses, nor the clangour of a trumpet, nor the roll of a drum, nor the crackling of a conflagration, nor the wheels of engines, nor the tolling of a bell, nor the groans of death,—but a deep and troubled sound, in which all these bore a part. I shuddered, and hurried towards my home for refuge; but, as I reached the end of the lane that opened into the street, I perceived a number of persons assembled in front of the admiral's house. Some of the neighbours, disturbed by the circumstance, had come to their windows with lights, by which I saw that the crowd consisted of a detachment of the Swiss guards, and that the duke de Guise, and the Chevalier d'Angouleme, with several persons of quality, were among them. All this time the bell of the Louvre was ringing with a wild and dismal larum. I knew not what to think; but, perceiving a gate-way open in the street, I ran into it, and, concealed in the shadow within, I waited the issue of what was going on with throbbing anxiety. In this situation I heard the duke of Guise call impatiently aloud to some one in the house, " Besme, is it done?" and, in the same moment, this assassin, with his sword dropping blood in his hand, looked from a window, and, in a hoarse and agitated voice, answered, ' Yes.'— ' Then throw out the body, that we may be sure,' said the duke. In the same instant several persons, and among them Besme, brought the bleeding body of the old admiral to the window, and flung it into the street; upon which, Angouleme, taking out his handkerchief, wiped the face, and, having ascertained that it was indeed the body of the admiral, kicked it with his foot. At this moment, a frantic multitude of the bigotted populace came rushing to the spot, and exclaiming, ' The heretic! the heretic!' dragged it by the feet, to present it as an acceptable offering to Catherine de Medici.

"By this time the whole city was alarmed: the cries of fire and of murder resounded on all sides. The windows were lighted up; the shrieks of women, flying with their children, were heard in all directions. I mingled in the crowd, hurried from place to place with the stream. Doors were battered open, and the inhabitants barbarously murdered. At one place, the bloodhounds forced the gate of a large and stately mansion, and a band of them entered. The crowd in which I was, stopped without: we heard shrieks and entreaties, followed by groans and the screams of childhood, that pierced the heart. In this moment, a young female, the lady of the mansion, in the garb of sleep, came rushing out with a child in each arm, and holding an infant by its clothes in her teeth. A cry of horror and of nature burst from all who saw her; but some wretch behind levelled at her head a stone, and she fell, stunned by the blow. In the same moment, the wolves, who had burst into her fold, came raging and bloody from within, and trampled and stabbed the mother and her children till they were more than dead.

"From this spot they proceeded towards the bridge, in order to join in the attack on the Hugonots, who lived on the opposite side of the river; and I availed myself of an opportunity of stepping into an open door, to escape from these monsters. Such had been the consternation in my mind, that when I left this place, I knew not in what direction I ran, till, as I leant panting and breathless against the wall of a building, I heard several voices at a window above me: I looked up, and perceived that it was the Louvre; and the king, with the queen-dowager, and several of their attendants, in a balcony. By this time the day began to dawn; and a scattered and terrified multitude of the persecuted were seen flying along the quay on the opposite bank of the river. The king, in a transport of savage bigotry, called to bring him a long gun, and in an instant fired on the fugitives. I looked up to heaven;—the skies were cloudless, and the stars that yet were visible sparkled: but I thought that, surely, at those glorious windows of heaven, there are witnesses who mark, and will avenge, this crime.

"I had not, however, much time for reflection; for another herd of the persecutors were heard coming to wards the spot where I stood. I fled as fast as my faltering limbs would carry me; and heard them, as they passed under the windows where the king and his mother stood, shout with exultation, that was answered by an echo,—if it was not by the triumphant fiends of perdition, who, unseen of mortal sight, instigated their human agents in the business of this terrible night.

"In what manner I got to my lodgings I have been unable to ascertain, such was the perturbation of my spirit. I have but a confused recollection of passing dead bodies, hearing fearful yells of despair and exultation; for, when I reached home, I had thrown myself on my bed, and, worn out by what I had seen, had fallen soon after asleep. When I awoke, I felt as if I had experienced some inconceivably horrible dream; and endeavoured to persuade myself that the scenes I had witnessed were all visionary: but the old woman with whom I lived, and who was a fierce Catholic, soon after came into my room. The satanic expression of satisfaction in her haggard visage, made me shake anew with horror. Her complexion was of a hideous yellow, her eyes black and malignant, her nostrils distended with the insolence of cruelty; and she had in one hand a knife, with which she had been employed in some culinary office, and in the other a large rusty key belonging to the portal door. She began to felicitate herself, and the rest of the Catholic world, on the great service that had been done to religion in the preceding night; and, in relating some of the most dreadful circumstances that she had heard, she struck into the air with the knife, and grasped the key with the energy of a demoniac,—the living personation of religious bigotry.

"The impression which this fanatic hag's appearance had on my mind, induced me to change my lodgings; and I went to the village of St. Cloud the same evening, where I obtained an apartment in a lofty house not far from the gate of the castle, overlooking the vale of the Seine.

"After I had tasted a little wine and fresh water, I sat down at the window, oppressed in thought with the terrible recollections of the preceding night. Absorbed in the hideous confusion of its dreadful transactions, I leant, with my head on my hand, insensible to every object without, till I was roused by the cooing of a pigeon which had alighed at the window. The softness and affectionate sound of its tones, came upon my spirits like the dawning of the morning to the eye of the benighted traveller; and I looked out on the beautiful tranquillity of the landscape before me, with a sensation of freshness and pleasure that I had never before enjoyed. The waters of the river were brightly glancing in the low declining sun of the afternoon;—a soft haze overspread the whole face of nature;—a delicious cheerfulness dwelt, as it were, on the bright verdure of the vineyards;—and the lively motion of a water-wheel belonging to a mill at a short distance on the river, seemed in unison with the general benevolence of the calm luxuriance of a scene, which, in that moment, acquitted to my heart, if I may use so bold an expression, God and Nature, from having had any part in the crimes of Paris.'

CHAPTER XVII.

Observations of the Editor on the Characters of Mary Queen of Scots, and of Queen Elizabeth, her Rival.

SOON after the massacre of St. Bartholomew, or the Paris matins, as it has been called, to class it with the famous Sicilian vespers, our author travelled into different parts of Germany; but his notes are so unsatisfactory, that we can make no use of this part of his Volume. He appears, however, to have hastened into England, when he heard that Elizabeth had determined to bring the Scottish queen, whom she had held many years her prisoner, to trial. It will be recollected, that Mary had been induced, by her uncles of the House of Guise, at her marriage with Francis the Second of France, to lay claims to the throne of England, on the ground of Elizabeth's bastardy, her mother, Ann Boleyn, not having been properly married, in the opinion of the Catholics, to her father Henry the Eighth. After the death of Francis, Mary, at the solicitation of her people, left France, and went to Scotland; where the Reformation had made a rapid and wasteful progress. She was herself a sincere Catholic; and the court in which she had been educated, was not calculated to inspire her with very rigid notions either of personal chastity or public of virtue. Her religion was accordingly at variance with that of the major part of her subjects; and her conduct was not calculated to inspire them with any respect for herself, although her extraordinary beauty and elegant accomplishments rendered her an object of universal admiration for some time. It must however be admitted, that she was not particularly zealous; and that she even bore with considerable fortitude and great forbearance, the contumely with which her faith was assailed by the reformers. Nor should it also be withheld from the memory of this unfortunate princess, that, in the treatment which she received from her husband, Lord Darnley, whom she espoused soon after her arrival in Scotland, her feelings as a woman received great provocation. That she was privy to his assassination we think not improbable; but, as this has been questioned with great ingenuity, the charge may be abandoned: but it cannot be denied, that the event afforded her satisfaction. Her subsequent marriage with Boswell was itself a confirmation of her guilt; and her secret acquiescence in a league, formed for the purpose of extirpating the Protestants, justified her subjects in taking up arms against her and the party united to the Catholic cause. The result of this rebellion forced her to fly to England; and she entered the dominions of Elizabeth, her cousin, to which her claim had been so proudly advanced, as a fugitive and a suppliant.

Historians have condemned Elizabeth, for the manner in which she treated this ill-fated princess on her arrival in England; and have, with more generosity than discretion, imagined that it became her royal dignity to receive the queen of Scotland as an honoured guest. But magnanimity is not at all times wisdom; and, in this case, it would have been the extreme of folly. Elizabeth had a difficult part to perform. Those of her own subjects who were still adherents to the old religion, considered her as a usurper of the throne; and even many who professed the new doctrines, were not satisfied that her right was perfectly legal. All the great continental sovereigns, with the pope at their head, were her enemies; and, though not actually at war with her, only waited a fit opportunity to attack her with all their united powers. Was it therefore to be expected, that she would receive as an open, free, and honoured guest, the declared pretender to her throne, and an avowed enemy of the religion that she had undertaken to support. But, it cannot be questioned, that, for several years after the arrival of Mary, she treated her with all the distinction and consideration due to her rank; nor, in fact, until that princess, rendered desperate by the ruin of her fortunes, embarked in plots, having at once for their object the overthrow of Elizabeth and her own liberty, can it be justly said that Elizabeth took any step against her, that was not rendered requisite by a wise and patriotic policy. Beyond this, however, her treatment of Mary deserves reprobation; for, after having held her in captivity eighteen years, the guilt of bringing her to trial, and of leading her to execution on the scaffold, is unquestionably one of the most extraordinary events in history. It was however a crime, in which the whole English nation participated. Elizabeth can in no respect be considered as having committed a greater outrage on the decorum of national justice, in the public murder of the Scottish queen, than her counsellors who advised the trial, than the parliament who implored, or than the people who clamoured, that the sentence should be executed. Mary was sacrificed to the spirit of the age; and the odium of her death does not attach more to Elizabeth personally than that of any other victim of the laws, whose death-warrant, in her capacity of sovereign, she was advised to sign. But it is time that we should give our author's account of the event; and his notes being of considerable extent, we shall form them into an entire chapter.

CHAPTER XVIII.

The Trial of Mary Queen of Scots.

[A. D. 1586.]

"In the evening I reached Fotheringay, where the queen of Scotland was confined, and took up my lodging in a small ale-house which stands at a short distance from the castle-gate. It was dark when I arrived, and the house was filled with the servants attending the commissioners, thirty-six of whom had arrived in the course of the afternoon; and who, having waited on the unfortunate princess, delivered to her a letter from Elizabeth, commanding her to submit to trial, as a party concerned in Babington's conspiracy. The conversation among the servants when I entered the kitchen, where they were assembled, related entirely to this solemn business; and they were discussing, in their way, according to the custom of the English of all ranks, the merits of the case. The queen of Scotland had among them evidently a very considerable party, chiefly of the younger class, several of whom inveighed with great freedom against the treatment which she had received. From this conversation, desultory and rude as it was, and conducted, in some instances, with great heat and vehemence, I gathered, that Mary received the commissioners with great dignity, and perused the letter with undisturbed composure,—a satisfactory proof to her partisans of her innocence; but, to her adversaries, of her art and dissimulation. It was evident that these varlets had imbibed, in most instances, the opinions of their masters; and that they had collected, one with the other, a very circumstantial account of this important interview.

"When the Scottish queen had read the letter, she laid it on the table, the commissioners standing uncovered, with much respect in their deportment, before her; and, turning to Lord Walsingham, who was their oracle, said, in a firm but sedate manner, 'She wondered that the queen of England should command her as a subject, who was an independent sovereign, and a queen, like herself:' adding, 'I will not stoop to any condescension that will lessen my own dignity, or prejudice the claims of my posterity. The laws of England are unknown to me;— I am destitute of counsel; nor can I conceive how I can be tried by my peers,—for there is but one equal to me in the kingdom. With respect to the laws of your country, my lord, I have never enjoyed their protection; for, ever since my arrival in England, I have been treated as a prisoner.'

"In reply to this address, lord Walsingham urged her to submit to what was the determination of his royal mistress, otherwise the commissioners would proceed against her as contumacious. But she interrupted him with a degree of indignation, saying, 'I will rather suffer a thousand deaths, than acknowledge myself the subject of any potentate on earth. I am however willing to vindicate myself in a full and free parliament; but, for aught I know, this commission of yours is but a device to take away my life with a pretext of justice. My lord, I conjure you, in this business, to consult your own conscience; and remember, that the theatre of the world is much more extensive than the kingdom of England.' The vice-chamberlain Hatton, who was one of the commissioners, stepped forward at this moment, and, in a respectful and persuasive manner, said, 'Your majesty injures your reputation by refusing to submit to a trial, by which your innocence may be proved to the satisfaction of all mankind.' This observation made a deep impression on her; and, after a pause of two or three minutes, she said, 'Well, I will submit, on condition that I am admitted to protest of disallowing all subjection:' and they consented to enter it upon the record of their proceeding.

"Next morning the court met in the great hall of the castle, in which a number of the neighbouring gentry were present as spectators; but the crowd was not great. When the commissioners had taken their places, the queen came into the hall, leaning on the arm of one of her ladies; for she was afflicted with rheumatism, and appeared to be somewhat lame. Her demeanour was indescribably majestic; and the extraordinary beauty of her countenance, which had excited so much admiration in the days of her youth at Paris, was rendered peculiarly interesting by an affecting and pale expression of melancholy. All present received her with marked respect; and she was conducted to a seat under a canopy opposite to her judges. When the commission was read, as she had signified on the preceding evening, she protested against being considered, by submitting to a trial, as acknowledging any subjection to Elizabeth; and it was entered in the record accordingly. She was then accused of high treason against Elizabeth, in having been consenting to the conspiracy of Babington: and this charge was supported by Babington's confession; by the copies taken of their correspondence, in which her approbation of the design to assassinate the queen was clearly expressed; and by the evidence of her two secretaries, Nau, a Frenchman, and Curle, a Scotchman, who had sworn that she received Babington's letters, and that they had answered them by her orders. Their evidence was still farther confirmed by the testimony of Ballard and Savage, to whom Babington had shown these letters, declaring them to have come from the captive queen.

"To these charges, and this evidence, she made a sensible and dignified reply, which deeply impressed the court, and all present.—'As to Babington's confession, I must observe,' said she calmly, 'that, as it was extorted by his fears of the torture, it surely is not such as any tribunal, having impartial justice for its object, would admit as evidence. The letters ascribed to my secretaries are shameful forgeries: but why are they themselves not here, and as witnesses? They would not dare, in my presence, to persist in saying that ever I did authorize any such letters. That I have exerted my best endeavours to recover my liberty, I acknowledge; and I only pursued the dictates of nature: but any thought against the life of your mistress, was a thing too horrible to enter into my mind.'

"Several other letters were then read; in one of which the earl of Arundel, and his brothers, were mentioned. On hearing their names she burst into tears, and exclaimed, 'Alas! what hath the noble House of Howard endured for my sake! and she added, with fervent indignation, 'These letters, Lord Walsingham, are a base contrivance of your's: you have often practised, not only against my life, but that of my son's.

"Walsingham rose, and addressed her without the slightest tone of resentment. but with great force; and said, 'I am unjustly accused. My heart, before God, is free from malice. In my private capacity, I have never done any thing unbecoming an honest man; nor in my public, aught unworthy of the high place I hold in the state.'

"The anger of Mary was but a momentary fit of feminine passion; and she replied, 'I believe you are innocent, my lord; but give as little credit to the accusations of my enemies, as I do now to the reports that I have heard to your prejudice.'

"When the evidence had been gone through, the queen demanded that she might be furnished with a copy of the proceedings, and allowed an advocate, skilled in the laws of England, to plead for her: but the court refused her demands. Upon which she left her seat; and, on her retiring from the hall, the court adjourned to the Star-chamber in Westminster, where all the commissioners but two being present, she was declared guilty of the crime of high treason, and sentence of death pronounced against her."

CHAPTER XIX.

The Execution of Mary Queen of Scots.

"After some unaccountable delay, considering the determination at first shown to proceed against the queen of Scots with the utmost rigour, queen Elizabeth has at last consented to her execution; and the earls of Shrewsbury, Derby, Kent, and Cumberland, have arrived at the castle, with two executioners in their train, to finish this tragical business.

"These noblemen are naturally, I am told, of harsh and austere manners, but withal men of integrity; strongly attached, both by principle and policy, to the Protestant religion. It was late before they reached the castle; and Mary, at the time of their arrival, was engaged with her women at her evening devotion. She was aware of her sentence, and preparing herself for the worst; but her women still endeavoured to flatter her with an assurance that Elizabeth would not dare to carry it into execution.

"The four noblemen, immediately on their arrival, requested to be conducted into her apartment, and she received them with her wonted composure. But, without any extenuation of their severe duty, they showed her the death-warrant, and told her that it must be executed at eight o'clock next morning. She seemed to be none daunted, either by the communication, or by the abrupt manner in which it was delivered; but said, I am greatly surprised, indeed, that the queen of England has, with her own hand, consented to my execution:' and, laying her hand on the New Testament, which lay on the table before her, she solemnly repeated her abjuration of being privy to any conspiracy against the life of Elizabeth. She then requested that her confessor might be permitted to attend her; but this these austere noblemen, from a fanatical principle, refused: and she indicated by a wave of her hand, full of dignity and resignation, that she wished to be alone.

"On their returning, she ordered her supper to be brought in, of which she ate sparingly, comforting her attendants, who were overwhelmed with sorrow; telling them, 'that they ought not to mourn, but to rejoice, that she was so soon to be delivered from the miseries of this world.' Towards the end of supper she ordered all her domestics to come into the room; and, having drank to them, as they knelt around her dissolved in tears, she begged their forgiveness for any neglect or undue severity that she might have shown them; and, having divided among them what money she had still remaining, they retired, unable to control their grief from bursting into loud lamentations.

"When left alone with her women, she reviewed her will, and perused the inventory of her effects; and, after writing letters to the king of France and the Guises, recommending her servants to their attention, she went to bed at her usual hour, and passed part of the night in uninterrupted repose,—the remainder she spent in prayer and acts of devotion. Towards morning she dressed herself in a rich habit of silk and velvet, which, of all her wardrobe, she had alone reserved for this solemn occasion. The under-sheriff of the county was soon after admitted, to inform her that the hour was come; and that he must attend her to the place of execution. She then again parted from her domestics; and, supported by two of her guards, on account of her lameness, she followed the sheriff.

In passing through the anti-chamber, Sir Andrew Melvil, the master of her household, fell upon his knees; and, shedding a flood of tears, lamented his misfortune in being doomed to carry the heavy news of her unhappy fate to Scotland. 'Lament not, good Melvil,' said she, 'but rather rejoice, that Mary Stuart will soon be freed from all her cares. Tell my friends that I die constant in my religion, and firm in my affection and fidelity to Scotland and France. God forgive them that have long desired my end, and have thirsted for my blood, as the hart panteth for the water-book. Thou, O God! who art truth itself, and perfectly understandest the inmost thoughts of my heart, knowest how greatly I have desired that the realms of England and Scotland might be united. Commend me to my son; and assure him I have done nothing prejudicial to the state or the crown of Scotland. Admonish him to persevere in amity and friendship with the queen of England, and see that thou doest him faithful service;—and so, good Melvil, farewell;—once again, good Melvil, farewell: and grant the assistance of thy prayers to thy queen and mistress."

"In this place, she was met by the four noblemen, who, with great difficulty, were prevailed upon to allow Melvil, with her doctor, and apothecary, and two female attendants, to go with her to the scaffold. They were, however, overawed by the dignity of her manner, when, in answer to their refusal, she said mildly, ' I am, my lords, the lawful sovereign of Scotland, the queen-dowager of France, and the lineal heir to the throne of England.' They bowed: and she passed on to the great hall of the castle, where a scaffold was erected, covered with black cloth.

"Around the scaffold a number of soldiers were drawn, keeping an open passage to the door; and a vast concourse of persons filled both sides of the hall. A general expression of sorrow, and the sound of the passing bell, announced her approach. The sheriff entered first, followed by the lords: she came behind, at some distance, her train borne by Melvil. Her countenance was pale and serene, elevated by the spirit of martyrdom. A long lawn veil flowed from her head over her black mantle, and she held a crucifix of ivory in her hand. Her beauty, though dimmed by age, excited a universal sentiment of sorrowful admiration. It seemed indeed to many, as if her countenance was illuminated by an inward and a holy light: such was the awful effect of the composure of her look. She advanced to the scaffold with a majestic air; and, having mounted the steps, seated herself in a chair, that was placed on purpose, while the warrant for the execution was read. When this was done, the dean of Peterborough, who was without the rails which surrounded the scaffold, addressed her, in an exhortation to renounce the errors of popery; but she requested him to be silent, as she was resolved to die in the Catholic religion. The earl of Kent observing that, in her devotions, she made frequent use of the crucifix, said to her, that it would better become her to have Christ in her heart than in her hand; and she replied, with surprising presence of mind, 'It is difficult, my lord, to hold such an object in my hand, without feeling my heart moved for the sufferings of Him it represents.'

"With the aid of her two women she then began to undress for the block; and one of the executioners also lent his hand to assist them. She smiled, and said, 'I am not accustomed to undress before so large a company, nor to be attended with such servants.' Her two women, at these words, bursting into tears and loud exclamations of sorrow, she turned about to them, and put her finger on her lips, as a sign of imposing silence; and, having given them her blessing, she desired their prayers in return. The two executioners, kneeling, asked her pardon.—'I forgive you,' said she, 'and all the authors of my death, as freely as I hope forgiveness from my Maker:' and she then again made a solemn protestation of her innocence. Her eyes were then covered with a linen handkerchief; and she laid herself down on the block without fear or trepidation: and, whilst she repeated a pious ejaculation, her head was severed from her body, by one of the executioners, at two strokes of the axe."

CHAPTER XX.

Hareach in Switzerland.

AFTER the execution of Mary queen of Scots, Hareach went again to the Continent, where he remained many years, abstracted from the world, among the mountains of Switzerland. His book for several pages consists of nothing but descriptions of the scenery; and he seems to have found a strange pleasure, in conceiving that there was a species of sympathy between his spirit and the various aspects of the landscape. In one place, he speaks of the morning as eloquent to his heart with a thousand arguments to be cheerful: the singing of the birds,—the sparkling of the waters,—the glittering of the dews,—the freshness of the flowers,—the ploughs moving in the valleys, the flocks scattered over the uplands,—and all those various sounds and forms of liveliness, vigour, and beauty, which render the first fine mornings of spring so delightful. In another passage, he describes himself as seated, in summer, enjoying the breezes that fan the foreheads of the mountains, and contemplating nature in her masses and outlines, vast, distant, and sublime.—" A profound silence dwells in the air at this height;—no sound reaches me from the valleys;—the roar of the water-fall is not heard so high;—the forests appear but as the sides of the hills, darkened by the shadows of the clouds that are floating far below me. The city seems but as a desert spot of pebbles; and the stupendous piles of the Alps, extending on all sides, suggest to me awful ideas of a world destroyed: till the rising mist, filling the valleys, and insulating the hills into so many islands, affects me with a vague sense of danger, as if I was here alone on this solitary peak, and beheld another deluge overspreading the earth."

The description of his feelings, during the autumn, are expressed with still more enthusiasm.—" Beneath the shelter of this overhanging rock, I can trace the career of the blast, and fancy that I see, in those wide sheets of mingled hail and rain, the genius of the season heralding the approach of winter. A universal alarm pervades all nature. The waters come rushing forth;—the birds fly wildly from the groaning woods;—the cattle take refuge in the lea of the hedges;—the skies are troubled, and the lake is foul and dark." But, in winter, he assumes a more social tone; and expatiates, with hearty satisfaction, on the pleasure that he enjoyed in the cottage of a peasant, where he was one night obliged to take shelter from a severe storm.—" It was the best house in a little hamlet at the bottom of the mountain; and the inhabitants consisted of a cheerful old man, and his wife, a brisk and notable dame, who seemed to have an earnest enjoyment in the performance of her domestic duties. She set before me a plentiful meal of their common fare; and the good man, who was somewhat garrulous, was not sparing of his conversation. Soon after I had finished my repast, a traveller, passed the prime of life, entered; and, after a few short questions, the old man, with a shout, recognized a nephew that had, many years before, left them in the capacity of a servant to a French officer of high rank. It is impossible to describe the joy that his return occasioned. The uncle shook him by the hand, placed him in the great chair, stirred the fire, and called to his wife to fling on more wood,—all in one breath. She was no less overjoyed, and ran out to tell the neighbours. The old man asked a thousand questions about what the traveller had seen; but the neighbours coming in, he described them as they appeared, reminding him of who they were, by some little incident that had befallen them before he went away. Such as, that old fellow there, with the bent back, and the grey hairs, is Lucern, whom you well recollect a great clumsy rogue, that used to eat more, and do less, than any other reaper in harvest. This pretty maid is the daughter of Julia Delavie; but, blooming and smiling as she is, she will never be like her mother. Poor Julia died in giving her birth. Ah! look where Grisette comes: you may well remember Grisette, that used to be so kind to you when a boy, and to whom you promised a fine mantle for her old age. You are come in good time to give it; for, poor soul! her strength is not what it was; and we are all obliged to be as kind to her as our little means will allow. In this way the worthy Gaffa continued to introduce the villagers, as they entered to welcome the traveller home: till a spruce little antiquated thin old man made his appearance. He was the village-schoolmaster, and clerk of the church: and the uncle pointed out to his nephew that he still wore the same dress in which he had left him; and that his cloak, although the same, still looked as good as new. In the midst of this harangue, the pastor of the parish, a benignant and venerable character, made his appearance, and was received with a degree of unaffected, but touching, respect. The great chair at the fire-side, in which the traveller had been placed, was resigned to him; but he refused to take it, insisting that it was the stranger's due on that night. In the midst of all this kindness and congratulation, the old woman came in, dragging, with infinite good-humour, an old blind savoyard minstrel, which made her overjoyed husband snap his fingers with delight; and, in a short time after, when a flask or two of their best wine was emptied, the younger villagers began to dance with great glee to the savoyard's music. In this manner the night was passed; and the stranger, who had been so long away, amidst the gaieties and dissipations of distant cities, was welcomed back to the haunts of his childhood and simplicity."

CHAPTER XXI.

Some Account of the State of the Public Mind in London at the Time of the Trial of Charles I.

After a period of many years, in which we meet with nothing remarkable, nor, indeed, are we able to trace the movements of our traveller, we find ourselves suddenly transported into the most interesting scenes. Attracted by the report of an intention, on the part of Oliver Cromwell and the Parliamentary faction, to bring king Charles the First to trial, our author, together with a number of other strangers, led by curiosity to witness so extraordinary an event, left Paris, where it would seem he had resided some time, and came to London. They arrived on the evening of the day in which the House of Commons constituted the High Court of Justice, and nominated Bradshaw Lord President. Bradshaw, as our readers probably know, on being requested to accept this singular honour, hesitated; and Lord Clarendon insinuates* that his hesitation was feigned. Considering, however, the object of the office proposed to him,—no less than the trial of his sovereign, on charges which, if not true, a predetermination certainly excited to constrain to that issue, there is something like gratuitous accusation, in supposing him to have been actuated by any hypocrisy on so great an occasion. Indeed, the character which his lordship gives of Bradshaw, is the severest comment that can be made on his own partiality in this instance. He describes him as a gentleman of an ancient family, but of a fortune of his own making; not without parts; of considerable practice in his chamber, though little in the habit of frequenting Westminster-Hall; and of unbounded ambition: all qualities calculated to make the possessor hesitate to

---

* Clarendon's History, Vol. iii. p. 340.

accept a place of trust, which necessarily involved the hazard of fame, life, and fortune. But, as we profess only to extract our author's observations, we shall not involve the reader in any matter of controversy.

"When I had provided myself with lodgings, (says Hareach,) I walked out to view the city, and strayed by accident to where a numerous assemblage of the people was collected round the gate of an extensive pile of buildings, or sort of college, which they called Gray's Inn. On enquiring the cause of the crowd, an old respectable-looking man informed me that they were waiting the return of a deputation from the Parliament to Mr. Bradshaw, a counsellor.—'Is it understood,' said I, 'what is the object of their visit?'—'Some say,' replied my informant, 'that they wish him to be the chief-justice at the trial of the king.'—'Then it is determined that the king shall be tried?' exclaimed I, struck with the coolness with which the old gentleman had replied to my question.—'No doubt of it—and found guilty too:' was his answer. The tone in which this was uttered struck me still more forcibly; and I looked at him without speaking. He observed my surprise; and added, 'Do you think, sir, that they would venture to try the king if they were not sure of finding him guilty? His acquittal would be their own condemnation.'—'Of whom do you speak?' said I.—'Why, of those who take the management of this business—of whom else?'

"I knew not well what to make of my companion. His appearance bore the most favourable testimony to his respectability. He was plainly but well-dressed. His hair was white and flowing; his linen remarkably neat; his hands, without being so delicate as those of a gentleman of the same years, showed that they were not employed in hard labour; and the expression of his countenance indicated sincerity. I therefore ventured to continue the conversation, by observing, 'If it was so essential to find the king guilty, his death must be already determined; and it seems unnecessary to go through the formality of a public trial.'—'You are a stranger to our ways:' was the answer. 'Every thing must be done according to law; particularly if it be in any degree equivocal. Law takes off the responsibility of individuals, and acquits men of the worst actions to their own consciences. The assassination of the king would be as fatal to his enemies as his acquittal. No: he must be tried, and proved guilty. He will have fair play at his trial. The court will be well constituted: it will consist of honourable men: the impeachment will be properly drawn; and the evidence will, without any subornation or perjury, clearly and fully make out all the charges. As far as the trial goes, there will be nothing to find fault with. But,'—— and he checked himself, as having said too much: and I changed the conversation, by enquiring what kind of man Bradshaw was.—'O! a very clever fellow:' was the ready answer. 'He has been much employed by those who were subjected to prosecutions by the king's party. He is an able lawyer: and they don't want justice so much as law. But I doubt if he will accept their offer; for he is in good practice, and knows the world too well to give up the solid footing that he has acquired for the precarious emoluments of their favour.'

"While we were thus conversing together, a bustle in the crowd apprised us that the deputation was coming out; and, in pressing forward to see them, I parted from the old philosopher. The deputation consisted of three persons, whose appearance did not indicate any thing remarkable. They had the sedate and solemn look of men who had restrained, but not subdued, their passions. They were such as would not instantly resent an insult, but they would deliberately revenge it.

"The crowd received them with different feelings. The greater part with shouts, clapping of hands, and waving of hats: others, however, no less explicitly manifested their disapprobation of the popular proceedings by groans and hisses,—a circumstance that made me shudder; for I expected an immediate conflict between the opposite partisans: but, as the carriage with the deputies drove away, the crowd quietly dispersed.

"On returning to my lodgings, I fell in again with my old acquaintance, and told him how much I was astonished at the heat of party-spirit, which seemed to divide the mob, and yet was followed by no outrage. He smiled at the observation; and said it is only in the country and small towns that the population fight among themselves. Mobs in great cities will occasionally commit excesses; but battles between citizens, in their own streets, rarely indeed happen. They are too near their own property: the hostages that they have given to society are too immediately before them.'—' Then, you do think that even the trial of the king will excite no commotion in London.—' Nor his execution either, if that should be resolved on:' was the tart reply. 'Our property and families are dearer to the most loyal amongst us than the life of the king. Were they at a distance, I would not be answerable for the consequence.'

"It was by this time almost dark; and the old gentleman, turning suddenly into a street leading in a different direction from the way to my lodgings, wished me good night."

CHAPTER XXI.

The Trial of Charles I.

"BRADSHAW has accepted the office of Lord President of the High Court of Justice, and has been invested with great state: many officers, and a guard, has been assigned to him; and a noble house, belonging to the dean of Westminster, has been given to him for a residence. It is not intended now, as was at first proposed, that this new court shall only exist for the trial of king Charles, but shall continue, in all time coming, for the investigation of extraordinary offences* which the law has not defined,—in a word, a penal court of equity: and, certainly, if the English do intend to make their kings amenable to justice, some such tribunal is necessary.

"The proceedings of this singular conspiracy against the king overwhelm me with wonder. If the rebels are not honest men, they certainly do contrive to give a sublime character of lenity and justice to their proceedings. Harrison, a man much in the confidence of Cromwell, was sent to bring the king from Hurst Castle. He is a man of low birth, the son of a butcher, and originally bred a clerk with a lawyer. When the rebellion broke out, he joined the Parliamentary army, in which he at first obtained a cornetcy; and, by diligence and sobriety, was promoted to the rank of captain: he is now a colonel of horse.† He received the king with all proper outward respect, remained always uncovered in his presence, but watched him with extreme vigilance. As they were to lodge for the night at Windsor Castle, his Majesty requested that he might dine at Bagshot Lodge, in which Lord and Lady Newburgh, two of his most confidential friends, resided; and Harrison permitted a servant to be sent forward to apprise them of his coming. In the course of the journey, the king complained much of the horse which he rode; and, while he was at the lodge, Harrison provided another for him. Having spent three or four hours with much apparent satisfaction, though he was not suffered to be in any room without the company of six or seven soldiers, who allowed little to be spoken, except it was loud enough for them to hear it too, he took farewell of his hostess. Lord Newburgh was permitted to accompany the king several miles through Windsor-forest, till he was requested by Harrison to return. When they reached Windsor Castle, Charles appeared uneasy, and somewhat dejected; and words to the following effect showed the apprehension that was in his mind. 'The odiousness and wickedness of such an assassination and murder, would assuredly be

---

* Lord Clarendon. † Ibid.

fatal to the person who undertook it.'—Harrison replied with some degree of sternness, 'Your majesty need entertain no such imagination or apprehension. The Parliament has too much honour and justice to cherish so foul an intention. Whatever they resolve to do, will be very public, and in a way of justice, to which the world shall be witness, and will never endure a thought of secret violence.' But the king thought that they would not venture to produce him in the sight of the people, under any form whatsoever of a public trial.

"From Windsor the king was brought to St. James's Palace; and this morning he was conducted with great state before the High Court of Justice, assembled in Westminster Hall. It was an august spectacle, and every circumstance combined to render it most affecting. The vast size and great antiquity of the place; the veneration entertained for the laws so long administered there with unparalleled impartiality; and the hitherto irresponsible dignity of the prisoner's rank,—all tended to excite emotions, and awaken associations, of the most awful kind.

"When the king was brought in, the judges remained covered as he was conducted to the bar; and he also kept his hat on. His demeanour was serene and prepossessing; and he sat down in the chair provided for him with an easy composure. The judges looked at him with evident anxiety. After a pause of about two minutes, the ordinance of Parliament for the trial was read aloud, and the judges were called over, every man answering to his name as he was called. The president, Bradshaw, being the first, answered. The next was General Lord Fairfax; and no answer being made, an officer repeated the call a second time, upon which a female voice among the spectators cried, 'He has more wit than to be here.' This occasioned some disturbance and murmuring; but, when it subsided, and the impeachment was read, in which the expression was, and of 'all the good people of England;' the same voice, in a louder tone, answered, 'No: not the hundreth part of them.' Upon which, one of the officers ordered the soldiers to fire into the box from which it proceeded. But it was discovered that the offending person was Lady Fairfax, who, after some persuasion, was induced to leave the hall, to prevent any new disturbance. Order being thus restored, the articles of impeachment were then read to him, which, in substance, were to this effect: 'That he had been admitted king of England, and trusted with a limited power, to govern according to law; and, by his oath and office, was obliged to use the power committed to him for the good and benefit of the people: but that he had, out of a wicked design, to erect to himself an illimited and tyrannical power, and to overthrow the rights and liberties of the people, traitorously levied war against the Parliament, and the people therein represented.' It then mentioned his first appearance at York with a guard, his setting-up his standard at Nottingham, the time when the battle of Edge-hill was fought, and all the several battles fought in his presence; 'in which (it said) he had caused and procured many thousands of the free-born people of the nation to be slain; that, after all his forces had been defeated, and himself become a prisoner, he had, in that very year, caused many insurrections to be made in England, and given a commission to the prince, his son, to raise a new war against the Parliament and people; that he had been the author and contriver of the unnatural, cruel, and bloody wars; and was therein guilty of all the treasons, murders, rapines, burnings, spoils, desolations, damage, and mischief, to the nation, which had been committed in the said war, or been occasioned thereby: and that he was therefore impeached for the said treasons and crimes, on behalf of the people of England, as a tyrant, a traitor, and murderer, and a public implacable enemy to the commonwealth of England.'

When the articles of impeachment were read, the president Bradshaw reprehended the king, for not showing more respect to the court; and told him that the Parliament had appointed that court to try him for the several treasons and misdemeanours which he had committed against the kingdom, during the evil administration of his government; to the end that, upon the examination thereof, justice might be done.

"The king, without any alteration in his countenance, said, 'I would know by what authority the Parliament has brought me by force here; and who gave them power to judge of my actions,—for which I am accountable to none but God, although they have been always such as I need not be ashamed to own to the world. I am your king: you are my subjects, who owe me duty and obedience. No Parliament has authority to call me before them. It is not the Parliament of England that has done this; nor have you any authority from that Parliament to sit in this manner:'—and, after arguing in this strain for some time, he concluded, by saying that he would not so far betray himself, and his royal dignity, as to answer any thing they objected against him, which would be to acknowledge their authority; though he believed that every one of themselves, as well as the spectators, did, in their own consciences, absolve him from all the material things which were objected against him.'

"The president, with rather more warmth than was perhaps decorous, advised the king not to deceive himself with an opinion that any thing he had said would do him any good; that the Parliament knew their own authority; and would not suffer it to be called in question or debated. 'I would advise you,' said he, 'to think better of it before you are next brought here, and answer directly to the charge,—as you must be sensible what judgment the law has pronounced against those who stand mute, and obstinately refuse to plead.'

"The court then rose; and the king was conducted from the bar. As he was walking between the guards to the door, several of the spectators expressed aloud their compassion for his unhappy condition; but the greater part were loud in their imprecations against him, calling Murder and Tyrant. One of them, it is said, even spat in his face; but he only took out his handkerchief, and wiped it, as if it had been an accident."

CHAPTER XXIII.

The Execution of Charles I.

"The king was three times produced before the court, and as often persisted in refusing to acknowledge its jurisdiction. On the fourth day, as he was conducted from St. James's Palace to Westminster Hall, he was grossly insulted by the populace; and the mob and soldiers exclaimed as he passed along, 'Justice! Justice! Execution! Execution!'—but he preserved his self-possession undismayed. His judges having now examined witnesses, by whom it was proved, what indeed was notorious to the whole world, that he had appeared in arms against the forces commissioned by Parliament, sentence of death was pronounced.

"In returning down the hall from the bar, the multitude again reviled him with the most bitter reproaches; but he bore their insolence with great patience, saying, 'Poor souls! they would treat their generals in the same way for sixpence.' The people, however, were not all alike fanatical and base: some of them even shed tears as he passed; and one of the soldiers implored a blessing on his royal head. An officer who overheard him, struck the faithful sentinel to the ground before the king, who could not help saying that the punishment exceeded the offence.

"From Westminster Hall, Charles was conducted to the palace of Whitehall, where he desired permission of the Parliament to see his children, and to be attended in his private devotions by Doctor Juxton. These requests were granted; and also three days to prepare for the execution of the sentence. All that remain of his family now in England, are the Princess Elizabeth, and the Duke of Gloucester, a child of about three years of age. After many paternal and sensible exhortations to his daughter, it is reported, that he took his little son in his arms, and, embracing him, said, 'My child, they will cut off thy father's head: yes, they will cut off my head, and make thee a king. But, mark what I say: thou must not be a king as long as thy brothers Charles and James are alive. They will cut off their heads when they take them,—and thy head, too, will be cut off at last: and, therefore, I charge thee, do not be made a king by them.' The child, bursting into tears, replied, 'I will be torn in pieces first.'

"Every night during the interval between his sentence and execution, the king slept sound as usual, though the noise of the workmen employed in framing the scaffold continually resounded in his ears. The fatal morning being at last arrived, he rose early; and, calling one of his attendants, he bade him employ more than usual care in dressing him, and preparing him for so great a solemnity.

"The scaffold was erected in front of Whitehall, adjoining to the Banquetting-house, and covered with black cloth. It was guarded by a regiment of soldiers; and on it were seen the block, the axe, and two executioners in masque. The people, in crowds, filled the streets and windows to a great extent around.

"The king was led through the Banquetting-house attended by Dr. Juxton; and, on reaching the scaffold, he looked at the assembled multitude on all sides, and, perceiving how unavailing the attempt would be to make himself heard by so vast a number, he addressed himself only to those immediately around him; justified his own innocence in the civil wars; and observed, that he had not taken arms till after the Parliament had shown him the example;—that he had no other object than to preserve that authority entire which had been transmitted to him by his ancestors; but, though innocent towards his people, he acknowledged the equity of his execution in the eyes of his Maker, and owned that he was justly punished, for having consented to an unjust sentence upon the earl of Strafford, a nobleman of high distinction, who, in an early stage of these troubles, was impeached, tried, and executed, under the direction of Parliament. He forgave all his enemies, exhorted the people to return to their obedience, and acknowledge his son as his successor, and signified his attachment to the Protestant religion.

"This address made a deep impression on all that heard it; and the officer to whose care he had been committed acknowledged himself a convert.

"While he was preparing himself for the block, Dr. Juxton said, 'There is, sir, but one stage more, which, though turbulent and troublesome, is yet a very short one. It will soon carry you a great way. It will carry you from earth to heaven: and there you will find, to your great joy, the prize to which you hasten,—a crown of glory!'—'I go,' replied the king, 'from a corruptible to an incorruptible crown, where no disturbance can take place.'—'You exchange,' replied the doctor with emotion, 'a temporal for an eternal crown,—a good exchange.'

"The king having taken off his cloak, delivered his St. George, the ensignia of the order of the Garter, which he wore, to the clergyman, and said emphatically, 'Remember!' He then laid his neck on the block; and, stretching out his hands as a signal, one of the executioners severed his head from the body at one blow. The crowd in that moment uttered a convulsive cry, and recoiled backwards involuntarily, as if struck with horror. The executioner dropped the end of the axe on the scaffold, and bent over the body as if he looked at it; but his masque concealed the expression of his face. His attendant stooped; and, taking up the head, showed it at the three sides of the scaffold, exclaiming, 'This is the head of a traitor!'

"Many kings before this British monarch have suffered death for their offences against their subjects; but, since the days of Agis the Lacedemonian, he is the only one that has been sacrificed with the formalities of justice. His deportment throughout the whole of his trial, and this final tragedy, was sufficiently dignified; but it wanted that air of martyrdom which rendered the behaviour of his grandmother, in circumstances almost similar, at Fotheringay, so truly sublime. Mary seemed to consider herself as a martyr to the Catholic religion; and her extraordinary beauty diffused a halo around her, that must be imagined,—not described. Charles was no less a political martyr; and many of his faults must be imputed to the errors of his education. He lived at a time when the spirit and usages of the government were at variance with the spirit of the people; and governing by old rules and precedents, instead of accommodating himself to the changes of the times, he has fallen, and drawn down, as he sunk, the government and constitution of his country.

"Admitting that this monarch, who has so largely shared in the singular evil fate of his family, did deserve to die, I am not sure that the solemnity of a public trial and execution was judicious. The greatest tyrants, in their crimes against their subjects, are in general personally innocent, according to the grosser conceptions of the world; and it cannot be denied, that Charles Stuart, with all his dissimulation, was, in private life, an amiable character. It is the guilt, or the subserviency of ministers, that makes tyrants; and, however much it may conduce to impress the race of kings with a due sense of the responsibility of their awful trust, the trial and death of this prince are calculated, I fear, to do much harm to the liberties of the people. His private virtues will, to many minds, extenuate his public errors; and the conduct of his adversaries and judges has not been distinguished for such sublimity of virtue, as to take from this tremendous spectacle the dark and dreadful complexion of a crime."

CHAPTER XXIV.

The Funeral of King Charles I.

WE must now supply a few particulars from history. Those who took the management of the trial and execution of the king, certainly preserved a degree of consistency and decorum, that undoubtedly gave an air of solemnity and a colour of legal justice to their proceedings. The head and body, immediately after the execution, were carried into a room at Whitehall, where they lay exposed to the public view for several days, that all men might be satisfied that the king was not alive. They were then embalmed; and, being put into a coffin, were carried to St. James's Palace, where they lay in state, (if state it might be called,) some time, until the arrangements were completed for the funeral. In this interval, the Duke of Richmond, the Marquis of Hertford, and the Earls of Southampton and Lindsey, who had been members of the royal household, applied for permission that they might be allowed to perform the last duty to their deceased master, and to wait upon him to the grave; and their request was granted, on condition that, as it had been resolved to carry the corpse privately, without pomp or noise, to Windsor, where it was to be interred, they should not attend it out of town, but meet it at the castle on the day appointed for the funeral.

Accordingly, the coffin was committed to the care of four of those servants who had been appointed to attend the king during his imprisonment, by whom it was conveyed to Windsor; and it was that night placed in the apartment which had been formerly his bed-chamber. Next morning it was carried into St. George's-hall, where it remained till the lords came, who did not arrive till late in the afternoon. They immediately went to the governor of the castle, and shewed the order which they had from Parliament to be present at the funeral; and requested that the bishop of London, who was with them, might be allowed to read the funeral service. This, however, the governor positively refused; saying, that, as the Common Prayer Book had been put down, he would not suffer it to be used in any garrison where he commanded: and no entreaties, on their part, could induce him to swerve from this determination. They then went into the church, to make choice of a place for burial; but they found it so altered and transformed, all inscriptions,* and those landmarks, pulled down by which the different places were formerly known; and such a dismal mutation throughout the whole, that they knew not where they were; nor was there any of the old officers present, who could direct them to the places where any of the princes had been formerly interred. At last, a man belonging to the town, seeing their perplexity, stept forward, and said, that he knew the vault in which King Harry the Eighth and one of his wives lay: and in this vault the remains of the unfortunate Charles were deposited.

Upon the restoration of his son, it was generally expected that they would have been removed from that obscure burial-place, and solemnly deposited, with all befitting ceremonies, in the royal mausoleum of Henry the Seventh's chapel in Westminster Abbey; but, by this time, the Duke of Richmond was dead, and the Marquis of Hertford confined by infirmity and indisposition to his chamber. The Earls of Southampton and Lindsey, however, went to Windsor, with such of their own servants as had been present at the funeral; but so great was the confusion in which they found the church, that none of them could again discover the situation of the vault; and, after digging in several places without success, they abandoned the search.

During some recent repairs, under the direction of the Prince Regent, in our own time, the vault was found; and

---

* Lord Clarendon.

his Royal Highness went himself in person, and directed the coffin to be opened, when the head and body was found in a state of considerable preservation. It is mentioned by Lord Clarendon, that a plate of silver was fixed on the coffin, with these words only, "KING CHARLES, 1648;" and that the black velvet pall which was used in the funeral, was thrown over it at the interment. But, in the accounts of the examination of the Regent, no notice was taken of these things.

Before returning to the Book of our author, we cannot quit this subject without observing, that, however criminal the conduct of the adversaries of Charles the First may have been, the whole public circumstances attending his execution and funeral reflect great credit on the nation, and present a noble contrast to the rage and rashness which characterised the proceedings of the ancient Roman senate against their tyrants. This must be ascribed to the good sense of the people, and to the deference which all men in this country have been so long accustomed to pay to public opinion. There is, indeed, no surer guard of liberty than public opinion; for it is the only antagonist that can be opposed to the intrepidity of bad men, while it is the most effectual champion of the oppressed. From the moment that it was determined to put Charles to death, the most studious attention was paid to the forms of law; and to the private character of the commissioners appointed to try him, no material dereliction of morality could be imputed. They were, it is true, for the most part, men who affected a greater austerity of religious principle in their manners than the generality of the world; but it was an affectation characteristic of the spirit of the time; and the conduct of men is always, more or less, according to the original energy of their character, regulated by what is admired by the generality of their cotemporaries. Nor, though the tragical doom of Charles the First, considering the purity of his personal actions, must ever deeply excite and interest the sympathy of the loyal and humane, must it be gratuitously imagined, that his enemies were not, at least in their own opinion, actuated by the zeal of public duty. Posterity stands as it were on a hill afar off from these turbulent scenes; and history has explained the causes of many movements which presented a very different aspect to the parties engaged in the conflict. By the king's faction, the proceedings of the Parliament were felt as audacious, and resented as rebellion; while to the Parliamentary party, the king himself often appeared deceitful, unjust, and tyrannical; and it must be confessed that great blame might justly be imputed to them all. But, to suppose that virtue, on either side, was opposed only to guilt, is to embrace the feelings of a party, and to forfeit all that claim to the power of forming an impartial judgment—the right and inheritance of posterity!

CHAPTER XXV.

Sketches and Reflexions on the State of Italy and Greece; with Pictures of Turkish Manners.

[A. D. 1700–1745.]

IMMEDIATELY following the interesting circumstances which we have extracted, respecting the death of Charles the First, we find our author again wandering along the shores of the Mediterranean, and directing his steps eastward. He remained but a short time at any one place; and his observations resemble those of a common traveller. He speaks of Italy, however, as having recovered much of its former splendour, and makes one remark on this head which we think curious.—" I do not understand how it is," says Hareach, " that, although the arts have certainly declined greatly from the high state which they attained in the pontificate of Leo X. the general appearance of the Italian cities, at this time, is much more magnificent,—and yet the commerce of the country has fallen off. It would seem as if architecture is the last of the fine arts that attains maturity; and that a long period of painting and sculpture must elapse before a taste for ornamental building is properly formed in the public mind. Is the formation of this taste owing to the fictitious edifices with which the painters ornament their pictures?

"What augments (he observes) the pleasure of travelling in Italy at this period, is the interest inspired by the remains of ancient art and manners, blended with the magnificence of modern times. In this respect Italy excels every other country; but England alone is inferior to Italy: for the change of manners and religion in that kingdom have produced effects greatly similar to the vicissitudes of fortune, which have so altered the face of Italy. The feudal castles and the monastic remains of the English, possess an air of antiquity and a grandeur of mass, that can only be compared with the gigantic fragments of the ancient Romans. In other countries, the same sort of buildings exist, but not in the same picturesque state of decay and ruin; and therefore do not affect the poetical associations of the mind in the same manner. In France and Germany the monasteries and the castles are still inhabited, and still make a portion of the existing system of manners and institutions. But in England the castles are for the most part entirely in ruins, or only preserved from being so by the local attachment of the possessors; while the monasteries are altogether in a state of dilapidation: the remains and monuments of ages, and of a people, no more. It is thus in Italy. The relics of ancient magnificence have no affinity with the existing order of things; and, accordingly, in wandering amidst its interesting scenes, the traveller is constantly reminded of a great people, whose epitaph forms a splendid portion of history."

Soon after these reflections, we find a series of notes, which brings our mysterious author into Greece; and from these, with as few interruptions as possible, we shall continue to make such extracts as appear interesting or illustrative, either of his own feelings, or of the state of the country.

"I embarked at Leghorn in a Greek vessel bound for Smyrna; and for two days we had a pleasant passage along the Italian coast, and through the straits of Messina: but the wind soon after failed us, and we lay several days becalmed without motion. The sailors began to grow impatient; (for the modern Greeks, I perceive, have lost none of the quick sensibility of their ancestors;) and it was resolved that a religious ceremony, which one of them had seen performed in a former voyage with the happiest success, should be tried on this occasion. Thirty-eight pieces of paper were accordingly prepared, each inscribed with a holy name, and put into a new night-cap. These billets represented the persons on-board; and each of the Greeks drew one out of the cap, paying a piaster to the mate, to be delivered to a priest on their arrival in port, for behoof of the saints. As they were not very sure about the religion that I professed, they rejected me from participating in the ceremony; but a billet was drawn by one of the men on my account.

"The sailors, as they drew their papers from the cap, went to the stern of the ship, and, making the sign of the cross, kissed the billet, blew it into the sea, and prayed to the power whose name it bore to send a wind in poop. But their prayers were ineffectual; for the last billet was not a minute in the water, when a smart breeze came directly against us. In order to ascertain in what degree of veneration the saints invoked were respectively held, I procured a copy of the list, which I transcribed. The Trinity, the Virgin of Augusta, St. Michael, Jesus Christ, the Angel of the Annunciation, St. Anthony, St. Spiridion, St. John, St. Haralabow, St. Demetrius, St. Nicholo, St. George, St. Andrew, St. Vassilius, St. Vagilistus, St. Passandi, St. Theodosius, St. Paul, St. Anagiro, St. Leo, St. Lucas, St. Parastivi, St. Pandalemonos, St. Constantine, St. Nestow, St. Humphrey, St. Marianne, St. Savas, St. Athanasius, St. Gregory, St. Helena, St. Thomas, St. Cesto, St. Peter, St. Jerom, St. Paul, St. Gregorius, and the Holy Cross."*

---

* Galt's Letters from the Levant.

"After beating about for some time, the wind, in the course of the second day, shifted to the south, and blew quite a tempest, which obliged us to bear away up the Adriatic, and we came to anchor in the port of Zante; here, tired of my voyage, I landed, and resolved to visit the Morea, as the Peloponnesus is now called. With this intention, as soon as the weather permitted, I embarked in a small vessel for Corinth, where we arrived the following day: but, O! how changed that city since last I was there, and even then it was in ruins. The Turks had, about twenty years before, taken it from the Venetians. A few rude columns of a temple, and two or three shapeless fragments of building, are all the visible relicts of its ancient grandeur.

"At Corinth I fell in with two merchants of our nation going to Trepolizza, the residence of the Ottoman governor of the Morea, who has the rank of vizier, to offer him jewels for sale; and I determined to accompany them, having never, by accident, in all my various wanderings, come into the society of the Turks.

"The beauty of landscapes may not depend on the state of the weather; but, undoubtedly, the weather materially affects the sentiments with which we behold them. When we reached that part of the valley of Argos where the road winds under the ruins of Mycenæ, not a breath of air was stirring; the sun, sinking behind the mountains, was surrounded with clouds, that resembled vast masses of solid fire, the effect of which produced a slight sensation of awe, in addition to the other feelings which the tranquillity and beauty of the scene awakened. Before me lay the gulph of Argos; on the west side of which were several promontories, like the side-scenes of a theatre, extended in successive perspective to a great distance; and, on the east, the city of Napoli, with its abrupt cliffs, all glittering and vividly tinted with the setting sun, presented a magnificent spectacle. The plain immediately before me, with several ploughs in motion, and interspersed with hamlets, presented the cheerful images of industry and homes: but the sublime aspect of the heavens, and the consideration of being in a country where the moral change was still more mournful than the desolation that I had all day witnessed, gave a degree of solemnity to my reflections approaching to sadness. Here a proud-hearted people are the slaves of a race, who almost scorn to regard them as beings of the same species. The soil is sullenly tilled, and the harvest is niggardly. Such is the pestiferous influence of oppression! But, after all, it is not the oppressor, but the oppressed, that are to blame. That kind of tyranny, whether arising from laws or individuals, which overwhelms the liberties of civilized communities, such as the Grecian states once were, is but the embodied vices of the people."

We shall now, in contrast to these sentimental reflections, extract a description of a Turkish barber's shop at Trepolizza, being one of the few indications of good-humour that are scattered through the desultory pages of Hareach.

"In passing along the streets, I observed a Turkish barber's shop; and, being somewhat in need of assistance in his way, I went in. He was at the moment trimming and anointing an Aaron-bearded Mussulman. This shaver of the faithful was a middle-aged man, with a due portion of professional suavity of manners. He wore clean yellow leather boots, a scarlet pelisse trimmed with brown fur, and a huge muslin turban. In performing the mysteries of his art he was attended by a boy to hold the bason; and he tucked-up his pelisse behind. The floor of the shop being wet and sloppy, he was mounted on a pair of stately wooden pattens, to keep his yellow buskins clean. His operations, I can conscientiously say, were neatly performed; and he appeared to have a great run of business. At his door was a stage, on which his customers held their fumigations, and discussed the news of the day, with the dignified composure and gravity of their national character."

To this we must add the account of his introduction to the vizier of the Morea.

"The merchants having informed the vizier, while they were higgling with him about the prices of the gems

TURKISH BARBER.

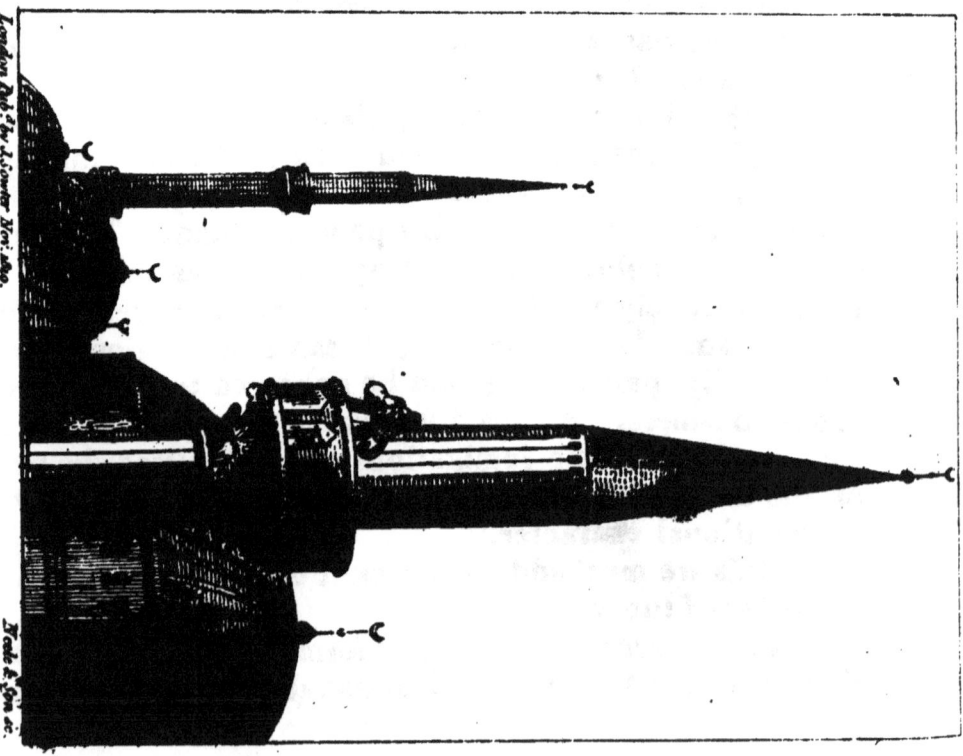
A MUEZZIM.

they have brought to sell, that they had come from Corinth in the company of a traveller from Christendom, his highness requested them to say he would be glad to see me; and I very willingly availed myself of the invitation.

"My name being sent in to the vizier, I was at once admitted to his presence. The room was showy and handsome, but not magnificent. In the farthest corner, on a sofa, elevated on a crimson velvet cushion, sat his highness. On his head was a stupendous turban; in his belt a dagger incrusted with jewels; and, on his little finger, a diamond ring of extraordinary value. In his left hand he held a string of small coral beads, which he twirled backwards and forwards during the greatest part of the visit. On the sofa beside him lay a pair of richly-ornamented pistols. Several officers were seated on the sofas near him, others stood on the floor; but I was afterwards told that those on the sofa were guests: for that, according to the etiquette of this viceregal court, those who receive the pay of his highness are not permitted to sit down in his presence.

"On my entering the room, the vizier beckoned me to sit beside him. Among other questions, he enquired if I had a wife; and, being answered of course in the negative, he said I was a happy man; for he found his very troublesome. Considering the probable number, this is not unlikely.

"Pipes and coffee were in the mean time served. The vizier's pipe was at least four yards long. The mouth-piece was formed of a single block of amber, and fastened to the shaft by a broad hoop of gold decorated with diamonds. While the pipes and coffee were distributing, a musical clock, which stood in a niche, began to play, and continued doing so until this ceremony was over. His highness, was served with his coffee by a gigantic officer; and, when he returned him the empty cup, he elegantly belched in his face.

"There is, undoubtedly, much grave simplicity in the character of the Turks; and their general humanity is greatly misrepresented in Christendom."

CHAPTER XXVI.

Hareach at Athens.—A curious Mahomedan Ceremony.

From Tripolizza our author returned, with the Hebrew jewellers, to Corinth, and embarked with them on the gulph of Egina, in a boat bound for the Piræus, the port of Athens. Here he left them, and walked to the city, where he found every thing so changed, and departed, as it were, from its ancient character, that he could recognise but few of the former ornaments of that once beautiful metropolis. His description of a Mahomedan ceremony, is worthy of being extracted from among his general reflections. It was occasioned by a great drought, which had continued so long, that great apprehensions were entertained of the entire failure of the harvest.

"Public prayers for rain are now ordered for nine successive days; and this morning they commenced. The first three are allotted to the Turks, the next to the Arabian slaves, and the last three to the Christians. The ceremony began this morning at two hours before sun-rise. The three principal emirs, with a boy before each of them, carrying the Koran on his head, and followed by all the Turks of the city, with their male children, walked in procession to a place among the ruins of the temple of Jupiter Olympius, which had been previously prepared; the emirs repeating, from papers which they held in their hands, a suitable prayer for the occasion, and the Turks responding ' Amen,' at the close of each sentence.

"After their arrival at the place appointed for the worship, the chief mufti delivered an appropriate discourse. His manner was simple, modest, and slow, but impressive. At the close of this discourse, a flock of ewes and lambs was driven close to the worshippers; and the Turks, all standing, the lambs were separated

from their mothers. The divided flock began to bleat; and the Turks addressed, at the same moment, a loud and pathetic supplication to heaven. Viewing the dry channel of the Ilissus, and the blasted appearance of the grass, and beholding the sun, which at that moment arose from behind Mount Hymettus, red and arid, like a shield of polished copper, it seemed to me as if all nature, feeling the destructive thirst, sympathised in the fears, and seconded the supplication, of man."

Our author soon after this left Athens; and, in looking back on the valley of Attica from a small khan, where he rested during the heat of the day, he indulges in some mournful reflections on contemplating the distant prospect of the Acropolis, and the ruins of the Parthenon, in that fortress.—" To the mere antiquary," he says, " yon celebrated city cannot but long continue interesting; and to the classic enthusiast, just liberated from the cloisters of his college, the scenery and ruins may often awaken admiration, and inspire delight. Philosophy may there point the moral apophthegm with stronger emphasis; virtue receive new incitements to perseverance, by reflecting on the honour which still attends the memory of the antient great; and patriotism there more pathetically deplore the inevitable effects of individual corruption on public glory: but to the wanderer, who rests for recreation, or who seeks a solace for misfortune, how wretched, how solitary, how empty, is Athens."

CHAPTER XXVII.

Hareach in Persia.—Permanency of the Asiatic Character.—A Tribe of Turcomans.—A Persian City.—A Caravansera.—A Cloud of Locust.—Domestic Manners of the Persians.—The characteristic Noises of a Persian City.

Soon after leaving Athens, we find, by his notes, that our Wanderer passed over into Asia Minor, led by a vague curiosity to review the state of those countries which he had visited in his youth. His notes of these devious excursions are extremely brief, and record little, but that he staid a day at one place, and, on the following, travelled alone through a solitary and desolated track to another. But he speaks of the Asiatic character as still unchanged.—"The revolutions of ages," says he in one part, " the vicissitudes of fortune, and the changes of government and religion, produce no alteration in these aborigines of the human race. They have descended, since the days of Trajan, from the palace to the hovel; and yet they still retain all their wonted love of ceremony in the reciprocities of social life."

He was drawn to make this observation from an incident which happened to him in crossing Asia Minor, of which we shall extract his own account.—" Having crossed the river a little way above the ruins of Ephesus, by a bridge of several arches, I entered a beautiful but lonely valley. The clear stream meandered cheerfully along, and the sides of the mountains, broken in some places into stupendous precipices, and in others scooped into fine holms and pastoral hollows, were here and there adorned with stately trees.

"After walking leisurely along, ruminating on my own fortune and out-cast condition, I fell in with a numerous train of camels, cattle, men, women, and children. Forgetting in the moment that I was in Asia, and being so long accustomed to the usages of Europe, I at first imagined it was a troop of country-folk going with their merchandise to a fair; but the camels, and the garb of the men, soon recalled my recollection; and I was agreeably surprised to find that these strangers were a tribe of Turcomans, who, like father Abraham and his household, roam over the vast unappropriated domains of Asia, and have no local habitation. During winter, they come into the narrow valleys; and, as the spring returns, they retire again towards the open country, passing the vicinity of the large towns about the end of Lent, at which time they dispose of their lambs and firstlings. This tribe consisted of about a hundred persons, men-servants and maid-servants, with their little ones; upwards of three score of camels, with a more numerous retinue of cattle, sheep, and goats, asses loaded with poultry in baskets, and other patriarchal chattels and movables.* I beheld, in this scene, the truth of the Mosaic descriptions in living testimony before me."

The next detached note illustrative of Asiatic manners relates to his arrival in Persia; by which it would seem that his long residence in Christendom had indeed materially affected his former habits.—" It would be impossible," he says, "to give an inhabitant of the cities of the West, particularly those of England, a correct idea of the first impressions which an Asiatic town is calculated to make upon him. Accustomed as his eye has been to cleanliness, and a general appearance of convenience in the exteriors of life, he feels a depression of spirits, and even strong emotions of disgust. Instead of houses with high roofs, well glazed and painted, and in neat rows, he finds them low, flat-roofed, without windows, placed in little connection. In vain he looks for what his idea of a street may be; he makes his way through the narrowest lanes, encumbered with filth, dead animals, and mangy dogs. Instead of smooth skins, and tight

---

* Galt's Letters from the Levant.

dresses, he sees rough faces masked with beards, and long flapping garments; and, for active people, walking about with an appearance of something to do, only here and there a gorgeous native,* stepping solemnly along in slip-shod shoes of the most delicate colour. —— * * *

"I halted at a small town where there is a superb caravansera, an order of buildings for the use of travellers peculiar to the Asiatics. These buildings consist of stables and bed-chambers, and are frequently erected by private persons, at their own expence, in the hope that so good an act in this life will meet with its reward hereafter. This edifice was originally built by an ancestor of the chief eunuch of the king, who, having heard that it was falling into decay, sent a sum of money to the magistrate of the town, to clean and repair it. The magistrate, however, instead of doing so, put the money into his own purse, and left the caravansera to its fate; it has, in consequence, fallen almost into ruin. The delinquency of the unjust magistrate has, however, not been long allowed to pass unpunished; for the eunuch, on being informed of his dishonesty, has procured him to be arrested, and, this afternoon, not only obliged him to refund the money, but ordered him to be severely beat on the soles of his feet. Caravanseras built and endowed by private persons, consecrated to hospitality, and the refuge of the stranger and the wanderer, have, in all ages, been held sacred in the East."

The following account of a cloud of locust, is worthy of being noticed.

"The weather for several days had been intensely hot; the air was like the breath of a furnace; and frequent whirlwinds raised the dust and sand in vast columns to the skies. I was seated in the shadow of the wall of a fountain, which a benevolent Persian had constructed for the traveller in the waste, when I was surprised by a rushing sound as of a strong wind. The air was presently darkened; and, on looking up, I saw a cloud spreading over the heavens, here and there semi-transparent, in other parts so dense and black as quite to eclipse the

---

* Morier's second Journey through Persia.

light of the sun. This, I soon found, was a flight of locust, by myriads of these predatory insects dropping around me. I was struck with a dreadful apprehension; and returned, shuddering with horror, towards the village which I had left. But I had not ran far, till, approaching the cultivated fields that skirted the desert, I saw all the villagers, young and old, out, and making a wild and clamorous noise, ringing upon their brazen utensils, to alarm the locust from settling. All, however, was of no avail: the plague literally came down in showers, entered the inmost recesses of the houses, were found in every corner, stuck to our clothes, and infected our food. The hedges and the corn-fields, which I had left in the vigorous green freshness of a promising harvest, appeared, next day, as bare as winter, and as barren as the waste. The villagers were overwhelmed with grief; and nothing was heard but the murmuring of the devouring insects, and the lamentations of the people. But, fortunately, a fresh and strong wind, in the course of the forenoon, rose from the south-west; and, in the course of two hours, not a vestige of them was to be seen."

A description of the domestic life of the Persians, may, like a farce after a tragedy, follow this account of the irresistible devastation of the locust.

"In the immediate vicinity of the house where I lodged lived an old morose Persian, who daily quarrelled with his women; and I could distinguish the voice of one particular female, whose answers, made in a taunting and querulous tone, never failed to throw him into a passion so violent, that blows were uniformly the result, and these were followed with corresponding yells and lamentations.

"Then, bordering on the garden-wall, scarce twenty yards from where I usually sat, was a society of women, five or six in number, the wives and concubines of a Mussulman. They were either dissolved in tears, sobbing aloud like children, or riotous with the most indecent and outrageous merriment. Sometimes they sang in the greatest glee, accompanied by a tambourine, and anon they quarrelled with all the virulence of the most shrewish women of Christendom. Accident once gave me a view into their yard, where I saw three women surrounded by children, seated on the bare stones, smoking. They wore a large black silk handkerchief round their heads, a shift which descended as low as the middle, a pair of loose trowsers, and high-heeled slippers. This, I believe, may be considered as a sketch of every Persian woman's dress within the harem in hot weather.*

"But every town and country has its own peculiar dissonance, and none are more characteristic than those of Persia. At dawn of day the muzzins are heard calling the people to prayers from the tops of the mosques: these are mixed with the sounds of cow-horns, blown by the keepers of the hummums, to inform the women, who always bathe before the men, that the baths are heated, and ready for their reception. The cow-horns set the dogs a-howling;—the asses begin to bray about the same time, and the cocks to crow, accompanied by the cries of children; while persons, calling to one another, and knocking at doors, complete this concert of discords."

CHAPTER XXVIII.

Pilgrimage to the Tomb of Noah's Mother.—A Journey to Mount Ararat.—Terrible Storm.—View of Ararat. —Reverie in contemplating the Mountain.

AFTER roaming from place to place through Persia, our author appears to have directed his steps northward, on a pilgrimage to Marand, where, it is said, that the tomb of the mother of Noah is still to be seen; but, upon inspecting the place, he was disgusted with the manifest impo-

---

* Morier's second Journey.

sition of this legend, and quickly left the town. Heedless of the course to which he had involuntarily directed his steps, he came to the village of Zenjirch, which he describes as beautifully situated amongst rocky hills of the most picturesque forms.—"The mountains here," he says, "do not wear that volcanic and barren appearance which they do almost throughout Persia. They were green to the very summits; and some heavy showers, that had fallen in the night, had given them a face of bright verdure, in pleasing contrast to the dark masses of rock, and the bare red soil in several places.

"Having heard at this place that I was not far from the great mountain of Ararat, where the ark rested after the Deluge, and on whose summit, beneath the everlasting snows with which it is covered, the remains of the primeval vessel are preserved till the world shall be again destroyed, I resolved to visit an object, every idea of which is associated in the mind with the most sublime recollections. About two hours' walk from the village I obtained a view of the mountain; but the weather was hazy, and it was too distant to be satisfactory. I rested that evening at the village of Khoi, and next day I pursued my solitary journey to Alanjeck, a mountain-fortress, the ancient Olana, which Strabo mentions as one of the treasure-cities of Tigranes and Artabasus. Here I obtained another, but still unsatisfactory, view of the mountain. Continuing my pilgrimage from Alanjeck, I descended towards the banks of the river Araxes, and stopped at the hamlet of Nasik, where a tremendous tempest, accompanied by incessant thunder and lightning, forced me to remain all night.

"For upwards of forty days, the country in this neighbourhood had not been refreshed with rain, and all nature was agasp, as it were, with thirst: but the deluge that fell in the thunder-storm was as if the windows of heaven had again been opened, and all the ministers of hail and rain were again busily emptying their vessels of wrath on the world. About sun-set the rain ceased, but the clouds lowered blacker and more dreadful; so that it was dark sooner by an hour than usual. All the inhabitants of the place were out, and alarmed, and knew not what to think of this appalling phenomenon. As they were standing together, infecting each other with their several fears and conjectures, we heard an awful noise, like the rushing of a great body of water, and ran towards a hollow in the valley, where we supposed the torrent was rolling; but, on approaching the spot, the moon, which by this time had looked from her chamber in the cloud, enabled us to see that there was nothing remarkable there: but still the noise increased, and seemed to be coming nearer and nearer. Nothing could be more tremendous: every one expected either an earthquake or a hurricane. In this fearful moment, the falling of some prodigious hail apprised us that the commotion was over our heads; and, on looking up, we could plainly discover the clouds impelled by two violent currents of air in different directions, whose concussion produced the noise that had so alarmed us.*

"Having passed the river Araxes next morning by a bridge of boats at Abasabad, I crossed the plain to Nakhjuwan; and the weather, which had all day been hazy, clearing up as I reached a rising ground above that town, I had a splendid view of the Father of mountains. Nothing can be more beautiful than its form,—more awful than its height. From an immense spreading base, the slope towards the summit is easy and gradual, till it reaches the region of snow, when it becomes more steep and abrupt. A slight cloud still hovered half way down its side; but the hoary summit rose high and bright in the clear blue ether of the evening sky. I sat down, and contemplated it as the resting-place of Omnipotence, when the work of destroying a world was done. A thousand sublime and floating images passed before my mind, to which I could assign no distinct form; and my imagination endeavoured to grasp them in vain: but they were only palpable to the feelings of the heart. I endeavoured to form a conception of the state of the old world on the eve of the Deluge; and the storm which I had experienced at Nasik assisted me in the attempt. I

---

* Morier's second Journey.

saw as it were before me the great edifice of the ark, sable with the pitch with which it was overspread, standing in the midst of a spacious plain, which had once been a forest, of which all the trees had been consumed in the construction of the vessel of deliverance; multitudes of men, women, and children, were assembled in various groups around, all in the noisy licentiousness of a great festival. The sun, which was declined towards the horizon, shone with his usual radiance on their flags, their shows, their pageants, and their dances. At the same time the moon was also above the horizon, but she dispensed no light. Suddenly, however, like the interposition of a dreadful hand, a black cloud fell as it were over the glorious face of the sun, and all was instantly darkened. The riotous multitude uttered a shriek of horror; their revelry was suspended, and they flew towards the ark; and, frantic with despair, wildly clamoured for admittance. The cloud, however, soon opened asunder; and the sun, then on the point of setting, looked out upon them again for the last time, and slowly sank beneath the horizon.

"The devoted multitude, as if ashamed at their panic, resumed their festivity with more alacrity, and laughed at the fears into which they had been betrayed: but the aspect of the heavens was changed. The light of the moon began to silver the edges of all things, and the increasing blackness of accumulating clouds gave a strange and funereal effect to the appearance of the earth.

"Still, however, the mirth and revelry continued. After some time a cry was heard at a distance of several persons coming furiously on horseback; and it was immediately understood, that they were flying towards the hills, a neighbouring lake having began to swell in an extraordinary manner, and the waters to overflow the land. This again suspended, and for ever, the riotous mirth; for the horsemen, without stopping, only giving an alarm, hastened on. In the course of a few minutes the noise of rushing waters was heard; and it was discovered that those of the lake, overflowing the adjacent country, were now spreading along the plain. The revellers were struck with consternation, and stood motionless and indeterminate; at last, however, they thought of the ark; but the waters now rolled in torrents between them and it, and they could not approach it. Now was their despair complete,—for a dreadful crash was heard over head. It was not thunder, and there was no lightning; but a sound, as it were, of terrible engines, and presently the rain began to fall. The darkness deepened; but still, at times, the moon held her wonted course, and threw an obscure and ghastly light upon the scene. Then it was that from all directions myriads of people came rushing towards the ark, those from the sea-shore crying out, ' that the fountains of the great deep were broken up, and the waters were rising upon the dry land.' But the stream of the lake was now risen to a raging river, and all access, even towards the ark, was far denied; and, in frantic resolution, the whole multitude fled towards the hills.

"In this moment I looked towards the ark, and I thought I perceived it move, or rather give, as it were, a shudder. I fixed my eyes upon it, and I was soon convinced that it was almost afloat. In a few minutes after, it turned, as it were, in the stream, and floated solemnly away.

"It passed down towards the ocean, and sailed over large cities, whose towers were still above the surface of the water on which thousands of the inhabitants were clustering and crying out for help. The deluge from the ocean was now coming over the land, and the ark was borne along through the valleys, and amidst the mountains, the sides of which were thronged with the inhabitants of the earth in despair. The sable ark moved awfully along. A mother and several children had reached the pinnacle of a rock, which had once been the peak of a lofty mountain. The children clung to her closely, as the water rose nearer and nearer. When it reached their feet they sprung in horror upon her shoulders, and, overborne by their weight, she fell, and was borne away.

"In this stage of my reverie, the tinkling of numerous bells roused my attention; and, on looking round, I saw a caravan of camels moving deliberately toward

Nakhjuwan. As the sun was now on the point of setting, I arose, and went towards them; and, being fatigued with the long journey I had travelled that day, I requested the drivers to give me some refreshment, which they did with the greatest readiness. Observing how much I appeared exhausted, they also placed me on the back of one of their camels, and took me with them into the town. These pilots of the ships of the desert, as the camels are picturesquely called by the Asiatics, are a simple and kind-hearted race: their life is almost constantly spent in travelling. From their infancy they are accustomed to be with the caravans; nor, indeed, without some such continued experience, could they trace their way across the vast plains and pathless wilds over which they transport the treasures and the commerce of so many nations: and, when they die, their tombless graves are on the way-side, or in the sands of the desert."

CHAPTER XXIX.

The Return of Hareach to Greece; his Journey to Mount Parnassus; with his Reflections on an Immortal Life and Death.—Conclusion.

From Ararat our traveller proceeded in a western direction through Armenia, and wandered for some time amidst those mountains where the ten thousand Greeks lost their way for about twenty-one days. He then approached the shores of the Black Sea; and, embarking at Trebazond in a small vessel, was landed at Kirpi, an inconsiderable port, two days' journey overland distant

2 P

from Nicomedia, where he again embarked for Constantinople. In this portion of his journal we meet with nothing deserving of any particular notice. Of Nicodemia he merely says, "The form of the mountains, and the aspect of the land, are unchanged; but the capital of Dioclesian is no where to be traced: a rude Turkish town is all that occupies the scite, and even that is in a state of great decay."

On the day of his arrival at Constantinople, he found a vessel bound for a port in the island of Eubea; and, having taken his passage in her, was, in the course of a week, landed, and reached the town of Negropont the same evening.

"This town," he says, "which now gives its name to the whole island, is situated on a point of land that projects towards the coast of Bœotia, to which it is connected by a bridge. The strait is here so narrow as to serve as a bridge to the fortifications. The irregularity of the flux and reflux of the sea here has, from time immemorial, been regarded as a wonder in nature."

From Negropont he went to Thebes, where he rested for the night and part of next day. He found nothing there that interested his feelings; and, with a dejected heart, lamenting the decay of civilization in the country, he travelled heavily towards Livadia. Whether his object in visiting this place was to fulfil his destiny, and renew his youth, by bathing in the waters of the cave of Trephonius, we are not informed. He speaks of the virtues of that famous spring in terms full of mystery, and the immortal prolongation of human life, as the most deplorable state to which the human being could be consigned.—"To witness," says he, "unseen, the errors and the sufferings of those we have loved, I have often thought, would be the greatest of all afflictions; and perdition can have no burning so dreadful, as that which must attend the guilty spirit, when, after death, he awakens among the souls of those who have died before, and learns from them that they were the invisible witnesses of all he did;—that those who expired, breathing affection for him, shun him with abhorrence;—and that those, who were as vicious in life as himself, and whom he affected in his days of sin to shun and condemn, recognise him with familiarity as their proper associate."

From Livadia he walked to the ruins of Delphi, and ascended Mount Parnassus; and, in his descent from the top of the mountain, he came to the monastery dedicated to St. John of Jerusalem, and took up his abode with the caloyers, as we have mentioned in the introductory chapter. The reader is now acquainted with the principal notes in the mysterious Book which he left.

CONCLUSION.

The volume of Hareach, for we still wish to retain the fiction suggested by the caloyers, contains various other notes respecting learned men, artists, and public characters; and, at some other time, we may possibly be induced to arrange them also into a narrative. However, for the present, this is sufficient. It will occur to the reader, that, hitherto there has been but little use made of the story of "The Wandering Jew," although few fictions are better calculated to afford a compendious view of the history of some of the most remarkable stages in the progress of the human mind. Should our attempt be approved, the design is susceptible of being applied in various ways; and the approbation of the public would induce us to extend it to historical views of other objects.

But, while we are satisfied with the originality of Hareach, we are not quite so well pleased with the merits of our own share in the task of selection. Original materials are often, by the incapacity of editors, deprived of all their force; and we are so well persuaded of our own defects, that we are not sanguine of receiving any particular approbation for the manner in which we have executed this undertaking. One thing, however, is certain; that the desire, on our part, to make up an interesting and instructive volume, was not wanting. Kindness therefore, on the part of the reader, for our exertions, is all that we can venture to hope for; and that amiable disposition will greatly tend, even to himself, to make our defects the less disagreeable.

We frankly acknowledge, that, when we embarked in this compilation, we did not anticipate so much labour as we have been obliged to perform; not conceiving that we should have found it necessary to supply the deficiencies of Hareach with so many references to other books. According to the cursory view that we took at first of his Volume, the contents appeared fuller of historical facts than we afterwards experienced, and the narrative seemed to be better connected. Such, however, is often the case: in editorial undertakings the original work falls off in interest as the task proceeds; and, at the conclusion, instead of appearing to deserve the encomiums set forth in the bookseller's prospectus, the new version is consigned to the world with very subdued hopes and humble expectations.

Without, however, saying too much respecting the consciousness of our own deficiencies, lest it should be suspected that we affect more diffidence than we really feel, we trust the reader will give us credit for the best intentions, nor impute to us any fault that is not very obvious. Richly as the page of history is stored with instructive lessons, the weakness of man is such, that few can avail themselves of the important moral with which public events are calculated to impress even the most humble individual of the lowest station. In our endeavour, we have applied to that great store-house of morality; and, in the magnificent tale of the fall of nations, and the fate of monarchs, we have, without any formal declaration of our design, exhibited examples applicable to all the various conditions of life. Towards the arrogance of the Romans, by which they were betrayed into those excesses that finally ruined their great and well-constructed empire, we have particularly attempted to direct the attention of the reader. This portion of our subject, treated with more formality, might have afforded greater opportunities for moral declamation. Eloquence, however, was not the object of our undertaking. Nor, indeed, in the limits to which we were prescribed, was there room permitted for any display of erudition beyond what the illustration of the subject immediately required.

But we have not addressed ourselves to the wise and learned: for the former do not stand in need of our instruction, and the latter would be offended, if we presumed to think they required our comments. Youth, the open-hearted, the ingenuous, and the generous, are the pupils that we desire to see in our portico, and the disciples to whom we address our lessons.

If, therefore, by our extracts from the Volume of Hareach, we can excite their curiosity to examine in riper years more attentively the different subjects on which we have touched, no small portion of our reward will be obtained. Over the page of ancient history the shadows of prejudice have so long fallen, that much is obscured; and, it is only by the lamp of enquiry and suspicion, that we can discover the truths concealed. History, in a word, has too long rested on the authority of individuals; and, when we speak of historical fact as being particularly venerable, we forget that it is often but the opinion of men who, in their day, were as partial and prejudiced as our own cotemporaries. Nevertheless, one thing is certain from history: that, if events did not take place exactly as they have been in general recorded, the character of human nature seems to have been in all ages the same. Greatness, whether of nations or of individuals, has depended much less on voluntary resolution than we are apt to think, in judging of the public events that happen in our own time. All the course of human affairs clearly appears to be under the management of some far higher influence than the wisdom of the men who most busily bestir themselves in the transactions of their respective epochs. Literally, the hero, the sage, and the statesman, whom we are so much in the practice of regarding as the main-springs of political and moral revolutions, are discovered to be but cogs of great wheels, whose movements and axles are hidden in the depths and darkness of time. To endeavour, therefore, to enter into the feelings of the cotemporaries who witnessed those great events on which we are taught by historians to dwell with so much wonder and interest, is at least an amusing method of correcting the presumption of our own judgment with respect to occurrences which immediately affect ourselves:—and this is the moral that the story of the " Wandering Jew " is peculiarly calculated to impress.

FINIS.

AN

ABRIDGMENT

OF THE MOST POPULAR MODERN

VOYAGES AND TRAVELS.

Illustrated with Maps and numerous Engravings. 12mo.

Vol. I. containing Voyages and Travels in EUROPE; Vol. II. in ASIA; Vol. III. in AFRICA; Vol. IV. in America; each Volume distinct and sold separate, price 5s.

For the Use of Schools.

By the Rev. T. CLARK.

This Work will enable the young Reader to acquire, in a concise form, a knowledge of all the material points of information contained in the most esteemed modern Books of Voyages and Travels in the Four Quarters of the Globe, without those repetitions which have rendered so many works of great literary merit trite and uninteresting.

www.ingramcontent.com/pod-product-compliance
Lightning Source LLC
Chambersburg PA
CBHW080327170426
43194CB00014B/2490